ECONOMIC AND POLITICAL
REFORM IN AFRICA

ECONOMIC AND POLITICAL REFORM IN AFRICA

ANTHROPOLOGICAL PERSPECTIVES

PETER D. LITTLE

INDIANA UNIVERSITY PRESS
Bloomington and Indianapolis

This book is a publication of

Indiana University Press
Office of Scholarly Publishing
Herman B Wells Library 350
1320 East 10th Street
Bloomington, Indiana 47405 USA

iupress.indiana.edu

Telephone orders   800-842-6796
Fax orders   812-855-7931

Manufactured in the United States of America

Library of Congress Cataloging-in-Publication Data

Little, Peter D., author.
    Economic and political reform in Africa : anthropological per-
spectives / Peter D. Little.
        pages cm
    Includes bibliographical references and index.
    ISBN 978-0-253-01079-7 (cl : alk. paper) — ISBN 978-0-253-01084-1
(pb : alk. paper) — ISBN 978-0-253-01093-3 (eb) 1. Rural development—
Africa. 2. Economic development—Africa. 3. Africa—Economic
policy. 4. Agriculture and state—Africa. 5. Sustainable development—
Africa. I. Title.
    HN780.Z9C6473 2013
    307.1412096—dc23
                                                        2013016718

1 2 3 4 5 19 18 17 16 15 14

In memory of Betty and Bill Little and Peter Branson

Contents

Preface

THIS BOOK TOOK much too long to complete! It perennially was on the back-burner, always precluded by more urgent commitments. It has hung around in partially completed form for several years and confronted lots of false starts and stops along the way. An important change in the project's pace came in 2007–2008 when I was awarded a Guggenheim Fellowship, which allowed me to commit full-time attention to the book for nine months. A research leave from the University of Kentucky in fall 2007 and a sabbatical from Emory University in spring 2011 helped me to finish the bulk of the research and writing. The lengthy gestation of this project means that I am indebted to many colleagues, institutions, and collaborations, which I will acknowledge in the rest of this preface.

To begin, the topical and geographic breadth of the project—case studies in six African countries (Ethiopia, The Gambia, Ghana, Kenya, Mozambique, and Somalia)—required an arsenal of partnerships, collaborations, and methods unusual for an anthropologist. It draws on key research and collaborative opportunities and partnerships that were afforded me during the past twenty-plus years. In many respects, the book represents a synthesis of my work since 1990. Within a five-year period in the early 1990s I was involved in two comparative research programs that greatly expanded my geographic and topical interests. Both were interdisciplinary, multisited projects. The first was a comparative study of contract farming in Africa codirected with Michael Watts of the University of California-Berkeley, to whom I am deeply indebted for many of the ideas reflected in chapter 1. This project allowed fieldwork back in Baringo District, Kenya, the location of my dissertation research, as well as research in The Gambia, West Africa, where I had not previously worked. In the late 1980s contract farming, a form of capitalist production that vertically links small farmers with the operations of agribusiness firms and processors, was just being introduced in various African countries and increasingly associated with the production of so-called nontraditional commodities. Contract farming (CF) came to symbolize the pro-business agendas so prevalent in the 1980s and 1990s, and provided a very convenient window into the intricate connections between global trade and transnational firms, on the one hand, and local politics and labor relations, on the other.

Field research for the chapter (1) on CF of nontraditional commodities was conducted in the export horticultural zones near Banjul, The Gambia, and Accra, Ghana, during 1993–1994 and partly supported by another comparative research project focused on peri-urban economies (described below). For the CF research a range of actors, including farmers, business owners, exporters, and policy makers, were interviewed at multiple sites, including farms, offices, and marketplaces. In Ghana field interviews were conducted with 83 of the approximately 500 farmers growing pineapples under contract at the time, and with key informants, such as traders, large-farm owners and managers, government officials, and chiefs. This fieldwork was supervised by Cyril Daddieh, currently of Providence University, and based on research modules that had been jointly developed by the two of us. I am grateful to Cyril for his hard work and intellectual inputs to the study. For the Gambian research, data collection focused on four related components: (1) horticultural traders; (2) communal vegetable gardens; (3) household (or "backyard") producers; and (4) large export farms and firms. Overall 93 small-scale farmers, 167 horticultural traders, and 12 owners or managers of large-scale export farms were interviewed in the Banjul peri-urban area during January–October 1993. Most of this fieldwork was supervised by Catherine Dolan, currently of Oxford University but at the time a PhD student at the State University of New York-Binghamton, and Isatou Jack, now a senior associate of International Relief and Development (IRD) based in Washington, D.C., but an independent consultant in The Gambia at the time. The study was based on a research module, interview guides, and questionnaires that I developed in consultation with Catherine and Isatou. I conducted the in-depth interviews with 12 owners or managers of export farms, in some cases with the assistance of a translator. I am equally indebted to both Catherine and Isatou for their assistance in the fieldwork and subsequent analyses of the Gambian data. I updated both the Ghanaian and Gambian materials through interviews in 2008 with researchers and policy makers and reviews of recent reports, statistical data, and literature.

A second interdisciplinary research program was on "Peri-Urban Economies in Africa," and I codirected it with Michael Roth, then of the University of Wisconsin but currently at Associates in Rural Development, Burlington, Vermont; and Douglas Graham of Ohio State University. This comparative study looked broadly at how livelihoods of peri-urban residents were affected by economic reform programs, especially with regard to land, labor, and credit markets. The peri-urban study hypothesized that the impacts of reforms were particularly intense in zones located near major metropolises, because of their heightened commercialism, active land markets, diversity of economic activity, and relatively good access to domestic and international markets. This research project included a case study of petty traders in the urban and peri-urban areas of Maputo, Mozambique, during 1991–1992, as well as in peri-urban areas of Accra, Ghana, and, again, in Banjul, The Gambia. In addition to interviews with market and government officials, wholesalers, shopkeepers, and transporters, data were collected through a random survey of 73 small-scale (petty) traders in Districts 2 and 4, two of Maputo's eight peri-urban districts, based on a questionnaire that I developed for the project. In these two districts five markets were covered: 7 de Abril, Malanga, and Xipamanine in District 2 and Ferroviário and 3 de Fevereiro in District 4. The unstructured interviews asked about the history of trade in the Maputo area, the content and nature of buying and selling relationships, perceptions of the effects of economic reforms, and other important information that was difficult to gather from the questionnaire-based module. The survey of petty traders was administered by Irae de Lundin, a Brazilian anthropologist, who at the time was a visiting faculty member in the anthropology program at Eduardo Mondlane University (EMU), while the unstructured interviews were conducted by me, with the aid of a translator, and Irae. I especially was fortunate to collaborate with such a capable researcher and with her anthropology students at EMU who assisted in the study, especially Antonio Timóteo Fanequisso, Simeão Lopes, Orlando Nhancale, Luciano Peres Norte, Amélia Mônica Sitoi, and José da Silva. The findings of this work are reported in chapter 2. Both the projects on contract farming and on peri-urban economies in Africa were sponsored by the Settlement and Resource Systems Analysis (SARSA) Cooperative Agreement based at Clark University and the Institute for Development Anthropology, with funding from the United States Agency for International Development (USAID) (grant no. DHR 5452-A-00-9083-00).

It should be noted that at the time of the Mozambique research the country was just coming out of a prolonged civil war, and the dicey security situation around Maputo effectively determined a study area with a circumference no more than 10 kilometers from city center. It was a "workable" and relatively safe delineation of a peri-urban space. As one colleague from EMU sarcastically noted, "the peri-urban research zone extends until you hear shots or find land mines."

Other chapters in the book report on more recent field research that I conducted in conjunction with other research projects. The materials in chapter 3 are based on a case study of community-based conservation around parks and conservation areas in pastoralist areas of Baringo, Samburu, and Kajiado Districts, Kenya, that was part of a larger comparative study on local institutions and natural resources management in Kenya. Fieldwork was conducted during the summers of 1995 and 1996, with follow-up research during summers of 2001 and 2006. Focus-group and key-informant interviews with a range of actors, including policy makers, NGO personnel, pastoralists, and local politicians, as well as archival research, form the empirical basis for the chapter. Although the majority of interviews for this chapter were conducted in rural settings, some were conducted in government and NGO offices in Nairobi and district towns, such as Maralal, Loitokitok, and Marigat, Kenya. This activity also was supported by the SARSA Cooperative Agreement.

Chapter 5, in turn, draws on an interdisciplinary study that involved fieldwork in four districts of South Wollo and Oromiya Zones, Ethiopia, during 2000–

2007. The project addressed the social and economic causes of food insecurity and poverty in the region. It relied on an unusually rich mix of quantitative and qualitative data from a multiple round (7) study of 416 randomly selected households during 2000–2003; ethnographic case studies of 62 of the 416 households with initial visits in 2001–2002 and repeat visits during 2004–2005 and 2007; and a series of detailed interviews with key informants and focus groups of male and female farmers and traders. The late and sorely missed Yigremew Adal of AAU, A. Peter Castro of Syracuse University, Priscilla Stone of Washington University, Kassahun Kebede, a graduate student at Syracuse University, and Mengistu Dessalegn of AAU also were involved in research design and data collection. I am very appreciative of their important contributions to the South Wollo study. This project was supported by the Broadening Access to Input Systems (BASIS) Collaborative Research Support Project based at the University of Wisconsin (grant no. LAG-A-OO-96-90016-00).

Chapter 4 and parts of chapters 3, 6, and 7 draw heavily on my ethnographic research among two specific communities in East Africa: Il Chamus agro-pastoralists of Baringo District, Kenya (see earlier discussion) and Somali traders of the Kenya/Somali borderlands. Some of this work was made possible by an interdisciplinary project, titled Pastoral Risk Management in East Africa (PARIMA), where I served as a co-principal investigator along with Abdullahi Aboud of Egerton University [Kenya], Chris Barrett of Cornell University, and Layne Coppock of Utah State University. It was supported by the Global Livestock-Collaborative Research Support Program (GL-CRSP) based at the University of California-Davis (grant no. PCE-G-00-98-00036-00). In addition to an Il Chamus site, the PARIMA project addressed risk-related strategies across five other sites in northern Kenya, which are discussed in chapter 6. The total sample in the northern Kenyan study was 180 households, or 30 households per site, and data were collected during 2000–2005. Unlike many studies in pastoralist areas, the sampling unit was an administrative area (called Location) that included both mobile pastoralists and settled households who pursued nonpastoral activities. Under this project I was able to return to the Il Chamus area of Baringo District for short research periods (two to three weeks) during the summers of 2001–2004 and 2006–2008.

My earlier research in Baringo relied on participant observation, case studies, and a study of 58 households during 1980–1981 and 1984. During the summers of 2003 and 2004 a subset of these households (or their descendants) were reinterviewed in order to gauge changes in wealth accumulation, education, migration, and other social and economic phenomena over an approximately twenty-year period. The Baringo work mainly was funded by the Social Science Research Council and the GL-CRSP.

Chapter 7 stems from studies of Somali traders that began in southern Somalia during 1986–1988 and continued in neighboring Garissa District, Kenya, during the summers of 1996–1998, 2001, and 2008. The core of the Somali work since 1996 has been detailed interviews and case histories of 69 Somali traders, data collection at keys markets, and interviews with NGO officials and policy makers. The follow-up work on the Somalia/Kenya border was conducted in collaboration with Hussein A. Mahmoud, who then was a PhD student at the University of Kentucky but currently is based at Pwani College–Kenyatta University, Kenya. I am deeply indebted to Hussein for all of his work and assistance, often under difficult field conditions. Most of the research on traders was funded by a research grant from the John D. and Catherine T. MacArthur Foundation with supplemental support by the BASIS project. In some of this work, I collaborated with the Organization for Social Science Research in Eastern and Southern Africa (OSSREA) based in Addis Ababa, Ethiopia. The earlier materials in chapter 7 are supplemented by more recent interviews with Somali traders and refugees during short visits to Kenya in 2004, 2006, 2008, and 2011.

During 2008 the writing of this book greatly benefited from visiting research appointments at the African Studies Centre, Kyoto University, and the African Studies Centre, Oxford University. Both institutions provided stimulating environments and opportunities to present portions of the book to colleagues and graduate students, which I like to think sharpened many of the book's arguments and findings. I particularly am indebted to both directors at the time, Ohta-san Itaru at Kyoto and David Anderson at Oxford, for inviting me to the centers and making the visits so productive and enjoyable. In addition, a generous fellowship from the John Simon Guggenheim Memorial Foundation, which I am especially appreciative of, allowed me to spend time at these centers and devote most of my efforts there to writing this book. While I am grateful to all of the above-mentioned institutions and funding agencies, individuals, and research projects, they are in no way responsible for the book and its contents. I take full responsibility for the book, including any flaws and inaccuracies.

The book's long maturation period also means additional colleagues and friends played important roles in its completion. In addition to those mentioned so far, the support of the following individuals is warmly appreciated: Edward Ackah, Abdel Ghaffar Ahmed, David Brokensha, Barbara Cellarius, Dejene N. Debsu, Michael Horowitz, Patrick Kakimon, the late Ivan Karp, Dickson Keis, Reuben Lemunyete, Clement Lenachuru, Jackson Lenapir, Eunice Lepariyo, Thomas Letangule, Nickson Lolgisoi, Hussein A. Mahmoud, Daniel Murphy, Irene S. Obeng, Matthew Richard, Thayer Scudder, Helen Simmons, Tegegne Teka, and Waktole Tiki Uma. Throughout the book pseudonyms are used for names of individuals who were interviewed during field research, and while they are anonymous I greatly appreciate the time and effort they provided under sometimes difficult circumstances.

Finally, I would like to acknowledge the support of my family—Ellen, Nelly, Katey, and Peter D—who endured more extended absences away from home for this book project than probably is warranted. While it may be little consolation for them, they always made returning home very special. The book, however, is dedicated to three individuals who played key roles in my first visit to Africa. The late Peter Branson took the initiative to find an undergraduate study program in the spring semester of 1974 that allowed a group of students to spend a largely unsupervised but amazingly wonderful semester in Kenya. Over a few Heineken beers at a bar on a cold wintry night in Washington, D.C., he persuaded me that the trip would be a very worthwhile experience. He was clearly correct, and it was a semester that changed my life! Although he never would have read this book (and I truly mean it!), I think that as a successful small business owner he would have appreciated the work's implicit support for Africa's small-scale traders and farmers, who often struggle against great odds as well as large competitors with deep pockets and political power.

The second and third persons that the book is dedicated to are my parents, the late Betty and Bill Little. Both were enthusiastic supporters as well as financiers of that first trip to Africa. I am forever grateful to them for their love and unstinting support of the different travels and directions my career has taken over the years. Both my parents and Peter are sorely missed.

ECONOMIC AND POLITICAL REFORM IN AFRICA

Introduction

What It Means to Be "Reformed"

I BEGAN TO THINK about this book about thirteen years ago on a short visit to Baringo District, Kenya, where I had conducted my PhD dissertation research during 1980–1981. I had not been there for almost three years when I visited in March 1998. Standing on the parched and badly receding shores of the district's namesake, Lake Baringo, a nearby young man explained that its retreat was evidence of "climate change." We subsequently engaged in conversation about environmental change, a discussion in which my new friend spoke of "community-based conservation" and "local partnerships" as ways to confront these new ecological problems. It is a language that often is displayed in nongovernmental organization (NGO) brochures and websites, a discourse he had obviously learned well. It also was apparent that he worked for one of the many NGOs in the area engaged in conservation programs. Indeed, during my three-year absence from the area NGO employment had become one of Baringo's few sectors of job growth.

Later that week I visited an old friend in a nearby settlement, only to learn that he had been "retrenched" by the government, a term that I heard more than once during this trip. It meant a loss of government ("salaried") employment, which for many in the area was the most secure means for the future. Simply no one voluntarily left government employment, even when s/he was engaged in private business and other activities. One juggled state employment with other ventures, which was (is) a growing necessity for many in Kenya, rather than resign. Finally, I visited the government compound in nearby Marigat town, the divisional headquarters of central Baringo, only to find that almost three-fourths of the offices now were occupied by a U.S.-based international NGO. Indeed, a foreign private group had quite literally taken over the public space once occupied by departments of the Kenyan government, where I once sat with "notebook in hand" studying local government archives. When I revisited the area in June 2002, the organization's large, multicolored sign still was prominently displayed at the compound's entrance, a symbolic pronouncement that the game had changed.

After that visit to lowland Baringo there was much to think about in terms of change. Transitions clearly had come to the area, consistent with the reform agendas of the 1980s and 1990s. The latter generally reduced, often awkwardly and inconsistently, the state's developmental role in Kenya and, in turn, heightened the prominence of private actors, including NGOs. African governments, such as Kenya's, had been pressured by the World Bank and International Monetary Fund (IMF), a major source of capital for governments in most of sub-Saharan Africa,[1] to undertake reforms and implement policies in the 1980s and 1990s that privileged nonstate groups, free trade, and market-led development. The market was "in" and the state was "out," and families in lowland Baringo were experiencing the stresses and uncertainties associated with these changes.

This book explores local experiences with neoliberal reforms like those described above, by focusing on case studies in six African countries: Ethiopia, The Gambia, Ghana, Kenya, Mozambique, and Somalia. It focuses on a set of these experiences or encounters, including multinational investment in contract farming (chapter 1), a biodiversity (wildlife) conservation program in remote locations (chapter 3), and a "democratic" experiment in a formerly single-party state (chapter 4). All the book's case studies are based on original ethnographic and survey-based field research and represent what Watts calls "globalized local sites" (1999: 22) where the global clearly is identifiable in a local setting. They show that different policy interventions opened African communities to increased global orientations and pressures, but also provoked rigid cultural boundaries, identities, and an explosive awareness of local histories and differences. Although they have a global context, these encounters with neoliberalism are played out in specific places: the hot fields of a contracted bean grower, the dusty offices of an activist or NGO, or the rutted streets of a peri-urban settlement. All of these come with their own social and political histories, but I argue that they are representative of larger processes prevalent throughout Africa.

An ancillary goal of this book also is to inject the study of pastoralism, which has been the center of much of my own scholarship, into current theoretical debates in anthropology and the social sciences about the state, neoliberalism, and development in Africa. As a topic, pastoralism often is treated in anthropology as a field in and of itself, complete with its own journals, such as *Nomadic Peoples* and *Pastoralism: Research, Policy, and Practice*. This disciplinary tendency has isolated the study of pastoralism from wider developments in the discipline and related fields. By comparing and theorizing about the impacts of reforms across a range of different political and cultural settings and livelihoods, including pastoralist and nonpastoralist, the book demonstrates that pastoralists are as affected by structural reforms and politics as are other communities.

This book recognizes the recent controversies and criticisms of the term neoliberalism, especially with regard to its lack of analytical precision and its broad applications to an array of social and politico-economic phenomena (Clarke 2008; Ferguson 2009; Gibson-Graham 2008). Similar to other grand ("totalizing") concepts—for example, globalization—it has become a catch-all term to describe almost any kind of recent social and economic changes even remotely related to market-based ideologies and/or interventions (Littlejohn 2010). Despite its crit-

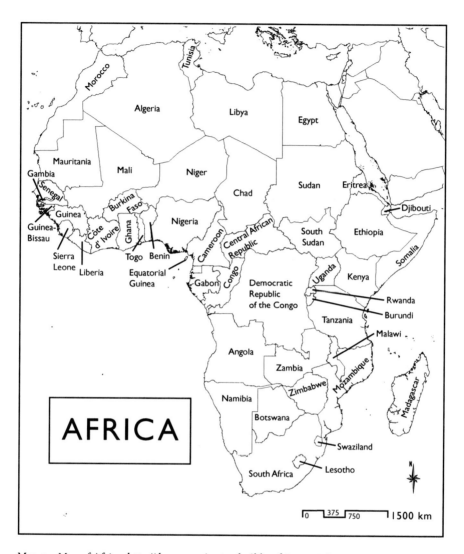

Map 0.1. Map of Africa. http://d-aps.com/carte.php?lib=africa_map&num_car=25457 &lang=en).

ics, the literature on neoliberalism has exploded in the past decade. Its use in the social sciences mainly is traced to the late 1990s, where in some cases it was conflated or combined with the term "globalization": for example, "global neoliberalism" or "neoliberal globalization." In a study of the term's usage, Peck et al. note that "of the 2500 English language articles in the social sciences that cite 'neoliberalism' as a keyword, 86% were published after 1998" (2010: 97). It clearly is a word that is strongly associated with a particularly recent historical period, but nonetheless provides an intellectual platform that helps make sense of the changes discussed in subsequent chapters.

What then is neoliberalism, and how is the term used in the book? Borrowing from Harrison's very basic use of the concept as "a project to expand and universalise free-market social relations" (2005: 1306), and Harvey's more detailed explanation as "liberating individual entrepreneurial freedoms and skills within an institutional framework characterized by strong private property rights, free markets, and free trade" (Harvey 2005: 2), I find the concept particularly useful in exploring the contradictions between what economic (neoliberal) reforms were supposed to do and what actually was (is) happening in local communities. According to these related uses of the term, much of what is described in this book are incomplete or hybrid forms of neoliberal intervention that are only partial in their impacts regardless of intention (see Peck et al. 2010). For example, rather than a constriction of the informal or unofficial sector in African towns as predicted by reform models, the nonwaged or informal sector rapidly grew in these locations even while neoliberal market policies flooded urban and peri-urban areas with cheap imported goods, which ironically then became the basis for many informal trading activities (chapter 2). A narrative that celebrates the growth of petty trade and the informal sector generally as an unleashing of a suppressed entrepreneurial spirit naively misunderstands the desperate urban employment situation in Africa. Indeed, estimates are that the informal sector accounts for 78 percent of non-farm employment, both urban and rural, as well as 93 percent of all new employment being generated on the continent (Meagher 2009: 399). In other cases, even with the imposition of reforms the state did not completely or even measurably retreat from control of its economy, institutions, and key actors despite a strong private sector discourse to the contrary (chapters 5 and 6).

In the book, the term "informal sector" often is used interchangeably with others such as "unofficial" or "unwaged" sectors, simply for lack of an easily communicated set of alternative concepts. Unfortunately, as it has been applied in the past informal sector implies a misleading separation from the so-called formal sector, usually defined as activity officially sanctioned and/or licensed by the state, rather than recognizing the interdependencies and linkages between the two. For this reason, the use of the term "informal sector" is controversial, especially among anthropologists (Hansen and Vaa 2004). As the book will show, the boundaries between formal and informal often are porous, especially regarding trade, where particular commodities at different levels in a market chain can move between the official and unofficial, and the linkages between the two sectors can be very strong. For instance, a set of commodities, such as gem stones or agricultural products, can enter a market chain through informal—even illegal— channels, but eventually be sold through state-licensed, formal retail outlets. In daily practice individuals and households often straddle the two sectors, engaged simultaneously in both official and unofficial or informal activities, and I will suggest that this straddling has increased as a result of the neoliberal reform programs of the past three decades. Furthermore, it will be argued that even the distinction between legal and illegal, the latter of which sometimes is conflated with the informal, is troublesome, since some economic practices discussed in the book, such as informal transborder trade, can assume a legal appearance even though it is essentially illegal in most countries (see chapter 7). In sum, when the term "informal sector" is used in the book it is not meant to imply a razor-sharp distinction with the formal sector nor a neat boundary between what is legal and illegal.

By providing ethnographic cases of how rural farmers and herders interpret and respond to different political and economic reforms through either formal or informal practice, the book integrates experiences across seemingly unrelated sectors, such as agriculture, governance, trade, and social services. It follows Ferguson's (2009) general suggestion of distinguishing between different uses of neoliberalism, especially its applications as a (1) pro-market, deregulated approach to the economy; and (2) political technique for ruling populations and producing responsible citizens. They are fundamentally different uses, but often are lumped together under the term "neoliberalism." As will be discussed in the book, neoliberalism defined the broad parameters of state projects of economic and political development that remain prominent in many African countries. As will be shown in the case of Ethiopia (chapter 5), the different uses (economic and political) of neoliberalism can result in contradictory practices on the ground that are both antimarket and antidemocratic despite rhetoric to the contrary. In the remainder of this chapter, the historical and intellectual background to this project and the book's organization are presented.

Dynamic Africa?

An added burden of a long-drawn-out project such as this one, especially when covering places like Somalia where events change with astounding rapidity, is the need to continually update the book. Indeed, Africa's social and politico-economic changes during the past five years (2007–2012) alone have not only pushed me to rewrite large parts of different chapters, but also to pitch the book in a slightly different manner than when it was first formulated following that trip to Baringo, Kenya. In the late 1990s through the mid-2000s Africa was considered to be on the extreme fringe of globalization in terms of trade, technology, communications, and other standard indicators. At the time, flows of technology, trade, and finance were minuscule, and they still are in comparison to other world regions (see Arrighi 2002; Ferguson 2007). Outside of South Africa, sub-Saharan Africa still has very few (if any?) McDonald's restaurants or official Nike athletic stores, both transnational corporations with graphic global symbols—the "golden arches" of McDonald's and familiar "swoosh" of Nike. However, since about 2006, cell (mobile) phone access has greatly improved across the continent, international investments—especially from China but also from other countries—have grown, and urbanization on the continent is accelerating at an unprecedented pace. In fact, sub-Saharan Africa now is the world's most rapidly urbanizing region and fastest-growing market for cell phones (Shah 2011). Africa's estimated 600 million mobile phones in use are more than in Europe or the USA (*Economist* 2011: 15). Change is prevalent, and much of it is related to global connections with other places and to the spread of neoliberal ideas and reforms.

The tempo at which foreign investors, especially from China and India, are cutting deals for minerals, farmland, and oil extraction, and rapid advances in telecommunication use have edged the continent slightly closer to the center of global action. Indeed, the "great recession" of 2008–2009, which did not have as serious an impact on African economies as in more advanced economies, along with increased trade and investment, has allowed some African countries (for example, Ghana, Botswana, and Mozambique) to experience recent annual economic growth rates in the range of 5–10 percent. One could argue that because their economies were not well integrated into the global financial and investment networks that unraveled during 2008–2009, they have been less affected by the recent economic turmoil. Thus, except in a few countries like South Africa, there was not the speculative real estate, overvalued stocks, and questionable financial products that came crashing down globally in the past few years. In fact, in my recent trips (2011–2012) to Nairobi, Kenya, and Addis Ababa, Ethiopia, I saw considerably more tall construction cranes in these two cities than in my hometown of Atlanta, the recession-battered capital of America's "new South."[2] Thus, to have been on the periphery rather than in the midst of global economic activity in 2008–2009 perhaps was a blessing rather than handicap for sub-Saharan Africa.

I do not want to exaggerate the magnitude of recent economic changes and gains and their impacts on Africa. The facts are that most Africans remain very poor and that eighteen of the world's poorest twenty countries still are found there (UNDP 2011).[3] The continent also still badly lags in investment, social welfare indicators, and Internet connectivity relative to other world regions, and "still only has around 1 % of world trade and GDP" (Littlejohn 2010: 87). Indeed, most of the changes mentioned above have benefited only a small minority of African citizens, and most have experienced declining rather than improving welfare.

The Age of Reform and Neoliberalism

For those of us whose research in Africa spans the past three decades rather than just the last five or ten years, the onset of neoliberalism, with its pro-market reforms and antistate rhetoric, marked an important watershed. No other region of the world was subject to so many and so aggressive a series of neoliberal reform experiments—both economic and political—as was Africa (Harrison 2010a). They generally can be traced to the early 1980s with the first wave of structural adjustment programs (SAPs) of the International Monetary Fund (IMF) and World Bank, the ultimate neoliberal tool for economic reform (see World Bank 1981 and 1984). In practical terms, the SAPs slashed public expenditures and employment and inserted market principles in many aspects of economic, political, and social life. For the zealot reformist, the market would serve as an "impartial arbitrator" that determines human welfare and success rather than leaving the outcomes to state bureaucracies and planners. In reality, however, the public/private dichotomy was found to be especially blurred in real economies and the market as subject to politics and manipulation as any other institution, despite strong ideological rhetoric to the contrary. As Berry notes, "the neoliberal ideal of an 'open,' competitive market in which exchanges take place free from the exercise of power and (mis)representation (i.e., 'transparently'), not only doesn't exist in practice (a point economic theorists readily concede), but is of questionable usefulness as a tool for explaining economic realities, in Africa and elsewhere, or as a conceptual blueprint for economic and political reform" (2007: 67). Notwithstanding its contradictions, the language of reform crept into local discourses, and its impacts on livelihoods and relationships were real, as the examples at the beginning of the chapter demonstrate.

The SAP reforms strongly embody pro-market principles that are at the core of neoliberalism, with the consumer "responsibilised to make wise and prudent choices in the free market" (Hyatt 2011: 107). The SAP interventions had profound effects on the institutions and livelihoods of rural and urban Africans and represented a break with the statist-led development approaches of the 1960s and 1970s. These reforms provided opportunities for a few, especially those favorably connected to the state, to freely pursue wealth accumulation through market-based opportunities and investments. However, they challenged the majority to live with inflated costs of living, reduced formal-sector employment, and a withered public sector that struggled to provide even minimal education, health, and welfare protection for its citizens. Whether or not these reforms and their effects were necessary steps to "right the economic ship" can be contested, especially since many African economies were in terrible shape in the early 1980s. What is less disputable is that they ushered in important restructurings of African livelihoods and labor and production relations and introduced new notions of individual responsibility and accountability. In part, this book is about these changes.

For financially distressed African states, there often was little recourse in the 1980s but to capitulate to different reform experiments (Arrighi 2002).[4] As noted above, the most intrusive were the SAPs, which streamlined the state and allowed the private sector, including NGOs, to assume many of its functions. They led to employee retrenchments as in the case of the Baringo family discussed earlier, privatization of state-owned corporations (parastatals), and elimination of subsidies on social services and agricultural inputs. State-led development was perceived as the problem rather than the solution, and the "invisible hand of the market" became the determinant of winners and losers, dictating which workers kept jobs and which firms survived. Ironically, many of the parastatals destined to be privatized or dismantled in the 1980s and 1990s had originally been established with funding and technical support from the World Bank, the same institution that later aggressively advocated for their elimination (see de Wilde 1967).

At the international level what started off as an economistic agenda of "getting the prices right" in the 1980s turned to a concern with governance and democracy in the 1990s (Harrison 2004) and poverty alleviation later on in the 2000s. The extreme state minimalist approach of the 1980s was tempered in the 1990s with a recognition by the World Bank and other international agencies that government had a role in poverty alleviation and development, but it had to be democratic and pro-growth (Williamson 2000). After ten years of disappointing results and anemic economic performance in Africa during the 1980s, it was time, in the words of Moore, to get "the state right" (1999: 61). A thin civil society, undemocratic and corrupt regimes, and a general lack of government accountability and rule of law were all perceived as crippling constraints to development and foreign investment and badly in need of reform. The common ideological premise was that only with good governance, democracy, and a vibrant civil society could Africa benefit from market-led policies and attract needed external investment. In short, it was poor governance, ineffective institutions, and weak judicial systems that were to blame for Africa's lost decade (1980s) and growing poverty, not the SAP policies that were imposed.

The most immediate and visible means of making government and its leaders accountable was by introducing multiparty politics and elections in previously single-party states (Ndegwa 2001; Abrahamsen 2000). Within a relatively short period of ten to fifteen years multiparty elections were introduced in the majority of African states, but the playing field often was so uneven and unfairly stacked against opposition groups that many contests only reaffirmed existing power structures. In this regard, the African state was brought back into the picture in the 1990s, but mainly to establish an enabling environment of democratic institutions, laws, and policies to promote investment and growth and to allow trade and markets to operate (on the role of judicial and institutional reforms in neoliberal policy, see Harvey 2005). Disbursements of foreign aid were withheld from states that resisted democratic reforms and external demands for good governance.

By the early 1990s donor-funded governance and democratization programs proliferated across the continent, including in Kenya (see chapter 4), and strong support was provided to civil society, including NGOs and other nongovernment groups (see Bratton 1997). The term "governance," as distinct from government, left the possibility of nonstate governance systems and rule; for example, corporate or NGO governance. In Kenya alone the number of NGOs grew by more than tenfold during the 1990s (Ndegwa 2001). African governments, in turn, were challenged to liberalize their own political systems or, as noted above, lose access to badly needed funds. Perhaps nowhere did external donors pursue political reform more vigorously than in Kenya. The country was (is) a staunch ally of Western nations, but the United States and several European countries had tired of the abusive and corrupt politics of its president, Daniel arap Moi. In fact, President Moi became a "poster child" for bad governance in the eyes of Western leaders, who relentlessly pressured the government to introduce multiparty elections, which it eventually did in 1991 (see chapter 4). Accountability and financial and political transparency emerged as development buzzwords in Kenya, as well as in other African countries.

Despite the promises of almost two decades of market-based reforms and the introduction of multiparty elections, poverty remained prevalent in Africa. Numerous reform programs had been attempted, with promises of impending prosperity, but most low-income Africans still experienced heightened hardship and risk even when demonstrating phenomenal ingenuity and resilience. Is the problem that neoliberal market reforms are not working, or is it that people just are too poor to benefit from market-based solutions? Could markets be made to work for the poor just as improved governance and democracy can enhance economic growth? Mainstream policy makers believed the answer to the second question was an emphatic "yes," and thus a new set of softer reform programs were launched on the continent.

To implement a market friendly but pro-poor approach to development, the World Bank initiated a new funding tool in 1999 called the Poverty Reduction Strategy Plan (PRSP). This mechanism required client governments to demonstrate in their development plans how poverty would be reduced in their countries. In effect, the poverty reduction plans or strategies increasingly formed "the contractual basis of the relationship between donor agencies and developing country governments" (Green 2006: 1109) and to qualify for these funds governments had to already have undergone SAPs (see Weber 2004). The neoliberal agenda of economic growth remained central with the PRSPs, and the new conditions initiated what Craig and Porter (2003) call "inclusive liberalism," with terms like pro-poor growth and pro-poor markets key to the new development discourse (also see Rutten et al. 2008). For some critics, PRSPs were merely "structural adjustment programs in disguise" that placed much of the blame for poverty on African states and their populations, rather than on flawed adjustment policies and programs (Bond and Dor 2007: 349; also see Gould *2005*).

Despite the fact that more than 80 percent of countries in sub-Saharan Africa undertook some type of SAP and PRSP, these interventions and their funders were never as omnipotent as some critics assumed. Certain African leaders, for instance, were able to shape their own agendas for political and economic gain and actually increase statist controls under SAP policies (Hibou 2004). As Harrison notes, "neoliberal development policy can entertain models of state expansion or expanded state remit in specific circumstances on the condition that the predicted effects of state action will be to release immanent free-market-like behavior in societies" (2005: 1307). To return again to former Kenyan president Moi, he was especially skilled in delaying or simply refusing to follow SAP recommendations even while making funders believe he was pursuing reforms (Murunga 2007; Brown 2001 and 2007; Ogachi 1999). He used external demands for democratic elections in the early 1990s to increase controls on rural communities through an ethnic-based divide-and-rule policy that expanded rather than reduced state controls and bureaucracies (chapter 4). Moreover, he held off on privatizing certain key state companies despite loan conditions that dictated their sale to the private sector.

The late prime minister Meles Zenawi of Ethiopia also has skillfully resisted certain donor-driven demands for reform. He led a massive liberalization of the economy with World Bank/IMF support, but has backed off donor recommendations for private land markets by keeping the ultimate control of land, and hence of farmers who live on it, in the hands of the state. Despite pro-market narratives, his policies increase state control of rural communities through mandates for continued auditing and monitoring of programs and the policing of farmer participation in development activities, including labor contributions (chapter 5). In both the Kenyan and Ethiopian cases, political leaders were (are) able to keep flows of foreign aid and loans coming into the country, even though they resisted key SAP conditions and used policy reforms to expand and consolidate their own political control of the country (chapters 5 and 6).

Throughout the past three decades in Africa, the flows of ideas, practices, and discourses related to economic and political reforms have moved at dizzying speeds, even though—as noted earlier—advances in global commerce and technology sorely have lagged relative to the rest of the world. New institutions, production relations, and forms of identity emerged or were reworked in unexpected ways. Local households and individuals survived austerity measures and often harsh conditions through informal activities, remittances, and unofficial trade networks—sometimes in illicit goods (see Roitman 2005; Nordstrom 2007; MacGaffey and Bazenquissa-Ganga 2000). Unofficial cross-border trade, which is largely invisible in official trade statistics, was one such strategy that allowed farmers, herders, and traders to weather political uncertainty and market volatility during the past two decades (chapter 7).

Development policy in Africa and elsewhere also has changed as even the international financial institutions (IFIs) (IMF and World Bank) recently have questioned their own assumptions about excessive deregulation and the state's role in the economy (see World Bank 2007a and 2009). A major annual report of the World Bank recently highlighted the need for "bringing the state back in" and how the "the 2008 financial crisis showed the pitfalls of deregulation and unrestrained markets (World Bank 2009: 330)." Some scholars are suggesting that we already are in a post-neoliberal era and pose the question: "what comes next" after neoliberalism (Hyatt 2011: 105; also see Peck et al. 2009)? For still others neoliberalism is just another cyclical phase in the history of global capitalism where the pendulum soon will swing back toward progressive politics and heightened roles in the economy for the state (Wallerstein 2008). The economic successes of China in the past decade and its growing presence in Africa also would suggest alternatives to IFI mandates and neoliberal prescriptions, but this generally has not been the case so far. As of 2010, thirty-four African states were still under PRSP prescriptions, and IFI reforms and policies maintained their strong influence on national development even in countries, such as Zambia, where China's role is prominent (Harrison 2010a: 2).

Contradictions and Connections

In almost every quarter of the continent economic and political reforms ushered in unexpected changes and contradictions as new political and economic spaces emerged in the public voids left by reforms and reduced state capacity. The stunning takeover of Kenyan government offices by an international NGO discussed earlier in the chapter is a striking example of this. These transitions have taken place in a global environment marked by the end of the Cold War, the lauded triumph of neoliberalism, and the end of one-party states in most of Africa. There is little question that these changes are at least partially interrelated. For example, the end of Cold War politics with the collapse of the Union of Soviet Socialist Republics (USSR) in 1991 reduced the geopolitical importance for the West of several African states, such as Somalia (chapter 7), while opening the way for the further spread of economic and political reforms, including in Africa. Four of the six countries addressed in the book—Ethiopia, Kenya, Mozambique, and Somalia—figured prominently in Cold War struggles on the continent, on the side of either the USSR (Mozambique, Ethiopia [post-1975], Somalia [pre-1978]) or the US and West (Kenya, Ethiopia [pre-1975], Somalia [post-1978]). The political and economic effects of the end of the Cold War even were felt in relatively remote parts of the continent, such as isolated rangelands of northern Kenya and southern Ethiopia, and among communities, such as pastoralists, often considered outside global influences (chapters 3–5 and 6).

Certain communities and organizations have resisted their encounters with neoliberal reforms, but in others they have accommodated the changes. The transnational Somali community in eastern Africa is a group that accommodated as well as took advantage of liberal trade and foreign currency reforms. Their trade and financial networks grew considerably since the 1990s as currency and trade restrictions in the region were lifted and they took advantage of different markets (chapter 7). Other communities, such as Maasai and Maasai-related pastoralists, have incorporated new democratic discourses to bolster their own political and economic agendas, while still others have pursued lucrative unofficial markets under the guise of free trade policies, thus avoiding state taxes and tariffs.

The types of encounters or interventions addressed here are associated with specific reforms, such as a policy to privatize wildlife conservation efforts or subsidize exports of nontraditional commodities. The reform may be an imposed *idea* about how a market should operate or a product be produced and exported, but it still has a practical, *material* context with real-life economic and social implications. African communities increasingly are exposed to these encounters in particular locales and have responded to them in both predictable and not so predictable ways (see Comaroff and Comaroff 2001; Mbembe 2001; Van Binsbergen and Van Dijk 2005).

The effects of the global agenda of neoliberalism are experienced in widely different sectors and activities, including those outside the normal gaze of most writers about neoliberalism in Africa. As Clarke notes, under the neoliberal paradigm "all people are or should be enterprising individuals" (2004: 62) and, I might add, whether it is in the context of welfare reform or an agricultural trade program. Thus, the impacts of these encounters are felt not just in the obvious spheres of social and economic life—trade and employment—but in a range of different areas of society. For example, how indigenous communities essentialize their own cultures for political purposes (Brosius 1999) or street traders pursue "illegal" activities in a liberalized market economy (Bayart et al. 1999) are as much the effects of neoliberalism as are free trade agreements. Each is a response to a particular policy reform and intervention that helps to explain their behavior, whether it is legal or illegal.

These encounters with the global are played out and filtered through layers of national, regional, and local histories and political structures. As noted earlier, these layers can result in very contradictory and unexpected outcomes. This is what happened in Kenya when a conservation program triggered a local political movement for land claims and increased political rights among marginalized pastoralist groups (see chapter 3). In this case, a global environmental group's community-based intervention to bolster declining wildlife populations opened political space for local groups and activists to voice concerns, from land rights and basic human needs to political participation and human rights. As chapter 3 will show, this kind of politicization can have chilling effects on international organizations and their funders whose intentions are conservation and development, not political activism!

Another contradiction of neoliberalism evident in Africa (and elsewhere) relates to open-border trade policies. Most countries, including those in the West, herald regional free trade initiatives as means to promote comparative advantage (i.e., allow each country to produce and trade what they do best) and expand market size. However, rarely do they fully implement them. Economic and political self-interest interferes with their implementation, as do recent concerns with global terrorism and illegal border crossings. Similar to the end of the Cold War, the onset of the global war on terrorism in the 2000s was a major historical marker that quickly sharpened the divide between those states considered friends and those perceived as foes of the West. East African states, for example, were encouraged to support free trade policies but also were pushed by the West to police borders against undocumented movements of people and goods. The contradictions between free market policies and fears about illicit border flows and criminality are especially apparent in the Sudanese and Somali borderlands, both considered havens for terrorist activity (chapter 7). These concerns grew after the U.S. embassy explosions in Nairobi, Kenya, and Dar es Salaam, Tanzania, in 1998 but took on added urgency after the tragedy of 9/11 (September 11, 2001).

For certain African states, such as Ethiopia, post-9/11 concerns provided a raison d'être for curbing the enormous cross-border trade in livestock and other agricultural products that especially benefit its pastoralist citizens, a community whose relationship with the Ethiopian state always has been problematic (see chapters 6 and 7). At the same time as fears about illicit border crossings were affecting policies, African countries were being encouraged to open their borders to investment and trade, including with neighboring countries. Thus, similar to the end of the Cold War in 1991, the global war on terrorism spearheaded major changes and contradictions in sub-Saharan Africa, especially regarding trade and border policies.

Narratives and Power

The power of discourse in social and political relations has long been recognized in anthropology, including in studies of economic development (Ferguson 1990; Escobar 1995). Borrowing mainly from the late French philosopher and social theorist Michel Foucault (1991a and b), scholars have shown how states and development agencies impose their own discipline, concepts, and languages, as well as "scientific" narratives in support of them, to disguise highly unequal power relationships and political agendas (Li 2009; Mitchell 2002). Harrison, for example, uses Foucault's concept of governmentality in the context of markets to show how market governmentality produces certain categories of "incentivised workers, consumers, citizens, entrepreneurs, and so on" (2010b: 24). In development how a group is categorized or labeled by policy makers and agencies is not just an academic exercise, but has real-life implications in terms of resource allocation and access, ability to pursue certain livelihoods, and participation in particular programs (Leach and Mearns 1996; Moncrieffe and Eyben 2007).[5] By moving beyond narratives and concepts to examine actual interventions and their responses in specific historical and cultural contexts, one can observe their effects on everyday lives and material struggles. This tactic also permits a focus on the state and development agencies that produce policy narratives, the programs and projects that result from them, and the ways that local communities resist, accommodate, and/or avoid them.

The book shows how certain narratives and terms, such as market competition and participation, have been hijacked by state and private organizations to promote agendas and policies that discredit local institutions and economic practice. As will be shown, they often are employed to pursue certain politico-economic proposals that increase controls on local populations and livelihoods, while also transferring lands and other resources to state and/or private investors. What is happening on the ground in several African countries under the guise of improving wildlife conservation and local economic benefits (chapter 3) or alleviating poverty and hunger essentially are large-scale land transfers from local communities to outside groups and investors (chapter 6 and conclusion).

Markets and their rewards are distorted by power, and it is those who are politically connected that benefit the most. Although the book is critical of the politics and narratives surrounding market reforms, its message is not an anti-market one. In fact, the actions of the herders, farmers, and small-scale traders discussed in this book are very *pro-market*. Rather the points to be made are that: (1) the logic of the market has penetrated into spheres of social life where it has not been before; and (2) much of the neoliberal discourse about the "free market" has been captured by advocates of a certain market model of large corporate business, where the logic is to eliminate competition—often with government or donor support—and control different markets and actors even when these actions are essentially *antimarket*.

The book also is *not antidevelopment*, although it does take issue with certain development narratives and policies that espouse a type of corporate model that constrains and diverts resources from many of the positive local developments occurring throughout Africa, including in the countries discussed in the book. Many of the real developments in Africa that are taking place, such as the phenomenal spread of mobile phone technologies discussed earlier and such related industries as mobile banking and financial transfer companies, are occurring without much assistance from the international donor community. The growth in livestock exports from the Horn of Africa is another development story that has emerged without international development assistance or government involvement, in part because much of it originates from stateless Somalia. Somalia, including the states of Somaliland and Puntland, exports more than 1.5 million live animals per year, making it one of the largest exporters of live animals in the world (chapter 7). In monetary terms, it is estimated that the Horn of Africa itself, including Somalia, exports an estimated US$1 billion of live animals and animal products with very little development or state assistance (Catley et al. 2013). While the trade does not usually benefit the poorest herders in the region, it is still a commercial accomplishment that has generated needed revenues for large segments of the population and region. Other positive developments discussed in the book include pineapple growers and cooperatives in Ghana who eventually benefited from World Bank and state assistance, and NGO programs in The Gambia that established village gardens of women who were able to tap lucrative hotel and, at least initially, high-value export markets (chapter 1).

Organization of the Book

The book takes seriously the charge of Kingfisher and Maskovsky (2008) for grounded empirical work on the effects of neoliberal reforms on everyday life. However, to understand the effects of neoliberal reforms in a comparative context, it is necessary to work across different communities and to address larger questions and scales than an anthropologist normally does. "Thick" ethnography of specific cultures is vital to the anthropological project, but for this work it was essential to push beyond the particulars of individual cases, to probe cross-cultural patterns and themes especially centered on labor, land, and market relations. The goal is to capture both the details of local livelihoods and relationships ("everyday life") and also provide a basis for comparison.

No doubt there is a tradeoff in ethnographic depth and knowledge when geographic coverage is expanded and multiple research sites—even countries—are included, but this breadth is necessary for the book's objective of identifying the comparative impacts of a global reform agenda. Although each of the chapters in this book is grounded in local ethnography, some rely more extensively on survey research than others, and still others capture larger geographic scales than is common in anthropology (see Preface for details on research methods).

Throughout the book the ubiquitous SAPs are a common thread. Each of the six countries discussed underwent an SAP program, and some of the chapters (especially 1 and 2) capture the early moments of the reform encounter, while others examine impacts over a longer and more recent time span (chapters 5 and 6). The next chapter (1) analyzes contract farming programs in The Gambia and Ghana that encourage farmers to pursue niche markets for nontraditional commodities—for example, so-called luxury vegetables (French beans and eggplants) and spices—in order to earn scarce foreign exchange and reduce dependence on traditional export commodities. By supplying wealthy northern markets and consumers with off-season produce for year-round consumption of fresh fruits and vegetables, the activity paradoxically means African farmers often confront poverty and food insecurity in their own locations. Perhaps nowhere are the effects of neoliberal reforms and capitalism more baldly felt by African farmers than with the imposition of contract farming.

In chapter 2 the growing phenomena of petty traders and informality in African cities are examined. It draws on a case study of peri-urban Maputo (Mozambique) that captures the period (1991–1993) just after the end of a prolonged civil war when pro-market reforms were being introduced. It shows how petty trade (informal sector) has become a survival mechanism for many in Maputo's peri-urban neighborhoods in a context of reduced formal sector employment and wages. Chapter 3, in turn, addresses how practices and discourses of rural development in East Africa are increasingly shaped by global concerns for biodiversity. Here the market and a pro-business approach are perceived as key mechanisms for improved conservation and livelihoods. What results is a complex web of government, NGOs, and private firms that manage and profit from biodiversity and nature-based activities. This encounter especially is revealing in the region's wildlife-rich pastoralist areas where communities use global concerns about the environment to shape their own agendas to protect lands and livelihoods.

The focus on Kenya continues in chapter 4, where multiparty politics and elections are discussed, with an emphasis on how they influenced local politics and identities in the home district (Baringo) of former president Daniel arap Moi. It shows how democratic reforms created new political spaces, identities, and alliances, including with international NGOs (INGOs), among previously powerless and marginalized groups, such as pastoralist communities. Throughout the country indigenous and minority groups sought increased political rights and representation, including in Moi's home district, where the Il Chamus community successfully sued the government in court for the right to have their own political constituency and representative.

Chapters 5 and 6, in turn, examine one of the inherent contradictions of the neoliberal reform agenda: the need to promote economic growth, while alleviating poverty and protecting the poor through social safety nets. In principle, poverty and hunger were supposed to be alleviated, not produced, under neoliberalism, with government-subsidized social welfare protection being the antithesis of the neoliberal reform agenda. Both chapters spotlight the fact that despite almost two decades of economic reforms, chronic food insecurity and poverty are prevalent in both Ethiopia and Kenya. Both governments are able to use neoliberal technologies of auditing, measuring, and labeling to pursue political agendas under the guise of helping the poor and hungry. In chapter 5 the Ethiopian state uses a narrative of "food aid dependency" to justify a top-down food aid welfare program, as well as the resettlement of local farmers from their customary homelands. Similarly, chapter 6 discusses how the Kenyan state uses narratives of pastoralist poverty to justify political actions under the guise of promoting economic growth and alleviating poverty, despite the fact that many pastoralists do not perceive themselves as poor.

In chapter 7 the Somali case is presented as an example of hyper-liberalization where politics and power relations are important but operate in the absence of a functioning state. It highlights a transnational community that is increasingly globalized and able to adjust to open trade policies and pursue its comparative advantage in a range of economic activities. Without a government but with a growing diaspora and a remittance, trade-based economy, the chapter suggests, the Somali business community has benefited from economic and political reforms in the region as it has been able to enter new international markets and invest widely in neighboring Kenya, South Sudan, and Dubai.

Finally, in the conclusion a summary of the book's key findings and themes is discussed, as well as their relevance for understanding development and social change in Africa. It does not offer solutions and prescriptions to Africa's development problems, but instead points to the positive local developments that are occurring, often without the support of development agencies, and to the practical lessons that can be learned from them. As the chapter and book generally reiterate, the impacts of neoliberal reforms can be revealed statistically, but more importantly, they can be told through the stories and actions of those individuals and communities who have experienced and lived through what can only be described as an era of postponed promise. The book is a testimony to their resilience and creativity.

1 "They Think We Can Manufacture Crops"

Contract Farming and the Nontraditional Commodity Business

IN MAY 1994 I sat at a meeting in the office of a large international development organization in downtown Banjul, the small capital city of The Gambia, West Africa. The conversation centered on the need to diversify the country's exports and its dependence on groundnuts, a traditional export crop whose annual export earnings had been declining for the past decade. The discussion eventually turned to how The Gambia, with its favorable climate, political stability, low labor costs, and relatively close proximity to European markets, could increase its role in the growing fresh fruit and vegetable and cut flower trade to Europe, an activity that already had achieved some success. A glossy, colorful brochure financed by a British aid agency was handed out; it included the caption *"Cut Flowers, The Gambia: An Opportunity to Invest"* (Commonwealth Secretariat and the National Investment Board, n.d.). Key questions raised at the meeting included (1) how could contract farming of "nontraditional" exports commodities (green beans, chilies, and cut flowers) play a role in this trade; and (2) how could beneficial links between Gambian farmers and international markets and businesses be forged?

Later in that same year I attended a similar meeting in Accra, Ghana, where policy makers again were praising the benefits of export diversification and the nontraditional export trade to Europe, which both were perceived as mechanisms for bolstering the country's economy and alleviating poverty. In this case it was argued that the country had relied too long on traditional export commodities such as cocoa, whose trade volume had improved little in recent years. Once again, the export of nontraditional commodities (NTCs) to lucrative markets in the West (Europe and the United States) was viewed as a means to diversify exports and achieve economic growth. The kinds of discussions at this and the Banjul meetings were not without financial consequences, as millions of dollars of development funds at the time were chasing nontraditional commodity programs in Africa, often relying on contract farming models for implementation. They were (and still are) pursued in the hopes of diversifying exports, enhancing the so-called private sector, and improving the welfare of small farmers by linking them with transnational firms (Helleiner 2002; World Bank 2007a).

In its most basic terms, contract farming (CF) involves the production of a commodity by a farmer under an agreement with a buyer, usually an agribusiness firm or food processor, at an agreed price and quantity. It has long dominated the agrarian landscape in high-income countries, such as the United States, but in the 1990s it was a relatively recent innovation in sub-Saharan Africa, where it remains both widely praised and strongly criticized (see Little and Watts 1994; Glover and Kusterer 1990; Sautier et al. 2006). In Africa CF operations sometimes are married with the production and trade of an NTC, which is defined as "a product that has not been produced in a particular country before . . . [or] was traditionally produced for domestic production but is now being exported" (Barham et al. 1992: 43). USAID alone supported more than twenty-five NTC programs in Africa during the 1990s that focused on niche markets, such as French beans, spices, and mangoes and pineapples, and often involved a contract farming model of production and marketing (Little and Dolan 2000; Ghana Private-Public Partnership Food Industry Development Program 2003). Like the community-based conservation programs that will be discussed in chapter 3, these ventures seemed like "win-win" situations: low-income African farmers gain access to advanced technologies and high-income markets, and private corporations and governments profit from cheap labor, abundant land, and favorable growing conditions.

Despite a very mixed record of delivering benefits to farmers in Africa, contract farming of NTCs is viewed as a "fresh hope for Africa's declining agriculture" (World Agroforestry Centre/NEPAD 2007: 1). In this chapter, I examine the experiences of contract farming of NTCs in the Banjul (The Gambia) and Accra regions (Ghana) of West Africa, both sites where horticultural exports and CF were strongly advocated and backed by international financial institutions and development agencies. In the early 1990s both countries were undergoing major economic reform and export diversification programs, and contract farming of NTCs was seen as integral to these efforts. Similar NTC programs were taking place in several other countries on the continent at the time, including Kenya, Uganda, Zimbabwe, and Burkina Faso, with the same Panglossian rhetoric about the benefits of CF farming and NTC trade. At the time the enthusiasm seemed warranted as exports of fresh fruit and vegetables from Africa to Europe were growing rapidly in the 1990s, especially during winter months, when European-grown produce disappears from the market (see Little and Dolan 2000; Little and Watts 1994). In practice, however, these were targeted investments for particular locales that took advantage of Africa's climate, cheap labor, abundant land, and donor financial incentives, but proved to be especially risky for smallholders.

By capturing the historical moment when farmers in both locations were first being introduced to contract farming of NTCs, the chapter assesses its local impacts on farmer welfare and labor relations; the ways that governments and development organizations (including NGOs) latched on to "niche markets" for NTCs as solutions to the two countries' economic crises; and the contradictions between the narratives of policy makers and the local realities of CF. It also addresses recent challenges to CF and horticultural exports presented by the growing dominance of supermarkets, new certification requirements for food imports from Africa, and changing consumer preferences in Europe.[1] Some of the unsustainable aspects of smallholder involvement with NTCs first observed in the early 1990s created problems throughout the decade and into the 2000s and eventually derailed what was seen by many as a promising union between small farmers and international business (Glover and Kusterer 1990; Little and Watts 1994).

The chapter will show that one country (Ghana) saw its exports of NTCs grow rapidly in the 1990s and 2000s, although accompanied by a sharp decline in the use of smallholders and contract farming. By contrast, during the same period The Gambia experienced a decline in both NTC exports and reliance on contract farming and small-scale farmers. The development narrative that small-scale farmers would greatly benefit from a close integration with multinational business and its modern technologies and management practices proved to be overly naïve regarding the economics and politics of CF, demands of global markets, and incentive structures of transnational firms themselves. In both the Ghanaian and Gambian cases large agribusiness firms and commercial farms moved away from contracting with smallholders and, instead, have expanded production of NTCs on their own large farms. As will be emphasized, this shift partially results from the imposition of stringent certification and food safety requirements by European importers and supermarkets that made very costly the monitoring of produce from smallholders, but the trend away from smallholder contracting was well underway even before this, including in Kenya and other African countries (see Dolan and Humphrey 2000; Okello et al. 2007; Minot and Ngigi 2004; and Sautier et al. 2006).

Another factor that accounted for the demise of small farmer contracting was the liberalization of land markets in both locations, which reduced the costs of land acquisition and allowed large farms to expand at the expense of smallholders. The cumulative effect of these forces further reduced the role for small-scale farmers in the NTC business (see Dolan and Humphrey 2000). The declining trend in the use of CF in the NTC export trade occurred despite the continued praise for contract farming and its benefits in development and government policy circles (Ghana Private-Public Partnership Food Industry Development Program 2003; World Agroforestry Centre/NEPAD 2007). Finally, as will be shown in the case of Ghana, small farmers ironically have been brought back into the NTC business because of strong state support and public investment programs, both pariahs of the neoliberal reform era but critical elements of the Ghanaian success story.

The Historical Context

The language and classification process of NTCs reflect a set of global changes that are closely associated with free trade policies and the structural adjustment programs that were discussed in the introduction.[2] This observation is especially relevant to Ghana and The Gambia, which were among the first "adjusters" on the continent to undergo wide-ranging structural reforms in the early 1980s. In the hopes of increasing trade revenues and reducing the state's role in agriculture, development agencies and their dependent African states heavily pushed for private-sector-led export diversification and NTC programs (see Mannon 2005; Minot and Ngigi 2004; World Bank 1989; Humphrey 2004). As implemented in practice, the concept of an NTC is ripe with contradictions and uncertainties since what constitutes a nontraditional export product changes both within and across national boundaries. For example, under a USAID trade program in Ghana in the 1990s the yam, a tuber crop indigenous to West Africa and a local food staple, is classified as a nontraditional export. On the other hand, cocoa, an industrial commodity introduced by the British in the last century, is considered a traditional export.

The contradictions are even sillier in East Africa, where in Uganda coffee and cotton are labeled as traditional products, but maize and some varieties of local beans qualify as NTCs because they have not been exported to overseas markets in the past. The whole range of "exotic" produce (for example, mangoes), high-value horticultural products (for instance, green beans and cut flowers), and spices—the so-called niche crops that have received such a strong endorsement from the World Bank (World Bank 1994 and 2007a)—mainly fall into the category of nontraditional. The dividing lines, however, are often blurred, and business entrepreneurs and politicians have been known to petition the government, often via an export promotion unit, to have a certain product reclassified as a nontraditional export in order to receive a subsidy or credit. Since the export of NTCs in such countries as Ghana is exempted from government export tariffs and is eligible for tax rebates, there are strong incentives to pursue this strategy (see Takane 2004: 31). Thus, a planner with one mark of a pen can reclassify an entire commodity regime, its farmers, and traders into a category worthy of investment and promotion and, as well be discussed later in the chapter, instigate agrarian changes with widespread social and political implications.

The notion of a NTC takes on a whole set of powerful associations in states such as Ghana and The Gambia. Table 1.1 lists some of these hidden attributes that were implicitly endorsed by the economic reform programs of the 1980s and 1990s. While production and trade in traditional export commodities, such as groundnuts (The Gambia) and cocoa (Ghana), symbolized the old statist policies and "backward-looking" programs of agriculture, the NTC business is seen

Table 1.1. Nontraditional versus Traditional Export Commodities

Nontraditional Commodities	Traditional Commodities
Private sector	Government
Progressive	Backward
Globally market-driven	Government monopoly
Assist economic reforms	Hinder economic reforms
Pro transnational corporations	Pro state-owned corporations
Wave of the future	Wave of the past

Source: Adapted from Little and Dolan (2000: 62)

as progressive, export-driven, and entrepreneurial. In short, it signifies a new market-savvy Africa with linkages to transnational companies, fiscally conservative budget reformers, and true believers in the benefits of global commerce.

The decade of the 1980s witnessed rapid increases in the involvement of low-income African farmers in the production of NTCs, including in Ghana and The Gambia. As prices for classical export crops, such as sugar and cocoa, fell throughout the decade, many farmers, with the active encouragement of their governments and development agencies, pursued high-value niche crops. In The Gambia, for example, the percentage of total foreign exchange earnings from groundnut exports fell from 45 to 12 percent from 1981–82 to 1991–92 (Hadjmichael et al. 1992). Although not as dramatic as the Gambian case, foreign exchange earnings from Ghana's traditional exports, including cocoa and gold, declined throughout the 1980s (ISSER 1992: 77). Confronted with these dismal trends, both states, with funding from international development agencies, pursued NTC production and export diversification programs. This often meant significant transformations in the organization of production and marketing among smallholders, including the promotion of linkages with agribusiness through contract farming mechanisms (see Little and Watts 1994).

In high-value commodity chains contracts are used to vertically integrate farmers into the market, ensure that there are regular supplies and a reliable market outlet for the commodity that is produced, and facilitate transfers of technology and inputs between growers and contracting firms. The underlying premise is that a contract is required for farmers to take on the added risks associated with a new crop and an unfamiliar and often very distant market. It also helps to ensure that the buyer has a predictable, reliable supply of the product. Contract farming is a common agrarian institution in high-income countries like the United States, but in places like Africa it is part of recent transformations in global commodity systems and trade. In its early stages contract farming arrangements between smallholders and large firms and farms were integral to Ghana's and The

Gambia's horticultural export trade.[3] In the case of the Accra area the main NTC grown by smallholders was pineapples, and in the Banjul region it was vegetables and fruits, mainly eggplants, chilies, green beans, and mangoes.

The growth in NTC exports from sub-Saharan Africa during the past twenty-five years, including from The Gambia and Ghana, is best illustrated through an examination of the global fresh fruit and vegetable (FFV) industry. This sector has involved strong participation both by agribusiness firms and African smallholders. The destination for most of Africa's horticultural produce, including FFVs from The Gambia and Ghana, has been Europe. Aggregate exports from sub-Saharan Africa showed large annual increases during the 1990s, especially from Kenya, Zimbabwe, and South Africa, but large declines in the 2000s (World Bank 2007a). Part of the reason for the recent drop in FFV exports from sub-Saharan Africa is the emergence of Morocco and Egypt as key exporters of winter vegetables to Europe. These two countries hold considerable transport advantage, with their close proximity to Europe, over sub-Saharan African locations and, consequently, have taken over a large percentage of market share (World Bank 2007a: 6).

In terms of The Gambia and Ghana, table 1.2 shows the export record for FFVs in the countries also is mixed. For comparative purposes, data from Kenya, which is one of Africa's earliest and most important exporters of FFVs, are included in the table. Overall FFV exports (mainly pineapples) from Ghana continued to grow during 1989–2002, but declined in The Gambia by almost 75 percent during 1993–2002. The Gambia, which was one of the early participants in the trade, clearly has not kept pace and has lost market share to other West African countries, including Mali and Burkina Faso (see Friedberg 2004), and the above-mentioned North African competitors. In addition to the increased competition from nearby countries, other reasons for The Gambia's poor performance include decreased air and sea transport links to Europe; the increased demands for certification and product safety by European importers; and widespread financial problems among export firms. In contrast to The Gambia, the export market in Ghana has benefited from a growing demand for its main NTC export, pineapple; its demand in Europe grew at 5 percent per annum during 2000–2003 (Ghana Private-Public Partnership Food Industry Development Program 2003: 8).

Associated with the emphasis on nontraditional exports were extensive changes in the economic policies of African states and the international donors that supported them. As was discussed in the introduction, in the decade of the 1980s national governments in Ghana, The Gambia, and several other African countries confronted both nightmares of national bankruptcy and an international community that viewed excessive state intervention as the main problem. The decade marked the beginning of a radically different approach to development. The economic reform programs introduced in The Gambia and Ghana during 1983 initiated some of the earliest and most comprehensive pro-market policies on the

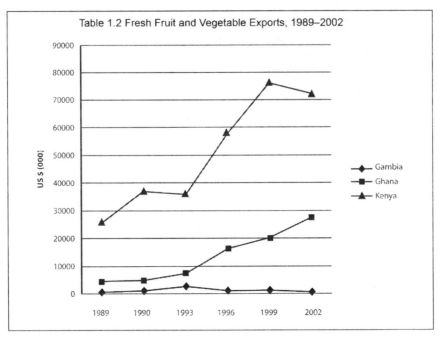

Table 1.2 Fresh Fruit and Vegetable Exports, 1989–2002

Source: FAO Trade Statistics (1989–2002).

continent. For The Gambia this meant strong reductions in fertilizer subsidies for rice production, the country's key food staple, which resulted in reduced fertilizer imports from 5,500 to 600 tons from 1984 to 1990, a steep fall in domestic production, and a growth in rice imports of more than 300 percent in that period (Mosley, Carney, and Becker 2010). Since the reform programs in both Ghana and The Gambia were instigated and supported by the International Monetary Fund (IMF) and World Bank, they went by the same name, the Economic Recovery Programme (ERP). Indeed, the IMF and World Bank were driving forces, and NTC export activities found a prominent place in the reform packages in both countries. The importance of production and marketing flexibility and the perceived failures of the state in most agricultural export ventures were stated reasons for a new private-sector-led strategy (see World Bank 1989 and 1994). Both countries had large state-owned juice-processing companies that failed in the 1980s, only to be replaced by private-sector initiatives during the 1990s. As will be shown, the market-led reforms in The Gambia and Ghana sharply increased the role of the private sector in key export industries, especially in the FFV trade.

Strong fiscal and other incentives encouraged investment in the production of NTCs, and by the early 1990s both Ghana and The Gambia established export promotion councils and regularly participated in European trade shows to promote their exports. In The Gambia one marketing campaign included a picture of a ripe mango and eggplant on its promotion brochures, with the caption: "The Gambia means more than beautiful beaches and friendly people" (field notes, May 1993). The Gambia is well known as a winter escape destination for Europeans, especially British tourists, but it also wanted recognition for its exports of fresh fruits and vegetables. For both countries the NTC business was to usher in a new era of "catalyzing export diversification towards more sophisticated sources of advantage" (Ghana Private-Public Partnership Food Industry Development Program 2003: 3).

The Push for Nontraditional Commodities

The promotion of NTCs in Ghana and The Gambia, therefore, occurred against a backdrop of sweeping economic reforms that reduced the state's role in agriculture and elevated the participation of the private sector. It should be noted here that the term "private sector" and its meaning are especially problematic in the context of many economic activities, including the NTC business (also see chapters 3 and 7). In the Gambian case, many of the small export firms had strong investment from key government officials, the same individuals who were publically deciding on public support and policies to promote NTC exports. Like many NTC firms in Ghana, they also depended heavily on extension services, infrastructure, and market concessions from the government (see Little 1994). The idea that the private sector can somehow be neatly distinguished from the public sector simply is incorrect, whether one is speaking of the actions of an NTC contracting enterprise or an NGO (see chapter 3). Ghana and The Gambia both were held up as success stories of good economic adjusters and models for other African countries (Hadjmichael et al. 1992; Sahn 1996). Although this label is no longer applied to The Gambia, especially after its military coup in 1994, Ghana maintains a reputation as a very good reformer and economic performer despite the presence of strong critics (Aryeetey and Kanbur 2008). In July 1994 The Gambia experienced a bloodless military coup that overthrew the government of President Jawara and replaced him with a 29-year-old soldier, Yahya Jammeh, who remains in power today (2012). After this event the involvement of many Western development organizations, including USAID, ceased temporarily, and those that resumed operations in the country did so at significantly reduced levels of support (Loum 2002; Radalet and McPherson 1995).

In the early 1990s, both Ghana and The Gambia were being heralded for their enabling business and investment environments (Aryeetey et al. 2000; Konadu-Agyemang 2001; Radalet and McPherson 1995). The international community generously rewarded their governments with massive amounts of foreign aid, making them at the time (1990–93) among Africa's and the world's largest recipients of assistance in per capita terms (Konadu-Agyemang 2001; Radalet and McPherson 1995). Ironically, despite the favorable reputation and significant external resources provided The Gambia, public disenchantment with the ERP was an important factor in the overthrow of the government in July 1994 (see Loum 2002). Although the elite in the former Jawara regime were being enriched through illegal land deals and state-financed investments, including in the NTC export sector, the structural adjustment program "failed to increase living standards for the majority of the rural poor, even if a widespread deterioration was avoided" (Cooke and Hughes 1997: 99). Ghana, in turn, confronted several political challenges in the 1990s, including multiparty elections, but avoided the turmoil that marred The Gambia (see Boafo-Arthur 2007).

The production of NTCs is done on a relatively large-scale basis in the key peri-urban areas of both Accra, Ghana, and Banjul, The Gambia. I will first describe the setting for NTC production in the Accra area and then address the Banjul situation.

Approximately 25 kilometers north of Accra is Ghana's pineapple belt, where smallholders, traders, and large and small firms all compete for part of the lucrative European pineapple trade. It is a zone of several thousand hectares of well-drained, fertile soils with moderate slopes that are conducive to pineapple production. It extends west-to-east about 35 kilometers between the main towns of Nsawam and Aburi in the Eastern Region of southern Ghana. Many pineapple growers in the area during the 1990s had an informal purchase agreement with a particular exporter (s) or large farm, which then sold to an export firm. In addition, at the time there were another approximately twenty large farms growing the fruit as well, with leased land holdings as large as 300 hectares.

Pineapple production and exports from Ghana have taken place since the 1950s but began to receive special attention in the late 1980s with the state's push for export diversification. In 1989 the government established the Export Finance Company Limited of Ghana to assist with the export of nontraditional commodities, such as pineapple, and created tax incentives and other policies to promote its exports (see ISSER 1992: 139–144). An earlier study by the Ghanaian-based Institute of Statistical, Social and Economic Research (ISSER) showed that the initial response was positive but not spectacular: "In 1989, 61 agricultural commodities [including pineapples] featured in the non-traditional commodities that were exported. . . . The foreign exchange earned rose from US$21.17 million in 1989 to US$28.78 million in 1990, an increase of about 36 percent" (ISSER 1992: 77, cited in Daddieh and Little 1995: 3). The growth in pineapple exports, however, was considerably better than for most other NTCs. From 1990 to 2002, the export value of the fruit increased even more, with growth of about 400 percent during the period (see table 1.3). By 2002 pineapple was the country's most important nontraditional horticultural export, accounting for 24 percent of total horticultural exports (Trienekens et al. 2004: 4).

Table 1.3. Fresh Fruit and Vegetable Exports, 1989–2002

	Volume in ($000)					
Country	1989	1990	1993	1996	1999	2002
Gambia	610	900	2,710	1,070	1,166	671
(vegetab. amt)	(440)	(670)	(2,100)	(350)	(35)	(289)
Ghana	4,375	4,830	7,490	16,260	20,086	27,714
(pineapp. amt)	(2,097)	(3,830)	(5,180)	(9,051)	(11,593)	(15,520)
Kenya	26,001	36,817	36,190	58,128	76,447	72,550

Source: FAO Trade Statistics (1989–2002).

The large-scale promotion of NTCs in The Gambia first took hold in the late 1980s. The country attracted transnational investment at the time and emerged as an important regional exporter of horticultural produce to Europe (Little and Dolan 2000). Similar to Ghana's exports, the most important destination for Gambian produce was Europe, especially the United Kingdom (UK). Despite widespread enthusiasm for the new exports, annual earnings from NTCs never exceeded US$3 million during 1990 to 2002, and they even experienced a steep decline after the mid-1990s (see table 1.3). A government policy paper published in 1993 laid out an investment plan and an objective to increase horticultural exports to dalasis 100 million (US$11.64 million) by 2000 (Gambia 1993: 20), an amount that the sector never came close to achieving. There were fifteen large firms—many with their own farms—exporting NTCs from The Gambia in 1994, but only two firms in 2004 (World Bank 2007b). The more successful of the two firms, which survived the export bust, is a wholly owned subsidiary of a British supermarket chain. It has a sophisticated irrigated farm of 400 hectares, including 50 that are certified for organic production; its own shipping and refrigeration facilities at the Banjul International Airport; and a permanent workforce of more than three hundred employees (ibid.: 107). Similar to the Ghanaian case, there also has been a strong tendency for large farms and export firms to decrease purchases from smallholders.

As with Ghana, the export of The Gambia's horticultural produce was (still is) a prominent element in the state's export diversification program (Gambia 1993: 17–18; World Trade Organisation 2004). As recently as 2005, high-value horticultural (NTC) production and trade were still being trumpeted as a very viable export diversification industry for The Gambia despite the massive decline in exports. One report, for example, notes that "there is a good opportunity for stimulating [horticultural] production to augment levels of exports and foreign exchange earnings in guaranteed markets abroad. . . . With increased freight space in aircrafts, weekly exports could easily be doubled" (Entreplan 2005: 25). Another equally optimistic study argues that "the main potential for developing non-traditional exports is in the area of horticulture" (McKay 2005: 1206). Flash-back to about fifteen years earlier and one finds almost the same hyperbole used to describe the promise of NTC exports from The Gambia (see FAO 1992). Indeed, these recent assessments take no note of the historical legacy of declining exports, nor do they consider the reasons for this downward trend.

Thus, the strong pro-market ideology associated with NTC trade has blink-ered the Gambian state and private-sector advocates alike to the realities of a sector that is badly in decline. To its disadvantage, the country now competes for air and shipping space with larger countries such as Ghana, whose exports are con-siderably greater and a higher priority for international shippers (see table 1.3). In fact, the growth in pineapple exports from Ghana has impacted the limited sea and air shipping space available for Europe's other West African trading partners, including The Gambia (Agro-Ind 2002). Nonetheless, the Gambian state and its development sponsors still amazingly encourage exports of NTCs to Europe as a development strategy for the country, while maintaining policies that reduce ex-port taxes and tariffs on inputs, and subsidize infrastructure and marketing ser-vices for exporters.

From Smallholder to Large-Farm Production

Who is involved in the production and trade of NTCs in Ghana and The Gambia? What realities underlie an industry that has received the praise of so many differ-ent organizations? When horticultural exports began to take off in the 1980s, it was assumed that village smallholders, especially women growers in the case of The Gambia, would be able to participate in this growth. Toward this goal, there were several initiatives on the part of NGOs and development agencies that spe-cifically targeted women's gardens in The Gambia, in the hopes that they could benefit from the contract farming of NTCs (Daniels 1988; FAO 1992; Planas 1990). The garden schemes themselves usually received land from the local *alkalo* (chief) and were managed by a small committee (eight to ten members) comprised mainly of women. They are found in peri-urban settlements around Banjul and range in size from 2 to 15 irrigated hectares, with an average of twenty-five to thirty-five members (see Little and Dolan 2000). This section compares and contrasts dif-ferent production regimes, including women's village gardens, involved in NTC production in each country and shows how they have changed over time.

The production of export horticulture in both countries is comprised of vari-ous production and institutional arrangements involving farmers, traders, and firms of different scales. Actors range from small-scale merchants attempting to export on their own to large corporations with sophisticated technologies that are vertically integrated with the operations of large European buyers. As this section will demonstrate, there are remarkable similarities between the two countries in the history of NTC production and trade, but also important differences in policies and scale of production and trade.

Contracting with Smallholders

The general conditions for successful CF ventures include a labor-intensive commodity that can be grown by smallholders and a market that cannot easily be met through open market purchases. Both of these conditions are found in the Accra and Banjul cases. In both examples the emergence of CF schemes were based on new labor-intensive, niche-market commodities (NTCs) that could be processed or airlifted fresh to seasonal markets in Europe. Moreover, in both areas contractual arrangements between small farmers and buyers ranged from informal buying arrangements to formal written contracts, although the latter were the exception.[4]

Elements of contract farming were initially invoked in two different types of production arrangements in the Banjul and Accra regions. In Banjul export firms initially contracted with the communal gardens of women farmers mentioned earlier and with mainly male commercial growers on farms of 2–5 hectares. On the other hand, in Accra they contracted with small farmers (mainly male) on holdings of 1–2 hectares and with male commercial growers on farms up to 10 hectares (see Daddieh and Little 1995). These relationships changed over time. Although firms and large farms often initially contracted with surrounding smallholders to meet export orders, they eventually abandoned them as they developed their own farms and increased production using waged labor. This pattern of excluding smallholders in favor of production on large units using waged labor has been documented in other sub-Saharan countries, especially in Kenya (see Dolan and Humphrey 2000).

In terms of production relations, marked gender differences were prevalent in both sites. In the Banjul region more than 90 percent of contracted farmers on the communal vegetable schemes were women. Export firms preferred to contract with them and/or hire them as laborers for their own farms because they were perceived as good and docile growers. The careful harvesting and weeding of labor-intensive specialty vegetables, such as green beans, were (and still are) perceived to be female activities, a stereotype that also explains why large farms mainly hire woman vegetable pickers. In numerous interviews with Gambia farm managers, these qualities and characteristics of women growers and laborers—for instance, "careful vegetable pickers"—were highlighted (for Kenyan examples of such gendered stereotypes, see Dolan 1997).

In contrast to the Gambian case, pineapple farming in the Accra region predominantly is a male activity, and the work involves laborious field clearing, husking of fruits, and planting of heavy pineapple suckers/young seedlings. More than 80 percent of contracted pineapple growers are males, and the hiring practices of large farms favor male over female workers, an almost complete inversion of the Gambian pattern (Daddieh and Little 1995; Conley and Udry 2004).

In both countries small-scale entrepreneurs, often young males ages 22–35 years, emerged early on in the horticultural boom. They started by buying produce from smallholders, and the more successful ones eventually invested in their own farms of up to 20 hectares in the Accra and 5 hectares in the Banjul cases. In the Gambian case, they began to replace women gardeners as important sources of produce for the export business by 1992–93. Horticultural production in The Gambia depends on irrigation, which greatly increases capital requirements for NTC production in the country. By contrast, pineapple production in Accra mainly is rain-fed. During 1993–94 about sixty of these itinerant male traders and/or commercial farmers operated in the Accra area, but only ten in the smaller Banjul region. In the Gambian case small-scale horticultural producers usually relied on no more than four or five exporters, although there were fifteen registered export firms in 1992–93 (Little and Dolan 1993). However, in the Accra area there were about seventy-five registered exporters during most of the 1990s (see Daddieh and Little 1995).

By 2004 options by Gambian smallholders for selling had become even more limited. As noted earlier, only two export firms remained in the NTC business by then, and they procured from smallholders only when extra supplies were needed for an export order (World Bank 2007b: 107). At this time most export firms and small-scale commercial growers had either gone out of business or shifted their trade to local and regional markets (personal communication, Isatou Jack, October 1, 2011). In contrast to the CF operations in The Gambia, a majority of small-scale pineapples farmers in Ghana contracted with more than one exporter and often changed purchase agreements after only one or two years (Daddieh and Little 1995). As with the Banjul case, producer prices were usually determined prior to the production season, and some inputs were provided by the exporter.

Small-scale farmers in Ghana had pineapple plots of less than 2 hectares, often located near an export company's farm. As noted earlier, most of these growers and the laborers they hired were male. At the start of the season the exporter and farmer ("outgrower") usually agreed on a price and fixed an amount that would be purchased, although there was variability in these arrangements. The firm's workers would come to the farmer's field and spray the pineapples with a chemical that hastened maturity and then would arrange to harvest the fruits within three to four days. The laborers usually wore the chemical sprayers on their backs. The larger export firms/farms also transported the fruit to their warehouses, where it was boxed and prepared for export (Daddieh and Little 1995). For smaller exporters the farmers usually had to harvest the fruit themselves and then seek out the exporter to transport the produce. Not surprisingly, most growers preferred to deal with large farms/firms rather than the small-scale traders mentioned earlier, who were seen by some farmers as "unreliable" (field notes, June 1994). In most cases farmers were not compensated until after the pineapples were exported and sometimes not until the exporter was paid, which could take two months or more (Daddieh and Little 1995: 42–43).

There were problems, however, with the more flexible buying arrangements in Ghana. Farmers sometimes had little knowledge about the individual with whom they contracted, and thus deception and payment defaults were common (Daddieh and Little 1995). Reports of nonpayment from small traders were more frequent in the Accra than in the Banjul region. As discussed earlier, young male entrepreneurs hurriedly rushed into the NTC business with little experience of the pineapple sector and often quickly confronted serious financial difficulties. When the inexperienced businessmen had their produce rejected by a large export firm after procuring supplies from farmers, smallholders often suffered. The traders would cut their losses by reneging on their payment agreements with local farmers.

Occasional stories were heard in the Accra region about unbearably long delays in payments, reduced payments based on false claims of product quality, and other problems with buyers (based on field notes, June 1994):

> The exporters do cheat and only pay ½ the money some times. They only select the best fruits and leave the others. (Male farmer, age 65)

> When payment did not occur, the exporter was always telling us of problems with airplane failures. (Male farmer, age 43)

> When exporters wish to reduce the agreed price per kilo, they give excuses that their flight failed them. (Male farmer, age 50)

> There are periods when they do not show because the plane didn't arrive due to bad weather, or when there was enough fruits in Europe. (Male farmer, age 37)

> The exporter came to spray but did not harvest all. I asked for compensation but they didn't budge. (Male farmer, age 29)

> An exporter came to spray but did not harvest and all the fruits got rotten. I cannot do anything because I am scared of the exporter. (Male farmer, age 45)

These comments show the very unequal relationships between buyers and growers and the vulnerability of the latter group. The exporters control most of the information about the export business and can use excuses that smallholders are unable to verify, like "airplane failure" or problems in the European market, to renege on payment. (For similar stories about airplane mishaps in Kenya's horticultural export trade, see Dolan 2001.) These outrageous tales involved both large and small firms/traders, but were more frequent among the latter. About

20 percent of farmers in 1994 reported that they no longer grew pineapples for export because of difficulties with buyers, especially in collecting money. In one case farmers who were not paid even "impounded an exporter's transport vehicle because he had been unduly delinquent in paying them. It took the intercession of the local chief for a payment arrangement to be negotiated and for the truck to be released" (Daddieh and Little 1995: 43).

Ghanaian smallholders face special risks and vulnerabilities because of the technologies associated with pineapple ripening, which can limit their ability to negotiate alternative markets. As noted earlier, after the employee of an exporter has sprayed the fruit with a ripening chemical, growers are compelled to market their pineapples almost immediately. If the exporter does not return to purchase and transport the pineapples, as one farmer explained, "the fruits can rot in the field" (field notes, June 1994). If the grower suspects fraud, then she/he either must sell to another exporter/trader or unload the produce on the local market for about 50 percent of the export price. At times smallholders have to compete with each other to secure a buying arrangement with an exporter, which further reduces their negotiating power and, consequently, the price they receive. In some interviews farmers revealed tales of having to bribe buying agents to secure a purchase agreement (Daddieh and Little 1995: 45). Thus, despite the boom in the Ghanaian pineapple business, a large number of farmers had withdrawn from the NTC trade during 1992–94, in order to concentrate on the less lucrative but more secure domestic market. Many of these dropouts had experienced negative experiences with one or more exporters.

Both Ghanaian and Gambian contract farmers complained about the negative effects of Economic Reform Programme (ERP) policies in their countries. Gambian farmers were most concerned about the retrenchment of family members from government jobs during the early 1990s, while Ghanaians voiced concerns about inflation, especially for consumer goods and farm inputs. There was a general feeling in both countries that "a lot of goods are available but they are too expensive for us to buy" (field notes, June 1994). Small-scale pineapple farmers in the Accra region also complained about the elimination of fertilizer subsidies under the ERP. Daddieh and Little describe a meeting between farmers and government officials regarding a new World Bank program that required local farmers to cover the full costs of inputs, even after government subsidies for agriculture already had been drastically reduced:

> The outspoken chief, for instance, rose to his feet to let it be known by the delegation that even if Mr. Rawlings (the President) himself were standing in front of him, he would repeat his assertions to his face. . . . He insisted that farmers do not have the money to contribute to these proposed projects. He provided much needed comic relief when he said that he had not even given his wife "chop money" that day. He went on to allege that the government had constructed a road for the benefit of Combined farm (the leading pineapple

grower-exporter) under PAMSCAD (Programme of Actions to Mitigate the Social Costs of Adjustment). How could the government construct a road for a single individual and then turn around and ask for contributions when it comes to smallholders? Several farmers also wanted to know why the government has handed over the sale of fertilizer to private individuals who were profiteering at their expense. (1995: 62–63)

The meeting went on for several hours, and government officials were forced to defend the World Bank–sponsored economic reform program, arguing that farmers now had to rely on themselves and confront "the forces of demand and supply." At one point a government official explained how the farmers needed to abandon their old ways of thinking. "No government, he asserted with confidence, including Cuba and China, practices socialism anymore. Cuba is going the capitalist way" (Daddieh and Little 1995: 63).

As illustrated here, local officials had learned the new discourse of neoliberalism and were warning farmers that the market dictates of supply and demand would increasingly affect their welfare in the future. They had to be accountable and responsible for their own welfare. The reduction in state support for smallholder farming, however, was being implemented at a time when the state was reducing import tariffs and export taxes and increasing support for large firms and farms involved with NTCs. That the candid chief, in his remarks, made reference to government assistance for one large commercial farm in the area indicates an astute local awareness of how uneven and unfair the implementation of policy reforms was in this sector.

Thus, despite an improved macro-economic environment in Ghana, economic reforms were taking a heavy toll on the most vulnerable actors in the pineapple commodity chain, and the ones who absorbed most of the risks associated with growing NTCs: small-scale farmers. Ghanaian smallholders were feeling considerable hardship under the economic reform program, especially as prices for agricultural inputs were increasing considerably faster than pineapple prices. In several interviews among the eighty-three farmers in the study's sample complaints about inflated prices for agricultural inputs were common, and they perceived it as a key reason why "the welfare status of farmers is not improving as expected" (field notes, June 1994). This inflationary trend continued throughout the decade, and by the late 1990s growers were using only about 10 percent of the recommended fertilizer applications on their pineapple fields due to the high costs of the input. As a result, pineapple yields and farmer incomes were suffering badly (Conley and Udry 2004).

The ability of farmers to participate in Ghana's growing NTC business was heavily dependent on having access to capital to purchase expensive inputs, including planting materials and agro-chemicals. Unlike the Gambian case, where groups of low-income gardeners on village schemes could share production costs, pineapple production was carried out on individual farms. The following excerpts from farmer interviews point to the cost woes associated with pineapple farming (based on field notes, June 1994):

> I would like to grow for export but have no money to buy inputs, which are very expensive. (Female farmer, age 50)

> The pineapple business is capital-intensive so only those with capital can reap the huge profits. (Male farmer, age 42)

> I could not go into pineapple farming because I did not have enough money. (Male farmer, age 60)

> The pineapple business is strenuous and needs a lot of capital. (Male farmer, age 34)

Small- and medium-scale pineapple growers received little financial assistance from the government until the late 1990s, and exporters provided only the minimal support that ensured their own operations were profitable. In fewer than 25 percent of recorded cases did Ghanaian exporters provide credit to smallholders with whom they had purchase agreements. Thus, after the initial onset of the pineapple boom, it has been large farms and better-off smallholders who have participated and benefited. For example, Daddieh and Little note "income benefits from pineapple production are very unevenly distributed. In general, a middle stratum of farmers is emerging whose steadily increasing incomes depend on growing export-quality pineapples" (1995: ix). The accrual of benefits from pineapple farming to a better-off class of farmers continued into the early 2000s (Conley and Udry 2004: 19). For example, field studies conducted in 2002 (Takane 2004) and 2003–2004 (Victor 2007) showed that pineapple farming mainly benefited farmers with middle-sized commercial farms (2–10 hectares) who could afford the relatively high costs of planting materials and agro-chemicals. By 2004 smallholders who wanted to produce pineapples for export had to compete with large commercial farms that were expanding into more accessible and better endowed areas, which made it even more difficult for poor households to pursue NTC production (Victor 2007: 435).

Similar to the Ghanaian case, a small-scale grower in The Gambia must grow for an export farm or firm if she/he wants to participate in the export trade. Interviews with Gambian exporters revealed their initial reliance on village gardens for procuring supplies while they were developing their own farms. The most common contracted crops were eggplants and chilies, but a few schemes grew green beans, a crop that mainly was cultivated by large farms using hired labor. Exporters indicated an initial preference for contracting with women-managed communal gardens for labor-intensive crops, such as chilies, since labor costs for these crops are high. As the export farm sector grew, partially aided by liberal land policies and concessions (Roth et al. 1994), attention shifted from small-scale gardeners to production on large farms. Thus, while 45 percent of export firms and commercial farms were contracting with smallholders in 1989, the figure had dropped to about 25 percent in 1994 and to almost nothing by 2004 (Little and Dolan 2000; Barrett et al. 2004; World Bank 2007b).

When they purchased from gardeners (usually women), Gambian export firms did not deal directly with individuals, but instead worked through a management committee. The contract with the group would specify the amount of land to be allocated to each contracted crop and the inputs that the exporter would supply. For example, an exporter might agree to buy all chilies from 0.8 hectares and all eggplants from 0.6 hectares of garden land. It then was at the discretion of the scheme committee to allocate quotas and responsibilities among its members. Usually plot owners who wanted to grow a contracted crop would be allowed to do so, and allotments were usually distributed equitably. Each woman gardener, for instance, might produce contracted crops on less than 0.02 hectares and utilize the remainder of the plot for local vegetables. In contrast to the Ghanaian situation, seeds, fertilizer, and technical advice were provided by the exporter, and the costs of inputs were subtracted from the final payout. Payments to the gardener usually occurred only after the exporter was reimbursed, which meant delays of up to six weeks. Therefore, similar to the Ghanaian smallholder, the Gambian gardener by forgoing payment was actually, and perversely, providing a type of credit to the exporter.

Contract growers on communal gardens also complained about some of the stringent quality requirements that were imposed by exporters. The following statement from a woman gardener highlights the kinds of problems they confronted:

> The exporters ask us to grow chilies and to harvest them when they are green. Then they don't come to pick them up and pay us. We have a lot of problems with these exporters. There is no local market for green chilies so we will not grow them unless we have a written contract. (Field notes, February 1993)

As the above text indicates, most of the risks in these deals were absorbed by the growers, the poorest and least powerful actors in the NTC market chain. Other farmers in The Gambia explained how they were left "to feed green beans to cattle" when exporters rejected their produce on quality grounds (field notes, May 1994). With the exception of the tourist hotel market, there is very little local demand for green beans.

Small Commercial Growers and Absentee Farmers

As noted earlier, an important phenomenon in both the Accra and Banjul regions was the emergence of small-scale commercial growers. They were important throughout the 1990s, although by 2000 they had virtually disappeared from the Gambian NTC trade. Initially, small-scale commercial growers sold their produce to large export firms, although a few joined with other small traders to export the produce themselves. As noted earlier, they often started in the business by initially contracting with small-scale producers until they established their own farms. These young entrepreneurs mainly were male and had access to non-farm income through waged, including government, employment and/or self-employment in the urban center (see Victor 2007). For the Gambian exporter, these commercial growers were perceived as more reliable and market savvy than communal gardeners.

In contrast to growers on communal gardens, the category of young contract farmers (mainly male) grew in importance in The Gambia during the 1990s. They had become integral to the operations of several export firms. As Little and Dolan explain, they often "operated like mini-export farms, relying on hired farm managers and hired labor, and utilizing expensive farm inputs for market production. The difference is that they do not export directly themselves but rather they grow under contract for larger export firms who then sell overseas" (1993: 58).

Like other contract growers, these small commercial growers also had problems in meeting the demands of the international market. One Gambian male grower approximately 35 years of age lamented the demands of the European market:

> The supermarket chains in Europe know nothing about farming or the needs of farmers. They only want a certain size and color of vegetable and think that a farmer should be able to produce this every time. They think our farms are like factories where we can turn out a bean of 10 centimeters every time. Farming is not like factory work. (Field notes, May 1993)

Although they earned considerably higher incomes than other contract smallholders, these small commercial growers grumbled like other growers about nonpayment and the rejection of produce by export firms. The same was true for Ghana's small-scale commercial growers and traders (Daddieh and Little 2005).

Large Farms and Exporters

As noted earlier, smallholders were integral to the establishment of the NTC business in The Gambia and Ghana, including the development of the large-farm sector. As Takane notes in the Ghana case:

> The export companies initially relied on smallholders and commercial farmers for procuring produce. Within a few years, however, they concluded long-term land lease contracts with traditional rulers and established their own large-scale plantations. By 2000, the procurement of produce via direct production was the primary strategy adopted by most exporters.... Procurement from smallholders was the last option. (2004: 35)

My own observations in 1993–94 already questioned the continued role of smallholder participation in the NTC trade, since there already was evidence at the time of their marginalization in the activity (Little 1994; Little and Dolan

2000). In The Gambia exporters especially were vocal about the unreliability of smallholders. Their most common complaint related to scheduling problems and how most communal gardeners did not work on their vegetable plots until after they harvested their main food crop, rice. By the time they were ready to harvest their contracted vegetable, the exporters complained that it was already January or February and well into Europe's winter export season. A second and related factor that exporters voiced was the difficulty of coordinating their harvest schedules with the demands of the export market. Exporters frequently complained that even after harvest agreements were reached, farmers might be delinquent because of other agricultural demands or a social commitment, such as a wedding. On more than one occasion exporters harped that they could not fill orders or meet commitments for air cargo space because vegetables were not harvested on time. Once cargo space is reserved, the exporter has a window of about two days to procure the required amount of fresh produce.

Similar to the Banjul case, the decreased reliance on smallholders by Ghanaian exporters already was in motion by the early 1990s. As in The Gambia, many companies were just beginning to develop or expand their own farms to supply produce for the export trade. Small-scale farmers saw the development of large farms as a threat to their own livelihoods and voiced concerns about the trend:

> I had a verbal contract with an exporter but after harvesting twice the exporter stopped buying. It stopped when the exporter got his own farm and since he increased his own production he will not buy mine. I will continue to produce for local market but do not like this. (Male farmer, age 41, field notes, June 1994)

> No exporter has contacted me this year (1994) because they have enough of their own fruits. (Male farmer, age 40, field notes, June 1994)

Thus, in both Ghana and The Gambia the state's emphases on export diversification and private sector development, tactics that were strongly encouraged by international development agencies, often squeezed smallholders out of NTC activities. In some cases, there was a stated preference for large-scale over small-scale farms. For example, in The Gambia an agribusiness firm hired by one development agency recommended that farms with less than US$1.5 million in start-up costs and 100 hectares of irrigated land not be encouraged to engage in the NTC business. In 1994 those requirements would have excluded all exporters in the country but one (Little and Dolan 2000). As recently as 2003, a donor-sponsored NTC program in Ghana revealed a similar bias in favor of the large-farm sector, in this case arguing that contracting smallholders should mainly be used to help by absorbing the "risks of losses in production or low quality products" (Ghana Private-Public Partnership Food Industry Development Program. 2003: 25).[5] In other words, a prudent financial strategy is to contract out production to smallholders when risks are high, so they, rather than large farms and/or export firms, can incur production losses. Caught up in the heightened neoliberal, pro-business fever of the time, governments in Ghana and The Gambia did not dispute such recommendations despite their negative impacts on smallholder welfare (see Little and Dolan 2000).

Almost twenty years after espousing the merits of private-sector contract farming schemes and a reduced role for the state (World Bank 1989), the World Bank itself acknowledged the problems of relying heavily on an unfettered market to distribute benefits and ensure a role for smallholders in agricultural export programs. For example, its own staff admitted that "increased vertical coordination led to the shift from contract farming with smallholders to large-scale estate production in agroindustrial farms. . . . While contract farming favored larger farmers, poorer households participated as farm workers" (World Bank 2007a: 131). This is exactly what happened in both the Gambian and Ghanaian cases. This same World Bank publication goes on to suggest that government (public sector) initiatives are needed to help smallholders compete in the lucrative NTC export business. Indeed, the kind of thinking reflected here represents a marked departure from the World Bank's and IMF's earlier positions, when the state was the "villain" and an unrestricted market was the solution (see World Bank 1981 and 1989). Chapters 5 and 6 on social protection and poverty alleviation programs will further revisit these kinds of contradictions and the recent changes that have been made to ensure that the poor do not become poorer.

INCREASED DIFFERENTIATION

By the 1990s the commercial farm sectors in both countries already had experienced significant differentiation as smaller, less capitalized firms dropped out and larger farms prospered.[6] This trend toward heightened concentration, coupled with an approximate farm failure rate of about 25 percent between 1988 and 1993 in the Gambian case, highlights the risks associated with export activities even among the wealthiest exporters. Overall more than 85 percent of the licensed horticultural export farms/firms operating in 1994 had dropped out of the export business within ten years (Agro-Ind 2002; World Bank 2007b). Reasons for the high failure rate include decline in air space capacity and transport from The Gambia, lack of capital, European certification polices on product safety and traceability (discussed later in the chapter), poor production and storage technologies, and weak relationships with European supermarkets (Agro-Ind 2002).

As indicated earlier, one of the surviving enterprises in The Gambia was a subsidiary of a UK-based agro-business firm that had its own import business and was well integrated into the supermarket business of Europe. The firm is cleared to package their own produce in The Gambia and directly ship to European supermarkets, which avoids the high costs of labor for packing in Europe (see Agro-Ind 2002). Both Gambian and Ghanaian export firms with long-term relationships with European importers and supermarkets were better equipped to overcome stiff international constraints and costs related to the new demands for product certification. They also could invest in or have access to technologies that remained prohibitively too expensive for small-scale exporters.

In Ghana the number of large farms of 50+ hectares growing pineapples increased from twelve in 1994 to more than twenty in 2002 (Daddieh and Little 1995; Trienekens et al. 2004; Ghana Private-Public Partnership Food Industry Development Program 2003). According to Trienekens et al., "the larger plantations [in Ghana] have a vertical integrated business from farm to port. They have direct contact with their customers in Europe, have their own trucks and own shaded pack houses" (2004: 4). These kinds of large, vertically integrated operations were largely absent in 1994. While farms were larger in Ghana, the benefits of the export trade were more equitably distributed than in The Gambia. In Ghana the two largest farms/firms controlled less than 50 percent of exports in 1994 and less than 25 percent in 2002 (Daddieh and Little 1995; Trienekens et al. 2004). Despite their successes, by 2006 export farms in Ghana were experiencing considerable competition in the global pineapple market, especially from Costa Rica, which raised some doubts about their sustainability in the future (see Wageningen University/Michigan State University 2007).[7]

DUMPING PRODUCE AND COMPETING WITH SMALL-SCALE TRADERS

The extent to which product dumping by large export farms affects local markets in Africa rarely is acknowledged (see Little and Dolan 2000). The unloading of subquality export produce on local markets depresses local prices, and consequently incomes, for small-scale farmers and traders. The dumping of produce on local markets is widely practiced by large NTC farms in Ghana and The Gambia, as well as in other African countries (for example, Kenya). Many small-scale farmers in these countries tenaciously complained of this tactic. For example, "about 78 percent of farmers in our Ghana sample viewed this unfavorably and saw it as a threat to the competition and the long-term sustainability of their own farms" (Daddieh and Little 1995: 45). Comments from Ghanaian smallholders confirm this:

> Large farms can sell on local markets and, thus, our income is reduced. (Male farmer, age 42, field notes, June 1994)

> The exporters are increasing their local sales, so they can swallow our local market. (Male farmer, age 27, field notes, June 1994)

> Large farms are able to capture our customers with low prices. (Male farmer, age 60, June 1994)

In Accra the dumping of non-export-quality produce on local markets helps larger firms/farms meet their cash flow needs, which are a problem since export payments can be delayed weeks or even months.[8] Similar complaints about large farms were voiced by Gambian farmers. In this case the large export farms went so far as to grow some crops, especially tomatoes and peppers, strictly for the local market. The strategy allowed them to maintain laborers and financial viability in the off-season when sales to Europe decline. For the Gambian exporter, there also is a small but relatively lucrative trade in fresh vegetables and fruits that focuses on the country's twenty or so tourist-quality beach hotels. They can sell non-export-quality produce to this market, in addition to unloading produce on the local market. As Little and Dolan note, "the hotel trade is increasingly attractive because it represents a relatively 'up-scale' local market, where the consumption of high-quality, high-value produce is widespread. The hotel trade is a convenient market to 'off load' second-quality produce that is not export grade, but is still above what can be obtained on the local market" (1993: 43). Although the hotel trade is a relatively small market, it is better insulated from competition than the export trade. Several large export farms in the 1990s tailored their annual planting schedule to accommodate both the export (primarily) and local markets (secondarily).

To tap the local market, The Gambia's two largest export farms in the early 1990s established outlet wholesale stores at the region's two largest wholesale markets. As Little and Dolan emphasize, "most export farms recognize the importance of the local market for absorbing non-export-quality produce, and for buffering against some of the risks and competition associated with export trade. By opening their own wholesale outlets on the local market, the two largest exporters in the country directly compete with local producers and traders" (1993: 36). To observe the contrast between lively, brightly dressed women traders with their colorful produce at the markets and rigid male employees of a large export firm with their newly constructed wholesale stores, cash registers, and books of invoices and receipts was stunning to say the least. Many local traders and farmers were vocally upset by this trend and felt the government should take action to protect their market positions (field notes, May 1994). However, state and donor support for the NTC business not only encouraged large-farm dominance in the export trade, but also indirectly facilitated their prominence in local markets to the noticeable disadvantage of small-scale merchants and farmers.

SMALLHOLDERS AS CONTRACT LABORERS

Low-income smallholders increasingly work on large farms as casual laborers, especially since many no longer grow crops under contract. As stated earlier, pineapple farming requires heavy work in preparing fields and planting pineapple seedlings, and farm managers favor male over female workers. By contrast, the hiring preferences of export farms in The Gambia favor women workers, especially for weeding, picking, and packing activities. Gambian men, in turn, mainly

are hired for field preparation and irrigation work and some become field managers, who easily are identified by their company shirts. Women packers and vegetable pickers sometimes wore white shirts and scarves provided by the firm. One
Gambian farm manager indicated that in comparison to men "women are more
reliable and diligent vegetable pickers" (field notes, February 1993). They are particularly favored for harvesting chilies and green beans, both extremely laborious
and tedious chores.

Work conditions in The Gambia were very difficult, and shifts of up to ten
hours were not uncommon in peak export months. While women accounted for
the bulk of employees, they held less than 10 percent of skilled or management positions, which were reserved for men. Not surprisingly, Gambian female workers
on export farms earned considerably less than men, even though they provided
most of the labor. For many unskilled workers, labor was compensated on a piece-
rate basis—for example, per area weeded or units harvested—which can be very
exploitive. It was a practice that some private companies encourage, to pressure
workers, as one firm noted, to "significantly improve productivity" (Landell Mills
Associates 1989: 65). However, several local chiefs in the 1990s protested against
this exploitive practice of piece-rate work, which "is not the local custom" and is
undesirable to villagers (see Little and Dolan 2000).

Unlike in the Accra area, waged employment on large farms in The Gambia
often was tied to the original land concessions awarded by local chiefs. With active
intervention by government, either large farms directly acquired land by having
it officially "titled" by government authorities or they leased it from village chiefs.
The titling of land, especially in the export agricultural zones, was encouraged
under the country's ERP, but most farms preferred to locally lease land. When an
exporter approached a village to acquire land for export activities, they frequently
arranged with the alkalo to employ local laborers in exchange for the use of land.
In return for hiring villagers the company was allowed long-term lease arrangements of twenty or more years. In some cases, the contracts were for more than
100 hectares of prime farmland.

The employment-for-land agreements did not always encourage stable work
relationships between the firm and village. Disputes over land were frequent, and
on more than one occasion villagers vehemently protested to government about
land deals. In fact, the issue was so "hot" in 1993 and 1994 that very few officials
wished to discuss it with us, and coverage of land conflicts in local newspapers
was frequent (see Little and Dolan 1993; Jallow 1994). In one editorial in a Gambian newspaper the writer questioned whether an alkalo is a "profiteer who can
sell common land to the highest bidder, often to Germans, Lebanese, British and
wealthy Gambians" (*Daily Observer* 1994). The same article went on to recommend that "the government look humanely and swiftly at the land question, for
land is closer to the heart of a Gambian than gold and should be treated with re-

spect, honesty and consistency" (ibid.). Studies of land tenure and rights during the time confirm the increased tension over land in the horticultural growing areas and the resentment over private deals that certain alkalo made with Gambian and foreign investors (see Roth et al 1994). Only two months after this newspaper account was published the government was overthrown and land grabbing in the peri-urban area was noted to be one of the factors (see Loum 2002; Cooke and Hughes 1997).

As noted earlier, the customary land tenure system in Ghana's pineapple belt was characterized by a great deal of flexibility and accommodation in terms of land uses and leases. In 1994 only 12 percent of farmers felt land acquisition was a serious problem (Daddieh and Little 1995). Chiefs were willing to entertain a variety of rental arrangements, some of which entailed employment agreements similar to the Gambian cases discussed above (ibid.: 27–28). However, this changed with the growth of the large-farm sector, and by the 2000s land had become a serious issue. In a 2007 study, Victor notes how smallholders are losing land to large farms in the pineapple belt: "Within the Ghanaian context, the main effects of the introduction of export cropping has been the significant deterioration in access to land as smallholder food crop farms are being consolidated into larger scale export crop farms" (2007: 436). The increased demand for land in the area has meant that smallholders who still are able to grow pineapples for the export trade are pushed into less accessible and less favorable areas (see Takane 2004).

Certification and Other Recent Challenges

Concerns from Europe over food safety, pesticide residues on produce, and, more recently, treatment of farm workers (including use of child labor) resulted in the imposition of new requirements for NTC production in Africa. These new regulations generally have made it more difficult for small-scale farmers to participate in NTC production and trade, including the lucrative FFV trade. One early action by European importers, in response to consumer pressure, was the creation of EurepGAP (Global Partnership for Safe and Sustainable Agriculture), an association of food importers and retailers "ensuring quality, safety and labor standards and providing international verification across a wide range of agricultural production sectors" (Ghana Private-Public Partnership Food Industry Development Program 2003: 3). To sell to European supermarkets, which control more than 70 percent of the market for African produce, exporters now have to be EurepGAP-certified (see Dolan and Humphreys 2004).

Bias toward Large Farms

For small-scale pineapple growers in Ghana, the cost of a required EurepGAP audit per year is 300 British pounds, which is equivalent to about 70 percent of an average farmer's income (Brown and Sander 2007: 9). This rule alone has pushed many small independent producers out of the export business altogether. In terms of International Food Sanitation Safety (IFSS) requirements, which have been stringently applied on European food imports since 2000, foods must be traceable to the source of production for supermarkets to sell them. As large supermarkets in Europe, such as Sainsbury, have pushed for more of the sorting and packing of produce back onto horticulture-producing countries because of reduced labor costs, the hygiene of hired workers has been a special concern in packing operations, including in The Gambia and Ghana. In some cases they are subjected to random pathogen swabs of their hands when packing fresh produce for export to ensure that germs are not transmitted (Okello et al. 2007: 15). Along with the exclusion of thousands of African smallholders in the NTC trade because of certification requirements, IFSS mandates also effectively "have screened out smallholders in all these [African] countries (ibid.: vi)." While it is not possible to gauge the number of African smallholders who have been affected by these import restrictions, it is estimated that more than 50 percent of small-scale green-bean growers in Kenya have dropped out of the NTC business since the 1990s (ibid.).

An ironic twist to this story is that in addition to protecting European consumers, certification mandates such as those imposed by EurepGap also were supposed to safeguard laborers and small-scale farmers from exploitive work practices, but in the end further marginalized smallholders because export firms stopped buying their produce. Small-scale cultivators, in effect, are unable to absorb the costs of certification, including the costs associated with fair trade certification, and thus have exited a trade that once held some promise for alleviating poverty (see Dolan and Humphreys 2004).

Similar to producers in other African countries, large farmers in The Gambia and Ghana have been better able to better respond to the new trade environment than have smallholders. As Barrett et al. note for The Gambia, "large farmers have many advantages over small producers, including the documentation to prove where the produce originated" (2004: 32). They also now question whether they can continue smallholder purchases because of the risk of losing access to the European market if a problem occurs and traceability is required. Their general response so far has been to avoid procuring supplies from small-scale growers. In Ghana a comparable trend has developed in response to similarly stringent certification requirements (see Takane 2004). Thus, certification requirements in Europe have pushed large farms/firms in both countries to further decrease purchases from small-scale growers.

State Intervention to the Rescue?

Ghanaian NTC producers have fared considerably better than their counterparts in The Gambia, in part, because of the active support of the state and, ironically, the World Bank. The Ghanaian story goes as follows. In response to a request by local pineapple farmers, the government—with financing from the World Bank—supported a smallholder-led pineapple scheme in 1999, which included a smallholder-owned limited export firm (Yeboah 2005). It included many of the same villages where we had worked in 1994–95 (see Daddieh and Little 1995). This venture was spurred by members of five local farmer cooperatives in the pineapple belt who were very concerned about their declining position in NTC production. They wanted to continue to participate in the activity by being able to compete with large-scale farms and exporters (see Yeboah 2005). Their members also formed cooperatives "to enhance their ability to attract help in producing and marketing their produce" (ibid.: 81). After considerable discussion among themselves, they approached the government for assistance.

With World Bank approval and financing, the state supported the cooperatives and "helped them jointly form Farmapine Ghana Limited, which was 80% owned by the cooperatives and 20 percent by two export companies" (Trienekens et al. 2004: 5). For the World Bank, the main architect of Ghana's austere economic reform program, it was an implicit admission that contra private-sector enthusiasts, public support and intervention often are needed to ensure market competition and a role for undercapitalized small-scale farmers. As noted earlier, a recent World Bank report (2008) even admits that the NTC export business, especially with new certification requirements, usually favors large-scale farmers over smallholders, such as happened in Ghana. The report even argues that "further efficiency gains [for NTC farmers] will require public sector support to deliver the necessary public goods, foster institutional innovation, and secure competitiveness. Because efficient markets do not always secure socially desirable outcomes, complementary policies are often needed to ensure smallholder participation" (ibid.: 133). The Farmapine project and its farmers clearly benefited from public support and financing.

The members of the Ghanaian smallholder-led scheme are not the poorest farmers in the area but, instead, are better-off local farmers with sufficient capital to produce under contract for the Farmapine Limited Company. However, they are considerably less well-off than the large commercial growers and exporters in the area. According to Trienekens and Willems, "Farmapine has over 200 members, all of whom own between 0.5 and 10–15 hectares" (2007: 48). A U.S.-based NGO with considerable experience in export-based agricultural systems also worked closely with the cooperative and its members, and its assistance was critical to Farmapine's success (ibid.). Within a few years of its establishment, Farmapine was earning a profit, and soon it became the second-largest exporter of pineapples in Ghana (Yeboah 2005). Overall the positive role played by collective action (cooperatives) and state and international development support demonstrates in the Farmapine case that smallholders still can participate in the NTC trade, but under a different institutional model than the previous one that effectively excluded them.

Summary

This chapter has examined the different trajectories of contract farming (CF) and the NTC business in two West African countries, Ghana and The Gambia. Although CF and NTC diversification programs are showcased as solutions for sub-Saharan Africa's agrarian deficiencies, they often involve fewer farmers, generate lower incomes, and incur greater risks than their enthusiastic supporters suggest. As the chapter has shown, something as small as a luxury vegetable (NTC) entails a set of global relations, symbols, and labor processes that encompass bankers, peasants, and development bureaucracies in a complex market arrangement. It creates an inviting picture of modernity and progressiveness that can drive state and donor agency policies and investments, but equally disguise what actually is taking place on farms.

Where smallholders have benefited from the NTC business, as in the case of Ghana, it has required state investment to even the playing field with large-scale operations and ensure their continued participation. Despite periods of prosperity, the production of high-value NTCs has witnessed wide swings in economic fortunes for small-scale growers who have seen their roles diminished over time. In the next chapter we turn to another segment of the population, urban-based petty traders, who often hawk fresh produce and whose numbers, unlike contracted smallholders, grew considerably after the imposition of economic reforms.

2   "Everybody Is a Petty Trader"
Peri-urban Trade in Postconflict
Maputo, Mozambique

A COMMON SIGHT IN Africa's sprawling urban and peri-urban areas is the widespread proliferation of petty traders, hawking items from foods to cigarettes to cheap imported electronics. These street hawkers and other self-employed traders represent the fastest-growing segment of the labor market in Africa, attracting the unemployed, the displaced, and the impoverished as well as those seeking to supplement declining wage incomes (ILO 2002; Brown et al. 2010; Hansen and Vaa 2004). Under the economic reform programs described in the introduction, it was assumed that these informal activities would eventually disappear—or at least decline in importance—as private investment grew and nonfarm industries and formal sector employment expanded. This has not been the case and, in fact, the phenomenon has accelerated in the 2000s as cities in Africa have grown faster than in any other world region, but industrialization and job creation has been disappointingly minimal. Moreover, spiraling inflation and declining real incomes make it difficult even for those with salaried employment to subsist without holding multiple occupations, including petty trading. As Mamdani points out in the case of Uganda, economic reforms and restructuring turned waged workers and others into "part-time hawkers" (1990: 438).

This burgeoning petty trade sector, often euphemistically labeled the microenterprise, or informal sector, has been praised by some as a sign of a healthy, private sector that is growing with pro-market reforms (De Soto 2000). Economic optimists might say this reflects a growing new entrepreneurial class and vibrant microenterprises, which emerged with pro-market reforms and the unshackling of state constraints. However, it seems a wide stretch of the imagination to view masses of unemployed street hawkers, flashing cheap consumer products at passing vehicles, as productive microenterprises. In fact, the petty trade sector's growth is more symptomatic of larger structural problems that leave many individuals with little choice but "to trade to eat" and pursue other survivalist strategies. In the case of highland towns of northeastern Ethiopia, for example, Gebre-Egziabher and Demeke found that more than 50 percent of unregistered ("informal") microenterprise owners were based on petty trade or informal service provision. They cited a lack of alternative livelihoods (including farming) as the prime motivation for initiating their activity (s) (2004: 14). Unlike other world regions that have experienced rapid urbanization, the growth of sub-Saharan African cities has not been associated with significant levels of industrialization. In most cities on the continent, the percentage of self-employed workers or what often is called the informal sector accounts for about 70 percent of employment and up to 90 percent in some countries (ILO 2002; UNDP 2006b). In fact, the informal sector is estimated to account for about 90 percent of new jobs in cities, and within it "street traders are one of the largest sub-groups . . . after home-based and domestic workers" (Brown et al. 2010: 666–667).

In this chapter I continue the urban and peri-urban focus of the previous chapter, but instead of highlighting commercial farmers in West Africa the emphasis is on petty traders in a southern African location, Maputo, Mozambique. Like the NTC growers discussed in the previous chapter, small-scale traders, many of whom operate on the street, also were assumed to significantly benefit from pro-market reforms and open trade policies. By exploring the social and economic aspects and strategies of petty trade and traders in the Maputo area during an early period of economic reforms (1990–93), I show the survivalist and opportunist strategies that many peri-urban residents pursued under increased uncertainty and poverty. As a nation, Mozambique was just coming out of a prolonged civil war in the early 1990s when fieldwork was conducted, and at the time it had the dubious distinction of being one of the two or three poorest countries in the world (UNDP 2006b). In this period the government was eliminating state-owned companies, controls on foreign investment, and domestic and export market regulations (Pitcher 2002).

The chapter will show that the growth in self-employed ("petty") traders was symbolic of the strains, as well as new opportunities of this early period of adjustment. Some of the larger traders in the Maputo area benefited from market liberalization, but for many others petty commerce was a desperate response to unfavorable access to land and waged employment and to reductions in urban services and subsidies. As the story will show, the poor majority of traders eked out a living that is paltry by almost any measure, selling a multitude of items, both food and cheap imported goods (matches, batteries, and cigarettes). These inexpensive products flooded the country's urban and peri-urban markets as trade liberalization opened up domestic markets to imported products from China and other Asian countries (Lyons et al. 2008). Since 2000, the percentage of informal urban trade accounted for by cheap manufactured imports from China and other Asian countries has grown considerably and largely has replaced food products as the main hawking category on the streets of many African cities, including Maputo (ibid.: 198).

History and Background

Mozambique experienced a starkly different economic and political history than what was described for The Gambia and Ghana (chapter 1). In the early 1990s many parts of peri-urban Maputo still experienced occasional armed incidents between government forces and the rebel group, RENAMO (Resistência Nacional Moçambicana [Mozambique National Resistance]), which was receiving support at the time from apartheid-ruled South Africa. Details of the brutal tactics of RENAMO and its support from the past South Africa regime can be found in Hanlon's account (1986). Mozambique was a country that even in the African context had witnessed a level of economic and social hardship and destruction that was unusually harsh. In 1991 state and public corporations (parastatals) in Mozambique still dominated most sectors of the economy, especially in banking and transport, and Western development agencies were just beginning to flood the area with foreign aid. The Cold War was over, and Russian technical assistance and advisors had been replaced by U.S. and other Western contractors and consultants. Mozambique was in the initial stages of a fairly ambitious development and economic restructuring program that was to gain momentum in the 1990s and 2000s (see Hanlon 1996; Pitcher 2002).

On the throes of a painful period of market-oriented reforms, Mozambique entered into a full-blown economic adjustment program with the International Monetary Fund (IMF) in 1990. However, prior to that it had been implementing limited reforms, in part to curry favor with the United States and World Bank. By the late 1980s it was already receiving high praise from the World Bank and IMF for its targeted economic policies and increasingly open markets (Hanlon 1991: 142). Because of Mozambique's former role as a USSR client in the Cold War era, Western nations desperately wanted the country to succeed in its economic reform efforts, and, as in the case of Ghana, massive amounts of foreign aid flowed into the country.

Thus, the historical moment of field research in the Maputo area during 1991–92 was an extraordinary and informative opportunity. A focus on the self-employed sector in the early 1990s, especially peri-urban traders, provided an excellent lens into the effects of neoliberal changes during a period of significant political and economic transition.

Unwaged Labor Market

A household survey of peri-urban Maputo in 1991 showed that most self-employed men were in informal service and trading activities and women in commercial vending, especially in cooked food sales (Graham et al. 1991: iii). Overall more than 70 percent of those involved in self-employed activities engaged in some kind of trade, which might mean selling individual cigarettes or batteries on street corners or produce in a public marketplace. The percentage of Maputo's total employment that was engaged in so-called informal activities was greater than 75 percent (ibid.). The majority of Maputo households (> 50 percent) at the time with a member employed for wages also had another member who was self-employed on a part-time basis. With the cost of living rising and wage incomes declining, it was necessary for households that were fortunate enough to have a member employed to supplement income through informal activities. In Maputo at the time men were about four times as likely to be employed for wages as women (ibid.).

A similar employment pattern generally holds for the 2000s, except that the percentage of the labor market accounted by the unofficial (informal) sector—including self-employed traders and workers—has actually grown to account for more than 90 percent of the economically active population. For example, a 2005 study of the Mozambique economy shows that "less than 10% of the active population has a formal job, and thus the informal sector absorbs 90% of the economically active population in Mozambique" (UNDP 2006b: 36). Similarly, a national study on employment, including in Maputo, shows a similar pattern where most employment gains in the 2000s have been in self-employed informal activities, which compared to the 1990s also means a "higher percentage of the working people hold more than one employment" (Bruck and van den Broeck 2006: 29). The lack of employment and the need to supplement wages even for those with salaried positions has meant that many males have entered trading activities once dominated by women, including street food sales (Agadjanian 2002).

In the formal wage sector of Maputo average incomes were painfully low in the early 1990s, which explains the need to pursue multiple income-earning activities. Reported weekly incomes of 8,000–10,000 metecais (mt) (US$ 4–5, at an exchange rate of US$1 = 2,000 mt) at the lower end of the formal labor market were well below a household's basic subsistence and housing costs at the time. Even at the higher end of the waged labor market, where average incomes were 20,000–25,000 mt (US$10–13) per week, households usually required at least one other member (usually the principal woman) to be self-employed, often as a part-time trader (Graham et al. 1991).

This heavy reliance on informal activities is also true for other parts of Africa, especially in urban and peri-urban areas (see Brown et al. 2010; Bryceson and Potts 2006; Hansen and Vaa 2004). For example, in the same part of The Gambia (Banjul region) that was discussed in chapter 1, it was found that about 65 percent of households were headed by "informal workers" (Wadda and Craig 1993: 17–18). These were males or females that were self-employed in trading or other activity and without a formal wage contract or employment agreement (ibid.: 67). More recent research from The Gambia shows a comparable pattern, with informal workers accounting for about "85 percent of employment in non-agricultural enterprises" (Heintz et al. 2008: 25). In fact, it is suggested there that "physically able persons . . . spend their days selling a few packets of cigarettes because there is no better alternative" (UNDP 2006a: 37). Thus, whether on the streets of Banjul, Maputo, or another African city one finds very high levels of unemployment where much of the workforce is pushed into poorly remunerative and unproductive petty trade activities.

Trade and Traders

Opportunities to be a petty trader in Maputo were shaped by the country's post-colonial socialist policies and, more recently, by its pro-market reforms. Here a petty trader is defined as a small-scale merchant who is self-employed and has gross sales of less than $100 per week. Most of them have sales considerably less than this amount. The petty trader can trade on the street or operate within a public marketplace, or utilize both venues.

Prior to 1987 domestic commerce in Mozambique was highly centralized and controlled by the government, with most foodstuffs, including fruits and vegetables, sold through a network of "bonded shops" (*lojas vinculadas*) and consumer cooperatives (Little and Lundin de Coloane 1993). Efforts to control the production and marketing of fruits and vegetables in the peri-urban areas were implemented through state programs that encouraged production around Maputo, and a government corporation for fruit and vegetable wholesaling (called E. E. Hortifruiticula). Considerable amounts of parallel trade in fruits and vegetables existed, and the state's ability to control the diversion of produce into private markets declined during 1980 to 1987. Some street traders, called *dumba nengue,* were adept at avoiding state controls, although as recently as 1991 they were still being harassed by government officials for avoiding regulations and permits.

"Dumba nengue" literally means "to rely on your feet," an apt defense against government officials who tried to halt street trading and against South African–based militias (RENAMO) who ravaged villages until the early 1990s (see Magaia 1988). According to Issacson, the term itself comes from a "southern Mozambique proverb whose point is 'you have to trust your feet'" (1988: 2). In the peri-urban markets of Maputo in the early 1990s dumba nengue simply meant street traders, those who work on their feet.

To acquire food and other necessities, urban consumers relied heavily on informal distribution networks that often drew on real and fictive kinship ties with government retailers. One woman trader explained how she used to hide an empty bag at night near a bonded retailer managed by one of her relatives, and return early in the morning to collect a bag filled with produce and other foods (field notes, October 1991).

Throughout the 1980s, war-induced instability in Mozambique also exacerbated the scarcity of food and the inefficiency of controlled markets. Security problems associated with the presence of RENAMO bandits restricted travel in the outer fringes of the peri-urban belt during 1991 and 1992, and even then movements of produce from certain peri-urban zones to Maputo urban markets occasionally were halted due to insecurity. One peri-urban market about 12 kilometers from the city center was attacked during 1991, and accounts of skirmishes in other markets were occasionally heard. Economic instability was coupled with a strong dose of political volatility.

The system of controlled food distribution in Maputo was subject to shortages, distortions, and graft by officials who were well placed to gain preferential access, especially during periods of acute scarcity. This practice, of course, fostered the creation of a parallel market with high transaction costs and its own set of inefficiencies. Traders told stories of how well-to-do clients would pick up their produce at designated secret locations in the late hours. They explained the different risks that were involved in this illegal activity, especially the fear of being reported by a neighbor or—even worse—being picked up by the police. As a first step in market deregulation, the state lifted price controls on the fruit and vegetable trade in 1985. With the initiation of the Programa de Rehabilitação Económica (PRE) in 1987, the nature of trade in vegetables and fruits changed and private markets were actually encouraged rather than discouraged.

In the Maputo region several types of petty or small-scale traders can be distinguished by scale, market orientation, and location. Within each broad category of commerce important distinctions also are found. In Maputo, for example, the term "dumba nengue" covered—and still covers—all kinds of street trade, including (in order of importance) the sale of drinks and local foods, agricultural products, manufactured goods (including soap, matches, and cigarettes), wood and building materials, and local crafts. Other traders sell at booths within the formal marketplace, but more commonly they hawk in the open areas outside the market or in the adjoining streets and sidewalks. By doing so, they avoid taxation and regulation by the municipality and thus are able to offer cheaper prices to consumers. According to discussions with Maputo's traders, the selling of small manufactured products in the streets and outside the markets grew rapidly after the advent of liberalization policies and the flood of cheap imports from Asia and neighboring South Africa. Almost 25 percent of our sample of self-employed traders in Maputo had moved to the peri-urban areas during the past ten years. These migrants often engage in petty trading activities because of the very low start-up costs (US$50 or less) and because access to agricultural land and more lucrative forms of employment are very limited (also see Jenkins 2004).

Special Case of Dumba Nengue Traders

Street traders (dumba nengue) of the Maputo region provide an interesting case of hawkers who over a long period have adapted to difficult circumstances. Their clientele in the early 1990s mainly were low-and middle-income urbanites, and an increasing number of the traders were males, especially recent migrants. However, females were still the majority of food vendors and traders (also see Agadjanian 2002). Dumba nengue traders generally were younger (average age of about 32 years) and were less likely than other Maputo traders to be members of market organizations, such as informal credit groups. As noted earlier, the growth in street trading in Maputo began in the late 1980s, when the government relaxed its restrictions on hawking and petty trade. In contrast to an average of over seven years of trading experience for the general population of traders, dumba nengue actors had been in commerce for an average of less than five years.

The street traders confront certain risks because of the unofficial nature of their business and because licensed market traders view them as unfair (illegal) competition and often work against them. For example, licensed vendors are quick to alert police and market officials of the location and identification of street traders in their area. Dumba nengue hawkers also confront risks of violence and theft on the street. One Maputo woman who had been trading at a neighborhood market in 1991 explained the situation:

> There is no conflict in the business. But there are those that work without a proper license and run the risk of being caught by the police. When this happens they usually pay something and go away without big trouble. Many times these traders know the routes of the police and can go around them and make big money, but there is always a potential risk with this enterprise. There is obviously a potential conflict between those traders paying taxes and those that don't, but the business goes on. (Field notes, November 1991)

The average weekly incomes of Maputo's dumba nengue traders were very low in 1991 ($11.64) (see table 2.1). Their average incomes also were nearly 15 percent lower than other traders in Maputo, with the average incomes of the poorest 40 percent of street traders equivalent to about $2.61 per week, or $0.37 per day. The latter is equivalent to less than half the average income of the poorest of Maputo's vegetable traders and about 20 percent of what street traders in Banjul, The Gambia, earned at approximately the same time (see Little and Dolan 1993). Among traders in the Maputo area dumba nengue hawkers were the most vulnerable to poverty, and trading for them was a survival strategy that was only partially successful.

The dumba nengue trade depended heavily on consignments from better capitalized suppliers who used the hawkers to sell their goods. The supplier provided a quantity of the products, such as cigarettes and cheap textiles, on consignment to the street trader and then collected revenue after they were sold. Street traders received a small commission from the sales, and some even charged 2–3 percent higher than agreed prices and could keep the difference for themselves.

Table 2.1. Socioeconomic Characteristics of *Dumba Nengue* Traders, Maputo, Mozambique, 1991

Indicator	Average figures (n=73)
Average weekly income (US$)[1]	11.64
Average income of those Earning < US$7.50/week	$2.61
(% total)	(40%)
Average education (years)	2.09
Average years of trading	4.73
Average household size	7.91
Average age (years)	32.3

Source: Author's analysis and data; adapted from Little and Lundin de Coloane (1993: 5).
Notes: 1. $1=2,000 metecais (mt) (in 1991).

Dumba nengue traders often were required to take out loans from the supplier, in order to receive the products, and they were restricted to selling only their supplier's items. In some cases the relationship between seller and buyer resembled an employer/employee arrangement, where their commission on sales (less than 3–5 percent) that they were allowed to keep could be considered a wage. In short, the ubiquitous "street kids" who sold cigarettes and other cheap consumer goods at traffic stops in downtown Maputo often were (are) "employees" working for a larger trader on a type of wage basis.

Social Differentiation

As the preceding discussion implies, there were considerable social and economic differences among peri-urban traders in the Maputo region. While most were poor, this was not always the case. Wide differences are revealed in levels of education and income, as well as in work experience. Gender also was a key principle of social differentiation. Since private trade was heavily constrained in Maputo until the late 1980s, more than 50 percent of traders who were interviewed had been engaged in commerce for less than five years.

Gender

Women comprised the bulk of produce traders in Maputo (about 95 percent of total), but as noted above there were certain high-revenue trading activities where men were conspicuously dominant. The tendency for males to pursue and, in some cases, squeeze out women from lucrative trading activities is common, and peri-urban trade is no exception (see Dolan and Humphrey 2000; Hansen and

Vaa 2004). In Accra, Ghana, for example, Overa notes that males "increasingly performed tasks associated with food-provision that—in this part of Africa—used to be done primarily by women, such as sitting on the roadside selling small heaps of onions or tomatoes, and helping women cooking and hawking snacks and 'street food.' Men now even carry food on their heads" (2007: 540). In Maputo's remunerative (cooked) food trade a growing number of sellers also were male (approximately 33 percent), and they earned considerably higher incomes than other traders. In contrast to the dumba nengue traders, merchants selling cooked food and drinks earned the largest average incomes, with very few earning less than 15,000 mt ($7.50) per week. Many of these processed food traders were school "leavers" or former government clerks or secretaries who were retrenched under the PRE program (for a similar pattern in other cities of sub-Saharan Africa, see Brown 2006). Many have relatively high levels of education, with an average of 5.33 years per trader, and several had completed secondary school as of 1991.

The vast majority of women traders (more than 70 percent of total) reside in households that are headed by their husbands. The notion that most successful women traders in Africa are highly independent and head their own households is simply not borne out in the Maputo case. Thus, while female traders may have considerable discretion over how they allocate the income earned from petty trade, they usually are not heads of households nor do they differ significantly in marital status from other women in the Maputo region (see Graham et al. 1991).

Education

With the exception of those male food traders discussed above, the level of formal education among traders in the peri-urban areas was extremely low, with an average of 1.7 years in Maputo. Even those relatively educated traders who stayed in government saw their real incomes decline so drastically during those years that they often were forced to trade on a part-time basis just to meet living expenses. One woman trader who sold vegetables and prepared foods explained how the business environment in Maputo has changed: "Everything is very strange at present. Look at the situation when students come to us and ask for jobs and many in the trade now are well educated. It should not be like this, they should carry on with their education and become doctors but they make money, especially in processed (cooked) foods but only in that business" (field notes, November 1991). The pattern described by the woman is symptomatic of a miserable employment situation, where even educated youth have to pursue petty trade and/or multiple types of work. In other interviews traders commented on both this new educated type of trader and the recent rural migrants ("refugees") who compete with them selling outside the markets on the ground or on the streets (field notes, November 1991). The rural migrants ("refugees") often moved to the Maputo area to escape war in the rural areas and/or to seek opportunities in the cities.

Table 2.2. Income Distribution of Peri-urban Traders, Maputo, Mozambique

Income group (Weekly incomes)[1]	Percentage (n=73)
(I) (highest)	9.4
(II)	15.6
(III)	21.9
(IV)	53.1
All	100.0

Source: Based on author's analysis and field data.
Notes: 1. Income groups are: (I) > $25; (II) $15–24; (III) $7.5–23; and (IV) $0–7.5.

Notwithstanding differences in income levels, a relatively strong relationship between education and income is revealed. Traders with no formal educaion (48 percent of the seventy-three traders interviewed) earned weekly average incomes of 5,220 mt (US$2.61), while those with four or more years earned more than 45,000 mt (US$22.50). Although it is not entirely clear why this is the case, some level of education up to at least 4–5 years seems to enhance mathematics and literacy skills, which in turn have a positive effect on small-scale trading enterprises. A similar relationship between a modest level of education and increased incomes of petty traders also is found elsewhere in Africa, in this case urban Ethiopia (see Gebre-Egziabher and Demeke 2004; Brown 2006).

Income Inequities

As noted above, differences in education account for some of the variation in trader incomes (see table 2.2). As table 2.2 reveals, more than 50 percent of traders are in the two lowest income groups, with less than 10 percent in the highest income category. In addition, more than half of the sellers (many of whom are dumba nengue vendors) earned only 7,641 mt ($3.82) weekly, equivalent to less than $0.55 per day. This low-income group, which comprised about 53 percent of sellers, earned only 18 percent of the total trading income of the sample. By contrast, the highest income group in Maputo, with less than 10 percent of the trader population, reaped close to 40 percent of total income. Thus, while the vast majority of Maputo traders engage in petty trade as a basic strategy for survival, a minority of the wealthiest merchants use it as an accumulation strategy to increase their wealth.

Employment and Survival Strategies

Many peri-urban traders in Maputo engaged in trade as their primary occupation, but many also pursued secondary livelihood strategies. However, the majority of Maputo traders did not farm, and if they did it was on extremely small plots. Almost 80 percent of petty traders in Maputo indicated that they mainly spent their trading incomes on food and household items, with only 18 percent indicating that they earned sufficient incomes to reinvest in their trading business. Their operations essentially were centered on basic subsistence needs. Most indicated that if they had sufficient access to agricultural land, they would not bother to trade (also see Jenkins 2004). In the Maputo area during the 1990s two important factors were at play that limited the importance of agriculture for most traders. These were that: (1) agricultural plots were very small (on average less than 0.2 hectare), so it was unfeasible to live solely on peri-urban farming, and (2) access to agricultural plots of any size was very difficult. Approximately half of the landless traders claimed that it was too difficult to acquire a farm, either because of high prices or because they did not have customary claims to the land. This has particularly been a problem for recent migrants or refugees to the area, who rarely gained access to land after migrating to peri-urban Maputo (see Jenkins 2004). Even among those who owned farms in the peri-urban belt, average farm sizes were minuscule and very inadequate for making a living.

As noted earlier, most traders lived in households with other income earners. This is a pattern that remains widespread in urban and peri-urban areas of Africa, where low wages and high living costs force multiple household members to be part-time entrepreneurs (see Brown 2006). In the Maputo case, most of these other workers were spouses or older sons and daughters of the trader. Not only did these other workers contribute income to the household but, in some instances, they earned more than the household member engaged in trading. An analysis of employment and income patterns of household members revealed that informal construction (> 40 percent) or related service work, followed by government work, were the most important sources of employment after petty trade. Men were much more likely than women to be wage earners or self-employed in nonagricultural occupations, such as construction or transport. Overall there were very marked differences in the gender division of occupations, with men controlling most government or professional jobs and skilled occupations and, as noted earlier, women engaging in market activities.

Informal Credit Relationships

Virtually no peri-urban traders had access to credit from formal institutions, such as banks. However, informal credit arrangements were widespread. For example, 45 percent of the seventy-three traders in our study received some type of minor credit from their suppliers. This was especially the case for street traders (dumba nengue), who, as mentioned earlier, often worked on a commission basis for a supplier. In some cases, the supplier provided the initial capital for establishing the business, and then regularly provided the trader with products on credit to

sell. In other instances, large wholesalers and/or transporters[1] also provided produce on a loan basis to their trader clients. Fruit and vegetable traders entered
into these arrangements with wholesalers to ensure a regular supply of produce
at a fair price. More than 30 percent of traders had some type of informal buying
arrangement with one or more suppliers. In one case it was reinforced by a written contract, but most involved verbal agreements. These agreements reflected a
general understanding that the trader would buy produce regularly from the supplier at current market prices rather than purchase from others.

Traders also widely participated in informal credit groups, in order to finance
a range of activities. They especially participated in *xitik,* which were informal
groups of ten to twenty traders that financed a limited range of activities. While
only 18 percent of all peri-urban households in Maputo reported membership in
an informal credit association (Graham et al. 1991), 55 percent of petty traders belonged to such groups. Informal credit was on a rotating basis where a trader made
monthly payments and every eleven to twelve months, depending on the number
of members, would receive a payout from the group. Xitik was the most important source of credit for all households in the peri-urban area. Credit funds from
these organizations primarily were utilized to purchase food and other household
needs and, secondarily, to invest in trading activities. In fact, about 66 percent of
xitik credit was used to purchase food and other household necessities, further
proof of the survivalist mode of most petty traders in the Maputo area (see Little
and Lundin de Coloane 1991).

Case Histories of Individual Traders

The diversity and experiences of market actors are revealed through case studies of individual traders. The stories of three Maputo merchants who were able to
adapt successfully to the chaotic conditions of the early 1980s and 1990s are presented below.

> Mama Lozi is an experienced vendor in her 60s (in 1991) who has been engaged
> in the business since she was a young girl. She came originally from nearby
> Gaza Province, Mozambique, and was taught the trade by her older sister.
> She has no formal education but speaks Portuguese reasonably well, and has
> emerged as the head of an informal group of traders at Xipamanine, a peri-
> urban market of Maputo. Mama Lozi also was an active member of several xitik
> and among the most respected traders at the market. She was a major advocate
> for the dumba nengue traders and wanted to allow them to work outside the
> formal marketplaces, since she herself had once worked as a street trader. With
> the relaxation of government restrictions, she has seen a spectacular growth
> in the number of traders working at Xipamanine. She claims there was an in-
> crease of about threefold just during 1988 to 1991.
> Over the years Mama Lozi has observed and/or experienced several changes
> related to trade. She noted that before independence Africans were required

to possess a special permit to sell agricultural products. At that time she used to sell tomatoes, kale, and *kakana* (a local plant used for medicinal purposes). When the government gained its independence in 1974, trade continued to be highly constrained by the socialist government of newly independent Mozambique. In the late 1970s she often had to sell vegetables on the parallel market because open trade was prohibited. However, she indicated that this was a pretty good business, because the government-sanctioned distribution centers (*lojas vinculadas*) could not meet local demand, so it was easy to find customers.

According to Mama Lozi, the PRE program greatly increased supplies and availability of vegetables and other foods, as well as the quantity of goods at the market generally. However, she noted that it also resulted in considerable inflation in food prices: "At present [1991] one can buy sugar, rice, and many types of food at the market . . . and that is good. But it also is bad because the money is not enough and everything is so expensive." Another change that this trader witnessed is the growth in the number of migrants ("refugees") involved in petty trade, which she said had greatly increased market competition and reduced incomes since the newcomers often sold goods cheaply. (It was unclear from the interview whether or not her real income had risen at all since 1988.) A final change that she experienced was the increased number of suppliers who brought goods in from Swaziland and Republic of South Africa (RSA). They were mainly males "because they are the ones with good contacts with suppliers in these countries." These traders often did not work through established networks; rather they supplied individual sellers on an opportunistic basis. According to her, they were trying to disrupt the existing relationships in the market by passing over the traders and wholesalers and directly contracting with individuals, including many dumba nengue/street traders to sell their imported goods. She did not think this is a good practice and said that it is mainly the new suppliers and new traders who participated in it. She noted: "A good relationship with a supplier makes the business function smoothly. In times of scarcity, for example, many traders have to go and look for products on the farms themselves; but when one has established a good contact with a supplier, he serves you even in times of scarcity." She felt the influx of manufactured goods—many of which were originally imported from Asia—and agricultural produce from RSA and Swaziland and the wholesalers supplying these to street traders was a threat to her own business and that of other local traders. (Field notes, February 1992)

* * *

Eliza is a 43-year-old woman who sells at a peri-urban urban market, called Ferroviário market, in the Maputo area. She moved to the Maputo region in the 1970s and worked in a government-owned factory until she lost her job in the 1980s. This was when she began her trading activities. She started on the street by selling fresh groundnuts, sweet potatoes, and cassava to workers around the docks and railway yards in the center of the city. On numerous occasions she was harassed by authorities, and once she was even arrested for engaging in street trade. This prompted her to move to the peri-urban settlements of District V in the 1980s, where she started to sell charcoal at small markets. "This was a dirty business and gave me health problems, so I decided to sell agricultural products, such as potatoes and onions," she explains. In the 1980s she moved to District IV and began to sell in an open area near the present market of Ferroviário. She helped to organize a group of traders in 1990 that successfully petitioned the municipality to establish a physical marketplace at Ferroviário, with stalls and storage space to place goods at night. By 1991 she headed an informal association of mainly former street traders. By then she had diversified into selling construction materials (timber and reeds) and firewood, in addition to vegetables. Eliza clearly was in that top 20 percent of vendors who earned a relatively reasonable weekly income by Maputo standards (in excess of US$12.50) and was not faced with the welfare and food security problems that confronted many other petty traders.

Eliza observed several changes during the twenty-plus years that she has been in business. The two most dramatic were the increased openness of commerce, especially the street trade, and the very high number of people engaged in petty trade—"everybody is a petty trader." Regarding the latter, she pointed to the lack of waged employment and low wages as reasons for this. She noted: "Many people are in the business of selling because there is a decrease of opportunities for jobs. Women used to be traditionally in this activity, but at present even men are entering because there is a lot of money to be made there (at least that is what they believe) and opportunities for jobs are decreasing. Even the specialization for women that used to be for certain trade, such as selling coconuts and tapioca, is disappearing: now anyone can enter this trade. Many of the new traders are refugees and displaced people, but many are also local residents who have either lost their jobs or who want to improve their economic situation by working two activities." Another change that Eliza observed was increased numbers of hawkers who sold prepared foods (breads, cooked rice, and vegetable stews) at the markets and in the street. She noted that a large number of young men recently had been attracted to this trade. (Field notes, February 1992)

* * *

Trader three, Jonas, was a male 38 years old who worked as a supplier and transporter. His father had been a miner in the RSA, and when Jonas was around 25 years of age he joined his father there and worked in a factory. With savings from this employment—and possibly with a loan from his father—he bought a used pickup truck in 1984 and went into the transport business. At first he restricted his informal transport business to moving the goods of Mozambican miners in South Africa to their homes in Gaza and Maputo Provinces, in southern Mozambique. He used these trips also to bring in radios, clothes, and some agricultural products, such as maize and rice, to sell in Mozambique. Business was good, allowing him to purchase a second pickup truck in 1986 and a motor pump to irrigate his 3-hectare farm in Chokwe, a village about 80 kilometers north of Maputo.

In the late 1980s Jonas began to supply the Maputo market with agricultural products, both from his own farm in Chokwe and from RSA. In 1990 he bought a large truck, which was used to transport agricultural products and people from neighboring Gaza Province to Maputo city, manufactured goods from RSA to Maputo and Gaza, and agricultural products from RSA to Maputo. In 1991 he maintained a list of traders in Xipamanine and dumba nengue hawkers whom he regularly supplied with tomatoes, potatoes, and onions. He used his profits from transport and trade to invest in his farm in Chokwe, which he had expanded by 1991. He said the security situation in 1991 still hampered transport links between Maputo, RSA, and Gaza Province (southern Mozambique). However, he emphasized that one had to take risks to stay in business, so he did not let insecurity halt his activities. "One has to be very careful and take advantage of government escorts," he exclaimed. Jonas also acknowledged that the number of individuals engaged in transporting agricultural products from RSA and Swaziland to Maputo grew rapidly during 1988 to 1991. Most wholesalers who brought in goods from neighboring countries did not own transport at the time but, instead, hired it locally. (Field notes, November 1991)

The three Maputo traders discussed above exemplify successful entrepreneurs and provide real-life context to the statistics discussed earlier. Their interviews highlight many of the changes in trade that occurred with the reforms of the 1980s and 1990s, including the increased presence of street hawkers, loss of waged jobs, inflation, and liberalization of regional trade. The kinds of risks and uncertainties that Maputo's hawkers faced in the 1990s were significant.

Other important themes can be gleaned from the different trader interviews. First, the complaint that there is growing competition and lower profits because of the proliferation of informal street traders is heard from the female market traders, but not from Jonas, because he has benefited by supplying them with his imported goods. Desperate job prospects and retrenchments, as well as growing numbers of "migrant" traders (including dumba nengue) crowd marketplaces and limit the prices that established traders, such as Mama Lozi and Eliza, can charge customers. In Jonas's case, however, he has used dumba nengue traders to hawk imported goods, and their growing numbers have strengthened his bargaining position with them. The effects of recent economic reforms are viewed as part of the reason for excessive numbers of individuals whose only job prospects are as full or part-time hawkers in the informal sector. As noted above, Jonas benefited from this change because it created a pool of the unemployed and street traders who could sell for him at reduced commissions.

Second, there is the mention of cross-border trade with South Africa, a wealthier country with an advanced agricultural and industrial sector that produces agricultural surpluses and a range of manufactured goods. This theme is highlighted in interviews with two of the traders. In Jonas's case unofficial trade with RSA and, more recently, cheap imports from Asia have benefited his business. Mozambique's proximity to sub-Saharan Africa's wealthiest nation means that traders are able to benefit from a geographic advantage, just as Somali traders in the Horn of Africa are able to do the same because of favorable proximity to the Middle East and Kenya (see chapter 7). Throughout Africa international borders provide important opportunities for unofficial trade, especially in an era where unemployed youth have little options but to engage in informal trade of both legal and illicit goods (see Meagher 2003 and 2010; Raeymaekers and Jourdan 2009; Roitman 2005). The RSA/Mozambique borderlands are no exception to this pattern (Peberdy 2000).

A third theme highlighted in the case studies is the growing number of young males (often educated) moving into trading activities normally associated with females. This is highlighted in the case studies of Mama Lozi and Eliza and is generally viewed as an unusual trend, but also a troubling one in some respects. As noted earlier, this same pattern is observed elsewhere in Africa and has been linked to the negative employment effects of SAPs (see Overa 2007).

Finally, although most traders were unaware of what specific reform programs were underway at the time, their narratives provide glimpses of what it was like to be in the informal sector during a period of reform and restructuring. Their responses point to the amazing resilience and resourcefulness of many traders who confronted economic and political volatility. In Maputo the reform program was to gain considerable momentum and, I might add, criticism later in the decade (Hanlon 1996). However, the symptoms of the economic reform packages in terms of inflation, cheap imports, and a growing unofficial sector already were evident in the early 1990s.

Thus, the political and economic turmoil of Mozambique provided many daunting challenges, but also opportunities for petty traders. In particular the two Maputo women, Mama Lozi and Eliza, managed to weather the considerable market and political uncertainties of the 1970s and 1980s, in part by relying on strong ties with suppliers and customers. These two traders represent older and relatively more prosperous vendors among those interviewed. They both had "graduated" out of the dumba nengue trade but still experienced poverty and hardships in their new trading activities. Jonas, in turn, reflects the very small class of highly successfully market actors of the 1990s, who accumulated start-up capital in South Africa, and invested in transborder commerce. He continued to be heavily involved in transporting agricultural products to market from RSA and, to a lesser extent, from his own farm in nearby Gaza Province. With improved transport and security, this type of business has grown in recent years, and many street traders continue to hawk goods and produce that are imported vis-à-vis this and overseas trade (Peberdy and Crush 2006).

Traders' Perceptions of Economic Reforms

As noted earlier, economic policy reforms had a strong but uneven impact in the Maputo area. The findings of the survey of seventy-three traders and discussions with a range of key informants, including market officials and wholesalers, generally confirm this. Since many of the market-oriented policies were already underway by the late 1980s, it was possible to discuss them with traders and record their perspectives. The interviews clearly show that the type and magnitude of economic reforms and changes at the time were unprecedented, but their impacts were mixed. To quote one approximately 60-year-old woman trader from Xipamanine neighborhood, Maputo: "The government is not doing much, but at least they leave us in peace to carry on with our trade." This perception was shared by many traders in 1991, although many would have liked for the government to invest in improving market facilities, storage, and transport networks and to create jobs.

Approval of some of these market reforms did not always translate into a perception that incomes and welfare had improved much. For example, when queried about whether or not their welfare had improved during 1988 to 1991, the majority of Maputo's traders claimed it had not. They said that trade was more profitable in 1988 before the relaxation of street trading regulations. However, divergent voices were expressed, in part reflecting the heterogeneous nature of the sector. From the perspective of most marketplace vendors, trade was better when there was less competition from street traders. Migrants and refugees who were willing to sell produce and goods at very low prices annoyed the established Maputo traders. With the influx of migrants at the time, as well as with reduced restrictions on petty trade, marketplace vendors often were (are) undersold by street traders.

Many licensed traders, however, pointed to other reasons for a decline in their profits. They believed that a rapid increase in prices, a result of currency devaluation under the PRE program and imports from neighboring countries, such as RSA, reduced their incomes. Because many traders also consumed their food inventory and mainly used their revenues to cover basic living costs, rapid inflation was seen as the major negative change during 1988 to 1991. If one looks at the income of the poorest group of petty traders at the time, there is little doubt that inflation jeopardized their ability to purchase basic foods for subsistence (see table 2.1).

Traders did not point to this trend, because it did not really begin until later in the 1990s, but the government's encouragement of South African investment in the past fifteen years resulted in the establishment of large South African supermarket chains in Maputo that would have diminished the role of local produce traders. In the late 1990s the South African supermarket chain Shoprite established an outlet in Maputo, and while it was supposed to source produce from Mozambique farmers and markets, much of its produce is imported from South Africa (Nair and Coote 2007).

Other complaints about the reform program relate to the retrenchment of workers by the government. Indeed, 38 percent of traders who indicated negative effects from reform policies pointed to this painful outcome. Traders consistently complained of falling market shares due to the infusion of new traders into the market, and they often blamed government downsizing for this. They believed that the increased competition from street traders threatened their own welfare.

Summary

As Africa's urban and peri-urban areas rapidly grow and public sector employment declines even more without comparable growth in private-sector jobs, the size and complexity of the part-time and full-time trading sector will continue to increase. What economic reform programs did in Mozambique was to reduce formal-sector waged employment, which was usually in the public sector, and devalue the local currency and wages of those who still maintained a job. These policy changes aggravated food costs for urbanites who depended on imports and pushed many to pursue informal-sector activities, such as petty trade. However, the government also liberalized domestic trade, which accelerated the number of street traders, but also bombarded the market with cheap imports from Asia and RSA. In Maputo petty trading can offer a way out of unemployment and dire economic difficulties: a quick strategy for earning money that requires relatively little capital investment. The heterogeneous nature of trader populations meant that some were economic "winners," while most lost out from the reforms.

The proliferation of petty traders in peri-urban Maputo and elsewhere in Africa is an unhealthy symptom of underdevelopment, as well as an implicit symbol of resistance to harsh economic reforms. Indeed, employment problems and low incomes are important reasons for the growth in petty trade in Maputo, specifically, and Africa generally (see Brown 2006; Bryceson and Potts 2006; Hansen and Vaa 2004). With access to farmland and adequate employment so very difficult, peri-urban residents enter the street trade in order to survive. While petty trading allows this group of traders to survive—albeit at very low levels of welfare— it represents a large underclass of unemployed and underemployed. To view it as a burgeoning class of private sector entrepreneurs, as some policy analysts do, paints an unrealistically rosy picture of a dire employment situation.

In the next chapter the themes of pro-market reforms and their local effects on households and communities are continued, but with a focus on environmental programs and the new configurations of private partnerships that manage them. It shows how pro-market reforms and rhetoric similar to those discussed in this and the previous chapter have impacted wildlife conservation and the pastoralist communities of Kenya who reside in biodiversity-rich areas.

3   "We Now Milk Elephants"
The Community Conservation Business in Rural Kenya

An elderly Samburu woman on the hot, dusty plains of northern Kenya explains to a visiting group of government and development officials that pastoralists have learned the value of wildlife. She notes unabashedly that "we now milk elephants like we do our cows—they provide us with income to buy food" (field notes, January 1995). The mixed crowd of state officials and development workers nod approvingly, discussing among themselves how local wildlife conservation efforts and enterprises in the area clearly have benefited local communities. This is exactly the kind of language the visitors wanted to hear, as the explicit goal of community-based conservation in Kenya and elsewhere in East Africa was to make nature and wildlife "pay," thereby encouraging communities to better conserve the region's rich biodiversity. In the era of pro-market reforms, a successful conservation program is one "linking business with nature" (USAID 2006).

At around the same time in another area of Kenya—the predominantly Maasai district of Narok—groups of young men, political leaders, and government officials clash over who should control a nearby rich forest zone of biodiversity. Should it be the central government, the county council, or the local pastoralist community? Unlike the other example noted above, this one involves violence, with frightful images of ethnic targeting, a stark contrast to the "win-win" scenario that advocates of community-based conservation (CBC) claim (see Dietz 1996). Nonetheless, both examples speak to a recent process of commodifying rich, biodiverse landscapes of Kenya, which, on the one hand, justify expanding conservation schemes with further restrictions on how local communities can utilize their lands and, on the other, create a market for biodiversity that can generate profits for investors and businesses but also violent contestations. Although these two examples take place under different circumstances, they combine similar themes of pro-market and pro-business approaches to conservation, a pattern that has become prevalent throughout eastern and southern Africa (see Igoe and Brockington 2007).

This chapter explores the book's theme of neoliberal reform in the context of biodiversity conservation in Kenya. It argues that Kenya's rich wildlife sector did not escape anti-statist actions and the effects of pro-growth reforms that characterized other sectors, such as agriculture and trade, which were discussed in the two previous chapters. In the Kenyan context biodiversity effectively equates to wildlife, especially the charismatic megafauna (e.g., elephants) and carnivores (e.g., lions and leopards) that are at the center of the country's lucrative tourist industry and a focus of the global conservation community. Similar to the luxury vegetable (NTC) business discussed in chapter 1, the drivers of market demand here also are affluent Westerners and Asians who visit as high-paying tourists and/or generous supporters of conservation. By expanding markets for tourism and conservation, economic reforms in the environment sector have profoundly affected Kenya's wildlife sector and the communities that reside in wildlife areas.

This chapter traces the ascendance of conservation reforms from the early 1990s to the 2000s, by which time most local conservation-based activities were gauged in terms of private-sector partnerships. It will show how international conservation organizations, private wildlife advocates, and development agencies have used the rhetoric of community empowerment, sustainability, and participation to advocate private-sector partnerships between communities and investors that often end up marginalizing the communities they are supposed to assist. Under the rubric of CBC, a particularly popular model in eastern and southern Africa (see Hulme and Murphree 2001), private controls on communal lands and resources were expanded well beyond the boundaries of national parks and protected conservation areas, representing a type of land grab but under the auspices of an environmental ("green") label (for descriptions of "green" land-grabbing elsewhere, see Vidal 2008; Zoomers 2010). The chapter's conclusion revisits the increasingly politicized nature of wildlife conservation in Kenya and the ways that local communities have used globalized discourses about indigenous rights and biodiversity to challenge environmental agendas.

Communities, Companies, and Conservation Reforms

The Kenyan government revised its wildlife policy in 1996 after a prolonged process that included external pressure from donor agencies (see Juma et al. 1993; Richardson 1996; KWS 1997b). In contrast to the earlier policy that focused on conservation in protected areas (national parks and reserves), the new directive explicitly advocated partnerships outside protected areas between rural communities and government, private-sector firms, and NGOs. Its goal was to improve and extend conservation beyond national parks and game reserves (Kenya 1996). To quote from a Kenya Wildlife Services (KWS) document, the principle of the new policy was to "give people an economic return from the wildlife living on their land and the wildlife will thereby assume a value in the community's eyes and encourage the application of sensible conservation practices" (KWS 1997b: 9). KWS is the government agency responsible for the country's wildlife resources and for operating its national parks and game reserves. The community-based program of KWS was an integral part of the new policy, and it advocated for participatory approaches, linking conservation with social and economic development objectives. Donor agencies, especially USAID and several prominent international nongovernmental organizations (INGOs), rushed to support the initiative. One estimate shows that the five largest international conservation NGOs, the so-called big five or BINGOs (big international NGOs) that includes World Wildlife Fund (WWF) and Conservation International (CI), received an estimated 70 percent of the $300 million that USAID allocated to conservation programs in the 1990s (Dowie 2006: 9). The BINGOs obviously have benefited immensely from increased donor funding for CBC, including in Kenya.

The partnership mandate targeted pastoralist communities for the obvious reason that they reside where wildlife are found. It is estimated that up to 75 percent of Kenyan wildlife annually migrate outside protected areas, usually onto the lands of pastoral communities (see Western and Gichoi 1993; Lamprey and Reid 2004). In the words of one conservation group working in northern Kenya, the fate of wildlife conservation "is inextricably linked to the fate of local pastoralist communities" (Northern Rangelands Trust 2008: 1). What is not acknowledged, however, is that while local partnerships may be a worthy goal, they usually reflect very unequal power relations, with the local community often having little clout to negotiate the terms of the partnership (for an Ethiopian example of this pattern, see Harrison 2002). Thus, rather than partnerships, many of these become patron-client arrangements with the powerful patron company or INGO dictating the terms of the arrangement and monopolizing most of the critical information.

The new, softer approach to pastoralists and conservation represents an ironic twist, since the policies of most East African countries, including Kenya, have been and continue to be blatantly anti-pastoralist (see chapter 6). In fact, pastoralist development itself has become a significant development category in the past ten years. Although most development agencies and governments earlier had shunned pastoralism as a marginal economic activity, many were hurriedly developing and funding programs for pastoralist groups in the 2000s (for example, see Hodgson 2011; and WISP [World Initiative for Sustainable Pastoralism] 2010). No doubt for many pastoralist communities this attention is a very welcome development since many still lack basic health, water, and education services. The attention to pastoralist development is from not only wildlife conservation advocates, but also groups concerned with humanitarian needs, human rights, poverty alleviation, and even climate change issues (McPeak et al. 2012). In Tanzania alone there are more than one hundred NGOs dealing with pastoralist (mainly Maasai) issues (Hodgson 2011).

The goal of KWS was (is) to expand the areas under conservation protection, which meant converting communal pastoral areas into community wildlife sanctuaries, land trusts, and/or ecotourism ventures through a CBC model. Terms like community driven, participatory, and local empowerment were used to describe the new CBC approach (Kenya 1996; Northern Rangelands Trust 2008), but virtually all the initiatives were instigated by outside parties rather than pastoralists themselves. How participatory could they then be? Despite strong rhetoric about community improvement, KWS's and most other conservation organizations primarily are concerned with environmental conservation and, secondarily, with local social and economic development. For obvious reasons, some key pastoral leaders opposed the new initiative since they saw it as further intrusion by conservationists onto their lands (Rutten 2004).

In 1997 the Enterprise Development Fund (EDF) was established at KWS's new Partnership Programme. The initiative was funded by USAID, and its mandate was to fund private enterprise projects related to wildlife conservation. To participate in the EDF program, communities usually had to provide game scouts (young men) to guard against poaching and agree to certain land-use restrictions in key wildlife areas, including keeping some of their lands free of livestock, crops, and human settlements (see Rutten 2002). Many pastoral communities were approached by private tour operators and investors to establish partnerships, which would allow the enterprises to access EDF funds. For a community-based venture to be eligible for EDF support, it needed a commercial plan demonstrating that the entity was financially sustainable. This often implied a marketing arrangement or contract with a private firm. As noted in a KWS annual report, the goal of the Partnership Programme was "to involve local communities in conservation as an economic enterprise" (KWS 1997a: 14). Many of the enterprise loans from USAID were relatively large for start-up Kenyan businesses, with some enterprises receiving more than US$30,000 in their first year (Lent et al. 2002: 6). Contrast this with some of the very small, local camping and animal-viewing initiatives that some Maasai communities south of Lake Magadi, Kenya (Kajiado District) had started with minimal funds and had annual operating budgets of less than a few thousand dollars (field notes, June 1995). In the pro-business parlance of the era, Maasai and other pastoralist beneficiaries were referred to as "project customers" (ibid.: 1).

Wildlife conservation was an easy sell to international constituents. Funding pledges to KWS from development agencies and conservation advocates reached $96 million by 1996, with additional promises in excess of $300 million through 2006 (McRae 1998: 510; Were 2005: 239). During some years, KWS had more funds for equipment and field operations than some key ministries, such as agriculture and health, and many civil servants resented this (field notes, July 1995). The strong initial support for KWS was a reflection and, some might argue, an ethical contradiction at a time when budget cuts under Kenya's World Bank/IMF–imposed structural adjustment program (SAP) reduced education and health services (see Richardson 1996). In an environment of economic restructuring, private groups were perceived as preferable to public institutions, and an important goal of KWS restructuring was to forge partnerships with the private sector. Under the SAP reforms the state increasingly delegated responsibilities for wildlife management to INGOs and private enterprises. The Conservation of Biodiverse Resource Areas (COBRA) project, a USAID-funded CBC activity at KWS with the unfortunate acronym of a deadly poisonous snake, even used INGOs to help train community members to serve as game scouts, and "some of those trained play the roles that KWS rangers do in national parks and reserves such as revenue collection in the community sanctuaries" (Kahata and Imbanga 2002: 18). The boundary between private and public responsibility and accountability was increasingly blurred in the country's key conservation areas.

During the 1990s and 2000s, KWS and its INGO partners actively brokered deals between private firms and local communities to encourage investment in local conservation-based activities. As Barrow et al. note, "community conservation has been promoted as a way to reduce government investment in conservation areas. . . . It fits the budget reform and SAP programs" (2000: 10). Accordingly, the emphasis on the private sector was claimed to reduce public expenditures and generate revenues for local communities who, in exchange for a range of different benefits, would agree to delegate large segments of their lands for conservation purposes. In reality, however, the model often worked differently. Private partnerships with communities sometimes led to exorbitant profits for private businesses while providing little in the way of benefits to the community itself. Rutten, for example, estimates that one of the contracts, between a Maasai group ranch and a private tour operator,[1] netted as much as a 75 percent return in one year, with a payment to the community equivalent to only about 15 percent of what the private company earned (Rutten 2002: 26–27). The contract in question required that the Maasai community set aside more than 5,000 hectares of their grazing land for the exclusive use of wildlife and tourism, or about 20 percent of their entire territory.

COBRA (1992–98) and its follow-on project, Conservation of Resource Areas through Enterprise (CORE) (1999–2005), embodied this commitment to private-sector partnerships and a pro-business approach to wildlife conservation. COBRA and CORE, with total funding in excess of $20 million, supported a network of mainly INGOs to stimulate enterprise development based on nature-based activities (see Lent et al. 2002). The CORE project especially embodied the pro-business and market-based approaches to managing and conserving Kenya's rich biodiversity. It provided about US$4 million to fund enterprise capacity building with a goal to nurture and broker nature-based enterprises in pastoralist communities of Kajiado, Laikipia, and Samburu Districts (ibid.). For some observers, the merits of the private-sector approach was seen as "questionable," in part because (1) it depends heavily on transitory funds (subsidies) from wildlife enthusiasts and donor agencies and (2) private partners did not always meet their investment obligations (see Rutten 2004; *Daily Nation* 2004). Referring again to a community-based Maasai enterprise bordering Amboseli National Park, the private partner in this case allocated only about 10 percent of the investment funds and built 12 percent of the lodging facilities that were stipulated in the contract, although in this case the community had set aside 7,000 hectares of grazing land for wildlife and tourism use (Rutten 2004: 12–13).

Private-sector partners benefited considerably under CBC programs, but they also heavily relied on project-subsidized infrastructure, training, management, and security (ibid.: 29). Indeed, even the most positive evaluations of the CORE and COBRA programs noted that many of the community-based projects and enterprises relied on external grants and subsidies to remain viable (Watson 1999; Lent et al. 2002). In this sense, private business could tap private funds, as well as state and public donor support and subsidies when conditions warranted it. In effect, they had the best of both funding worlds. This practice of subsidies was widespread despite the official narrative that the private sector could provide a model of wildlife conservation absent of subsidies and public funds.

The Politics of Biodiversity Conservation

By the 1990s conservation groups, including KWS, found themselves confronted by increasingly politicized pastoral communities whose lands they were encroaching upon. The new era of multiparty politics in the early 1990s witnessed highly publicized efforts by Kenyan communities to reclaim lands lost to agriculture and wildlife conservation (see chapter 4). One of the better known and most tragic cases, Enoosupukia of Narok District, was briefly alluded to at the beginning of the chapter. It was an incident in the 1990s between Maasai herders and mainly Kikuyu farmers in a highland, resource-rich location of Narok District called Enoosupukia, and it involves a complex set of issues interlaced with land and national politics (Matter 2010). In the Enoosupukia case many non-Maasai farmers had settled in the area during the 1960s through the 1990s and had purchased or leased land from Maasai and Dorobo families.[2] Narok politicians, especially Member of Parliament William ole Ntimama, played the environmental card by emphasizing that despite their land titles, these "nonnative" farmers had to be removed to protect a biologically diverse forest and watershed (see ibid.). The need to protect local forests and a catchment zone for town water supplies, as well as respect the rights of indigenous people, demanded their removal. In this case, the twin banners of indigeneity and conservation of biodiversity were raised to pursue political ends, and the actions resulted in attacks by Maasai youth that left seventeen farmers dead (see Dietz 1996; Klopp 2001).

The Enoosupukia tragedy was enmeshed in the harsh ethnic politics that accompanied Kenya's first multiparty elections in more than twenty years. Not only in Enoosupukia but throughout the Rift Valley and elsewhere in Kenya, violence was widespread after the 1992 elections, and much of it involved land conflicts that pitted Kalenjin or Maasai against Kikuyu (Klopp 2001). In Enoosupukia Kikuyu farmers indicated that until the local member of parliament (MP) stirred up ethnic hostilities and questioned their legitimacy to remain in the area, they lived peacefully among local Maa-speakers (Matter 2009). According to Matter, "the displaced residents argued that they had been targeted for eviction by the local MP, who sought revenge for their disloyalty in the 1992 general election" (ibid.: 5). This same MP was said to incite the violence of 1993 in the location and subsequent eviction of Kikuyu settlers from the area on the grounds that they were destroying the local environment.

Later in 2002 the Narok County Council gave eviction notices to all farmers who remained in Enoosupukia after the struggles of the 1990s. Most Kikuyu farmers already had departed following the violence of the 1990s, but some of them, as well as Kisii families from a neighboring district, had remained. Similar to the Kikuyu, Kisii are Bantu speakers and culturally distinct from Maasai. To ensure their removal, the Narok County Council in 2005, with support from the Kenyan army, evicted more than one thousand non-Maasai farmers from Enoosupukia, once again using environmental conservation as its rationale (Schmidt-Soltau 2006: 19). With little political representation in the Maasai-controlled Narok County Council or other local government institutions, they were unable to resist the eviction notices. By 2006 Maasai herders and their cattle had moved into the area and were using it for grazing (ibid.). Similar incidents to those at Enoosupukia have been observed elsewhere in Africa, where nonindigenous communities have suffered under the guise of environmental conservation and indigenous peoples' rights (see Dove 2006).

Another well-known act of resistance also involved Maasai pastoralists, but this time it included the Amboseli National Park area of southern Kenya. Here a local attempt was made in 2005 to recover Maasai territory from Amboseli National Park, which is among the best known and most profitable parks in Africa (see Ngowi 2006; Mynott 2005). In the Amboseli case, CBC programs and enterprises have been encouraged in the area since the 1980s (see Rutten 2002 and 2004). The attempt by Maasai to recover their lands from Amboseli National Park and turn control of the park over to the Maasai-controlled Kajiado County Council received support from the government of President Mwai Kibaki. The political gesture by Kibaki was viewed as a strategic move to garner Maasai support for a crucial referendum on a new constitution that Kibaki and his allies strongly endorsed (Mugonyi and Otieno 2005; for a detailed discussion of the controversy surrounding the national referendum, see chapter 4).

Confronted with the possible loss of a key conservation area like Amboseli, the response from the conservation community was rapid and definitive. For example, David Western, a former head of KWS and early advocate of CBC (Western et al. 1994), is quoted as saying that if this claim is honored "every other national park and reserve . . . risks being erased on a political whim at a moment's notice" (Holden 2005: 215). Almost immediately after Maasai leaders initiated the claim in 2005 large numbers of herders began to graze their cattle in the park: "Western reports that last week he counted 15,000 livestock" (ibid.). Maasai leaders around Amboseli warned that should the government fail to return the area to the Maasai people, "we will deploy parallel gate fee collection officers, dispatch our Morans (young men) to manage the park and return all the wildlife roaming freely on our private land to the protected land in Amboseli and Nairobi" (Mutai 2005: 1). The dispute over the ownership status of the park was held up in Kenyan courts for several years after Kibaki officially de-gazetted the park in 2005, which removed its protected status as a conservation area, and returned control of the land to the Maasai-controlled Kajiado County Council. A recent court ruling that Kibaki's action was illegal means that Amboseli may regain its national park status and return to the control of KWS (*Business Daily* 2010). Regardless of the legal outcome, the spate of spearings of elephants and lions by Maasai in the area in recent years demonstrates just how tense the situation around Amboseli remains (see Pflanz 2008).

As the above examples illustrate, conservation initiatives opened up considerable political space for local leaders and communities to push grievances and claims, often with chilling effects on conservationists and their sponsors. In the Amboseli case, Maasai leaders drew on the narrative of "participatory" community-based conservation, along with the fact that abundant wildlife graze their lands, to reclaim rights that had been lost with the establishment of a national park. "Participation" and "community empowerment" are terms that frequently are splashed across many INGO web sites. However, they can have powerful effect when their meanings are seriously interpreted and invoked by disadvantaged communities, in this case to validate claims to customary lands and water points that were lost to conservation activities.

In many cases Northern donors and INGOs are blinkered to the complex political dynamics that are associated with environmental conservation in Kenya, as well as in neighboring Tanzania (see Hodgson 2011; Neumann 1995).[3] Pastoralist communities are able to draw on resources and assistance from a range of different international actors, including human rights bodies like Minority Rights Group (MRG) International and the United Nations Human Rights Council (see

UNHRC 2007; Centre for Minority Rights Development [CEMRIDE] 2006), to pursue local political claims and agendas. As will be discussed in chapter 4, international pressures for democratic and political reforms in Kenya also fueled local power struggles, which in certain areas have become entangled with the politics of environmental and indigenous peoples' movements.

Thus, the emphasis on improved governance and democracy lent support to the CBC model since it emphasized local participation and the delegation of control and responsibility to local levels. Some leaders of politically marginalized groups, including many pastoralist and former hunter-gatherer groups, used the advent of multiparty politics (democracy) in the 1990s to increasingly invoke their new democratic rights as underrepresented indigenous peoples (see chapter 4). The linking of human and indigenous and minority peoples' rights to environmental/biodiversity debates symbolized a new political strategy that groups like pastoralists and other politically marginal groups now could pursue (see Igoe 2006).

In Kenya the distinction between "indigenous" and "minority" is constitutionally important. As this chapter has shown, claiming indigenous status for Maasai and other pastoralist groups is important for making claims to land against nonindigenous residents without strong historical claims to a particular area. This distinction between indigenous and so-called outsiders has been at the heart of much of the land conflict and violence in Rift Valley Province, Kenya, as tragically illustrated in the Enoosupukia case. However, the term indigenous does not have any special constitutional, and in some cases legal, status in Kenya, a country that did not support the recent UN Declaration of the Rights of Indigenous Peoples approved by the UN General Assembly in 2007. By contrast, minority does have political significance in Kenya's constitution. If a minority group can demonstrate that they are denied political representation by their elected MP from a larger ethnic group, they can make the case for a separate political constituency and elected MP (interview with Kenyan human rights lawyer, September 2008). In the 2000s several small Kenyan communities have employed this political strategy in the courts and National Assembly (parliament), but with very mixed results. The issues that surround the minority and indigenous labels remain politically sensitive and hotly debated in Kenya's electoral and judicial systems (see detailed discussions on the subject in chapter 4).

In their rush to decentralize wildlife management and work with community-based organizations, KWS and its international sponsors failed to recognize the undemocratic nature of many local groups that they supported. This deficiency is a common problem with many decentralized environmental programs in Africa, where elite capture of benefits is widespread (see Ribot and Larson 2004). For example, the case of the Il Ngwesi CBC project of Laikipia District, Kenya, shows how decentralization can sharpen local, undemocratic tendencies to the benefit of a few elite gatekeepers. This project involves an eco-friendly lodge that charges foreign visitors more than $400 per night for accommodation, a cultural center, roads and other infrastructure, and a core conservation area of 8,675 hectares in the home area of the pastoral Mukugodo, a hybrid group of Maa (Maasai) speakers. A total of twenty-eight local residents are employed in either the lodge or the conservation area, just a fraction of the approximately six thousand people who reside in the area (Equator Initiative 2011). An agreement was signed between a project committee from the Mukugodo group ranch and a Nairobi-based tour operator to manage and run the enterprise, but most of the community members who were involved in the activity were local notables and their family members who worked for the enterprise (see Ashley 2000; Salomon 2000). In the words of one resident from the area, "they are the ones and their children, who were given jobs at the lodge and conservancy" (field notes, March 2011).

USAID funded the Laikipia project, and its staff members praise it as a highly successful example of "linking business and nature" (USAID 2006), but the results of different studies point to a different story. One evaluation, for instance, notes that

> its control and earnings benefit only a small section of the community, having minimal effects for poorer community members (Ashley and Hussein 2000). For instance, employees of the lodge are for the most part chosen from committee members. The management of the bandas, and the beneficiaries of employment and benefits, are almost exclusively men. On the surface the tourist bandas appear to be a community initiated and managed project, but the idea for the project, the money, the marketing, and the management have all come from outside the community. (Salomon 2000: 32)

In another assessment of Il Ngwesi and five other CBC enterprises in Kenya, it is noted:

> A new report demonstrates that though communities in Kenya have devoted substantial portions of their own land to the wildlife conservation on which ecotourism businesses are based, they have reaped minimal gains from such ventures. Instead, they have ended up enmeshed in exploitative partnerships with various private investors. (Mbaria 2007: 9)

The recent closing (September 2011) of one of Kenya's premier and most expensive ecotourism lodges, the Shompole Lodge, due to a dispute between private investors in the lodge and the local Maasai community and its conservancy further raises the issue of who benefits from community-based conservation schemes and lodges. This exclusive, eco-friendly lodge is located in a large, community-managed conservancy of 10,000 hectares in the Rift Valley south of Nairobi, where some of the world's wealthiest individuals have stayed while on safari in Kenya. It also is an area where there have been long-standing disputes between Maasai group ranches and private companies seeking to gain control of the scenic and wildlife-rich lands (see Galaty 2013). In a newspaper article on the closing of Shompole Lodge and other community conservancies, Muiruri questions KWS's policy of encouraging partnerships with private investors for the management of Kenya's wildlife and conservation lands, suggesting that "some conservancies have taken advantage of the local people's ignorance to details in contracts to defraud them of their rightful share of profits" (2011). While there are no data on the actual distribution of benefits between the community and the Shompole Lodge that might point to unfair treatment, the facility remains closed as of July 5, 2012. A well-known safari firm that markets the lodge notes on its website that "Shompole Lodge was closed down until further notice in September 2011 pending an agreement with the local community on its future as well as that of the Shompole Wildlife Conservancy in which it is located" (Gamewatchers Safaris 2012).

In the case of the Il Ngwesi lodge, the relatively large grant of approximately US$178,000 provided by COBRA in 1996 and the local community's commitment of about 80 percent of its group ranch land to wildlife conservation has generated neither economic benefits for the majority nor the anticipated conservation benefits (see Ashley 2000; Ashley and Hussein 2000). A similar tale of skewed economic benefits from CBC activities is found near the world-famous Maasai Mara National Reserve in southern Kenya (see Thompson and Homewood 2002).

To ensure that wildlife is protected in its CBC projects, KWS effectively outsources security and animal control work to community groups. Through extensive training programs usually funded by INGOs or development agencies, local herders are trained to serve as community rangers and to report poaching to district game wardens and park officials (see KWS 1995 and 2007). Many of them are equipped with radio networks and weapons, and often they are linked directly into the KWS wildlife security system. They wear similar uniforms to those of KWS game rangers and in many cases have better equipment than their government counterparts, a point that also has been noted by others (Kahata and Imbanga 2002). Indeed, the number of donor-funded CBC programs that were allocated for the training and equipping of game scouts suggests that these investments merely disguise an expansion of policing and local controls on conservation despite the enticing rhetoric about community partnerships, empowerment, and participation (see Laikipia Wildlife Forum 2004).

The rapidity with which community lands outside of parks and reserves have been converted into a range of different control mechanisms, including land leases, land trusts, and community conservancies or sanctuaries, is truly astounding. In the late 1990s, when many CBC activities only were just beginning, COBRA's investments were responsible for about 110,000 hectares of private and communal lands being placed under some form of conservation control (Kahata and Imbanga 2002: 18). By 2002 its follow-on project, CORE, had brought an additional

97,100 hectares under conservation controls (Lent et al. 2002: 4), while another recent conservation effort—the Northern Rangelands Trust—hopes to eventually extend some level of control to as much as 625,000 hectares of northern Kenya (see Northern Rangelands Trust 2008). Along with the growth in private conservation trusts and controls has come the establishment of small, luxury ecotourist lodges, usually managed by Europeans and catering to wealthy international visitors. Such large increases in land under conservation represent significant losses of communal pastoral grazing areas and alternative livelihood activities, such as dryland farming. That most community-based conservation schemes are located adjacent to existing protected areas strongly suggests that these ventures merely represent an extension of existing national parks and reserves.

Land acquisitions for conservation, or what can be called green land-grabs, have been fueled by funds from donor agencies, European and U.S. charities, wealthy Western philanthropists, and international conservation organizations. It is a different kind of land-grabbing than recent cases of African governments (including Ethiopia and Mozambique) leasing out large chunks of local farmers' and herders' lands to foreign companies for agricultural investment (Von Braun and Meinzen-Dick 2009). Nonetheless, there are similarities in terms of their potentially negative impacts on local livelihoods between the two types of land-grabbing even though the former is done in the name of environmental conservation and the latter in terms of national food (and ethanol) needs and profits. In one case, a key conservation INGO in the region has piloted a conservation mechanism called "land trusts"[4] that convert large parcels of communal lands of northern Kenya into protected conservation areas as joint land-holding trusts. On its website the INGO solicits U.S. dollar contributions from donors to "adopt an African acre" of land in East Africa at a rate of US$35/ acre that can then be used to purchase/lease land for conservation, including for the establishment of conservation-based land trusts (African Wildlife Foundation [AWF] 2011). This is a sophisticated marketing approach for soliciting private conservation funds, with parallels to international charity groups who solicit donations to "adopt" an impoverished child or needy school.

In the case of Tanzania, where this type of green land-grabbing and public outsourcing of conservation management to private groups is especially pronounced, the same INGO referred to above has used funds to take over a former state ranch in a pastoralist area and operate it as an exclusive conservation area (Igoe and Brockington 2007: 438). The organization also recently drafted a memorandum of understanding (MOU) with KWS that will "support the institutional development of the Kenya Land Conservation Trust (KLCT) as an institution that will support landowners in conservation in wildlife habitats outside protected areas" (African Wildlife Foundation/KWS 2007: 4). The same draft MOU also establishes principles of collaboration for enterprises that benefit both local communities and conservation (ibid.: 5). With such MOUs—and KWS has many such agreements—KWS increasingly outsources the management of wildlife habitats and wildlife itself to a range of private actors, including INGOs, tourist companies, and foreign investors. There even was a suggestion in 2004 that debt-ridden KWS itself might be sold to a group of private investors, although this possibility was subsequently dismissed after opposition from the Kenyan public (see Koteen 2004; Mbaria 2004). By using conservation land trusts, community conservancies and sanctuaries, and other innovative land-based mechanisms, conservation groups can protect areas for wildlife conservation and upscale tourism without the political entanglements of creating additional national parks and reserves, such as the still-contested Amboseli National Park.

Thus, what has surfaced as a twenty-first-century conservation model in Kenya is a complex and often contradictory mix of private investors, wealthy Western conservationists, private corporations, NGOs (international and national), local community groups, and an accommodating state agency (KWS). What also have emerged are new strategies of both local political resistance and strategic accommodation among local communities. In the next section, the ways in which these strategies and institutional configurations unfold in different geographic and cultural contexts are examined.

Local Cases

How have these different environmental reforms, including the promotion of business-based approaches to biodiversity conservation, affected communities in Kenya? To answer this question, we look at examples from three locations that reflect different mixes of state and private actors, as well as market and political forces.

1. The Amboseli area, Kajiado District: As noted earlier, this is a well-developed tourist destination with a world-famous national park at the base of Mount Kilimanjaro, sizable populations of wildlife, and several community-based conservation schemes;
2. Wamba Divison, Samburu District: It borders a well-known wildlife reserve, Samburu National Game Reserve, and has an active community wildlife movement that has been spurred by outside investors—including European ranchers from nearby Laikipia and Isiolo districts—donor agencies, and INGOs.
3. The Lake Baringo–Bogoria basin, Baringo and Koibetak Districts: It has a moderately well-known national reserve, Lake Bogoria National Reserve, and freshwater lake, Lake Baringo, with a conservation area around it, but considerably fewer tourist attractions and CBC activities than either Amboseli or Wamba.

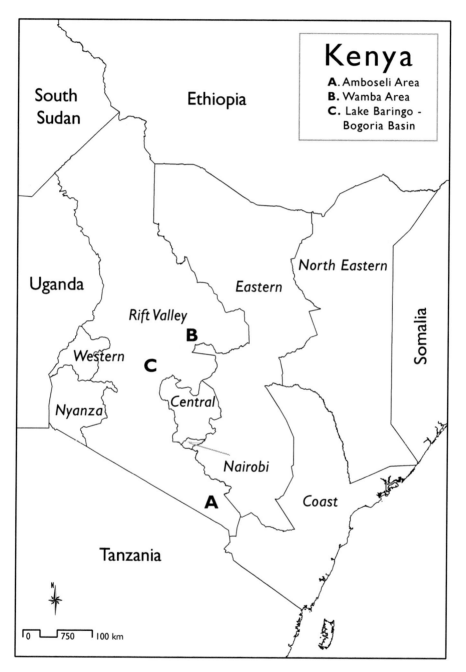

Each of these areas is inhabited by a Maa-speaking pastoralist or agro-pastoralist group. Maasai reside in the Amboseli area, Samburu in the Wamba area, and Il Chamus in the Baringo-Bogoria basin. Except for the Il Chamus who reside in a district (Baringo) largely comprised of Kalenjin speakers (Tugen and Pokot), Maa peoples are the majority population in the different locations. About 75 percent of the enterprise funds from the COBRA and CORE programs were allocated to tourist-related enterprises in popular wildlife areas of Kajiado (especially the Amboseli area), Laikipia, and Samburu Districts (see Lent et al. 2002). These allocations effectively excluded the Lake Baringo–Bogoria basin, which plays a relatively minor role in the country's lucrative tourist trade despite recent efforts to establish community wildlife conservancies and to improve tourist destinations.

In each of these districts conservation groups sought partnerships with group ranches since they were seen as convenient organizations with control of large expanses of land. However, in reality these entities were poorly organized and undemocratic and had performed miserably in developing livestock resources and improving pastoralist incomes. Nonetheless, they were allocated important functions in wildlife conservation by KWS and others for the simple reason that they were one of the few community-wide organizations available. The allocated tasks were blatantly at odds with their original mandate of encouraging commercial livestock production among Kenya's pastoralists (see note 1, this chapter). As Ndung'u observes, for community wildlife conservation "the group ranch has been the major institution of collaboration. . . . KWS is using the Group Ranches as points of entry for WDF [Wildlife Development Fund] projects" (Ndung'u 1997: 25).

The Amboseli Area

The Amboseli National Park hosts about 200,000 bed nights of visitors per year, and its gate (entry) fees were about US$3.5 million in 2004 figures. It generates the second-largest amount of revenue among parks and reserves in the country, behind the famous Masai Mara National Reserve (Bulte et al. 2008: 398). Six Maasai group ranches (GRs) are in the immediate wildlife dispersal area of the park. These include Mbirikani, Kuku, Kimana, Olgululi, Eselengei, and Rombo ranches, and collectively they comprise an area of about 503,000 hectares, or 503 square kilometers (Meguro 2008). Three of them—Kuku, Kimana, and Mbirikani—contain important wetlands near the park's borders to which elephants migrate, but where irrigated farming is rapidly increasing (Rutten 2003). The Maasai group ranches were the first to be formed in Kenya, and those in the Amboseli area date from the 1970s. Among the six ranches Kimana is the most popular tourist destination and the location of the first community wildlife sanctuary in the area (see Rutten 2002).

The history of CBC in Kimana GR has been described in several different publications and reports, so I will just briefly summarize some of the key events associated with Kimana (Rutten 2002; Mburu et al. 2003; Salomon 2000). To begin, a community wildlife sanctuary in Kimana was first discussed in the 1980s because of its critical importance to the Amboseli ecosystem. By 1994 several different conservation groups and private tour operators, as well as KWS, were in discussions with the community about the establishment of a CBC enterprise. The KWS department, with COBRA support, was keen on reaching a conservation agreement with the Kimana GR because the area: (1) contained important wetlands near the park, (2) hosted a number of Amboseli's resident elephant population during the year, and (3) comprised land-use activities, especially irrigated agriculture, that threatened the park's wider ecosystem (USAID 1997: 66). In 1994 KWS approached the committee of the Kimana GR with the idea of establishing a community wildlife sanctuary. Initially, group ranch committee members were very skeptical about a wildlife sanctuary, since the community already had lost key dry-season grazing and water resources in 1973 when Amboseli National Park was established (field notes, June 1995). To counter their reluctance, KWS financed trips for committee members to an ongoing CBC project near the Maasai Mara National Reserve, Narok District, where a Maasai community there had created a sanctuary and was said to be benefiting from wildlife conservation activities. The Narok project is noted for raising local incomes and improving wildlife conservation and was (is) a favorite stop on KWS and COBRA/CORE–funded tours of CBC schemes (for a contrasting perspective on the benefits of Narok's community wildlife projects, see Thompson and Homewood 2002).

After the trip to Narok the Kimana committee agreed to establish a community sanctuary with a core land parcel of 2,750 hectares for the exclusive use of wildlife and tourists (Rutten 2004: 13). In return, KWS provided Kenya shillings (Ksh) 4.2 million (US$65,000) for infrastructure in the sanctuary and encouraged the GR to form a partnership with a private tour operator. Under an initial agreement with three firms Kimana was to be paid a fixed annual amount of Ksh 50,000 ($833) for allowing the businesses to operate tented camp facilities (ibid.: 14). Not exactly a lot of income for a community with considerable livestock wealth, where a good-sized bull fetches upward of $300–400.

Despite a promising start in 1996 that included the awarding of the prestigious International Tourism Project of the Year by the British Guild of Travel Writers (KWS 1997a: 15), the Kimana sanctuary soon faced many problems. By 1998 profits to the community were well below what had been expected, and in the following year a serious drought struck the area (Rutten 2004). GR members, in search of grazing for their starving animals during the 1999 drought year, moved their livestock into the sanctuary in violation of the conservation contract. The action greatly upset tour operators and "tourists who wanted to see game not cattle while on a game drive" (ibid.: 16). However, the tactic confirmed for Kimana residents that pastoralism must remain the key priority and still is the most lucrative activity. Despite large infusions of project funds and a modest level of revenues from tourism, economic and ecological realities still overwhelmingly favored pastoralism over other uses of the land. For example, Muthiani shows that livestock earned Kimana community members about eight times as much per hectare as did wildlife in 1999: $21 versus about $2.60 per hectare (Muthiani, cited in Rutten 2004: 16).[5] By the end of the decade, the Kimana CBC project was in serious trouble.

Part of Kimana's problems stemmed from the highly inequitable distribution of revenues from the Kimana scheme. According to Salomon, "the major criticism of the sanctuary management by the Maasai community is that financial control rests with the wealthy and powerful members of the community. For many members of the Group Ranch, the only widespread benefit derived from the sanctuary is livestock grazing, and this activity conflicts with the tourism industry" (2000: 31). This finding is further confirmed by additional studies that indicate "a major problem in Kimana . . . has been that the leaders of the Group Ranch do not distribute the revenues equally" (Mburu et al. 2003: 66). In fact, only 13 percent of group ranch members claimed to have received any cash benefits from the project, while some stakeholders enjoyed "huge returns (mostly the private partner and some elite persons within the community)" (Rutten 2004: 19, 29). As noted earlier, in their "rush" to organize communities, KWS and other conservation groups often reinforced local inequities and power relations by supporting GR committees.

In 2000 the Kimana committee agreed to a contract with a subsidiary of a European hotel chain that effectively gave the firm control of the entire sanctuary, including responsibilities for gate fee collection, security, and the tented camp sites. Rutten notes:

> The final terms of the lease were: a monthly rent of Ksh 200,000 with an annual increment of 10 per cent; a Ksh 250 bed-night fee for each client and visitor landing at the Kimana airstrip; all locally available and qualified manpower to be hired from among the group-ranch members; and an agreement to purchase local produce. Here it should be recalled that initially the size of the sanctuary was put at 2,750 ha (6,793 acres). After the Kimana members agreed to the idea of a sanctuary, the size was increased to 6,000 hectares (about 14,000 acres) [apparently without most community members knowing about this]. (2004: 16)

Since tourism remains highly volatile in Kenya, especially after the country's postelection violence in 2007 and recent concerns about random bombings following Kenya's invasion of Somalia in October 2011 (see chapters 4 and 7), the Kimana community is absorbing considerable risks. In return for allocating their best grazing lands for conservation and tourism use, annual payments to Kimana residents are highly dependent on visitor and bed night numbers, which can fluc-tuate greatly from year to year. This is especially the case if there is political strife as there was in 2007 and earlier in 1991–92 and 1996–97. While Kimana is still referred to as a CBC activity (see Kahata and Imbanga 2002: 6), the community currently has little to do with the management of the sanctuary and effectively serves as a "landlord" for outside investors (Rutten 2004: 13).

Despite the new more lucrative contract, Mburu et al. (2003) show that Kimana GR members still earn considerably more revenues per hectare (about 200 per-cent higher) from pastoralism and agro-pastoralism than wildlife conservation. This discrepancy partly is explained by low annual payments resulting from the high operating costs of the private tour operators. The Kimana sanctuary itself is not financially sustainable without external assistance and grants despite the strong rhetoric about its market-based approach to conservation (ibid.; Bulte et al. 2008). In short, "nature as business" requires public support for Kimana and many other CBC enterprises.

Despite considerable conservation investments around Amboseli, negative attitudes toward wildlife and conservation still persist. In fact, Maasai communi-ties in the vicinity of Amboseli Park still view wildlife more as a livelihood con-straint rather than a benefit (Rutten 2004; Campbell et al. 2003). In most cases they would prefer that wild animals be kept off their lands (Mburu et al. 2003: 19). In fact, contrary to KWS's wishes, Maasai are pursuing subdivision and private land titles, which directly conflict with wildlife conservation plans for keeping the rangeland open (Rutten 2004). From the perspective of local Maasai, private titles would better protect them against the expansion of the park and other pro-tected conservation areas than would a group land title, an indication that they still view protected conservation areas as threats to their land.

Historically, Maasai around Amboseli also have used poaching to protest against park policies. Several rhinos and other valued species were killed by Maa-sai when the park was first established and the government failed to deliver on the water supplies and infrastructure that it had promised (see Lindsay 1987). These kinds of protests, including the damaging of tourist facilities by Maasai youth over disagreements with private firms, have occurred intermittently during the past 10 years. For example, a recent dispute (2008) with a private tour operator over access to dry-season grazing in a community sanctuary near Amboseli re-sulted in the killing of four elephants and the wounding of another 10 in the area. An international uproar by conservation groups immediately was voiced (Pflanz 2008). Yet, the government's continued outsourcing of conservation responsibili-ties to private firms and INGOs means that these kinds of conflicts are likely to grow with increased competition over land and persistent ambiguities over the different institutional roles and who actually is in control of wildlife management and conservation in Kenya.

The Wamba Area

Wamba Division is located in lowland Samburu District, the home of the Maasai-related Samburu. It represents a new frontier for community conservation activities. The area borders Laikipia District to the south, where a lucrative tourism industry with accommodations often exceeding US$600/night has been built up on large European-owned commercial ranches,[6] Isiolo District to the east, and the pastoral areas of Marsabit District to the north. With its close proximity to high-end tourist facilities and its status as a critical dispersal area for migratory elephants and other wildlife species, Wamba is seen as critical for wildlife conservation and tourism in the entire Laikipia/Samburu/Isiolo ecosystem. However, like much of northern Kenya, Wamba suffers from poor security and infrastructure, especially when compared to tourist sites in neighboring Laikipia and the Amboseli area. On the positive side, it offers significant populations of wildlife in relatively uncrowded landscapes and fewer land-use and political problems than in Amboseli.

The potential for wildlife conservation activities in Wamba has not gone unnoticed by INGOs, donors, and private enterprises and investors. Despite the presence of a nearby national reserve (Samburu National Game Reserve) and tourist facilities, pastoralists of Wamba are relatively inexperienced in dealing with the different actors and interests in Kenya's wildlife sector (interview with KWS official, July 1997). Thus, conservation groups and investors were able to establish themselves quickly in the area and without the kinds of political problems and resistance characteristic of Maasai areas to the south. Between 1995 and 2008 five community wildlife sanctuaries, one large umbrella conservation trust, two high-end tourist lodges (with plans for an additional three facilities as of 2012), and numerous wildlife and ecological monitoring activities were established in the area (see KWS 2007; Northern Rangelands Trust 2008). One large INGO even set up a conservation program in the area to work closely with Samburu communities, development agencies, and private foundations, including U.S.-based zoological groups, private charities, and wealthy philanthropists (see African Wildlife Foundation [AWF] 2008; Northern Rangelands Trust 2008). Indeed, Wamba is a "growth area" for CBC activities, and INGOs and tourist and conservation groups from nearby Laikipia and Isiolo districts have been driving forces behind their establishment and that of the recent Northern Rangelands Trust (NRT) (see http://www.lewa.org). The NRT includes large parts of Samburu (including Wamba Division) and Laikipia Districts and small parts of neighboring districts, such as Marsabit and Baringo. These mainly European-owned enterprises, as well as Nairobi-based companies, strongly encouraged Wamba communities to reserve large parts of their group ranches solely for wildlife and tourism use, in exchange for different social and economic benefits.

There are several good reasons why European-owned enterprises in neighboring districts would want to support conservation activities in Samburu District. These include the following: (1) Laikipia/Isiolo elephants seasonally migrate to Wamba and can be poached while there; (2) enterprises can expand their safari business to include visits and overnight stays in neighboring Samburu, providing a more uniquely "African experience" than what is available on a European ranch; and (3) if Kenya ever does change its highly contested wildlife utilization laws to permit sport hunting again, Wamba would be a convenient nearby area for trophy shooting. Regarding the last point, considerable public debate over the topic of wildlife user rights (i.e., safari hunting) has occurred in Kenya during the past twenty years, and the board of the Laikipia Wildlife Forum (LWF), which represents the interests of the district's mainly European commercial ranchers and conservation enterprises, has been a major advocate for lifting the hunting ban (see Mbitiru 1997; Laikipia Wildlife Forum 2004; *Daily Nation* 2004: 12). The government ban on wildlife hunting in Kenya was initiated in 1977 due to real concerns about declining wildlife resources and poaching. That the LWF is in favor of its lifting and the start of commercial hunting is hardly surprising, since its members would stand to benefit immensely if the ban was ended.

Laikipia District, especially the western part of the district, is not only a key conservation area, but also the scene of prolonged conflict and insecurity since the mid-1990s. Reports of the Laikipia Wildlife Forum seem almost oblivious to the land conflicts and violence in the area, but frequently do mention the need to increase trained and armed rangers in the area (Laikipia Wildlife Forum 2006). In addition, a movement by Maasai activist groups and leaders in 2004 to reclaim lost lands in Laikipia from the early twentieth century left a very uneasy feeling among European landowners and conservation enterprises in the district. Using the argument that the original 99-year leases were to soon expire, the Maa-speaking community formally petitioned the government that their former lands should be returned to the community (MAA Speaking Communities of Kenya 2004). However, the state and its courts ruled on behalf of the Laikipia ranch owners and tourist operators with the argument that the leases really were for 999, not 99, years. For Samburu and other Maa groups who were forcibly evicted from the district, the ruling was very unpopular and demonstrated for them that Laikipia District remains strongly tinged by a colonial legacy. As recent as 2011, Samburu herders were evicted from a former ranch of 17,100 hectares in the west of the district that had been purchased by two conservation INGOs for the purposes of giving "a chance for Kenya to create its newest national park, and stimulate tourism" (Survival International 2012).

Group ranches held little importance in Wamba when I first conducted interviews in the area during the summers of 1995 and 1996, especially when compared to their long legacy in the Amboseli area. They were unknown to most Samburu residents at the time, and even as recently as 2006 many local herders were unaware of the boundaries of the ranches and their purposes (field notes, June 2006). At a meeting of the Samburu County Council to discuss the establishment of a community wildlife sanctuary on group ranch lands, some elders even confused a group ranch for an administrative unit, such as a sublocation or location, and most had little idea what a group ranch was or the where ranch boundaries were located (field notes, July 1995). The KWS and other government officials were embarrassed by many responses at the gathering, since group ranches had been in the area for fifteen years, at least on paper.

However, as previously noted, group ranches provide a convenient local structure for KWS, INGOs, and private conservation groups to implement their programs in pastoral areas, including in Wamba. The first community wildlife sanctuary in the area, called Namunyak Wildlife Conservation Trust, was established in 1995 through a joint conservation agreement between two Samburu group ranches, Sabach and Sarara. In this arrangement the group ranches—which had not been legally formed or registered at the time—agreed to reserve a core conservation area of several thousand hectares for the exclusive use of wildlife and tourists, in return for a portion of the benefits that might accrue from tourist-related activities. The legal work for the sanctuary, including the formal adjudication and registration of the ranches, was funded by a European-owned conservation group in neighboring Isiolo District. Among the ten members of Namunyak's initial board of trustees three were Europeans and the others were Samburu elites and politicians from the district. In fact, the Namunyak group's own description notes how a nearby commercial ranch played a "leading role in the formation of the Namunyak Wildlife Conservation Trust . . . [and] has continued providing technical support" (see Equator Initiative 2003: 4). Not surprisingly, the commercial ranch, with its own lodge, uses the sanctuary for wildlife viewing by its high-paying international clientele.

The legal basis of the sanctuary is the trust mechanism (see note 4, this chapter), and following its formation Namunyak Trust entered into a commercial agreement with a well-known Nairobi-based tourist firm. The tourist operation established an expensive tented camp facility in the sanctuary, where more than forty Samburu were employed as game scouts or employees of the private firm (Equator Initiative 2003: 4). Unlike the Kimana project in Amboseli, representatives of Namunyak community—albeit most of these are elites—were involved in its management.

The combined area of the Namunyak sanctuary is 31,000 hectares, with a core conservation area of 2,000 hectares that is reserved solely for conservation and tourism use. According to one local resident, the entry of KWS and the idea of a Namunyak conservancy originally were resisted, especially after a local politician claimed that KWS wanted to create another reserve like the Samburu National Game Reserve (field notes, July 1995). Similar to the Maasai of Amboseli, the Samburu had lost access to important pastures and water points after the national reserve was established (Samburu County Council 2008). At an initial meeting about Namunyak, one Samburu elder noted "we feared that they might turn our group ranch into a national park" (field notes, July 1995). To allay the concerns of Wamba residents, KWS took a group of Namunyak residents to visit the same community sanctuary in Narok District that Kimana Maasai earlier had visited. After the visit, KWS officials noted that Samburu could see how income could be earned from wildlife conservation and CBC activities (interview with KWS official, field notes, July 2001).

Although there is little social and economic data on Namunyak, available information is not encouraging. For example, one source notes total payments of only $12,105 to its eight thousand members in 2002, which is about $1.50 per member and $6.00 per hectare for the core conservation zone (see Equator Initiative 2003). For a pastoral community that depends on high-value livestock, this is a minuscule amount of revenue (see McPeak and Little 2006). On a per hectare basis it is even well below the minimal revenues that were reported for the Kimana community sanctuary. Focus group interviews conducted in the district in 2001 support these findings. When asked to list their main sources of income, groups of Samburu herders listed wildlife last among a range of eight different revenue-earning options (see Smith and Little 2002).

Despite the questionable economics, community sanctuaries have spread throughout the area, with an additional four formed in Samburu District since the establishment of Namunyak. These were all established during 2002–2006, when tourism was on an upswing in Kenya, only to fall precipitously in 2007–2008 following the country's postelection violence (Fletcher and Morakabati 2008) (also see chapter 4). The new community sanctuaries have received funds from several private and government sources, including the San Diego Zoo, St. Louis Zoo, USAID, and several private foundations and individuals. Annual operating budgets of each of the new sanctuaries is less than $75,000, while that of Namunyak was $120,000 in 2007 (Northern Rangelands Trust 2008).

In 2005 the "supra" wildlife trust, NRT, was created with the goal of combining private conservation units, group ranch-based CBCs, and community wildlife trusts into a single management unit (Northern Rangelands Trust 2008). In total the new trust is to encompass more than 600,000 hectares, and its board and corporate structure includes several Europeans, including one who currently serves as executive director of the trust. Once again, the initiative came from the same Laikipia- and Isiolo-based enterprises that had helped to establish Namunyak and other community conservation schemes in northern Kenya. According to its website, the Northern Rangelands Trust "facilitates the development of community-led conservation initiatives in northern Kenya. It promotes the collective management of ecosystems in order to improve human livelihoods, bio-diversity conservation and rangeland management" (ibid.).

The rapidity with which the trust was established and able to attract considerable international funds is amazing for a region where building a mere 10 kilometers of tarmac road can take several years to complete. If the trust achieves its goal of protecting the greater Laikipia-Samburu ecosystem for wildlife use, a relatively large amount of Samburu rangeland, in excess of tens of thousands of hectares, will be withdrawn from pastoral use. This is not necessarily a bad outcome as long as a majority of community members are aware of its consequences and participate in the trust's decisions, and the benefits from the trust are distributed fairly and equal or exceed those from other uses of the land, including pastoralism. However, current evidence and observations from community-based wildlife activities in Samburu and elsewhere in Kenya show reason to be concerned.

Lake Baringo–Bogoria Basin

In contrast to the Amboseli and Wamba (Samburu) areas, the Lake Baringo–Bogoria basin does not host the megafauna or carnivores that affluent tourists wish to see. It has important biodiversity resources, but they are mainly avian species, including more than four hundred species of birds and one of the largest host populations of pink flamingos in eastern Africa (Odada et al. 2006; Baringo County Council/Koibetak County Council 2007). Rare antelopes, including large herds of the endangered greater kudu, and a few lions and other wildlife also can be found. Lake Baringo is one of only two freshwater lakes in Kenya's Rift Valley and has resident crocodile and hippopotamus populations. Lake Bogoria National Reserve, in turn, contains large numbers of endangered greater kudu antelope, as well as large populations of pink flamingos. Despite these attractions, the basin attracts far fewer tourists than either the Wamba/Samburu or Amboseli areas, where relatively easy access for viewing elephants, buffaloes, and lions is found.

Certain characteristics of the basin, however, make it very appealing to conservation advocates despite its limited appeal for tourism and private investors. First, Lakes Baringo and Bogoria represent two of Kenya's four international Ramsar wetland sites. A Ramsar site is a global designation for a threatened body of water or wetland that has exceptionally strong biological and economic importance, and its use is covered under an international convention (Odada et al. 2006). Second, as noted above, the Baringo-Bogoria basin is a critical migratory stop for pink flamingos and other migratory birds and is one of the most biodiverse avian zones in Africa (ibid.). Third, as mentioned earlier, the area has Kenya's largest resident population of the rare greater kudu antelopes. Finally, the basin is experiencing severe environmental degradation and erosion that has made its designation as a Ramsar site important for its protection. For example, the lake's water color is now reddish-brown, and the average depth of Lake Baringo has dropped by more than 70 percent since the 1960s from 8 to 2.5 meters (ibid.). This loss of depth is blamed on high rates of sedimentation (World Bank 2005a). Excessive sedimentation is facilitated by the lake's proximity to the eroded and steep slopes of the Tugen Hills where soil runoff into the lake and deforestation in the basin's upper catchment are very high. Recent widespread flooding of the Lake Baringo basin in 2012 shows the extent to which the upper catchment has been badly degraded, facilitating excessive runoff there and destructive floods in the lowlands.

Notwithstanding these problems, the Baringo-Bogoria basin is considered a rich, biodiverse area of national and global significance from the perspective of conservation biologists (Kenya Agricultural Research Institute 2007; Omwega and Norgbey 2004). Yet, with fewer market opportunities for tourism in the area, the basin is a strong challenge for a neoliberal conservation model based on community participation that advocates linking nature with business investments. An added constraint is that one of the key tourist attractions in the basin, a natural hot spring next to Lake Bogoria, which might have been the basis for a community-managed tourist facility, was appropriated in the 1990s by then-president Daniel arap Moi. His private firm included it as part of a private hotel and spa originally called the Lake Bogoria Hotel and now the Lake Bogoria–Spa Resort. It is the largest and most luxurious of the three lodges in the Baringo-Bogoria basin, with twenty-one rooms and twenty-three small cottages that cater to international tourists. Not surprisingly, the resort has attracted resentment from the local Endorois community, and the lodge has done little to contribute to local conservation activities.[7] In fact, it has diverted much of the very limited water from a nearby seasonal river that recharges Lake Bogoria for use in its swimming pool and for other resort needs (field notes, September 2008). In effect, funds for conservation activities in the basin largely depend on public sources, including donor-funded development projects, and outright subsidies and cash transfers, which are counter to a market-based approach to conservation.

Despite these challenges, INGOs, development agencies, and the state are expanding the amount of land under conservation protection and encouraging community conservation enterprises in Baringo District.[8] The latter set of activities especially has faced constraints. For example, during most of 2006–2007, two tourism projects in the basin funded by the World Wildlife Fund (WWF), a curio shop and a cultural center, were open only sporadically and reported only minimal revenues (field notes, June 2007). WWF is subsidizing the enterprises, including the employment of staff, since their success is deemed critical to gaining local conservation support and discouraging local herders from moving their cattle into the Lake Bogoria National Reserve (World Wildlife Fund 2008; Baringo and Koibetak County Councils/World Wildlife Fund 2007). Other attempts at implementing a market-based approach to biodiversity conservation in the area also have met with only modest economic gains. For instance, a UNEP/GEF project

that helped to establish the Lake Baringo Community Boats and Excursion enterprise with more than twenty members faced financial problems in 2006–2007.
Originally intended to cater to the limited tourist trade at Lake Baringo (Avramoski 2004), it was only marginally operative during 2006 to 2008, except during peak holiday periods for tourism, the Christmas and New Year celebrations
(field notes, September 2008). However, as of 2012 this community-managed enterprise was still in business, and there is a recent donor-funded initiative to promote tourism in the region, so local tourism and business hopefully could improve in the future.

The goal of another recent environmental project in Baringo and neighboring Koibetak Districts, the World Bank/GEF–funded Kenya Agricultural Productivity and Sustainable Land Management Project (KAPSLM), has taken a different
tack (World Bank 2005a). While recognizing the significance of the Baringo-
Bogoria basin and proposing "to conserve biodiversity, especially the rare and
endangered species in the project area and its environs" (Kenya Agricultural Research Institute 2007: 29), it advocates cash payments for ecological services (PES)
rather than enterprise development. PES recognizes that in the absence of tan-
gible economic benefits to land users, straight cash transfers are the next best option for compensating local communities in return for their efforts to conserve
valuable environmental resources. A report on the project claims that

> the PES approach is attractive in that (i) it generates new financing, which
> would not otherwise be available for conservation; (ii) it is likely to be sus-
> tainable, as it depends on the mutual self-interest of service users and pro-
> viders and not on the whims of government or donor funding; (iii) it is likely
> to be efficient, in that it conserves services whose benefits exceed the cost of
> providing them, and does not conserve services when the opposite is true.
> (Schmidt-Soltau 2006: 9)

In the case of the Lake Baringo–Bogoria basin, a conservation tax on visitors/
tourists would have to be combined with donor or government grants to support
PES, since the area does not attract the required volume of tourists and businesses
to finance it alone. As of 2011, the PES program has not been implanted.

Another constraint to CBC in the Baringo-Bogoria basin relates to boundary and land-use conflicts between the different groups in the basin. They are special problems in the northwestern and southern parts of the basin, where Il Chamus compete for grazing and water with Pokot and Tugen, respectively. Some Il
Chamus leaders actually view community wildlife sanctuaries as a mechanism
for improving security and halting land encroachment by neighboring communities, especially heavily armed Pokot (see chapter 4). Their focus is on an insecure, remote area along the eastern shore of Lake Baringo, where greater kudu,

hippotamus, lion, and zebra are found. It also is an area that has drawn the interest of the Northern Rangelands Trust, which has begun to develop it as a community conservation area (see discussion below). Once a conservancy is established and armed rangers are there to police the area, Il Chamus feel they might be able to peacefully graze their animals nearby. The presence of armed rangers might also halt further encroachment by Pokot (interview with Il Chamus elder, June, 2007). From the perspective of local leaders, the motivation for establishing a wildlife conservancy on the site is about defending boundaries and improving security rather than enhancing conservation.

Despite the constraints discussed above, the idea of a community wildlife sanctuary on the eastern shores of Lake Baringo attracted outside interest from other groups and projects, in addition to NRT (see Pricewaterhouse Coopers 2005). Originally, a United Nations Environmental Programme (UNEP)/Global Environment Facility (GEF)–funded program in the area, the Lake Baringo Community-Based Land and Water Management (LBCLWM) project (2001–2005), encouraged the establishment of a community wildlife sanctuary near the Il Chamus settlement of Rugus, the same location of interest to the NRT. Project officials applauded the community's support for a sanctuary there as proof of their (1) buying into a community-based conservation approach and (2) appreciating the need to conserve the area's biodiversity (see Omwega and Norgbey 2004). The project, of course, had little idea about the real security concerns and the reasons why Il Chamus might be receptive to a community wildlife sanctuary at Rugus. Similar to the Maasai and Samburu cases discussed earlier, the LBCLWM project arranged for local leaders to visit CBC activities outside their area, in order to demonstrate how benefits can be derived from wildlife conservation (field notes, October 2008). In this case, they visited the community wildlife sanctuary at Il Ngwesi, the costly CBC project discussed earlier.

In 2008 the NRT financed a survey of the proposed Ruko conservancy, the name derived from *Ru*gus and *Ko*milion villages, and the clearing of a landing strip for airplanes to bring in tourists (field notes, June 2008). Despite the promotion of a conservation sanctuary by NRT and LBCLWM for at least three years, most local residents still do not know about it. Interviews with key leaders of the Il Chamus community indicated that even some of them knew little about the proposal for a conservation sanctuary in their area, and were alarmed that it would remove some key grazing areas from pastoral use (field notes, September 2008).

Nonetheless, the Ruko Community Wildlife Conservancy was established on 19,000 hectares of lakeshore land in Il Chamus territory as part of the Northern Rangelands Trust's network of community wildlife schemes. In 2011 Rothschild's giraffes were reintroduced to the conservancy after being absent from Baringo for about forty years (Northern Rangelands Trust 2011). Because of the area's insecurity and lack of infrastructure, the only visitors to the area tend to be the few, wealthy tourists who stay at the small but very exclusive lodge and the tented camp on Lake Baringo's Ol Kokwe and Samatian Islands, respectively.

Summary

This chapter has shown how neoliberal reforms in conservation took hold in key biodiversity areas of Kenya. They fostered unlikely alliances between pastoralists, private business, and conservation groups, and have instigated community-based investments that extend conservation controls over large parts of the country's rangelands. Despite a new, "community-friendly" approach to conservation, negative attitudes toward wildlife conservation and KWS persist among communities in many wildlife areas of Kenya, including around the well-known Amboseli National Park. It is not that community-based conservation (CBC) schemes are inherently negative, since their basic tenet of providing increased revenues from wildlife for local communities is an admirable goal and they have had favorable impacts on local livelihoods and biodiversity elsewhere in Africa (see Hulme and Murphree 2001). Rather, the chapter suggests that the model often has been hijacked by private investors, overly zealous conservation groups, and, in some cases, local elite who channel the bulk of the benefits to themselves or, in the case of conservation NGOs, to the preservation of wildlife often at the expense of local pastoralists and their lands.

Pastoral communities have not been without agency in these highly contested struggles over land and resources. They have been able to draw on discourses surrounding "indigenous peoples" and biodiversity conservation to advance their own political interests and to make claims to lands that have been lost to conservation (see chapter 4). As the chapter has pointed out, when the CBC language of political empowerment and participation is taken seriously by pastoral communities, it can make for uncomfortable relationships with their international supporters and funders. That the Kenyan government increasingly delegates conservation responsibility to INGOs and private investors, who in turn "contract" with local communities for large expanses of prime water points and grazing for wildlife and tourism use, establishes an uncertain context for both pastoral livelihoods and biodiversity conservation.

In the next chapter we continue the focus on Kenya but turn our attention more explicitly to the local effects of political reforms and the advent of multiparty democracy. The emphasis again is on pastoralists of the Rift Valley, who are among the country's most politically marginalized communities. As will be shown, these political changes also are closely tied to the reform agenda that donor agencies pushed in Kenya and elsewhere in sub-Saharan Africa.

4 "They Are Beating Us over the Head with Democracy"

Multiparty Elections in Rural Kenya

A RECENT HEADLINE FROM the British Broadcasting Corporation (BBC) celebrates a "Landmark ruling for Kenya nomads." The account tells the story of a "historic court ruling" that awarded the same Il Chamus pastoral community discussed in chapter 3 the right to elect their own parliamentary representative (BBC 2006). The court case is one of several pending in the Kenyan courts where small indigenous (minority) groups argue that because they have been so dominated by politically powerful ethnic groups, they require their own special political representation. They require this recognition, it is argued, to benefit from the democratic reforms that have swept, often violently, through Kenya and other African nations. In some cases, these political reforms, which have been externally pushed by Western nations and development agencies, have given political voice to marginalized groups like Il Chamus, but in others they have created what Nasong'o and Murunga call "democratic dictators" (2007: 8) where leaders further consolidate their power and punish opposition groups. The legal victory for Il Chamus, which drew wide acclaim from international human rights groups and media, is a good example of a favorable outcome of Kenya's democratic reforms, at least in theory if not practice (Akinyi and Dzuya 2008; Stevenhagen 2007; Minority Rights Group [MRG] International 2008; International Work Group for Indigenous Affairs [IWIGIA] 2007).

Recent political changes in Kenya and elsewhere in Africa are part and parcel of the neoliberal reform programs discussed in previous chapters that opened economies to market-based "discipline," global competition, and increased private-sector involvement. For international donors, including the World Bank and USAID, poor governance and undemocratic rule were perceived as constraints to free markets, and thus political reforms were necessary to stimulate economic growth. One Oromo herder of southern Ethiopia whom I interviewed in January 2004 complained that the push for democratic reforms by outsiders and the government was so strong that it was like "they are beating us over the head with democracy" (field notes, January 2004). The new political reforms often were imposed by certain donor countries, including the United States, as quid pro quo for economic assistance. In Kenya's case widespread corruption also was highlighted as a failure of governance and an impediment to economic reforms (see Brown 2007).[1]

The wave of political reforms in Kenya, both rhetorical and real, brought contradictions and tired political strategies, including vicious ethnic politicking as leaders strongly appealed to primal loyalties. The Enoosupukia case discussed in chapter 3 is a good, albeit tragic, example of this. Throughout the country in the 1990s there was the revival of ethnic-based political associations, such as GEMU (Gikuyu, Embu, and Meru groups), and frequent warnings by politicians about the dangers of "ethnic strangers" in their home areas (this pattern sadly continues with equal vengeance, see Branch and Cheeseman 2009; Murunga and Nasong'o 2007). Many entrenched and battle-savvy national leaders, especially former president Daniel arap Moi, saw ethnicity as a convenient vehicle to (1) mobilize support among rural constituents and (2) sharpen (often violently) existing ethnic cleavages. While these leaders often negotiated political deals in the confines of Nairobi's luxury hotels and modern office towers, their machete-wielding followers wreaked havoc in the rural areas, especially in the lead-up to and immediate aftermath of multiparty elections in the 1990s and 2000s (see Klopp 2001; Rutten et al. 2001; Waki et al. 2008). The terrible and well-publicized post-election violence of 2007–2008 brought the country to the brink of collapse, but widespread ethnic-based violence was associated with every multiparty election beginning with the first contest in 1992. By capitalizing on and promoting ethnic divisions in the 1990s, Moi and his cronies could point to "tribal" clashes as a reason why Kenya was not ready for Western-style democracy.

This chapter continues to examine the local effects of policy reforms by examining democratic reforms in former President Daniel arap Moi's home district, Baringo. Instead of focusing on Moi's own group, the Kalenjin-speaking Tugen, it takes the perspective of the previously mentioned minority group, Il Chamus, and explores the ways that they have negotiated a changing and highly unstable political landscape. Their example, as illustrated in the chapter's opening story, speaks to many aspects of contemporary politics in rural Kenya, especially how political reforms have affected indigenous or minority ethnic groups as well as contributed to explosive ethnic conflicts (for the Kenyan distinction between indigenous and minority status, see chapter 3). The chapter captures both the turbulent period of the 1990s, when the ruling and sole political party, Kenya African National Union (KANU), begrudgingly gave into demands for multiparty democracy, and the post-Moi period (post-2002), when increased political space allowed Il Chamus to seek their own political representation, a strategy that invoked considerable violence against them. As the chapter will show, small groups like Il Chamus have been forced to seek strategic alliances with other minority groups in Kenya, as well as draw support from INGOs concerned with human rights and democracy. The chapter concludes with a discussion of the country's new constitution approved by a national referendum in August 2010 and its implications for such minority groups as Il Chamus.

Identity-Based Politics

Ethnic-based claims to "ancestral lands" or forests, often unfairly grabbed by private investors and companies, increasingly appear in Kenya's popular press.[2] They often invoke identities that were thought to have "disappeared" in the past, in some cases even prior to colonialism. Carrier, for example, provides an interesting case of how certain Mukugodo Maasai of Laikipia, Kenya, in contexts of extreme poverty and land shortages, have revitalized their Yaaku identity, a cultural marker that had been suppressed for decades because of Maasai hegemony and Yaaku's association with the low status occupation of hunting and gathering. He suggests that they are pursuing this tactic, in part, to validate claims to a valuable local forest. The original Yaaku were an ancient Cushtic-speaking people who had occupied the Laikipia area prior to Maasai. Today there are very few elderly Mukugodo who can speak the Yaaku language. Although their Maasai connection had been emphasized throughout the past century, some Mukugodo are reconstructing "a Yaaku identity, and demand greater rights to the Mukugodo forest" (Carrier 2011: 246). Like so many recent struggles by Kenya's minority groups to reclaim lands and forests on the basis of ethnic-based legacies, the Yaaku/Mukugodo have received strong support from local and international NGOs and activists.

In such popular dialogues as the one discussed here, ethnicity, tradition, and history are openly debated, contested, and at times reinvented with drastic political and economic implications (see Little 1998). Baringo is no exception to this pattern, and public debates about who were the first residents and what groups can claim which lands and forests have taken place since the colonial period. However, these discussions and claims reached special significance with the onset of democracy and multiparty election in the 1990s, as the right to vote, and for whom, was closely tied to territory and ethnicity.

In a regional context the Baringo basin, the homeland of Il Chamus, contains some of the most important grazing and water points in Kenya's Rift Valley between Lakes Naivasha and Turkana (a distance of about 600 km) (see map 3.1, chapter 3). The area was heavily contested by most of the important pastoral groups of the nineteenth century, including Samburu, Maasai (Laikipiak, Uasin Gishu, and Purko sections), Turkana, and Pokot, and was among the most turbulent regions in precolonial East Africa (Lamphear 1992: 33).[3] They sought seasonal control of the basin with its perennial water sources, which in the nineteenth century would have provided relatively easy access to important Maasai-controlled grazing areas further south around Nakuru and Naivasha (Anderson 2002). This part of the Rift Valley and areas to the south currently remain highly disputed and contested as evidenced by the violence that followed Kenya's 2007 elections.

The core aboriginal population in the area are called Keroi and still referred to locally as "true" Il Chamus. The Keroi were in the area by at least the eighteenth century and were Maa speakers, like the larger Samburu and Maasai (see Little 1992a). Throughout the nineteenth century the Il Chamus community received immigrants and refugees from the so-called Maasai wars of the nineteenth century and from other conflicts in northern Kenya. They also incorporated members from nearby Kalenjin communities, including the Keiyo, Marakwet, and especially the Tugen. Fluidity and flexibility characterized relationships at the time, and oral historical accounts of the period rarely acknowledge particular territories as belonging to specific groups. Today one can trace local families and clans in the area to both "living"—Tugen, Rendille, and Turkana—and "vanished"— Uasingishu Maasai, Laikipiak Maasai, and Il Toijo—identities. The latter represent groups who no longer form coherent communities; instead, their members have been incorporated into other groups. Even with this plurality of identities, local political relations in the area still acknowledge the original claims of Keroi, and contemporary local elections almost always invoke at least one Keroi candidate. The heightened public discourse about who is indigenous and who are ethnic strangers in the Rift Valley that was discussed in the previous chapter bolstered Keroi status even though demographically they are very small relative to other Il Chamus clans, accounting for less than 5 percent of the group's population of about 27,500 in 2009 (Abraham 2012: 6).

As was true for other groups in northern Kenya, the advent of British colonialism forced Il Chamus to accept more of a corporate identity and territoriality than at any previous time in their history. Assuming a certain identity was the key to laying claims to land, even when traditions had to be modified, even invented. With the onset of British administration in the area in 1904, many Il Chamus moved out of their original settlements in the wetlands south of Lake Baringo and for protection purposes established residences near British outposts. As Lamphear (1992: 68) points out, "guarding the Il Chamus" was one of the important functions of the Baringo colonial station, and the Il Chamus took advantage of their status as loyal allies of the colonial state. They started to graze their cattle on lands that had previously been used by Maasai and others, while they relied on the state to help mediate disputes with larger groups in the region. During this period, the British used Il Chamus warriors on three occasions in military campaigns against Pokot and Turkana, each time rewarding them with cattle for their assistance (ibid.). In turn, Il Chamus did not hesitate to call on the colonial state for assistance in disputes, especially in altercations with Pokot, who also were expanding their own territories.

Land Politics: Old Disputes, New Contexts

Land, the commodity that has figured so strongly in ethnic relations and struggles in Kenya (see Haugerud 1995; Klopp 2000), provides a convenient window for exploring history and politics in Baringo District, Kenya.[4] The colonial state established the Carter Land Commission (CLC) in the mid-1930s to investigate "native" land rights and resolve disputes, and different ethnic communities—including Il Chamus—were asked to provide evidence. Thousands of pages of documentation and testimony were produced, a perverse testimony to how Africans had to openly debate and negotiate their identities and land rights with British administrators (see Kenya Land [Carter] Commission 1934). At these deliberations Il Chamus elders emphasized the pastoral orientation of their economy and their close ties to Maasai. Elder spokesmen even used the "ole" prefix in their names, an ethnic marker characteristic of Maasai but rarely used by Il Chamus. Association with Maasai assured a special niche within the colonial schema of ethnic politics since there was little doubt that Maasai sections could invoke historical claims to most of the surrounding areas. In their discussions before the CLC Il Chamus emphasized their economic needs "to accommodate their expanding cattle herds" and their historical rights to important grazing areas near the Laikipia Plateau (ibid.: 253). (This is the same Laikipia area described in the previous chapter, where considerable high-end tourism on white-owned private ranches currently takes place.) The reasoning of Il Chamus was accepted. Official boundaries were drawn up that gave them rights to key pastoralist resources and formally tied their culture to a piece of territory.

Despite the colonial ruling, Il Chamus continued to lose lands to Tugen, and by the time of Kenya's independence in 1963 about 75 percent of a critical grazing zone called Arabel had been lost (FAO 1967: 1). The Tugen community assumed considerable power from the 1970s onward because their leader and parliamentary representative, Danel arap Moi, was first vice president 1966–77 and then president 1978–2002. By the mid-1980s highly prized Arabel and Ngelesha highland grazing areas near Laikipia District were fully occupied by Tugen. In 2002 the locations were combined and placed in a newly formed administrative unit, Mochongoi, under control of the Tugen community. As Joshua, an Il Chamus elder, explains, "we fought it but we could no nothing" (field notes, June 2007). He lamented that they did not have the political clout of Tugen with their powerful member of parliament (MP), President Moi.

Mochongoi Division was formed by the Moi government in 1998 to make room for settlement by members of his Tugen community and to punish his political opponents—mainly Kikuyu—and their leaders. The division was carved out of the Marmanet forest zone along the Baringo/Laikipia District border and into Laikipia District itself. To the strong protests of Laikipia District's leaders, the state formally annexed the area at the expense of Laikipia's residents and their lands and placed the new division within Baringo District. The political maneuver effectively increased the size of President Moi's home district by about 5 percent. All this was being done at a time when the state was undergoing SAP and was supposed to be shrinking government, rather than creating new administrative units with more government employees. To pursue this tactic, the state not only de-gazetted parts of a government forest reserve but also expelled about two thousand Laikipia villagers, mostly Kikuyu residents. Many of the displaced had been issued title deeds to their farms in the 1970s and 1980s, which the state did not recognize. Their evictions were viewed locally as a political ploy by Moi to weaken his Kikuyu opponents, since most displaced residents were Kikuyu members of the opposition political party, the Democratic Party (DP). Local politicians also saw it as a move to bolster Baringo District and Moi's campaign for *majimboism,* a region-based form of federal government, in the run up to the 2002 presidential elections (for a discussion of majimboism in Kenya, see Anderson 2005 and 2010). As Njeru points out, the main complaint of Laikipia's leaders was that the government annexed the Marmanet forest without proper consultation and it was then "transferred to Baringo District" (1998: 24). Laikipia's politicians took their case to the courts, even arguing that the state would lose considerable revenues from the loss of forest-based revenues from a state forest reserve. The transfer of lands took place despite these protests.

The government forest of Marmanet in Mochongoi was opened for settlement through a government-sponsored program in 1996, two years before it was formally annexed to Baringo District. The project was to be solely for lowland Baringo households in the district who suffered from poverty and food insecurity. Il Chamus, who were important allies of Tugen and other Kalenjin groups at the time, were promised large numbers of plots in the scheme, but in the end only twenty out of more than two thousand plots, or about 1 percent, were allocated to them. Tugen, in turn, were given more than 96 percent of the plots, and most of these went to individuals from the more prosperous Tugen Hills rather than to impoverished lowlanders as was the original intention. In the words of one local Il Chamus leader:

> Can you imagine when the old man [Moi] created Mochongoi Division, we were given very few plots there? The entire Il Chamus people and area were given only 20 plots (10 for Mukutan; 10 for this side). The Tugens from Kabartonjo and elsewhere in the highlands were given thousands. Our people took the few farms and a few moved there. We were very upset to receive so few plots. We felt let down—why have an MP and he cannot represent us? (Field notes, June 2007)

The government's settlement scheme in Marmanet formally excised any administrative controls by Il Chamus to Arabel (including Ngelesha), with the location officially being moved to the district's new, Tugen-controlled Mochongoi Division. This action further reduced Il Chamus territory by about 10 percent. As a possible defense, Il Chamus leaders recently have sought the old colonial maps to demonstrate to the current regime of President Mwai Kibaki and the law courts that Arabel and the Ngelesha area are part of their traditional homelands: "We would like to get those old colonial maps that show Arabel and Ngelesha were part of Njemps Location. They seem to be very hard to get—we have tried but cannot find those maps. We know those colonial boundaries would show that these areas were part of our location" (interview notes, June 2007). Evidence of the old colonial boundaries and divisions, which, as was noted earlier, were contested when first imposed by the British, is now ironically sought in defense of "traditional" territories. This strategy of relying upon colonial boundaries and maps in contemporary land and forest disputes in rural Kenya is not unusual (see Klopp 2002).

Il Chamus also lost land when a state-supported irrigated settlement scheme was established in the lowlands in 1988. Not surprisingly, this venture also mainly was for Tugen. It allowed more than one hundred families to settle in eastern locations of Il Chamus territory near Lake Baringo. Like his predecessor and Kenya's first president, Jomo Kenyatta, Moi was rewarding members of his own ethnic group (and his political clients!) with state-supported projects and land acquisitions. It only became worse and more flagrant when multiparty democracy was introduced and ethnic-based leaders, such as Moi, needed to reward even more of their group for their political support with projects and assets. In the words of a respected Il Chamus chief in the area, "the Tugen have settled here and we are being pushed—we are being encroached on all sides and are losing our land. We must stay here since this is our land? Where else will we go?" (field notes, June 2007).

As a result of such assaults on their land rights, a strong local movement by Il Chamus for an independent political constituency began to emerge. As will be shown in the next section, the consensus by the late 1990s was that only if they had their own MP and constituency could their lands and livelihoods be protected. But to achieve this, they had to make their case before the courts and the Kenya Election Commission that under the current political system, with a Tugen MP in central Baringo, they were denied their constitutional right of political representation. Their legal position was an implicit admission that ethnic-based politics, with all its inherent divisiveness, had become the norm for newly democratic Kenya.

"Nobody Will Speak for Us"

More than sixty-five years after the Carter Land Commission, another national event provided a strategic opportunity for Il Chamus and other marginalized ethnic groups to petition for improved land and political rights. The venue was the Kenyan Constitutional Reform Commission (CRC) with its highly publicized hearings in Nairobi during 2002–2005. This media-focused platform allowed local communities, especially those that had participated little in national politics, to openly present their cases for representation and retribution for past grievances, including losses of land. Constitutional reform in Kenya had been discussed since the onset of multiparty elections in the early 1990s, but now it was openly debated in a government-sanctioned forum. Since it was first mentioned, constitutional reform has been strongly encouraged by Western countries but could only be seriously considered after President Mwai Kibaki succeeded Moi in 2002.[5]

The formation of the CRC represented an attempt to reform Kenya's outdated constitution, an effort that pitted opposition politicians against the new Kibaki government. President Kibaki had campaigned on promises of constitutional reform. The daily hearings of the CRC were covered by local media, including online versions, and like the CLC deliberations in the colonial era, they provided public space for indigenous communities to vent about land losses and other injustices. In Baringo the CRC hearings were the subject of daily conversation and reflected an optimistic sense that open political discourse was possible in the post-Moi era.

There were two Il Chamus, including a woman, among the more than five hundred delegates who were nominated by political parties and government to participate in the CRC debates. Politically underrepresented groups, such as Il Chamus and Okiek (a Kalenjin-speaking community of former hunter-gatherers from the Mau forest of Rift Valley Province), presented their cases for both political recognition and the recovery of "ancestral lands." In contrast to the past, however, Il Chamus were allied with other pastoral groups and hunter-gatherers, some of whom formed NGOs and citizen groups. One such citizen group was the Pastoralists and Hunter-Gatherers Ethnic Minority (PHGEM) Network, which made a joint appeal to the CRC on behalf of Il Chamus and other pastoralists and hunter-gatherers, including Okiek, Maasai, and Samburu. The group emphasized the historical abuses that pastoralists and hunter-gatherers have suffered in Kenya since the colonial period. Their leaders wanted a new legal framework that would assist them to regain lost lands and forests, and they viewed a new constitution as the vehicle for achieving this. PHGEM collectively presented a memorandum to the CRC that outlined their demands and recommendations for what a new constitution should include (Pastoralists and Hunter-Gatherers Ethnic Minority [PHGEM] Network 2002: 2). To support their case, the document acknowledged international (UN and ILO) protocols and proclamations and drew on global discourses about indigeneity and human rights. It even referred to a legal case in Australia that ruled in favor of aboriginal populations and their land claims (ibid.: 4–5). In the memorandum, PHGEM leaders highlighted the state's failure to protect their communal lands and resources by showing how the Kenyan government favored rights of private corporations and tourism interests to the detriment of pastoralists and hunter-gatherers.

At some point during the early 2000s Il Chamus leaders began to refer to themselves as a minority rather than an indigenous group because of (1) difficulties surrounding the term "indigenous" in Kenya and Africa generally and (2) their interactions with global minority rights groups that used the term (for example, the Centre for Minority Rights Development [CEMIRIDE]). Being identified as a minority group also was a strategy for attaining political representation in Kenya. I had not encountered the term in any of my previous work among Il Chamus (see Little 1992a), but its use became prevalent post-2002. During the CRC hearings, the "minority" rather than "indigenous" label was preferred by Il Chamus, a good indicator of their strategic use of global discourses.

Other minority (indigenous) groups in Kenya pursued similar strategies and alliances with global human and minority rights groups, although many used the terms minority and indigenous interchangeably. More populous groups, like the Maasai, preferred to call themselves indigenous rather than minority peoples. As Lynch notes with reference to the Kalenjin-speaking Okiek and Sengwer groups:

> Leaders have consciously employed the "global discourses" of "marginalisation," "minority rights," "indigeneity," and "environmental protection." These discourses have enabled these political actors to enter new international arenas of action, including the internet, international conferences and African Commission on Human and Peoples Rights. These discourses have also strengthened their community claims via references to international human rights legislation, and have enabled political actors to forge links with new allies, representatives and patrons, including NGOs like Minority Rights and Survival International. (2006: 57)

In the 2000s Il Chamus also took on the important label of "pastoralist," which has emerged as a recognized political identity in Kenya and elsewhere in East Africa and is reinforced globally through networks of organizations and sponsors (see Coalition of European Lobbies for Eastern African Pastoralism 2011; WISP 2010). The formation of pastoralist NGOs and pastoralist parliamentary groups in government reinforced the public value of a pastoralist identity. The cause of pastoralists also received strong support from international human rights and environmental groups who provide funds and publicity in support of their cause (Cultural Survival 2006; Coalition of European Lobbies for Eastern African Pastoralism 2011). As was discussed in chapter 3, some of the motivation for this stemmed from concerns about wildlife conservation since significant wildlife resources are found on pastoralist lands. Other reasons involve real concerns for drought and food insecurity, which have ravaged pastoralist communities in the past decade, and the lack of basic human services and infrastructure that still plague pastoralist areas (see McPeak et al. 2012). Il Chamus themselves, as they had done during the Carter Land Commission (CLC) hearings, highlighted their pastoral heritage at the CRC gatherings, although many no longer practice mobile pastoralism. The response of an Il Chamus woman leader when questioned by a Samburu friend about the pastoralist heritage of Il Chamus indicates the changing context: "We are pastoralists, even though we farm and do not move with our animals like we used to. We are pastoralists" (field notes, June 2006). She was very firm in her defense of the pastoralist identity, as are most other Il Chamus.

Il Chamus' concerns about the need for constitutional reform also were included in a memorandum presented to the CRC by the MAA Pastoralists Council (MPC), an organization that represents the views of the larger Maa-speaking (Maasai) community. It includes the four groups discussed in chapter 3—Il Chamus, Maasai, Mukugodo Maasai, and Samburu. Of course, the Maasai, who number more than 800,000 in Kenya based on the most recent census (2009), were the dominant force in the alliance. The MPC's document that was presented to the CRC highlighted the political marginality and considerable land losses suffered by Maa-speaking peoples. It stated that "of all the Kenyan communities, the MAA speaking peoples have suffered the most from constitutional dispossession that displaced them from their ancestral lands and territories, dispersed them into inhospitable arid lands, fragmented them and set a pace a process of community disintegration that continues to date" (MAA Pastoralists Council [MPC] 2002: 1). Local Il Chamus leaders recognize the significance of the MPC in unifying the greater Maa community, but also point to the dominance of Maasai leaders in the organization. One educated Il Chamus who works in Nairobi stated: "We do collaborate with other Maa groups but their situation is different and we are very small. They have their own set of problems—we have ours" (field notes, September 2008). As will be shown later in the chapter, the petition by Il Chamus for an independent political constituency was compelled to emphasize the uniqueness of their cultural identity vis-à-vis Maasai, a marked departure from the strategy they employed during the colonial and most of the postcolonial periods.

It should be noted that earlier political alliances among Maa speakers and other pastoralists date back to at least the 1950s. In the period leading up to Kenya's independence in 1963, pastoralists of the Rift Valley, including Maasai and Samburu, formed a political coalition with Kalenjin-speaking groups because of fears of marginalization under an independent state dominated by the country's two major ethnic groups, Kikuyu and Luo. They formed KADU (Kenya African Democratic Union) party and advocated for majimboism that would give Maa and Kalenjin groups (including former pastoralist and agro-pastoralist communities, such as Nandi, Kipsigis, and Tugen), control of a key region, the Rift Valley Province (see Anderson 2005). Under the federal style of majimboism the different regions of Kenya would be given political representation and considerable autonomy to develop their own areas, which greatly would benefit the resource-rich Rift Valley Province and its Maa and Kalenjin communities, who could claim it as their indigenous homelands. Kenya's dominant Kikuyu and Luo communities could not make such a claim. To counter the majimboism movement and partially allay the fears of Rift valley residents, the first president of Kenya, Jomo Kenyatta, appointed several Kalenjin and Maasai politicians to cabinet posts in 1963–64. Later in 1966 he appointed the Rift Valley Province's and Kalenjin community's Daniel arap Moi of Baringo District as his vice president. KADU was dissolved and its members joined with the ruling party, KANU (Kenya African National Union) soon after the country's independence, and the issue of majimboism or regionalism simmered until the democracy movement of the 1990s. In 1982 Kenya officially became a one-party (KANU) state with an amendment to its constitution that made it illegal to form political parties.

As noted earlier, when the democracy movement took hold in the early 1990s, ethnic-based political alliances reemerged or formed for the first time, including a coalition of mainly pastoral and agro-pastoral groups from the Rift Valley called KAMATUSA. It was (is) comprised of Kalenjin-speaking (KA) groups, Maasai (MA), Turkana (TU), and Samburu (SA) who at the time strongly backed Moi's KANU party. As might be expected, it became an important political force on the national scene in the 1990s, and within it Il Chamus identity was ambiguously linked to Maasai, Samburu, and Kalenjin elements—all heritages that they can claim on historical grounds. With their strong-handed reliance on ethnicity and tradition, KAMATUSA leaders, including President Moi himself, emphasized the similarities between Kalenjin peoples and Maa groups, and used the political alliance's historical claims to Rift Valley lands to stigmatize opposition politicians and instigate fear into Kikuyu and other "stranger" farmers who resided in the Rift Valley Province but could not claim it as their ancestral lands. Recall the Enoosupukia incident discussed in chapter 3, where Maasai evicted mainly Kikuyu families from a highland area of Narok District. As the election violence of the 1990s and 2000s demonstrated, Kikuyu who lived in the Rift Valley had very good reason to fear for their property and their lives. Indeed, several hundred lost their lives, and more than 150,000, with Kikuyu being the majority, were displaced from their homes in the Rift Valley during pre- and postelection violence in the 1990s and 2000s, and especially in 2007–2008 (Waki et al. 2008). In the postelection violence of 2007–2008 more than 250 Kikuyu died in just one Rift Valley district, Uasin Gishu District (ibid.: 50).

To return again to the CRC hearings, an initial draft of the constitution, called the "Bomas draft" after the Nairobi venue (Bomas of Kenya) where the meetings were held, was produced in 2003. It included many of the concerns of PHGEM and MPC (see Okello 2003). Most pastoral groups, including Il Chamus, were pleased because it emphasized:

(a) affirmative action in employment and education opportunities, with a preference for pastoralist and other ethnic minorities;
(b) delegation of responsibility to local communities for land and resource allocation and a ban against private land sales in pastoralist areas; and
(c) the establishment of a federal type of government based on regionalism (*majimboism*).

However, when the draft document went to Parliament in 2004 for debate it was drastically revised by a handful of powerful MPs, and most of the recommendations of PHGEM and other ethnic minorities were removed. The constitutional document that emerged from parliamentary discussions, called the Wako draft after the key MP and attorney general (Amos Wako) who spearheaded the revisions, removed many of the recommendations of the Bomas draft, including those of PHGEM and MPC. The new draft maintained little of the language about decentralization and communal land rights of pastoralists; instead, their areas and political decision making were to remain under the control of the central state. Most Il Chamus were very disappointed and felt the Wako draft reflected the views of the ruling elite and dominant ethnic groups (especially Kikuyu) who largely control the economy and political system. Not surprisingly, the people in power were supportive of a strong central state rather than a federal-style system of governance. In a 2005 report by the London-based NGO Minority Rights Group (MRG) International, the situation was described in the following terms: "This proposed new constitution ensures that the lot of the poor remain unrecognized and further exposed to the whims and machinations of the mighty" (Minority Rights Group International 2005: 1). Thus, after approximately two years of passionate debate and lobbying, the revised constitutional document that was to serve as the basis of a national referendum offered little political progress for Il Chamus and other marginalized groups of Kenya.

To counter the parliamentary position, PHGEM and MPC actively campaigned against the Wako draft. In October 2005 Il Chamus leaders, including two prominent chiefs, attended a major political rally for the greater Maa community at Suswa, northern Narok District, a sacred area with important significance for the Maa community. Il Chamus respondents said that they sent their leaders to attend the Suswa meeting to show solidarity for a united Maa position against the Wako draft of the constitutional document (field notes, June 2006). The collective statement from this gathering of different Maa communities came to be known as the Suswa Declaration. This political mobilization by Maa speakers around the constitutional vote was unprecedented, and many Il Chamus leaders acknowledge its importance as a democratic experiment. According to a report by Cultural Survival: "The Maasai viewed the proposal [Wako draft] with great alarm, and subsequently a myriad of religious organizations, non-governmental organizations, community organizations, and civic leaders successfully spearheaded what one citizen called 'one of the fiercest civic education campaigns ever witnessed' in Maasai land (Cultural Survival 2006: 1)." When the national referendum for the new constitution was held in November 2005, it was soundly defeated by a vote of 58 percent opposed to 42 percent in favor. The results of the vote show that communities other than Maa speakers also had problems with the Wako draft of the constitution. As will be discussed later in the chapter, the debate about constitutional reform continued throughout the decade, and a new constitution was finally approved by a national referendum in August 2010. The new document has many positive aspects, but it leaves unresolved the issue of political representation by small minority groups, such as Il Chamus.

An ironic but beneficial outcome of the political reforms that swept through Kenya during 1990 to 2005 was the channeling of external resources into local communities and organizations, including those that eventually formed NGOs. Emboldened by the new political space opened up by these changes, newly formed civil society organizations (CSOs) and NGOs helped to instigate meaningful political dialogue and campaigns, including the constitutional reform movement discussed above. The phenomenal growth of these kinds of groups during 1990–2005 also was instigated by large injections of foreign development funds that increasingly preferred nongovernmental over governmental channels (Gibbon 1995). As was noted in the introduction and chapter 3, this was standard practice during the neoliberal reform era, and resulted in a massive proliferation of NGOs in Kenya and Africa generally. The added resources from international human and indigenous rights groups and environmental groups, including those described in chapter 3, also bolstered local CSOs and NGOs, and many of these groups represented minority and pastoralist interests. Environmental and indigenous peoples' concerns had become intricately coupled and increasingly politicized in the wildlife-rich areas of Kenya.

During this era of reform, however, Il Chamus continued to lose. By 2008 an entire administrative sublocation had been lost and another approximately 15 percent of their territory was unusable due to periodic raids by well-armed cattle riders, mainly the Kalenjin group—the Pokot. These attacks forced Il Chamus out of most of their eastern locations, especially after April 2005, when seven residents were killed and more than two thousand cattle were stolen during one large raid. In the words of Solomon, the attacks left the community in a desperate situation:

> Nobody will speak for us in parliament and get the publicity (in newspapers) that you need to get help and action. During the previous regime we really have

been squeezed on all sides. I do not know why they are trying to finish us. We have been loyal friends of the government and have never disturbed anybody. We just want to live in peace and help our families. We are not armed like the Pokot, so we depend on the government to help us but we do not know why they are doing nothing. We complain to them about these raids but they do nothing. . . . They are profiting from these raids and the government is doing nothing. They must be benefiting. (Field notes, June 2007)

The bewilderment of being abandoned by the government and unprotected against neighboring groups was a source of strong contention by Il Chamus who for the past century viewed themselves as peaceful and loyal allies of the state, both colonial and postcolonial. Even before the onset of colonialism European explorers, such as Joseph Thomson, referred to the community as "most pleasing natives" and a pleasant contrast to "the ferocious and arrogant warriors of Masai country" (Thomson 1887: 234). For Thomson and his caravan, the community was perceived as an island of tranquility in a turbulent sea dominated by Maasai. As we walked together along the banks of the Molo River 15 kilometers south of Lake Baringo, on a clear, hot morning in late September 2008, Solomon's conversation again centered on the government's inaction against Pokot attacks:

Why are they doing nothing—we have always been supportive of government, unlike other groups in the area. We have IDPs [Internally Displaced Persons] and refugees from this problem of insecurity. Are they not IDPs? Yes, they are and the government is doing nothing about it. Our people from there are so many at Eldume, Kailerr, Ngambo, Salabani and many places. Where are they to go and why has not the government done anything about this? (Field notes, September 2008)

In his low-toned voice, Solomon went on to explain how because of the IDP problem and excessive cattle concentrated in the area, his village now has little food or grass for their own animals. Not surprisingly, the Il Chamus community for the first time began to purchase weapons and arm themselves for protection, a common practice among most pastoralist groups of northern Kenya since the 1980s.

Long before these recent problems, Solomon's father, who was a well-respected subchief and leader, and other elders advocated for group ranches in the 1970s as a means to secure their boundaries against larger groups, such as Tugen and Pokot. However, these were never implemented by the government because of contentious border disputes and the costs of surveying and adjudicating the lands. Throughout the 1980s and 1990s they lost lands to some of the same groups (Pokot and Tugen) who ironically were their allies in the KAMATUSA coalition.

Other Il Chamus elders confirm Solomon's claims about the reluctance of the government to do anything about Pokot encroachment despite the increased violence in the area. Leleleboo, a man about 50 years old, states:

We are not armed like them (Pokot). They are very large in numbers and we cannot do anything about them. They want our land for grazing their animals. In the past year or so it has been almost every few weeks that there has been a raid. We think that because rains are good they raid more. It also is an election year (2007) and we think that may have something to do with it. We think that it might have something to do with us requesting a constituency. That upset the old man's [Moi's] son. We wonder why the government and the MP are not doing anything about it. We have sent people to Nakuru [capital city of Rift Valley Province] to complain and even to the old man (President Moi). We do not understand why they want us to get finished. And the Tugen just seem to be quiet and neutral and we do not understand why. We suspect that there might be something behind this—some politics. Perhaps if we had our own MP this would not be a problem. We could have somebody who could stick up for us in parliament and speak for us. (Field notes, June 2007)

Recall from chapter 3 that some Il Chamus leaders went so far as to seek protection against further land losses by supporting the establishment of a community wildlife sanctuary staffed with armed rangers. The sentiment of many in the community is that since the Pokot already have taken over the area east of Lake Baringo around Rugus, the area might as well be registered as a reserve with Kenya Wildlife Service (KWS). The Rugus area is near the border with Pokot-controlled territories in the Lake Baringo basin, and few Il Chamus have resided or grazed their animals there in recent years because of insecurity. It now is registered as a community sanctuary by the Northern Rangelands Trust (NRT), the large conservation group that coordinates conservation sanctuaries throughout north-central Kenya. Another university-educated leader, Joseph, suggested that the establishment of a conservation area at Rugus would mean that if the Pokot attack the area "they will be attacking KWS and the government. . . . KWS will have armed rangers there and that will be good" (field notes, June, 2007).

As was pointed out earlier, Il Chamus often sought support from the state for protection against larger groups. Unfortunately, now this help is no longer available, and, ironically, concerns about biodiversity conservation and minority rights may provide the most viable political spaces to pursue alliances and political action. As of 2011, some initial work by conservation groups on infrastructure in Rugus has been completed, but insecurity has constrained the implementation of a community wildlife program in the area.

New Political Options in the Post-Moi Era

Since President Moi announced his retirement from politics in 2002, the strategy of the Il Chamus community has been to seek their own political constituency, which would have to be carved out of Moi's former central Baringo constituency. Recall the local concerns about how "nobody will speak up for us" in Parliament.

If successful, a constituency would provide Il Chamus with their own MP, who would represent them nationally. Yet, to formally petition for an independent political constituency was a risky strategy given the extent of political violence in the Rift Valley since the 1990s. Such a tactic would unlikely have been pursued while Moi was still in power, but his departure provided a convenient opening, as did the public debates about democratic and constitutional reforms. Efforts to gain political representation began earnestly after President Daniel arap Moi announced his retirement in 2001, although some discussions about political representation had begun as early as 1998 (field notes, June 2005).

With Moi's retirement, his son, Gideon, was designated by the ruling KANU party headed by his father as the heir apparent to the Central Baringo constituency. Although Gideon Moi was elected to the parliamentary seat unopposed in 2002 after another Tugen and Il Chamus candidate withdrew, local resentment emerged almost immediately. A major complaint was that he never visited the area, not even when the community suffered from food problems and attacks by Pokot raiders. "Our MP does not visit Il Chamus much because he is involved in so many businesses. Now he is getting a helicopter so now maybe he can come and visit more," one Il Chamus civil servant sarcastically noted (field notes, June 2007). The incredible wealth of Moi and his family, including Gideon, is a well-known phenomenon in Kenya that is frequently highlighted in media and Internet accounts (Nsehe 2011). Local feelings about Moi's son were strong enough that several Il Chamus leaders began to explore alternatives to representation by him, including a formal request for their own MP.

A group of four local leaders turned to a small law firm in Nairobi managed by an Il Chamus lawyer, to seek legal advice and possible courses of action. Using a set of clauses in the Kenyan constitution (pre-2010) that allow a minority group to have their own constituency when it can be shown that their political rights are denied by their elected official(s) (MP), the Il Chamus lawyer and his associate wrote up a formal petition to the government on behalf of the group and the entire Il Chamus community. They presented their written petition against the government to the High Court of Kenya on March 12, 2004 (field notes, June 2007; also see Mbatia 2006). The legal document listed 19 separate declarations in support of a political constituency for the Il Chamus (Kenya 2006). Three of the most important include:

> A declaration that the fundamental right of representation in the National Assembly of the Republic under the provisions of Section 1A of the Constitution of Kenya, has been effectively denied to the Il Chamus Community;
> A declaration that the constitutional machinery for the representation and protection on minorities, including the Il Chamus, to wit the provisions of Section 33 of the Constitution of Kenya, has not been implemented by the Constitution as required;

> A declaration that the statistical chance of an Il Chamus candidate being successful as a Member of Parliament in the present Baringo Central Constituency is in practice so minimal as to effectively prevent any such membership of Parliament by such candidate for the foreseeable future (as it has been prevented in the past 40 years). (Ibid.: 3–4)

The formal petition also included reference to indigenous groups and their political rights elsewhere in the world, including Eskimos (Inuit Peoples) of Canada, as well as the different United Nations and International Labor Organization (ILO) proclamations (especially Convention 169 passed in 1989) and international forums about the rights of indigenous people. Clearly, the applicants were well versed in the global indigenous and minority peoples' movements and the international legislation in support of them. The Il Chamus lawyer who assisted in the case against the government has been a prominent spokesperson for the community and their rights. He was the lead advocate in a famous case in 2004–2006 where the Il Chamus community successfully sued the government for introducing the invasive bush *Prosopis juliflora* into their rangelands,[6] and, ironically, he recently (2011–2012) served as a member of the Independent Electoral and Boundaries Commission (IEBC), a government body charged with recommending constituency boundaries under the new constitution.

International NGOs and human rights groups rallied on behalf of the community's appeal for their own political representation, and national and international media covered the event as well. Internet technology allowed the political drama to be played out across national and global stages, including coverage on the BBC (see quote at the beginning of this chapter), and a few local leaders could draw on the publicity and support to solicit external funds and other resources for their case.

Despite their strong cultural and historical ties to Maasai and Samburu, local leaders used a strategy that highlighted the cultural distinctiveness of Il Chamus. This approach was taken to counter the government's initial position that they merely are a subgroup of Maasai and thus do not need their own political representation (field notes, June 2007). The government's case against an independent political constituency argued that Il Chamus are not a distinct community but are "a Masai clan in Kenya. . . . Representations cannot be based on clans" (Kenya 2006: 44). However, in the words of a prominent former chief, "we are not like them [Maasai]—we are a distinct culture" (field notes, June 2007). To counter the government's claims about their autonomous ethnicity, Il Chamus claimants presented ethnographic books and articles, including some of my publications, as evidence that they are "a uniquely cohesive homogenous and culturally distinct minority" (Mbatia 2006: 2).

According to interviews with individuals involved in the case, the courts initially accused Il Chamus leaders of promoting tribalism in Kenya. The legal advocate and his team countered that accusation by showing how under the current political system their democratic and constitutional rights for political representation were not possible without their own elected leader (field notes, September 2008). The legal application against the government and the Electoral Commission of Kenya (ECK) argued that "the present Baringo Central Constituency be divided by the next Boundary Commission into two separate constituencies . . . so as to prevent the present electoral marginalization of the Il Chamus from continuing" (Kenya 2006: 20). They tried to make the case that it was not about ethnicity or tribalism, but allowing the community to participate in the democratic process that accompanied the change to multiparty elections.

Sadly but not unexpectedly, the Pokot raided the Il Chamus community within a month after the formal paperwork for a political constituency was submitted to the ECK. The suspicious timing of the raid was not lost on most residents in the area. One prominent Il Chamus leader, Lenekariapo, suggested that Kalenjin (Tugen) politicians "paid the Pokot MP to hire some young thugs to steal the animals and harass people. Many people feel that this was not a coincidence and when it happened people immediately thought that it had to do with politics." Another community member remarked, "the raiders who went after the Salabani [Il Chamus] people and their animals came through the Tugen area, so that is why we say the MP [Gideon Moi] must have instigated the attack. They must have had help. But political issues can never be proved. Nobody will ever know" (field notes, June 2006). The attacks even forced one respected Il Chamus government chief who was targeted by local raiders to relocate out of the area, in this case moving to Kajiado District, where he was given accommodations by distant Maasai relatives. As was noted earlier, the failure on the part of the government to do anything greatly damaged local trust in the state, and even a small delegation of women leaders visited the provincial commissioner, Nakuru, almost immediately after the raid in 2004 to plead for security assistance. Like other local appeals in the past five years, it met with little positive reaction from the state. The security situation remained bad through 2009 and only slightly improved in 2010 and 2011.

To bolster their own security and protection, some local leaders in 2007 sought an alliance with the Maa-speaking Samburu who border Baringo District to the northeast. Their population is about five times the size of Il Chamus, and they also were suffering from Pokot raids. As one Il Chamus civil servant, David,[7] who is based in Nairobi, indicated:

> The PS [permanent secretary] in Lelewa's [another Il Chamus civil servant] ministry is a Samburu and we have talked with him about helping each other against the Pokot. It is something which could be good and we are exploring this. We have very good relations with the Samburu and are related to them. I have talked a lot about what can be done—and we will try to organize the

moran [warrior age set] to better defend their lands in the Kiserian/Mukutan [Pokot] border areas. . . . This raiding thing involves a lot of politics and the Kalenjin in the area are being quiet and politicians are not helping. (Field notes, June 2007)

Despite the attacks, active lobbying for political representation continued, and educated elites from Baringo, including the individuals quoted above, have been important advocates. Most of them had earned tuition bursaries (scholarships) from the government and university degrees, a clear advantage of living in former president Moi's political constituency, where many local residents were provided tuition support by the government or by Moi himself. Many of the university-educated Il Chamus elite owned homes or rented apartments in the country's capital city, Nairobi, or the provincial capital of Nakuru. The political constituency movement also received strong support from other segments of Il Chamus society, including youth and elder; rich and poor; and male and female. However, most of these community members knew little about the specifics of the electoral petition or the larger national movement for increased democratic representation by the country's minority (indigenous) groups.

In their struggle for political representation, Il Chamus clearly benefited from political coalitions formed during the constitutional reform debates and the national exposure that these alliances received. As one journalist noted, these alliances represented a distinct break with Kenya's political status quo: "Names such as Ilchamus, Wakaa, and Sengwer communities, which few Kenyans had heard of featured prominently. These are communities marginalized by past regimes almost into oblivion" (Okello 2003: 1). Other journalists from the national press provided similar national exposure for the Il Chamus: "The true minority and marginalized communities in Kenya include the Malakote, the Harti and Issack [both Somali clans], the Elmolo, the Shanikila, the Waata and the Njemps [Il Chamus]. Their condition is worse than that of the other poor Kenyans because they have no representation in Parliament and the local authorities" (Ahmed 2008: 1; also see Lesamuti 2005). When asked about the media attention surrounding their cause, most Il Chamus leaders were generally pleased but acknowledged that it did not ensure success. For instance, David noted: "We hear about these things and know about minority rights groups and that they are writing about us—and hear that they are reporting about us even in the USA. On the ground these things have not made a difference" (field notes, June 2007).

Despite frequent setbacks, Il Chamus and other politically underrepresented groups skillfully took advantage of the political space created by recent reforms and their increased links to global NGOs and organizations. Their participation in the previously discussed constitutional reform meetings showed the importance of alliances with similar underrepresented groups and with global human and minority rights groups.

During my fieldwork in the summers of 2006 and 2007, the political representation issue was hotly debated in Baringo, and in several interviews the importance of having large numbers of registered voters was noted. Comments about the area's population were common, since many respondents felt that a large population could be an important factor in determining whether the government might award them a political constituency. (It ended up that in the Il Chamus case, lack of political representation, not population, was the key factor—at least in the initial court ruling.) One school principal from the area remarked:

> There are so many Il Chamus, maybe 50,000. We do not know. They are everywhere. We do want our own constituency because the previous two governments did little for this area. Moi was better [than Kenyatta] but still did not do much. The government should give us a constituency because they want us to vote NARC [a political party in Kenya] [he laughs as he says this] . . . We are a minority group and now we can be given our own constituency. Maybe the next time we can be given a district. (Field notes, June 2007)

In an election year, such as 2007, it is not unusual for the government to promise new administrative districts or political constituencies to attract votes, but this is unlikely to have been a key factor in the Il Chamus case. The momentum for political representation preceded the 2007 election and, as was indicated earlier, the government representatives and elected officials actually were against it. However, elsewhere in Kenya the promise of new political constituencies and administrative units to foster local support has been a strategy of President Kibaki and before him, President Moi. At a national level more than 60 new districts were created in the two-year period leading up to the presidential elections in December 2007 (Akinyi 2007: 1), and overall the number of administrative districts in the country grew from 47 in 1994 to more than 220 in 2009. It is a clever political tactic to reward ethnic and clan-based followers with new administrative units, such as administrative districts and divisions, although it can serve to further divide rather than unite the population. The practice resulted in the subdivision of the original Baringo District into six new districts during 1994–2009, with both the Moi (through 2002) and Kibaki regimes advocating the strategy under a narrative of bringing government services closer to the people. However, similar to the awarding of political constituencies, this approach rewards political followers and boosts public employment for them, while also increasing the reach of the state. The latter outcome is strongly counter to the neoliberal policies of the 1980s and 1990s that favored a reduced government and is symptomatic of political regimes that place survival over other goals, including the welfare of its citizens.

Unfortunately, arguments for new political constituencies and districts, including in Baringo, largely are couched in ethnic terms, with the explicit assumption that only a member of the same ethnic group can provide effective parliamentary representation for her/his community. Thus, when queried about the possibility of combining Il Chamus with Mochongoi Division, the Tugen-dominated administrative unit that was formed in the late 1990s when Baringo expanded, to form a new constituency, Nelson remarked on the problems and disadvantages this would promulgate for Il Chamus:

> The former President Moi and his son, Gideon, are not happy with the idea of an Il Chamus political constituency and they want the constituency to be combined with Mochongoi. . . . If we have to be combined with Mochongoi, we will lose an election to Tugen and it will be just like the past. Il Chamus elders met last week with the Commissioner of Elections, a Maasai from Narok, and we will meet again with the person next week in hopes of gaining our own constituency. (Field notes, June 2007)

As this quote points out, ethnicity remains the main recruiting mechanism in the era of democracy and multiparty politics, even among small groups like Il Chamus. Efforts to bolster tribal numbers and create ethnic-based constituencies are symptomatic of this pattern. The Moi regime was particularly skillful in playing the ethnic card by pitting different groups against each other and using state resources to create new districts and administrative posts for his allies, while punishing opposition groups through state-sanctioned arrests and harassment. The postelection turmoil of 2007–2008 was largely along ethnic divisions and sadly demonstrates just how little has changed since the introduction of democratic elections in 1992.[8] Leaders still continue to use ethnic differences to instigate violence, as well as to create new political constituencies and administrative units. This pattern does not bode well for Kenya's future.

Victory in Theory

In December 2006 judges in the High Court of Kenya ruled that Il Chamus should have their own political constituency, and in July 2007 a second judicial hearing confirmed this ruling. The original judgment noted:

> With due respect in this matter we have formed the view that the ECK has not fully grasped its constitutional role. ECK has viewed the Il Chamus claim to representation as a tribal or clan claim. It is not and the Constitution does support their claim. Their claim stems on special interest as a minority under s 33 of the Constitution and as embraced by the community of interest criterion under Section 42 and also and as that of an indigenous and distinct community and on the additional ground of inadequate representation. In a democracy such as ours, representation most of necessity be a major instrument for participation that should enable the voice of a minority group to be heard in official bodies. Participation is the lifeline of democracy. (Kenya 2006: 78)

The legal ruling concluded with a mandate for the ECK that the "Il Chamus claim be processed" (ibid.: 115). The victory was perceived as an important milestone for a minority community that had held so little political power, and much celebration took place in Il Chamus. At the victory celebrations in Baringo District, leaders of several Maa groups (Maasai, Samburu, and Mukugodo) and supportive NGOs and INGOs were in attendance, including Mzee ole Kaparo, the Speaker of the House in Parliament and a Mukugodo MP. Moreover, international media also reported on the judicial outcome, including the story by the BBC. In Kenya the Maasai-based NGO, Mainyoito Pastoralist Integrated Development Organization (MPIDO), which is funded both locally and internationally, also highlighted the achievement of the Il Chamus in gaining their "own electoral constituency to reduce their marginalization and facilitate their democratic representation" (Mainyoito Pastoralist Integrated Development Organization [MPIDO] 2007). Moreover, Minority Rights Group (MRG) International, a large international human rights group based in London, proclaimed the victory on its website with the statement "that the Ilchamus qualified as special interest group under the current constitution" (2008: 6).

Despite the favorable verdict and widespread publicity, Il Chamus still remain without their own MP as of 2012. As the key Il Chamus legal advocate in the case explained to me, "In Kenya it is one thing to win a ruling and another to actually get something done. We won in theory but in practice still no commission [or constituency] has been formed. . . . We are a marginal group and nobody listens to us even when we win our case" (field notes, June 2007). By 2008 the lawyer was busy seeking a second court case to force the ECK to act on the ruling and implement the new constituency before the next set of national elections.

A further development recently occurred that places an additional roadblock toward Il Chamus' goal of national political representation. In August 2010 a new constitution in Kenya was finally approved, and it is a great improvement over the 2005 version, which, as discussed earlier, was voted down by the public. Although the document has strong and positive language in it about protecting the political and economic rights of minority and disadvantaged groups, it offers little guidance or recommendations for creating new constituencies for minority groups, such as Il Chamus (Kenya 2010a). The new constitution replaces districts with counties to be headed by democratically elected senators. It returns the country to the number of districts/counties (47) that were in place in 1994 prior to the period of rampant and politically motivated administrative growth. Importantly, it also reduces the power of the executive branch (president) by limiting its control of local and regional administrations and administrative appointments. These changes all are very positive. However, with the daunting challenges of implementing radically different political and administrative structures under the new

Figure 4.1. Il Chamus celebration of political constituency ruling. Photo by Stephen Moiko.

Figure 4.2. Il Chamus youth singing at constituency celebration day. Photo by Stephen Moiko.

constitution, it is highly unlikely that a political constituency for Il Chamus will be high on a national reform agenda, at least for the next few years.

A new constitution, however, has not stopped Il Chamus activists from continuing to make their political case, and many in the area still remain very disappointed that the earlier judicial ruling was not enacted. Very soon after the national referendum was approved, the Il Chamus were back in court in November 2010 with the same legal team as before, once again arguing that the decision of 2006 should be enforced and that "they should be given their own constituency" (*Daily Nation* 2010b). With the appointment of the Il Chamus lead lawyer to the IEBC body in 2011, the protests continued and grew even louder this past year (2012) when new political constituencies were recommended for the country, including for central Baringo (Thuku 2012). Il Chamus was not one of them, but, instead, a Mochongoi constituency was advocated that would include Il Chamus as a minority again to Kalenjin-speaking Tugen and Endorois. The situation was so tense in the area in February 2012 that armed skirmishes—with some loss of life—broke out between Il Chamus and the Tugen-related Endorois community, the latter a minority or indigenous group who also won an important court case against the Kenya government (see chapter 3; Human Rights Watch 2010). Both communities have been politically marginalized by the state, and it truly is tragic that they politically have been pitted against each other under the new constituency boundaries, even if it appears that the numerically larger Endorois are likely to fare better than Il Chamus. In the words of one Il Chamus resident: "With the creation of the new Mochongoi constituency, we will have nothing to gain as our Tugen [including Endorois] brothers will continue dominating us. We have been brought together again, yet we have nothing in common" (Kipsang and Cheploen 2012). As of July 2012 approval of new political constituencies and boundaries has not been finalized, but it almost is certain at this late date that an Il Chamus constituency will not be implemented prior to the upcoming national elections (March 2013).

If and when the Il Chamus ever have their own parliamentary representative, it will be interesting to observe what type of leader will be elected as the community's first MP. The favorable court ruling on a new political constituency in 2006 already provoked local interest at the time in the possibility of a parliamentary position. This is hardly surprising since the parliamentary posts in Kenya come with considerable power to enact legislation and disburse development funds, in addition to some of the highest salaries and benefit packages for elected officials in Africa and the world generally. If the favorable court ruling on behalf of Il Chamus is finally enacted, will the community elect an educated elite who resides outside the location but has good national connections? Or will it be a local leader who is more grounded in the community but has no important national connections? Based on discussions with members of the community, it is likely to be the former type of leader, who is familiar with national politics and has Nairobi-based allies. If this is correct, then it is a good indication of how important national representation is viewed locally.

Summary

This chapter has used the optic of one particular group, Il Chamus, to explore political change in the home district of former President Moi following the historic introduction of multiparty elections in the 1990s. The neoliberal agenda of economic and political reforms opened up new political spaces and possibilities for trans-ethnic and trans-national alliances, especially for indigenous minority groups. In Kenya, including in Baringo, it became possible to draw on global actors, such as international NGOs, and discourses in strategically important ways. Il Chamus seized on the opportunity afforded by democratic dialogue to purse political representation and an identity that distinguishes their political cause from other Maa-speaking groups in Kenya. They drew on the language of minority and human rights initiatives and built key alliances with national and international actors. Cosmopolitan leaders and lawyers with modern offices in Nairobi and important international linkages helped the community to achieve a national victory for representation.

Although Il Chamus professionals skillfully publicized the plight of the minority Il Chamus in national and international venues, in the end the Kenyan state maintained the upper hand. They have failed to achieve autonomous political representation despite a legal ruling in their favor and a supportive international context. With the complexities of implementing a new constitution and with planned national elections in early 2013, it is unlikely that the Il Chamus' political case will be revisited by the Kenyan government until at least 2014. In the next chapter, we turn to one of the tragic failures of the neoliberal agenda: the continued hunger and chronic poverty in many African nations—in this case Ethiopia—even after twenty-plus years of market-oriented reforms.

5   "The Government Is Always Telling Us What to Think"

Narratives of Food Aid Dependence in Rural Ethiopia

IN 2007 A large government billboard on a road in Amhara Region, Ethiopia, warily cautions rural residents about the harms of depending on food relief and developing a "dependency attitude." This same message is communicated at a workshop during the same year in the regional town of Dessie, South Wollo Zone, where government officials warn farmers about depending too much on food relief and not working hard enough on their farms: "That is the problem with South Wollo; farmers have received food aid for too long" (field notes, January 2007). Similar attitudes about farmers who are said to be "developing a dangerous dependency attitude" are expressed by officials throughout food-insecure regions of Ethiopia (government official, cited in Sharp et al. 2006: 48). Indeed, even among many members of the international donor community, a dependency syndrome among farmers is proclaimed with convincing authority but with little empirical data.[1]

The food aid industry in Ethiopia and the discourses and practices that surround it are fertile grounds for examining several of the book's key themes, including the contradiction between the benefits of pro-poor economic reforms and the reality of growing numbers of poor and hungry (Ferguson 2007). Ethiopia is governed by a coalition party, the Ethiopia People's Revolutionary Democratic Front (EPRDF), which was formed from different regional resistance movements after the successful overthrow of the harsh, militaristic Derg regime in 1991. Since that time, the government has held four rounds of often disputed multiparty elections, the most recent in 2010, and implemented economic reforms that dismantled state farms and cooperatives and liberalized markets but left land and some principal industries under state ownership. It also established robust ties with key Western countries, especially the United States and the UK, and with key development organizations, such as the IMF and World Bank, that have resulted in massive flows of external development assistance to the country (for example, see World Bank 2006). In 2008 it received more than US$3.3 billion in official development assistance (foreign aid), which makes it the largest recipient of foreign aid in Africa and the second largest in the world after Afghanistan (Global Humanitarian Assistance 2011). The country now is in pursuit of food self-sufficiency in basic cereals, increased agricultural exports, and accelerated rural development built on a massive mobilization program ("campaign") around the themes of economic growth and reduced dependency on food relief (Ethiopia 2005 and 2009). Most of these initiatives emphasize individual accountability, hard work, and responsibility, all key elements of the neoliberal reform agenda, while blaming dependency attitudes among farmers and herders for hunger and underdevelopment.

Despite pro-market reforms and massive amounts of technical assistance and external funds since the early 1990s, Ethiopia still remains the largest recipient of food aid in Africa and among the largest recipients in the world (Barrett and Maxwell 2005).[2] For instance, two recent droughts (1999–2000 and 2002–2003) alone resulted in imported food relief of more than US$500 million of food aid, and in some regions of the country more than 75 percent of the population received assistance during these emergencies (see FAO/WFP 2002; USAID 2003; Ethiopian Network on Food Security 2002). The state and its officials have put much of the blame on farmers' inabilities to overcome a dependency syndrome and pursue productive agricultural and resource management practices. That the country remains so food insecure and highly reliant on massive externally funded food aid programs represents a paradox for a country that boasts of improved macroeconomic performance, but is confronted with the need for massive public food safety net programs to keep millions of its citizens alive (see World Bank 2006; Brown and Teshome 2007).

This chapter explores the ways that dependency narratives and food security policies allow the Ethiopian state to remain in firm control of its rural populations, a tactic that has marked Ethiopia's political history since its Imperial Period (pre-1974). It does so while boasting of pro-growth reforms and free markets and a hospitable environment for large-scale foreign investment, especially by agribusiness firms. In 2008 government policy encouraged foreign investment in agriculture by loudly noting that the country had about 2.4 million hectares available for development by foreign investors, and already several private agricultural schemes of 5,000 hectares or more have been established in the past few years (Cotula et al. 2009; Oakland Institute 2011). Investors have come from as far away as India, Saudi Arabia, and China, all countries that confront their own shortages of arable lands. It will be shown in this chapter that despite official discourses emphasizing private markets, pro-business policies, and democracy, the state remains forcefully in command of its rural economy, and the narrative of farmer dependency reinforces this control. By looking at a key food-deficit area, South Wollo Zone of Amhara Regional State, it will be shown how a dependency narrative disempowers rural communities and badly misrepresents rural livelihoods. The dependency language underlies the country's recent massive Productive Safety Net Programme (PSNP), one of the largest social safety net programs in sub-Saharan Africa (Devereux et al. 2006), as well as supports the government's settlement and resettlement programs. By forcing most participants to work on public works projects—such as market feeder roads—in order to receive food and/ or cash, the state can claim that it is trying to both break a "handout mentality" among its farmers and promote economic growth.

Through detailed survey and ethnographic data collected during 2000–2007, the chapter also demonstrates that relatively few South Wollo households are excessively dependent on food aid. It will be shown that the arrival of food aid often is irregular and highly politicized, and during two recent droughts it arrived well after most of the damage to assets and livelihoods had occurred (see Little 2008a). In short, the uncertainties surrounding the *timing* and *amounts* of food aid have taught local farmers and herders not to depend too much on it.

Characteristics of South Wollo

South Wollo Zone of Amhara Regional State is located in the chronically poor and food-insecure area of northeastern Ethiopia. It is the center of the country's so-called famine belt and was one of the most severely affected regions in the well-known famines of 1973–74 and 1983–84 (see Wolde-Mariam 1984; Dejene 1990; Rhamato 1991). Compared to most other parts of highland Ethiopia, the area has smaller average farms, lower incomes, and is less food secure because it depends more on the short (*belg*) rains than other areas of Ethiopia (see Dejene 1990; Wolde-Mariam 1984). South Wollo was a key recipient of massive humanitarian efforts in the infamous 1973–74 and 1983–84 disasters, and it provided empirical materials for the well-known entitlement (famine) theory of Nobel laureate Amatrya Sen (Sen 1981; also see Baulch 1987). It also was one of the main affected areas during both the 1999–2000 and 2002–2003 droughts. If any area of the country would be expected to have a food aid dependency problem, it should be South Wollo.

Agro-ecology

The study region in South Wollo comprises four major agro-ecological zones: *wurch* (highlands above 2,800 meters above sea level [a.s.l.]), *dega* (highlands approximately 2,000–2,700 meters a.s.l.), *woina dega* (midlands approximately 1,500–1,900 meters a.s.l.), and *kolla* (lowlands below 1,500 meters a.s.l.). The area is approximately 120 kilometers from north to south and at its widest point is about 160 kilometers east to west (approximately 19,200 km^2). It is a particularly rugged terrain with very steep slopes; drops of 1,000 meters over a few kilometers are not uncommon. Most of the area has thick vertisol soils that require animal or mechanized traction to effectively utilize. No farmers in our study used mechanized

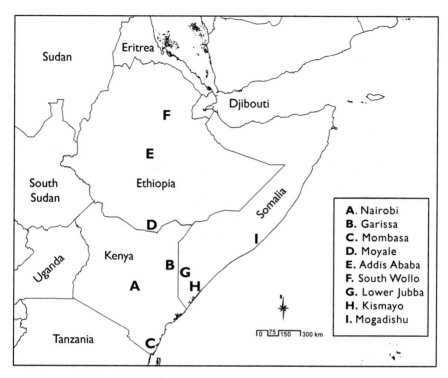

Map 5.1. Key places in Ethiopia, Kenya, and Somalia. http://d-maps.com/carte.php?lib=horn
_of_africa_map&num_car=25593&lang=en; map adapted by author and map key also com-
posed by author.

traction. However, all relied on oxen traction, with the exception of a few farmers who utilized horses. Because of strong cultural norms against women plow-
ing fields, many female-headed households, which comprise about 24 percent of
total households in the area, are forced to sharecrop out their farms to have them
plowed. This action reduces the harvest yield available for female-headed households by 50–65 percent depending on the terms of the sharecropping arrangement (see Little et al. 2006).

Culture and History

Ethnically the area is a mix of Oromo and Amhara populations with a large mix-
ture of Oromo migrating into the area during the sixteenth and seventeenth cen-
turies (for details on the history of highland Ethiopia and its populations, see
McCann 1995; Zewde 2001). Oromo are the largest ethnic group in Ethiopia and
Amhara are second. The population of the study area mainly is Muslim (> 85

Figure 5.1. Hillside farms, South Wollo, Ethiopia. Photo by author.

Figure 5.2 Family in South Wollo, Ethiopia. Photo by author.

percent), with the remaining predominantly Orthodox (Coptic) Christian. There are important differences in local social structure between the two main ethnic groups. The Oromo trace descent through male kinship lines (patrilineal), while the Amhara are generally bilateral (trace relations through male and female relations), which has important implications for settlement and inheritance patterns—especially for women.

Food insecurity and poverty in South Wollo have significant historical dimensions that are important to acknowledge. The 1973–74 famine killed between 40,000 and 80,000 people in one year alone and instigated part of the political unrest that unseated Emperor Haile Selassie (de Waal 1997: 106). Prior to the land reform that started soon after Haile Selassie's overthrow, only slightly more than 50 percent of households in the study region had access to their own farms. Other than administrators and family members of the imperial government who owned large estates, the few who owned land had to be "loyal subjects" of a local landlord or prince (field notes, January 2004). Instead, many residents were rent-paying tenants or sharecroppers on lands owned by the imperial government and its representatives.[3]

After the overthrow of the imperial government, a land reform program was implemented in the mid-1970s by the revolutionary Derg government that recognized peasants' rights to land, but kept ultimate ownership and transfer rights in the hands of the state. The Derg regime was headed by a military officer, Mengistu Haile Mariam,[4] who forged strong ties with the USSR and its allies, and who utilized very violent means to silence his critics and intimidate the population during the 1980s. After a prolonged civil war the Derg regime was toppled (1991) by a coalition of regional resistance movements that formed the EPRDF, which remains in power today. Additional land redistributions were conducted in 1992 and 1997, and approximately one-half of current households in South Wollo received the bulk of their land from these reforms. As noted earlier, the state maintains ultimate ownership of the land, and those farmers who temporarily leave their farms for more than two years will have their land repossessed by the local administration and reallocated to other households.

Poverty and Food Insecurity

By almost any statistical indicator large numbers of households in South Wollo are very poor. Among them female-headed households are more inclined to be poor than others. Per capita incomes (cash and subsistence values) in the area are less than US$50 per year for more than 80 percent of households, which is less than 50 percent of the average (US$104) for Ethiopia as a whole (World Bank 2002). And Ethiopia itself ranks among the poorest countries in the world according to a 2008 assessment (Global Humanitarian Assistance 2011). Even when compared with the poorest street traders (dumba nengue) of Mozambique (chapter 2) and pastoralists of northern Kenya (chapter 6), South Wollo farmers are very poor, earning on average less than $0.20 per day (Little 2008a).

Average land holdings are only 0.82 hectare per household in South Wollo, and even those in the largest land-owning quartile have an average farm size only of 1.72 hectares. More than 25 percent of households have average landholdings of less than 0.5 hectares, which is a minuscule amount of land for households who rely so heavily on rain-fed agriculture. On a national scale the average size of landholdings in eastern Amhara Region (including South Wollo) is about 20 percent smaller than in other rural parts of Ethiopia. The small land size and widespread hunger have led scholars to pessimistically refer to them as "starvation plots" (Rhamato 1991). In terms of ownership of oxen, the most valuable asset for a plow-based agrarian system, 35 percent of farmers did not own an ox and only 31 percent owned two oxen, the number that are needed for plow-based cultivation. With at least one ox, a family is said to be making some progress and can pursue *mekenajo*[5] rather than "beg oxen from others" (Stone and Kebede 2003: 32).

In South Wollo ownership of livestock, especially oxen, is associated with most key welfare indicators, including income, land ownership, labor availability, expenditures, and food availability. In the words of one local farmer, "The poor are without cattle, while the rich have cattle. In terms of soils and land there is not so much difference between rich and poor—soil is the same everywhere and everybody received some land through redistribution" (field notes, January 2004). Livestock ownership, therefore, shows a much higher degree of inequality than that of land. For the poorest 30 percent of households in the area, they "own virtually no animal assets" but almost all control some land (Roth and Mogues 2003: 6).

Differences in nonfarm income between poor and better-off households also show an interesting pattern in the area. Because waged employment is limited mainly to casual and unskilled work, which pitifully is compensated at about US$0.45–0.55 per day, it is pursued by the poor as a survival strategy, especially during droughts. In a similar fashion, nonfarm business opportunities in the region predominantly involve petty trading and other low-revenue enterprises, such as was the case in peri-urban Maputo (chapter 2), and consequently attract the poor (Gebre-Egziabher and Demeke 2004). As one farmer of Tebasit *kebele* (local administrative unit) explains, it is not the better-off individuals but rather the "poor who do petty trade in grain and lentils to improve themselves" (field notes, January 2004).

In addition to petty trading in grains and lentil, how else do the poor define themselves? According to Mulugeta, a 27-year-old male household head from Yedo, South Wollo, the distinction between rich and poor is as follows:

> The rich have many things: 2 pairs of oxen; food to feed family for 12 months of year (it takes a minimum of 10 quintal [810 kg] for me to feed my family for a year); have a mule and horse; can give out animals for share herding;

can give money and grain to others; own about 100 sheep; can educate children locally and even outside the area. The rich can go to Addis and there are many rich there. Rich go to town and even live in Addis and hire workers to run their farms. The rich also are building houses in towns and renting them (those houses being built in Dagolo are by the rich and they will rent them). If you are given a sheep by a rich man, you are like a servant to the person. He can call on you anytime, make you prepare *njera* [bread] and work on his farm—he can take the sheep back if you do not help him. The poor, however, are share herders; cannot feed their family . . . maybe only for 7 months or less per year; have few educated children; have no oxen; go to town for casual labor; and must use communal grazing for share herding. (Field notes, January 2007)

The same characteristics of better-off and poor individuals as indicated by Mulugeta were reflected in other conversations, reconfirming that the statistical profiles of household wealth and poverty discussed earlier, with an emphasis on livestock ownership, labor, and food self-sufficiency, generally are consistent with local perceptions. Interestingly, Mulugeta's antagonism about what the better-off can demand from the poor (even cooking njera) is revealed in several other discussions. In other cases, resentment by the poor against the rich also was revealed, in some interviews attributing their improved status to sorcery. Sentiments like these, were expressed in conversations: "we (poor) must do casual labor for the rich"; "people are poor because it is God's fate—god made some people gold (rich) and others bronze (poor)"; "the rich work hard to improve themselves and they support the poor—the poor are there to depend on other 'better off' households"; "rich people are from rich families—many got wealth from their parents"; and "the poor person's land belongs to the rich, since they take grain and money for the coming two to three seasons [through sharecropping] and the poor always remain indebted" (field notes, January 2004).

Drought and Food Aid Distribution

All eight research sites of South Wollo were strongly impacted by the 1999–2000 drought, and at least four were widely affected by the 2002–2003 disaster.[6] Massive amounts of food aid were imported in both periods, but the earlier disaster received the most international attention and food assistance (see Hammond and Maxwell 2002). During the early part of 2000 up to 75 percent of households in South Wollo received food aid at least once, and at the time it was among the country's largest recipients of external food on a per capita basis. At the peak of the 1999–2000 disaster about 1.2 million, or 50 percent of South Wollo residents, were receiving multiple allocations of monthly food aid (van der Veen 2000: 2). At a national level the region was impacted considerably worse than other areas of the country: "the already vulnerable areas of North and South Wollo, and East and West Hararghe in Oromiya Region were the most severely affected" (Hammond and Maxwell 2002: 26). About 10.2 million, or 16 percent of Ethiopia's estimated population of 62 million people at the time, required food aid in 1999–2000 (Lind and Jalleta 2005: 9), which is a considerably smaller proportion than those who needed it in South Wollo.

The 2002–2003 drought did not have as severe an effect in South Wollo as the earlier event. In our study area 57 percent of local households received some food assistance in 2002–2003, but most received it fewer than three times during the period. During this period only 5.8 and 10.8 percent of households, respectively, received food aid on a monthly or bimonthly basis, and even in these cases very few households received the recommended monthly allocation of about 50 kilograms of grain per family of five. At the national level 5.2 million, or about 8 percent of the country's population, required regular allocations of food aid (a total of 557,204 metric tons of food) during 2002, which is considerably smaller than the earlier figure for 1999–2000. However, the number of recipients and the amount of required aid had to be doubled by the beginning of 2003 "to avert a famine" (Ethiopian Network on Food Security 2002: 1).

The government of Ethiopia requires most food aid recipients, except where household members are too old, ill, or disabled, to work on public projects in exchange for food allocations. Part of the official thinking behind this is that free food distribution causes a "dependency syndrome," and thus recipients must work in exchange for relief rations. According to Lind and Jalleta, it is the government's way of "fighting what they label as the dependency syndrome. Policy requires aid recipients to work on public works in return for relief assistance (2005: 6)." Yet, in South Wollo most of the food-for-work (FFW) employment during 2000–2005 was highly erratic, and very few individuals found full-time work on these projects. During July 2002 to July 2003, for example, only 25 percent of households worked at least sixty days on FFW schemes, which is equivalent to about 22 percent of the available work days in the period. Very few earned food payments that exceeded more than 50 kilograms of grain every few months. Thus, while FFW is clearly widespread in the area, households are not overly dependent on it as a source of regular employment or food.

The current government has continued the pattern of using local administration to mobilize labor for conservation and public infrastructure work either on a food- or cash-for-work or a "volunteer" basis, a practice that was prevalent during the resistance period of the 1980s. Brown and Teshome describes how the mass "campaign" approach to mobilize labor and other resources is used in rural areas such as South Wollo:

> To push its development agenda, the government often pursues a "campaign" approach to implementing policies and programmes. This tendency partially stems from the perceived effectiveness of past mass mobilisation efforts and the belief that the state (and party) at all levels should act as a vanguard for development. Regional, woreda [district] and kebele [local] officials interviewed

for this research repeatedly stated that one of their key duties was to mobilise poor people and to change their mindset and attitudes. . . . The campaign to combat "dependency" exemplifies this approach as do recent plasma television trainings of farmers and teachers in woreda centres. (2007: 13)

In a similar fashion, Segers et al. (2008) describe how this mass mobilization approach to rural development and food security reflects key revolutionary themes of the former Tigray Popular Liberation Front (TPLF). Many former members of the TPLF control key positions in the ERPDF ruling party:

> At the discursive level, they [government officials] translate the popular discourse of joint revolutionary struggle by the TPLF and the rural population to the present-day development context. At the practical-administrative level they capitalize upon the historical legitimacy of a number of grassroots institutions initiated by the TPLF during the revolution. The discursive component of the mobilization of farmers for development essentially consists of appeals to the farmers' memories of repression by and resistance against the Derg. . . . Today's struggle for development, the argument runs, is equivalent to yesterday's struggle for liberation. (100–101)

These observations also hold true for what I observed in South Wollo, where military-like campaigns to combat food aid dependency and promote development are part of daily life, and local residents collectively contribute unpaid labor and cash to achieve development (*limat*). The labor is used to build feeder roads, plant trees, construct shallow water pans and soil erosion controls, and engage in other public work projects. As Harrison points out, to not volunteer for development work can result in cash fines or even the confiscation of farms (2002: 600). Many local farmers refer to those days when they engage in collective development work as "development days," and they often are unclear on the goals of these efforts. Because they also are required to make cash contributions for development, some view their contributions as a local tax: "We used to contribute one birr, but now it is three birr per month. We do not know its purpose since we do not get anything from it. Women contribute only for their country, for the sake of patriotism" (Castro and Mengistu 2002: 1).

A second female respondent from South Wollo similarly observes that "we are simply told that it is for development, and we should work" (field notes, March 2007). Much of this development work is done on a group basis, with the groups locally called *development budin*—a good indication of the extent to which development had infiltrated local language. In a lengthier explanation another woman, approximately 40 years old, explains how she participates in development work:

> We work for local development. This is not food-for-work. It is development work done through associations. We do things like plant eucalyptus trees. It is arranged by the chairman of the kebele. . . . I work on it myself through a

women's association. My husband works on it himself through male farmers' association. The children also work through youth associations. . . . There is no payment. They say it is development work. We work on Wednesdays and Saturdays in a week. We work until 12:00 o'clock PM. If the work is much, we work until 2:00 o'clock. But, if many people participate, we can finish work at 12:00 o'clock. Otherwise, we work until 2:00 o'clock. We have to work for local development. When we are told to promote development, we all participate in development work through our respective associations of women, farmers and youth. If we fail to participate, we will be fined five birr or ten birr. (Field notes, March 2005)

These interview excerpts reflect the ways that state officials strategically integrate popular themes of development and participation into their stated goals of defeating dependency and poverty. Indeed, the language of war that so often is used, such as combating or fighting, treats dependency and underdevelopment as "new enemies" of the people. For the Ethiopian government development and economic growth are key goals that must be achieved regardless of cost. Its heavy-handed style of implementation counters neoliberal notions of individual freedom and choice; instead, rural residents perceive that they have little option but to contribute labor and resources to the state's development initiatives. It also explains why some farmers do not see significant differences between the different governments that have ruled them since the mid-1970s. In the words of one male farmer from South Wollo: "They are always telling us what we think, and they are taking our time with their mouths, and with their mouths they reward us with words. A generation has passed since such promises started, but they still give us nothing but words" (field notes, July 2003).

Although the state attempts to maintain the appearance of a "free"-market, liberal democratic system, in reality it is heavily involved in the economy, and its semi-autocratic approach greatly restricts individual freedoms and political competition (see Aalen 2006). The Ethiopian government's recent attraction to the Chinese model of growth and development sans political liberalism is hardly surprising, nor is its receipt of numerous Chinese-financed infrastructure projects and investments (see Geda 2008; Qingfen 2011). As I will show below, the government's responses to local food insecurity and droughts reflect a strong capacity to intervene and influence political processes even at the lowest administrative levels.

During the disasters of 1999–2000 and 2002 food aid in South Wollo consisted mainly of allocations of wheat and, in a few cases, maize. The country rallied around the need to combat the potential famines, especially in South Wollo, and—as noted earlier—the government insisted that able-bodied farmers should work on public works projects if they received food aid. In South Wollo the allocation of food aid largely was and still is carried out through government administration, with the bulk of distribution managed by the state-affiliated body Organization for Relief and Development in Amhara Region (ORDA). A number of international NGOs, such as Concern International, Save the Children–UK and World Vision, are active in South Wollo but are involved in only a small proportion of actual food aid distributions. Not surprisingly, the Ethiopian government has a powerful and deeply entrenched state bureaucracy centered around food security and relief work, and its new Productive Safety Net Programme (PSNP) maintains an equally strong government presence (discussed later in the chapter).

The state and its local representatives are responsible for food aid planning, including annual estimates of need, and distribution and have always resisted heavy foreign involvement in their food aid business. Due to uncertainty of deliveries and amounts during recent relief efforts, it was not uncommon—in fact, it was the norm—for local officials to adjust participant criteria and prescribed food rations during emergencies. Hammond and Eggenberger (1999), for example, describe such a case in South Wollo during the 1999–2000 drought:

> Wereda officials and staff of the Organization for Relief and Development in Amhara Region (ORDA) say they have been instructed (by whom was not clear) not to distribute rations for households of more than five members. This was likely to have been made during the first half of the year when limited food availability did require a choice between reducing the individual household ration size and reducing the number of beneficiaries. . . . The effect is that individuals are currently receiving on average one half to two thirds of the ration prescribed for them in the NPDPM [National Policy for Disaster Prevention and Management] Guidelines. (3)

Following the 2000 drought one farmer provided this perspective on food aid distribution: "Food aid is not received on time. There are delays after it gets here. The rationing procedure is not good [they imply that some sort of discrimination occurs in the allocation]. We wish it could be improved" (Castro, Pankhurst, and Adal 2001: 5).

More recent interviews with farmers further confirm this lack of consistency and transparency in how food aid is distributed and how beneficiaries are determined. The current system vests considerable power in kebele officials, who for political reasons prefer to distribute to their clients and to as many families as possible, rather than target the neediest. The following excerpts from farmer interviews point to the ambiguities surrounding food aid distribution, as well as its blatant politics:

> I received food aid during September to November 2003. I was one of the few in the village who received food aid during this time. I get along with the PA [kebele] officials and they are kind to me. The PA Chairman decides on who gets food aid. . . . We eat when they give us. (Field notes, January 2004)[7]

> Now I do not receive any food aid from government because I do not have good relations with PA officials who decide on food aid distribution. Rich people have oxen and still get food aid and I want to know why. I have complained about this with others and even took the case to the wereda officials to protest . . . nothing has changed. (Field notes, January 2004)

> We received no food aid. It is given, but not to everyone uniformly. Some may be receiving it, but we are not. The officials think that we have assets—an ox or a camel. They want us to sell our assets so we can receive food, but we won't give them up. (Castro and Mengistu 2002: 11)

As the above examples suggest, there are considerable problems with how food aid is distributed in South Wollo, which further increases risks for food-insecure farmers who receive it. In the next section of the chapter, we look at ways in which the "command-oriented" state and its international supporters have attempted to improve the reliability of food aid delivery, especially for the chronically poor. The latter group is intended to include households and individuals who are so poor that they suffer serious food deprivation during both drought and nondrought times (i.e., throughout the year).

Food-Based Safety Nets

To improve the predictability and targeting of food aid distribution in Ethiopia, the international community heavily petitioned the government in 2003–2004 for a new approach to food security that would be more effective in addressing hunger and helping the poorest households to escape from chronic food insecurity (World Bank 2006; Brown and Teshome 2007). The previously discussed relief efforts associated with the droughts of 1999–2000 and 2002 showed serious problems with how food aid and food security programs operated in Ethiopia, including South Wollo. The international community wanted to see a large-scale social safety net program introduced that would guarantee food or cash for chronically hungry households, while helping them to escape poverty. The PSNP became part of the government's national food security program and emphasized public infrastructure activities for program participants who received food or cash to buy food.[8]

The government made it clear that all participants in the PSNP had to contribute labor for public works projects to receive food or cash unless they were disabled or elderly. This tactic was very much in line with the goals of reducing dependency-like behavior and increasing individual accountability. The international community, including the UK, the United States, Canada, and World Bank, pledged most of the funds for the PSNP's almost $500 million annual budget (Gilligan et al. 2008: 3). The program is designed to provide assistance to 8.3 million chronically food insecure, or about 13 percent of the country's population (Brown and Teshome 2007: 4). Only South Africa has a larger social safety net program in sub-Saharan Africa (Gilligan et al. 2008: 3).

The neoliberal undertones of the PSNP were strong, but heavily influenced by the state's particular top-down approach to development. At first the state was resistant to the idea of a safety net program because a massive public welfare program targeted at the chronically food insecure was inconsistent with its emphasis on economic growth and reducing dependence on food assistance. The program was broadened, however, to include agricultural diversification and resettlement components, both of which could be construed as supportive of pro-growth mandates (see Devereux 2010; Sharp et al. 2006; Ethiopia 2002 and 2009). A key premise of the program is that once basic food needs are met, households would take on additional risk and pursue more remunerative, market-oriented agricultural activities. The credit and agricultural inputs component of the food security program (called the Other Food Security Programme [OFSP]) is supposed to help them to achieve this and gradually escape from food insecurity and poverty (Ethiopia 2009).

The resettlement component, in turn, was very controversial, and most donors opposed it because of the potentially negative social and environmental impacts (see *Economist* 2004; Hammond 2008). Like the previous Derg regime, the government felt it had to resettle poor and "food aid dependent" households from drought-prone highlands to more favorable and less populated areas in the western part of the country, in order to break the food aid cycle and improve food security. The government's campaign target was to resettle 2.2 million people, but by 2008 only about 60 percent of that number had been resettled, and the activity was eventually stopped (Hammond 2008). Some households from our eight study communities in South Wollo had been resettled, but none of those in our sample of 424 households. Most residents who were interviewed strongly opposed resettlement, and the government wisely ended the program in 2010.

Under the PSNP the government insisted that food aid recipients do cash- or food-for-work, in order to build productive community assets. The program was intended to reduce rather than aggravate dependency-like behavior, so there were to be no "free riders" when it came to food or cash distributions. In this sense, even a public welfare program had to be productivity enhancing and not dependency producing—note the term "productive (P)" in the name of the program. The state eventually bought into the program because, as previously indicated, it would involve a massive amount of badly needed external funds and because they viewed it as broadly supportive of the government's campaign to overcome rural food aid dependency. To quote from a recent evaluation of the program: "The primary incentive was the Ethiopian government's strong ideological commitment to reducing the perceived 'dependency' of individuals and households on long-term food aid. The highest levels of the Government and ruling party saw the safety net as a way in which this cycle of dependency could be broken" (IDL Group 2007: 5). The program's goal was for the chronically poor to "graduate" from receiving food assistance after about two to three years of regular support.

Similar to most rural initiatives in Ethiopia, the state took a very top-down campaign approach to the new PSNP program. Counter to the serious concerns of its international funders, who favored a gradual approach, the government wanted the program to begin on a massive national scale that immediately targeted 8+ million chronically poor. Government officials provided mandates (quotas) for recruitment to the program and demanded that large numbers of the food insecure be weaned off assistance (i.e., graduate out of poverty and hunger) within a two-to-three-year period. This approach resulted in significant targeting problems as most local administrators opted not to include the poorest for fear that they would not be able to graduate from the program within two to three years (see Sharp et al. 2006; Brown and Teshome 2007). Instead, middle wealth households were targeted because local officials felt they had better chances of graduating from the program and meeting the government's dictated goals. They were expected to meet local quotas in terms of the percentage of program participants who no longer required food or cash aid. As Sharp et al. note:

> In the first year of PSNP operation (2005), Amhara Region took a policy decision to target the safety net on the "middle-class" category of households—i.e., neither the poorest nor the wealthiest, but those with some land and other assets who were likely to be able to "graduate" into food security with the support of the PSNP and OFSPs. Simultaneously, many of those excluded from the safety net, particularly the young and landless, were targeted for resettlement. This strategy has its own logic, but is clearly contrary to the targeting priorities of the PSNP as agreed between the government and donors. In response to pressure from donors and the federal government, and in the face of rising emergency needs and a high level of complaints from excluded households, the region reversed its targeting policy for the second year's targeting. For 2006, the woredas were instructed to ensure selection of the poorest. (2006: 18)

Although considerable improvements were made in the recruitment process, local officials still excluded certain very poor households, in some cases for blatantly political reasons (see Brown and Teshome 2007). Because the PSNP component of the food security program focused on the chronically food insecure, targeting was an important component of the activity. While targeting efforts were mandated to include the poorest households, there was considerable dissatisfaction and accusations of politicization about who actually was included in the PSNP. As with earlier food relief programs, the eventual decision of who should participate was largely left up to local kebele officials, although local groups of farmers also were supposed to play important roles in the selection process.

Unsurprisingly, tensions between kebele officials and local farmers and between households themselves over the selection process were prevalent. In fact, because of the auditing and monitoring of household assets, such as livestock, many nonparticipants openly discussed their dismay, while others even talked of hiding their assets to qualify for the program. The following remarks from local farmers speak to these problems:

> A constant evaluation of one's condition goes on. This is how they rank people. The rankings can change. They see your crop in the field, or they see your animals. It is in their hands. The kebele officials do it. (Male farmer, July 2003)

> We are too envious of each other's status. I belong to the third wealth category [which receives food aid], and others in the middle group wish they could negotiate to get food aid like him. . . . This sort of comparison results in "unhealthy thinking." . . . Envy increases these days. In imperial times people owned a lot of sheep. They did not count them. Now even a chicken is counted as an asset. (Male farmer, July 2003)

> The Safety Net program doesn't cover even 10 percent of the people that should be involved in the program. And these people who take part in this program, they don't even get their payment on a regular basis per month. Payments often are delayed for three or four months while people have problems. . . . The Safety Net program is something like a hand to mouth service. (Male farmer, January 2007)

> I know that it [PSNP] is helping and supporting people, but it does not include us because they say we are people of the "haves." I don't agree with that. . . . I always ask them to include us. They say people who have nothing are included. (Female farmer, March 2007)

Other farmers in South Wollo remarked about the political nature of the PSNP's selection process:

> [Under the PSNP program] some people just boycott work activities and because of this they stay at home, but at the end of the month they come simply to receive their payment. Such people are those who have some kind of relation with kebele officials and employees who do not want to work. . . . Even some people who were supposed to be included in the safety net program are not included because they thought that if they are registered for the program they would be taken to the resettlement program. So they declined. . . . But on the other hand there are people who were not supposed to get benefits from the safety net program. They were so courageous that they just got registered and now they are involved in the program. And some people who are included in the safety net program do not go to work but just let someone else go and do the job. So at the end of the month they just share the check; they share fifty-fifty or depending on the agreement. (Male farmer, March 2007)

PSNP and food-for work are all the same. The only difference is in terms of name—this one is called safety-net, that one is food-for-work. . . . Not all the poor are included in the program. . . . There was a criterion to select the poor and many people were recruited but the problem is that even in the first and second rounds many poor people were not included because of shortage of funding. There was only a small amount of money so only few people were included. . . . Yeah, last time for instance people were talking about many people who were relatively better off that were included but the poor were not. So people went to Dessie town to complain about the issue, but they were just told that to go to their kebeles and finish the case there. There was no change. They simply say that we did the selection in front of the community and it has already been decided and so we cannot do anything. In front of the community the kebele people select the poor saying that he is poor, that person is poor, and so on and so on. Then the officials write the names of the people selected by the community but later on when they transfer the document to another document they just change the names and include other names. In a village for instance, there are village representatives of the structure so they select their friends and people, who have no close relationship with such people, will be left out. The people who complained were the very poor . . . the poorest people who have nothing at all. (Female farmer, March 2007)

As these comments demonstrate, auditing, accountability, individual responsibility, and reduced dependency remain key principles of food aid programs in Ethiopia, including the PSNP. Kebele officials are expected to categorize and monitor families for food aid on the basis of need, but political factors assume a role, and those who are party clients and/or volunteer for local development work are likely to be selected. The auditing aspect, which is characteristic of many neoliberal reform programs, clearly is prevalent here, although its presence in food aid programs preceded PSNP. Farmers themselves openly discuss different auditing techniques that the government undertakes to select who receives aid and who does not. As the above cases illustrate, the continued auditing of local food security and wealth status and the uncertainty about who will or will not receive assistance create tensions and jealousies among local families. As early as 2001, the selection process associated with food aid distribution was perceived as divisive: "People in Wollo and elsewhere used to pray together. Now we cannot do that mainly because of food aid" (field notes, 2001).

As noted earlier, the government advocated resettlement as part of its national food security program, and many farmers clearly feared relocation. Resettling Amhara and Tigrayean households from highland areas, where the ruling EPRDF party draws most of its support, to lowland areas, where opposition parties are prevalent, can serve a political purpose by demographically diluting the strength of lowland opposition groups. Like the PSNP program, the government wanted to start on a large scale, targeting 2.4 million for resettlement during

2004–2008. By the time official word from the center reached local levels, kebele officials already were busily seeking "volunteer farmers" for resettlement. In some cases, a few of our South Wollo respondents initially felt that our study might be gathering information for the government's resettlement program. Even after we reassured them that we did not work for the government and that all responses would be anonymous, a few remained hesitant to speak to us. Such was the local apprehension centered on the issue of resettlement.

In 2003 discussions of resettlement already were taking place in parts of South Wollo outside our research location. Actual resettlement did not begin until early 2005, but the recruitment campaign started much earlier. As was mentioned earlier, resettlement ended in 2010. One elder male farmer remarked in January 2003 that "if you ask government now for land they will tell you to go for resettlement. Nobody here has left for resettlement but there have been local government meetings about it." He went on to say that he would refuse to go for resettlement—"it is better to be poor here and a hired herder, then to go for resettlement and die of malaria there" (field notes, January 2003). Note that most of the designated areas for relocation are in the malarial lowlands of western Ethiopia, which only adds to their unpopularity among highland communities of South Wollo.

The government emphasized that resettlement was strictly voluntary, but this was not always the case, and, as with other development programs, local officials were given quotas for resettlement (also see Hammond 2008). One young male farmer of 30 years from Tebasit, South Wollo, explained about the voluntary nature of the program:

> Government now wants the poor people to go for resettlement. But we refuse to do this and there have been meetings sponsored to discuss how good it will be if you are resettled. They say that the harvest in the resettlement areas is two to three times per year. Government says that they cannot keep giving food aid. They will take away food aid if farmers do not want to resettle. . . . Even if they offer me good farmland, two oxen, and food aid there, I will never agree to be resettled. The government is playing with us like a game and treats us like livestock. (Field notes, January 2004)

Along similar lines, another respondent from the same South Wollo village notes that "the government tells us that if we have a problem then we should go for resettlement. What can government do here now? Why should people go to resettlement to die?" (field notes, January 2004). As noted earlier, health issues are a major concern with resettlement, and several individuals when interviewed mentioned neighbors who had died due to malaria after Derg-sponsored resettlement in the 1980s.

Thus, the language of food aid dependency is used to justify radical and unpopular "solutions" like population resettlement. For policy makers to present an exaggerated picture of South Wollo as a food-aid-dependent basket case empowers them to advocate for resettlement and even package it as a humanitarian gesture. Yet, despite these official narratives about dependency, the empirical question remains: are rural households in Ethiopia excessively dependent on food aid? Do they modify their behavior because of a reliance on food assistance? The next section explores these questions in the context of South Wollo.

How Dependent Are South Wollo Farmers on Food Aid?

In their book on food aid, Barrett and Maxwell (2005) rightly point out that while empirical studies of food aid dependency in rural areas of Africa are scarce, the few available examples counter the presence of widespread dependency (also see Harvey and Lind 2005). In the rest of this section the charge about dependency raised by Barrett and Maxwell is addressed in terms of (1) its effects on local economic and social behavior and (2) its contribution to household and community food supplies.

Livelihood and Other Effects

What does the South Wollo data tell us about livelihood differences based on whether or not a household receives food aid? Contrary to the expectations of policy makers, food aid recipients are just as inclined, or even more so, to pursue multiple livelihood options as other households. There are few discernible behavioral differences in economic activities between those who receive food aid and those who do not. Based on data covering the 2002–2003 drought, table 5.1 shows that receipt of food aid did not have an important effect on the pursuit of different livelihood activities. In a comparison of food aid recipients with nonrecipients, several interesting patterns are revealed. For example, most households in both groups pursued some type of agriculture, and about the same proportion sold part of their farm produce, while a slightly higher percentage of nonrecipients (57%) versus recipients (51%) earned cash from the sale of livestock or livestock products. What is particularly noteworthy is that a much greater percentage of recipient versus nonrecipient households engaged in off-farm waged employment and petty business/service/trading activities. Much of this work involves difficult and low-status jobs that mainly attract desperate but hard-working individuals. These include migrant laborers who work outside the area on coffee farms or as street traders in an urban center and individuals who stay home to engage in local charcoal making and firewood cutting/selling. All of these ventures are miserably low-paying and "last resort" undertakings, and clearly an individual who is dependent on food aid for their subsistence would avoid them. The prevalence of this kind of work paradoxically is most pronounced during droughts, when food aid availability is higher than in other periods.

Table 5.1. Comparison between Food Aid Recipients and Nonrecipients, July 2002–July 2003.

Type of activity	% Food aid recipients (n=237)	% Nonrecipients (n=180)
Active farming	93	96
Sold crops from own farm	60	59
Earned cash from livestock	51	57
Received remittance income	15	7
Off-farm waged employment (mostly casual labor)	91	63
Petty business/service/ trading activities		
–make/sell charcoal firewood	28	1
–trade	9	14
–other	4	5
TOTAL	41	20
Reciprocal labor exchange	59	55
Contribute to social groups (mainly funeral associations)	99	94
Provide assistance to others	46	39

Source: Little 2008a: 866

Table 5.1 points to some of the research data that confirms the above findings. For example, it shows that food aid recipients are more than twice as likely as nonrecipients to be involved in nonfarm ventures. Moreover, there is a higher percentage of recipient versus nonrecipient households that earn income from three or more activities, a good indication that food aid does not have a negative effect on farmers' diversification strategies. In short, if food aid is supposed to reduce work and livelihood incentives—that is, create a "dependency syndrome" and make "people lazy"—the South Wollo data do not support this.

Another common premise about food aid is that it can harmfully replace or substitute for local practices of sharing, reciprocity, and mutual assistance, all customary forms of insurance for the poor. In the South Wollo study, however, the data do not support this pattern. For instance, participation in reciprocal labor-sharing exchange groups actually was higher for food aid recipients (59%) than for nonrecipients (55%). If we look at active participation in local community groups, such as funeral clubs, there also was little difference between the two groups. Moreover, when household heads and spouses were asked if they provided assistance to others during a thirteen-month period of 2002 and 2003, once again there were only minor differences between food aid recipients and nonrecipients. In fact, food aid recipients (46%) were more likely than nonrecipients (39%) to provide assistance to a kinsmen, in-law, and/or neighbor. When queried further on the topic, respondents indicated that the main types of assistance given were: (a) "provide loan or cash" (33% for food aid recipients versus 43% for nonrecipients); (b) "provide labor" (27% for recipients versus 14% for nonrecipients); (c) "lend/ share oxen or other livestock" (16% for recipients versus 14% for nonrecipients); and (d) "share/loan food and grain" (9% for recipients versus 19% for nonrecipients). Thus, based on the South Wollo findings it is apparent that there are only minor differences in livelihoods and mutual help ("insurance") behavior between the food aid and non–food aid groups. If anything, the former group expends a greater effort in assisting others than do nonrecipients.

Locational Considerations

Even community-level data on food supply dispute claims of food aid dependency in South Wollo. In both the 1999–2000 and 2002–2003 disasters food aid distribution reached a large proportion of the population, but amounts of food relief were too small or delivery too irregular to create excessive dependency even among the poorest. The quantities that were available to each kebele through direct transfers or public work schemes were as little as 50 kilograms of grain per household every three months, too small for most households to be excessively reliant on them. The erratic timing of relief deliveries to communities further discouraged dependency by most farmers.

The percentages of households who received food aid in different kebele during 2000 and 2002 are presented in table 5.2. Table 5.3, in turn, disaggregates household food sources during the second half of 2000, when food aid imports were highest.[9] In only two of the eight communities, Tebasit and Temu, was aid the most important source of food. Agriculture in these two sites is dependent on the short rainy season (*belg*) and is less reliable than in most of the other sites (see Little et al. 2006). The two best agricultural areas, Yedo and Tulu Mojo, received relatively small amounts of food aid, even during the worst (1999–2000) of the two droughts (table 5.2).

Despite relatively high levels of food aid imported into South Wollo in 2000, market purchases were considerably more important in local diets than food assistance. This helps to explain the multiple diversification strategies that farmers pursue to earn income. Even during the worst part of the drought, which was July–December 2000, food aid still was only the second most important source of food acquisition behind cash purchases. Informal conversations and observations confirm that at least some of the relief food was sold and/ or used by mem-

Table 5.2. Percentage of Households in Different Communities Who Received Food Aid during July–December 2000 and January–June 2002

	% of households who received food aid	
Research site (kebele)	July–December 2000	November 2001–June 2002
Chachatu	96%	27%
Kamme	98%	72%
Tulu Mojo	22%	17%
Yedo	32%	67%
Tebasit	100%	38%
Gerardo	45%	56%
Tach-Akesta	100%	72%
Temu	100%	29%
ALL	75%	47%

Source: Little 2008a: 868

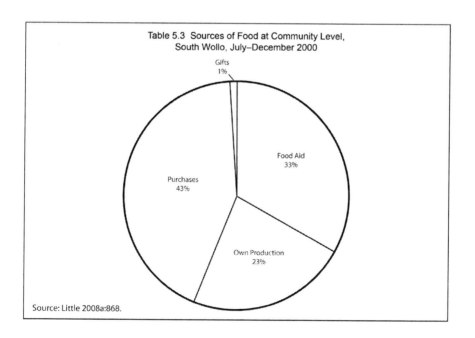

Table 5.3 Sources of Food at Community Level,
South Wollo, July–December 2000

Gifts
1%

Food Aid
33%

Purchases
43%

Own Production
23%

Source: Little 2008a:868.

bers to make local alcohol drinks. How much of it was marketed and/or used to make local brews to sell rather than consumed is not known, but the existence of these practices might further reduce the role of food aid in local consumption.

If one examines the entire twelve-month period between July 2000 and June 2001, which covers both the end of the 1999–2000 drought and the beginning of the recovery period, when food relief still reached more than 50 percent of households, the dependence on food aid is considerably less than in table 5.3. In this span food aid accounted for only 24 percent of total household food availability and less than 45 percent in any single community (kebele).

Patterns of food aid allocations during the 2002–2003 drought reveal even less dependence than in 2000. Almost half of the households received some food aid during the first half of 2002, but food aid was only the third most important source of food in the different communities, well behind purchases and own-farm production. Overall relief food accounted for less than 5 percent of total food available in the area, which is even below the low levels reported for other areas of Ethiopia in nondrought years (see Quisumbing 2003). Among the four kebele in South Wollo where at least 50 percent of households received food rations during January–June 2002, only one (Kamme) depended on relief for more than 5 percent of its total food needs. Like in the 1999–2000 disaster, the relatively high percentage of households who received food aid in 2002 did not equate to high levels of local dependency itself because of the small amounts provided.

Local Perceptions and Narratives

When discussing the role of food aid in their lives, most farmers confirm what the data show: that few perceive of themselves as highly dependent on assistance. Moreover, when it comes to the timing of food aid delivery there is equal confusion among respondents, and an almost "lottery-winning" reaction when they learn that it may be coming. As the head of one family, who at the time of the interview had not received food assistance for four months, remarked: "Now there is news that they [the family] will get food aid in the coming months" (Castro and Kebede 2003: 72).

The following cases based on interviews in South Wollo are typical of local perceptions regarding food aid:

> Idrissa is a widow who heads a household with two adolescent sons. She says that she gets along with local officials and they are kind to her. According to Idrissa, the chairman of the Peasant Association decides on who gets food aid and ranks villagers on their food needs. In the 1999–2000 drought she did not receive much food aid, but she is one of the few in her village who received food aid during late 2003, when conditions were better than in 1999–2000. Her sons worked for others as herders during the 1999–2000 drought so they could eat: "They worked for one year as herders." (field notes, January 2004)

Mesfin is a moderately wealthy male household head who says that he and his family received no food aid during the past year. "One has to be a friend not foe to get food aid." He has learned that it is better to look for other means to acquire food during a drought, including migration to other areas to work, rather than rely on food aid. (field notes, January 2004)

Ahmed heads a large family and has a daughter working in Djibouti (this case is drawn from Castro and Kebede 2003). He indicated at the time of the interview that the food situation was bad: "They are eating their seed and having to sell their cattle to buy food. The people are eating wood" (i.e., people are selling wood to buy food and survive, ibid.: 14). As of July 2003, Ahmed had not received food aid for a month, but prior to this he had been receiving small amounts monthly. The authorities were late in food deliveries, and his family received only 15 kilograms of food for the whole family, which lasted only about nine days. They sell wood and do other activities because they must buy the bulk of their food at the market. (ibid.)

As the above cases highlight, many local respondents who receive food aid rely more on local coping strategies than external assistance to meet consumption needs. Most received only small amounts of food aid per month and were unaware of amounts beforehand, as well as the timing of deliveries. Thus, in another example, a father with nine household members remarked: "I receive food aid for one person (10 kg) per month, which is very unfair. I have seven children but the government wants me to sell my livestock to feed my family" (field notes, January 2004). Along similar lines, another household head noted: "I received food aid until November 2003 but received only enough food for one person per month. PA [kebele] officials think I am rich" (field notes, January 2004). Finally, when asked about whether food aid makes them dependent and less motivated to work, an elderly farmer from Gerardo noted: "Some people may talk about it saying that it leads to people becoming less motivated to work and things like that—this is just rubbish" (field notes, March 2007). In short, the ethnographic interviews also challenge notions that households and individuals have developed a dependency syndrome because of food aid.

Despite strong evidence to the contrary, government, donors, and NGOs continue to support food security programs in Ethiopia on the basis of reducing food aid dependency among farmers. Kebede, for example, points to a USAID-funded and Save the Children–UK (SC-UK) implemented food security project in North Wollo in 2005 that was called Reducing Dependency and Increasing Resilience (RDIR) (2006: 586). The objective of the intervention was to increase local resilience by reducing household dependence on food aid and other forms of external assistance. At a national level the same misleading rhetoric is played out through the large, donor-funded PSNP, which as noted earlier is attempting to overcome food aid dependency in Ethiopia as one of its key goals. Although rural Ethiopia,

including both North and South Wollo, is very poor and in need of external resources, the materials presented here question the merit of assuming that their
residents are dependent on food aid.

Summary

There is little question that rural Ethiopia suffers from major food problems and
widespread poverty—and this was the case even before the economic and political
reforms of the 1990s. It is equally true that food aid has saved lives during emergencies and played a role in assisting households and individuals, especially the
poorest, to cope with major food deprivations in the country. Nonetheless, the
facts about food aid dependency and its implications in places like South Wollo
do not match local realities on the ground. As this chapter has shown, the dependency narrative empowers the state and international agencies to use radical interventions, such as the resettlement of highland populations into lowland areas
where there has been opposition to the current government. The assumed narrative of food aid dependency can be used to pursue such political projects that
have grave social and environmental impacts.

This chapter also has shown that despite official narratives few farmers are
foolhardy enough to depend on food aid in rural Ethiopia since its delivery is
nontransparent, uncertain, and poorly timed, and the amounts are insufficient.
The neoliberal themes of individual responsibility, accountability, and economic
growth are embedded in the PSNP initiative for the poor. By comparing livelihood and social activities among food aid recipients and nonrecipients in food-
deficit South Wollo, the chapter has shown that local livelihood strategies and
behavioral patterns have not been altered as a result of food aid deliveries and
strongly challenges the idea of food aid dependency. In the next chapter, the contradictions between local realities and pro-poor economic growth policies continue to be explored, but in the context of poverty-based programs in pastoralist areas of Kenya. As with the "food dependent" South Wollo farmers, the state
also uses narratives about pastoralists and pastoralism to justify political actions
under the guise of attacking poverty and promoting economic growth.

6 "Counting the Poor"

The Politics of Pastoralist Poverty Assessments in Kenya

Eᴛʜɪᴏᴘɪᴀ'ꜱ ᴇxᴘᴇɴꜱɪᴠᴇ ᴀɴᴅ expansive PSNP activity is a product of a new approach to poverty alleviation that uses both safety net and pro-market interventions to protect the poor, as well as to promote smallholder commercial agriculture. The implementation of Poverty Reduction Strategy Plans (PRSPs) in Ethiopia and other poor countries was an implicit admission that more had to be done to help the poor benefit from market-based economic growth (see discussion in introduction). To include the poor in development programs as required by PRSPs, it was necessary to identify who the poor actually are. This new, more humanistic approach to economic reform required that poverty be measured, mapped, and monitored. In the words of Maia Green, "poverty becomes not only a problem of the poor, but also their responsibility," and hence governments and donor agencies sought ways to measure, audit, and ensure compliance by the poor (2006: 1118).

In this chapter, I examine the issue of poverty among pastoralist populations in northern Kenya, a subpopulation that always registers high on national poverty radars. Counter to common orthodoxy, the materials presented here suggest that pastoralist poverty has been grossly exaggerated, in part to justify programs for settling and transforming herders into sedentary ("modern") citizens. A failure in poverty analyses to distinguish between settled ex-pastoralists, who often are desperately poor and hungry, and those who still actively practice pastoralism is at the core of the problem. Mobile pastoralists have always presented a dilemma for the modern nation state—and, I might add, for many development agencies as well. Rationales for transforming them into settled agrarian subjects are eagerly sought. It will be shown how neoliberalism's dual agenda of pro-poor economic growth and accountability facilitates a flawed understanding of poverty in pastoral areas that results in misdirected policies. Recall the discussion in the previous chapter of the ways in which misunderstandings about food aid dependency in Ethiopia justified drastic actions by the state, including the resettlement of the poor. In this chapter I also explore the power of labeling and how it can be used to disempower already politically marginalized groups, such as pastoralists, and intervene to force changes among them.

A comparative study of pastoral livelihoods in six different sites representing five different ethnic groups in northern Kenya, will show that most poverty in the region is associated with ex-pastoralists and other nonpastoralists rather than herders who still practice mobile pastoralism. By mislabeling pastoralists as desperately poor and blaming pastoralism for producing poverty and environmental problems, the Kenyan government is empowered to introduce radical alternatives, such as turning herders into farmers through sedentarization schemes, converting their lands into conservation or irrigation schemes, or selling off their lands to foreign investors. To borrow from James Scott, these painful actions make herders "legible" to governments and enable them to pursue modern livelihoods (Scott 1998). The association of mobile pastoralism with poverty also underlies state efforts to control and administer them, both strong challenges for many African states since at least the onset of colonialism.

The "Poverty Industry"

An increased focus on measuring (auditing) poverty as part of policy reform programs is widespread throughout Africa, not just in pastoralist areas of East Africa. For instance, the World Bank and other development agencies recently have funded massive surveys, such as the Living Standards and Measurement Survey (LSMS), to identify and quantify poverty in many African countries as part of ongoing Structural Adjustment Programs (SAPs). As a result, a virtual industry of research centers, consultants, and publications devoted to identifying, measuring, and monitoring poverty in Africa has emerged in Europe, the United States, and Africa. Evidence of the current popularity of the African poverty theme to academics and others is the fact that a recent issue of the prestigious U.S. science journal *Proceedings of the National Academy Sciences (PNAS)* includes a special section on sustainability and global poverty that is solely devoted to African poverty research. The coeditors in their introduction claim that "understanding African exceptionalism and contributing to its reduction is one of the grand challenges of sustainability science" (Kates and Dasgupta 2007: 16747). Editorial actions and statements like these imply that the scale and depth of poverty in the region is comparatively unusual and a challenge both to scholars and practitioners. For noble scientists wishing to study and try to alleviate global poverty, Africa therefore provides an ideal real-life laboratory for testing ideas with both intellectual and moral rewards.

As with most development planning, methods for identifying and measuring poverty rely heavily on economists and their arsenal of models, techniques, and indicators that usually privilege quantitative dimensions, such as incomes and consumption. In this new enthusiasm for poverty analysis and alleviation, scant attention is paid to inequality and to the economic and political structures that underlie and perpetuate poverty. Noneconomists at the World Bank and other organizations advocated participatory techniques for capturing the "voices of the poor," and these kinds of qualitative exercises were implemented in several African countries, but with little concern for identifying the structural inequalities that cause poverty (see Narayan 2000; also see World Bank 2011: "Voices of the Poor Project Team" website). By the mid-2000s an avalanche of literature on poverty measurements and methods had been produced. Africa was the center of attention for much of this work, since it was the only continent that had seen poverty rates grow in the 1990s and 2000s. The lens on Africa was further illuminated by the widespread attention to its poverty by global leaders and celebrities, such as Bill Clinton, Tony Blair, and Bono, as well as the publication of easily accessible books on the topic by Jeffrey Sachs (2006) and Paul Collier (2008).

Almost by default most of the scholarship and policy literature left unchallenged the underlying assumption that increased access to markets (especially export markets) was always a good thing for the poor. Indeed, there was little consideration that many segments of the poor lack the means, such as capital and education, to benefit from many markets, often leaving them disadvantaged or even more impoverished through exposure to markets. As Hulme and Shepherd caution: "A particular problem of contemporary poverty analysis, seeking to rapidly reduce poverty headcounts in an era of globalization . . . is to see 'the poor' as those who are not effectively integrated into the market economy. This leads to a focus excessively on the role that market forces can play in poverty-reduction" (2003: 404). What the emphasis on quantification and rigor did was to make poverty and "the poor" legible to policy makers and planners and objective realities that could be measured and counted (see Green 2006). Poverty was an enemy like food aid dependency, but first it had to be identified and measured, and then attacked and conquered through appropriate development interventions.

The PRSP model spread rapidly in Africa. It first appeared in the late 1990s, but by 2002 most East African countries already had completed the first stage of the reform process or what were called interim PRSPs (IMF/World Bank 2002; Abrahamsen 2004). In Kenya the PRSP was introduced in 1999 under a negotiated agreement between the government and IMF/World Bank, and the first plan was finalized in 2001 (Hanmer et al. 2003). The PRSP effectively became part of the conditionality of loans in Kenya and the framework for development policy in the early 2000s. To support poverty analysis, participatory poverty assessments (PPAs) were carried out in 10 districts or about 15 percent of the country's districts at the time and a new research department called the Poverty Analysis and Research Unit (PARU) was established in the country's Central Bureau of Statistics (CBS). When Mwai Kibaki replaced Daniel arap Moi as the country's president in 2002, his government decided to move beyond the PSRP with an economic recovery and pro-growth strategy called the Economic Recovery Strategy for Wealth and Employment Creation (ERSWEC) 2003–2007 (Kenya 2004). Many elements of the PRSP, however, were incorporated into the new program, and the dual focus on economic growth and poverty alleviation was maintained. Importantly, the newly created government department, PARU, was to be strengthened under the new program, and the IMF effectively recognized the ERSWEC as consistent with the principles of a PRSP. It did so by including the Kenyan document in its PRSP presentation, which showed that the country had met its poverty reduction conditionality and thus was eligible for additional IMF loans (IMF 2005).

With the creation of PARU, efforts to measure and monitor incidences of poverty were initiated during 2002–2003. PARU built on existing activities, such as the government's national Welfare Monitoring Survey (WMS), in its initial poverty-based research. Its first publications highlighted a range of different poverty indicators in its surveys, such as income, education, expenditure, and consumption (see CBS 2003). Another early action by PARU and its collaborators was the determination of a poverty level for the country equivalent to US$0.55 per person day (Kristjanson et al. 2005), which is barely one-half of the common measure (US$1.00) used in many low-income countries.

PARU's work meticulously documented the presence of poverty in each of the different districts and provinces of Kenya, correlating it with a range of economic and geographic correlates (CBS 2003). For the mainly pastoralist districts of northern Kenya their analyses showed that poverty rates were greater than 70 percent and that pastoralists were among the poorest subpopulation in Kenya (ibid.). In fact, the mainly pastoral province, Northeastern Province, was noted to be the poorest region in the country (see map 3.1, chapter 3). Poor access to markets and towns was highlighted as a key factor in explaining the prevalence of poverty there, as well as in other pastoral areas (ibid.). Because grazing in remote zones away from markets and towns is a key feature of pastoral livelihoods, it is not unexpected that analyses based on spatial access to markets and towns would reveal high rates of poverty in these areas.

More recent studies of poverty in Kenya arrive at similar conclusions about pastoralist poverty. For example, both Thurlow et al. (2007) and Okwi et al. (2007) found that lowland areas of livestock (pastoral) production had among the highest poverty rates in the country.[1] Okwi et al.'s study, in turn, applied GIS techniques to the government survey data and was able to map patterns of poverty in the country. Their analyses correlate spatial patterns of poverty with a number of standard indicators, including agro-ecology, distance to towns and roads, and levels of education. They concluded "that communities living in rangelands are likely to have higher poverty levels. Our results suggest that there appears a strong positive relationship between poverty and living in the rangelands" (2007: 16770). Since pastoralists are the main population living in Kenya's rangelands, the work directly implies an association between pastoralism and poverty.

Figure 6.1. Dry-season water point, northeastern Kenya. Photo by author.

Figure 6.2 Mobile phones charging in pastoral rangelands, southern Ethiopia. Photo by Dejene N. Debsu.

Pastoralism and Poverty

The association of pastoralism with poverty by development policy makers and analysts is not unique to development planning in Kenya. Generally herding populations fare poorly based on standard poverty indicators, despite their sizable but unrecognized contributions to national economies—as much as 10 percent of gross domestic product (GDP) in the case of Kenya (Behnke 2011). In a recent UN Food and Agriculture (FAO) publication, for instance, it is stated that "worldwide, pastoralists represent one of the poorest subgroups and among African pastoralists/agro-pastoralists the incidence of extreme poverty ranges from 25 to 55 percent" (Rass 2006: 1). The report goes on to note that there are 50 million poor pastoralists in Africa alone (ibid.: 66; also see White and Killick 2001: xvi).

In neighboring Ethiopia, which lies north of Kenya, similar associations between pastoralism and poverty are echoed (see map 5.1, chapter 5). Recent analyses from the country claim that (a) "pastoralists are poverty stricken, with minimal literacy rates, poor social services and a fragile ecosystem, submitted to unsustainable resource use practices" (Bekele 2008: 96); and (b) "pastoralists have remained the poorest of the poor and become more vulnerable to a growing process of impoverishment" (Ethiopia 2008: 6). In the Ethiopian case these mischaracterizations have resulted in development policies that can only be construed as anti-pastoralist despite the fact that the pastoralist sector annually accounts for more than US$200 million in formal livestock and meat exports and probably twice that amount in informal livestock exports (Devereux 2010; Little et al. 2010; Ethiopia Sanitary and Phytosanitary Standards and Livestock and Meat Marketing Program 2011). The government has made it clear that sedentarization of pastoralists is their medium-term goal, and most of their investments in the lowlands focus on irrigation and other alternatives to pastoralism (see Ethiopia 2008). These kinds of interventions greatly undermine mobile pastoralism in the country because they convert riverine and other valued pastoral lands into cultivation and other non-pastoral uses, often regardless of the high social, economic, and environmental costs. At worst they contribute to a self-fulfilling prophecy by aggravating poverty and food insecurity among mobile pastoralists where these problems had been held in check. The government also uses a narrative that equates pastoralist rangelands with economic "wastelands" and "vacant lands." The discourse is then used to justify and open the way for the leasing of thousands of hectares of pastoral lands to private agribusiness firms in the spirit of promoting foreign investment and economic growth (Cotula et al. 2009; for a similar approach by the government of Sudan, see Babiker 2013).

Part of the problem in poverty assessments of pastoralists, whether in Ethiopia, Kenya, or elsewhere, is that they usually fail to distinguish between poverty among pastoralists themselves and poverty in pastoralist areas. The latter is a spatial concept and does not directly associate poverty with pastoralism, but merely notes that it occurs in rangeland areas classified as pastoralist. The distinction is important and has significant policy implications, since many pastoral areas attract ex-pastoralists who may be casualties of violent conflict or drought, as well as other poor who migrate to the areas to seek petty trade and casual labor opportunities. In many cases they cluster in and around towns where limited employment, business opportunities, and social services are found.

In most area-based analyses, such as those mentioned earlier in the chapter, nonpastoralist populations are not distinguished from households who still practice mobile pastoralism. When this distinction is made the pattern of poverty looks very different, with most poverty found among town-based ex-pastoralists, casual laborers, and petty traders rather than among those who continue to practice mobile pastoralism (see Little et al. 2008). In fact, there is strong evidence that, counter to dominant narratives, pastoralists often are wealthier than neighboring groups who practice agriculture and other livelihoods, and importantly they often do not perceive themselves as poor (see Devereux 2010). Scott-Villiers (2011), for example, provides a wonderful example of the paradoxical nature of the "pastoralists as impoverished" dominant discourse. She uses a discussion from a regional workshop on pastoralist development in the Horn of Africa, held in Nairobi, Kenya, in 2009 to challenge the narrative. After participants of the region's pastoral communities had been lectured to about how much development agencies were doing to alleviate their poverty, one pastoral elder stood up and exclaimed: "We are not poor!" The elder then went on to explain that

> some people did indeed come to towns and settle there to obtain access to food relief, and they became separated from the traditional welfare system that still protected the majority. He talked about the wealth of the rangelands, the cattle and camels, sheep and goats. He gave the example of one district, statistically the poorest in Kenya, whose camel population is in the millions. "Camels are not counted in the statistics," he said. (774)

Although development practitioners at the meeting immediately contested the elder's statement, with one person even noting that "we have seen the poor people," the point had been made: pastoralists often do not see themselves as poor, and official statistics often understate their wealth (Scott-Villiers 2011: 775). If this truly is the case, then an important policy question becomes: should efforts not be focused on keeping populations in pastoralist livelihoods, since they experience less poverty than other livelihoods in these dryland areas?

A second factor that complicates poverty analysis among pastoralists is that herders often cope with risks by concentrating on herd growth and reproduction, not on market sales. This means that holding on to rather than selling productive animals is a rational strategy at certain times. The more animals an individual or household controls, the better their ability to cope with and recover from periodic shocks, especially droughts (McPeak and Gebru 2004). In most pastoral economies, including in northern Kenya, only 6–7 percent of herds and offspring are sold per year, and rarely are female animals ("productive capital") marketed unless conditions are very bad and cash for food is desperately needed (see Little 1992a). This strategic behavior means that herders' cash incomes, a common statistical measurement of welfare and poverty, may be especially low relative to the animal wealth they own (see Little et al. 2008).

A third reason for overstating the extent of poverty among pastoralists is that government statistical departments, such as PARU, usually fail to valuate own-consumption of pastoral products (especially milk), the value of herd breeding, and consumption and sales of hides and skins. They mainly look at sales of milk and live animals in income surveys. However, in addition to production for the market, pastoralism is geared to two goals: (1) herd growth to cope with and recover from droughts, which was discussed above, and (2) dairy production for own consumption. Neither of these goals relies heavily on markets, although this is not to say that markets are unimportant to pastoralists. They are and have been for a long time (see McPeak and Little 2006). The largest proportion of pastoral income derives from milk production, but the vast majority of this is consumed locally, and very little is sold on the market, except near urban centers (see McPeak et al. 2011). Since few national income surveys adequately account for the value of own consumption of dairy products, the value of breeding, and hides and skins sales, herders' incomes can be underestimated by as much as 40–50 percent (see Little et al. 2010). As Hatfield and Davies point out, "the value of livestock production in the drylands is often grossly underestimated in official statistics and thus does not attract the investment attention that it deserves. It is tempting to say that the under-valuation of pastoralism creates a self-fulfilling prophecy: by declaring it worthless and therefore justifying noninvestment, it has become economically unviable" (2006: 5).

A final factor for why poverty assessments among pastoralists generally are flawed relates to the multiple roles that livestock play in pastoralist societies. The value of animals, especially cattle and camels, goes well beyond immediate economic benefits, and they assume important roles in exchange networks, marriages, and other rituals. For example, the institution of marriage often represents the single largest transaction of livestock that a male (and his family) will make in their lifetime. It involves the transfer of bridewealth animals from the groom to the bride's family. Two key pastoralist groups of northern Kenya, Samburu and Rendille, who are discussed later in this chapter, require bridewealth payments of eight cattle and eight camels, respectively, to marry (Sato 1998). Rarely does a herder ever sell this large number of animals in a single transaction, although it is not unusual for a groom's family to make bridewealth payments over an extended period.

Other nonmarket transactions based on livestock are critically important for herders, including ritual gifts at birth and the naming of a child, exchanges between friends, loans to age mates and kinfolk, and raiding. The anthropological literature is full of examples of nonmarket exchanges in pastoral societies. For example, in her study of herd growth among Turkana, who are neighbors to both the Samburu and Gabra, Broch-Due found the following means for accumulating livestock: inheritance (25%); purchases (2%); raids (16%); direct exchanges (8%); delayed exchanges (7%); ritual gifts (8%); gifts from friends (10%); gifts from kin (2%); pregnancy fines (5%); and bridewealth (17%) (1990). In the Turkana example, with the exception of inheritance, marriage (bridewealth) payments are the second most important mechanism for building up herds. Important gifts of animals at other rituals also are important for the Turkana, as is livestock raiding (ibid.). By contrast, market purchases of animals account for only 2 percent of herd accumulation, a pattern that also is found in other pastoral societies of northern Kenya (see McPeak et al. 2011).

Livestock, obviously, have very important economic roles to play in pastoralist societies, but it is their role in social life and in establishing social relations that influences whether or not a pastoralist is locally perceived as poor. Without livestock a herder cannot manage critical social relations, which often serve an insurance function during periods of hardship, or participate in meaningful rituals. According to Sobania, "an individual without stock becomes isolated from potential pathways of cooperation and mutual insurance in times of hardship and must therefore survive outside the pastoral economy" (1979: 14). Oba reaches a similar conclusion by showing how without cattle a male Borana herder from northern Kenya cannot maintain his social obligations: "In effect, he loses his identity as a Boorana" (Oba 1996: 120). In short, the economic and social aspects of livestock are interdependent and supportive of each other, and both networks of people and animals need to be managed effectively to sustain welfare and avoid poverty (Little et al. 2008; and Broch-Due 1999).

"Measuring" Pastoral Poverty

This section draws on the previously mentioned study of pastoral economies at six sites in northern Kenya.[2] Their main characteristics are summarized in table 6.1, which demonstrates the considerable diversity in livestock ownership, climate, ethnicity, and market access in the region (also see McPeak et al. 2011). Ngambo is the site that has the best access to markets, located within 12 kilometers of a tarmac road connecting it with Nakuru (110 km), the administrative capital of the Rift Valley Province, and Nairobi (280 km), the largest city and market in the

Table 6.1. Sites Where Data Were Gathered

Site	Predominant ethnic group	Avg per capita livestock (TLUs)[1]	Average annual rainfall	Market access
Dirib Gumbo, Marsabit District	Borana	0.97	650	Medium
Kargi, Marsabit District	Rendille	6.98	200	Low
Logologo, Marsabit District	Ariaal/Rendille	2.49	250	Medium
Ngambo, Baringo District	Il Chamus	0.64	650	High
North Horr, Marsabit District	Gabra	3.61	150	Low
Suguta Marmar, Samburu District	Samburu	2.83	500	High

Source: Little et al. (2008: 591)
Notes: 1. TLU is defined as one head of cattle, 0.7 camel, or 10 goats or sheep.

country. However, Ngambo has the fewest livestock per capita and is the most diversified of the six, as well as the only community with any measurable reliance on irrigated agriculture. Kargi, in turn, has the poorest access to markets and infrastructure among the six sites and is heavily dependent on pastoralism. It is located more than 70 kilometers from Marsabit town, the district center of Marsabit District, over a very poor road. Although it is more than 550 kilometers from Nairobi—the key market destination for livestock sold in northern Kenya—Kargi also is the wealthiest in terms of livestock ownership. Among the six sites only North Horr—the second wealthiest in livestock—still practices a form of nomadism where the entire family moves to different grazing and watering sites. Most households in the region, including at Kargi, practice a form of semi-nomadism where there is a relatively fixed residence comprised of the bulk of family members, but mobile herd camps move around the rangelands for large parts of the year depending on local conditions and season.

Dirib Gumbo is the only site of the six that practices ox-plow agriculture, and its residents are Borana. It is isolated from other Borana-controlled grazing zones of northern Kenya and southern Ethiopia, so Borana here are heavily constrained in how they can manage their livestock and move with their herds. The site is located on Marsabit mountain about 8 kilometers from Marsabit town. Further south about 45 kilometers away is Logologo, which has a large Catholic mission station and relatively good infrastructure for a center of about 1,500 residents. It is located in the arid Marsabit lowlands along the main murram (unpaved) road between Isiolo center in the south and Marsabit town in the north. At a higher elevation to the southwest of Logologo is the Suguta Marmar site, which is located on the relatively cool, well-watered Leroghi plateau. This site is at the most southern end of Samburu District bordering Laikipia District, the commercial ranching and wildlife area that was discussed in chapter 3. It contains herds of zebra and migratory elephants at certain times of the year, but does not have the wildlife or tourism potential as the lowland parts of the district do.

The region of northern Kenya that encompasses the six sites has experienced considerable social, economic, and ecological changes in the past thirty-five years, particularly since the devastating droughts of 1973–74 and 1983–84 and the increased political insecurity of the 1990s and 2000s. Both sets of events have deep historical antecedents and have instigated different waves of pastoral sedentarization: pastoralists confronted with diminished herds and growing violence abandoned remote, insecure rangelands and moved into settlements and towns (see Little et al. 2008). Despite these problems, animal husbandry remains the main source of income in the region and a key element of cultural identity. In the remainder of this section, I assess poverty in the region according to a set of standard indicators employed in the literature and by governments, including the Kenyan government. I will show how many of these quantitative markers of poverty are highly questionable in the context of pastoralism. At a minimum they undervalue pastoral production and consumption, thus exaggerating the prevalence of poverty among mobile pastoralists (see Little et al. 2008).

Cash Income as a Proxy of Poverty?

The obvious point to begin with is cash income, which was highlighted earlier. Table 6.2 looks at different sources of income at the six research sites and uses a poverty marker of US$0.64, which roughly is equivalent to the regional daily wage of a casual laborer. This threshold is slightly above Kenya's official poverty line ($0.55), but is well below the global standard of $1.00 or $2.00 per day.

If we look at the amount of income in the table accounted by auto (household) consumption and herd breeding, it is apparent that the wealthiest sites are those that depend the least on cash incomes and the most on mobile pastoralism. Kargi has the highest total income, but on average cash income only accounts for 12 percent of it. Residents of North Horr, in turn, have the second-highest incomes, and cash also comprises a relatively small percentage of the total. Both sites, as reflected in the high figures for household consumption (in this case mainly of milk and, to a lesser extent, meat) and herd breeding, are highly dependent on herd-

Table 6.2. Income, Market, and Nonmarket Proxies of Welfare and Poverty, Northern Kenya, 2000–2002

SITE	Avg daily cash income per person (USD)	Avg daily value of auto-consumption per person (USD)	Avg daily value of herd breed. per person (USD)	Total daily value per person (USD)	% "poor" (less than casual labor wage rate of $0.64 daily)	Market access
Dirib Gumbo	$0.11	$0.15	$0.07	$0.33	73 %	Medium
Kargi	$0.16	$0.40	$0.57	$1.13	13%	Low
Logologo	$0.32	$0.18	$0.22	$0.77	60%	Medium
Ngambo	$0.13	$0.16	$0.18	$0.47	63%	High
North Horr	$0.11	$0.23	$0.45	$0.79	23%	Low
Suguta Marmar	$0.16	$0.10	$0.27	$0.53	70%	High
ALL	$0.17	$0.20	$0.29	$0.66	50%	

Source: Little et al. (2008: 594)

based incomes. That there is a relatively poor relationship between pastoral welfare and cash income challenges the latter indicator's use in local welfare measurements.

The case of Dhima of Kargi speaks to the problem of heavily relying on cash income as an indicator of welfare in northern Kenya. His example is one of high dependence on mobile pastoralism.[3]

Dhima and his household reside in the arid site of Kargi. In the study sample the household is among the wealthiest, in terms of livestock ownership. It controls more than 230 Tropical Livestock Units (TLUs)[4] comprised mainly of camels and goats, and maintains separate satellite camps throughout most of the year for both goats and camels. Dhima is 58 years of age and he has two wives and six children. His oldest son of 24 years of age and two nephews who also reside with the family do much of the herding at satellite camps, with occasional assistance from his 17 year old daughter. Other than periodically selling animals to purchase grains and other necessities, the household earns very little cash income and has little involvement with the cash economy. Ironically, while the households total income is very high, the component from cash is low. His family is in the poorest quartile of households based on cash earnings but among the highest in total income. In short, virtually all of the household's income stems from pastoralism and most is accounted by noncash income primarily from milk and, to a lesser extent, meat production. Thus, Dhima's sole focus is on managing the household herd and his household suffered very few livestock losses (< 10 percent losses) during the 1999–2000 drought, in part because the herds remained very mobile and were moved where water and pasture were available. For many households of northern Kenya the natural calamity resulted in losses of more than 50 percent of herds. (McPeak et al. 2011)

Dhima and his family clearly represent a case where cash income and expenditures are poor indicators of poverty and welfare. Contrast this example with households from Ngambo and Dirib Gumbo, who on average depend on cash earnings for 28 percent and 33 percent of their total incomes, respectively. Yet, they have very low overall incomes (cash and noncash) because of minimal earnings from pastoralism. Indeed, the findings in table 6.2 show that poverty is considerably more prevalent among settled households who depend more on cash incomes (for example, wages and petty trade) than among those—such as Dhima—who rely on subsistence-based pastoralism.

The case of Lewatachum of Ngambo illustrates the poverty among settled households, with minimal animals and few good income-earning prospects, that is reflected in table 6.2. It provides a stark contrast to the positive experience of Dhima.

Lewatachum is approximately 42 years old and his wife, Narapoch, is 30 years of age. They are both illiterate and neither received any schooling at all. The couple has four children, two boys and two girls, and all are under 17 years of age. Only one son aged 12 years is attending school. Even before the drought of 1999–2000, the family only owned two cattle and two sheep and both cattle died during the drought while the sheep survived. Three years after the drought ended they still had not been able to purchase or borrow any cattle but they had a herd of 2 goats and 5 sheep or the equivalent of less than one TLU (contrast this with Dhima's household herd of more than 230 TLU). Unlike other homesteads in the location, their household consists of a single thatched-roof circular hut with only a single, small thorn-fenced pen to keep their few animals. The physical appearance of a homestead can communicate much about the wealth of a local family, with the wealthiest families having multiple residential dwellings—one for each wife and her children—and large fenced holding areas for cattle and separate large pens for small stock. To survive, Lewatachum is a hired herder for one of the many wealthy absentee herd owners from the area, including the educated Il Chamus elite of Nairobi who were discussed in Chapter 5. They rely on cheap but skilled herders like Lewatachum to herd their local livestock, which can exceed 25 cattle and 250 small stock for the wealthiest urban-based owners. In return for his work, Lewatachum receives the equivalent of $0.40/per day and occasionally the bonus of a young sheep or goat kid. Remuneration is very minimal and thus his household is in the lowest quartile both in terms of cash and total income. Both he and Narapoch also pursue rain-fed farming on a farm of 1.2 hectare, but are only moderately successful two out of every five years. While it could not be confirmed, it is noted by others that Narapoch occasionally makes and sells local gin liquor, called *changaa*, to help the family meet living expenses. Her income from this activity could not be documented but the level of household expenditures and assets imply that it must be minimal. On different occasions when I visited Lewatachum, he clearly had consumed large amounts of changaa. Excessive alcohol consumption now is a major problem in the Il Chamus area. One important change that I observed during my intermittent visits during 1980 to 2008 is the replacement of low-alcohol beer (*busaa*) with potent changaa as the adult drink of choice. Excessive use of alcohol, which requires cash payments, is a further challenge that keeps sedentarized herders, such as Lewatachum, poor.

The case of Lewatachum, Narapoch, and their children exemplifies poverty among ex-pastoralists in northern Kenya and some of the low-income diversification strategies that they pursue. Unlike the earlier example of Dhima, in their case neither mobile pastoralism nor lucrative cash-earning options are possible. In effect, Lewatachum's household is trapped in poverty, in terms of both cash and livestock wealth.

What the data in table 6.2 do not reveal but is clearly apparent in the case of Lewatachum and his waged herding for absentee owners are patterns of inequality in northern Kenya. As noted earlier, recent poverty analyses in Kenya and elsewhere in Africa generally gloss over inequalities but, instead, focus only on the characteristics of poverty itself, using average or median incomes and other measurements. Indeed, discussions of wealth inequities usually are muted in many current analyses of poverty, including in Kenya, although these topics were widely addressed in the 1970s and 1980s (see Chilcote 1983; Leys 1974; Munoz 1981).[5] The large percentage of households in table 6.2, including Lewatachum's, that earn less than the wage for casual labor hints at the prevalence of inequality in northern Kenya.

Table 6.3 looks more carefully at patterns of inequality, especially the percentage of total income controlled by different strata of households. The findings generally show that inequities are higher where the dependence on cash incomes is large, especially reliance on salaried incomes with a reliable paycheck. For instance, across all six sites, 10 percent of households control 42 percent of pastoral/livestock-based income but 62 percent of cash incomes. An assessment of what

Table 6.3. Pastoral and Nonpastoral Income Distribution, Kenya, July 2000–
June 2001

% of households	All nonpastoral cash income (includes farming): % who control	All pastoral/ livestock income: % who control	Wage salary only: % who control[1]
Top 10%	62%	42%	93.44%
Top 20%	82%	63%	100%
Low 50%	2%	8%	0%

Source: Author analysis of Pastoral Risk Management (PARIMA) project data.
Notes: 1. Includes only April–June 2001.

proportion of income is controlled by the poorest 50 percent of households provides a better sense of how the poor fare vis-à-vis pastoral (livestock-based) and
strictly cash incomes. These households control a miserably low percentage (8%)
of pastoral incomes, but an even lower proportion (2%) of nonpastoral incomes.
In most of these cases, the poorest are ex-pastoralists or other nonpastoralists who
pursue petty trade, rain-fed farming (where possible), and casual labor, all activities that earn little cash income.

The presence of salaried income has the most dramatic effect on income inequality and it is highly sought out, although it benefits very few households in
the region. More than 90 percent of salaried income is controlled by only 10 percent of wage earners, which explains why the site that depends the most on salaried income, Logologo, also has the most unequal distribution of income. The
possibility of salaried employment is an important reason why pastoralist families invest in the education of their children, although the current availability of
salaried work in Kenya, even for those with secondary or postsecondary education, is very limited.

The example of Letikikon of Ngambo shows how important waged salary can
be for those few households who are fortunate enough to have educated members
in the work force.

Letikikon is an Il Chamus teacher from Ngambo, Kenya. He is 33 years old
and he lives with his wife, four small children, a niece, and his widowed
mother. He has taught at the primary school in Ngambo since the mid-1990s.
His salaried income places him in the top 15 percent of cash income earners in the study region and allows him to meet household expenses, as well
as provide occasional cash and food gifts to other relatives. While his father
practiced pastoralism, Letikikon relies little on livestock. Livestock-based in-

come accounts for less than 12 percent of his household's total income and per capita livestock holdings for the household are only 0.3 TLU, which is well below what would be considered viable for pastoralism (about 4–4.5 TLU per capita). Joshua's wife, who also graduated from a teacher's training college and is qualified to teach, does not work outside the household. Their household is now fully sedentary and rather than re-build and accumulate large numbers of livestock after the 2000 drought, he and his wife recently (2006) invested in low-cost rental properties in nearby Marigat town (based on McPeak et al. 2011). Joshua and his wife hope the revenues from rentals eventually will assist them with the education costs of their children, as well as permit additional investment in real estate.

Letikikon has moved away from a pastoralist livelihood but remains in the area and earns a relatively good income. Unlike the case of Dhima discussed earlier, his household is highly dependent on cash income, and because he has a relatively well-paying salaried position, cash income in this case is a good indicator of his household's welfare. Unfortunately, Letikikon represents a very small percentage (< 3%) of households with good salaried work.

There also are a small minority of households who earn relatively high incomes from both pastoral and nonpastoral income sources. Lelelo's household is a good example of this elite group.

> Lelelo lives in Logologo, Kenya. He is married with one wife and six children and had a herd of about 35 TLU in June 2000. Until December 1999 he worked outside of Logologo as a soldier and remitted income regularly to his household. At that time his animals were herded by his two older children and a son of his brother's with whom the household combined their animals. Beginning in 2000 he has received a pension from the government and this accounts for approximately 60 percent of the household's income. During 2000–2004 the household also earned income from food aid, livestock sales, and milk and meat production, with per capita incomes of these activities well above the average in the area (see Table 6.2). Lelelo and his household members do not intend to leave pastoralism and, in fact, since his retirement Lelelo has allocated much of his labor to livestock management. (Based on McPeak et al. 2011)

Similar to Letikikon, Lelelo received a regular monthly payment of cash, in this case from a government pension. However, unlike Letikikon, he continued to invest in pastoralism and pursue a mobile herding lifestyle. Lelelo's example illustrates a successful diversification strategy, but highly unusual in that he was one of only two individuals out of 180 households who received a government pension.

Improved Market Access and Location?

Mobile pastoralism requires space to take advantage of uneven patterns of rainfall and pasture productivity. In northern Kenya these conditions are most constrained near markets and towns, but favorable in relatively remote locations (see Little 1992a and 2003). Referring again to table 6.1, proximity to markets is poorly correlated with total income. In fact, the two sites with the highest overall incomes, Kargi and North Horr, have generally poor access to markets and towns. By contrast, both Ngambo and Suguta Marmar have very good access to markets and towns but, as pointed out earlier, considerably lower incomes than either Kargi or North Horr. This discrepancy occurs despite the fact that Ngambo and Suguta Marmar are the only sites with regularly scheduled livestock auctions, and they represent the two largest livestock markets in the study region. In both cases livestock traders are attracted to their markets from large parts of the Rift Valley and central provinces of Kenya. Nonetheless, average per capita incomes in Ngambo and Suguta Marmar are below some sites with poor market access, providing counterevidence to those who "focus excessively on the role that market forces can play in poverty-reduction" (Hulme and Shepherd 2003: 404). In short, the story from northern Kenya is one where mobile pastoralism must balance strategic searches for fodder and water in remote rangelands with the need to access town-based markets for selling animals and purchasing needed commodities (see Little et al. 2008).

Thus, the findings in table 6.2 challenge the common premise that geographic remoteness is an important cause of poverty in Africa (see Bird et al. 2002; Collier 2008). As was mentioned above, because the most productive rangelands often are in areas that are remote from market towns, geographic factors do not adequately explain patterns of poverty in pastoral areas (see Little et al. 2008). In fact, pastoral livelihoods seem to thrive in isolated areas where land-use competition is not severe, pastures and water are available, and population densities are generally low. The findings here also challenge a recent national assessment of poverty in Kenya that suggests geographic factors, such as distance to towns and health centers, are among the most important indicators of poverty (CBS 2003; Okwi et al. 2007). As was noted earlier, northeastern Kenya is a key location for Somali pastoralists but also the least urbanized in Kenya, with poor infrastructure and limited access to market towns.

Household Expenditures as an Indicator?

Cash expenditures also are frequently used in measurements of poverty, but are equally as problematic as cash incomes when assessing welfare among mobile pastoralists. This is for the simple reason that mobility, the key risk-management strategy of pastoralists, conflicts with excessive expenditures on housing, durable goods, and other large, costly consumer goods. Therefore, the motivation to spend cash for expensive but bulky consumer items is less than in sedentary communities.

The research findings from northern Kenya generally support this weak association between per capita cash expenditures and pastoralist welfare. For example, sedentary households in Ngambo have per capita expenditure levels that are higher than mobile households of Kargi, although the latter group is considerably wealthier. In communities like Kargi and North Horr, with relatively high levels of both livestock ownership and income, cash expenditures are relatively low when compared to other sites. This explains why households in North Horr, the site with the second largest per capita herds and incomes in the area, expends less cash on expenditures than households at any of the five other sites. Thus, like other market-based indicators, cash expenditures do not hold up very well as measures of welfare and poverty in northern Kenya.

Drought-Induced Poverty and Sedentarization

Many assessments of poverty in pastoral areas are influenced by drought episodes, even though their occurrences are a norm for the region. However, it mainly is during these disasters that global attention is focused on pastoral areas, often motivating actions that discourage mobile pastoralism and accusations that it is to blame for drought-induced hunger and poverty. Although drought has been a determining factor in the proliferation of poor stockless households—recall the case of Lewatachum—and the growth of impoverished settlements in the region, pastoralism is not the cause of drought-induced hardships. In the words of Little et al.: "In contrast to crises elsewhere, natural disasters in East Africa frequently spark calls for renewed efforts to transform—or even abandon—the area's prime livelihood system, mobile pastoralism based on nomadic or transhumant livestock production. . . . The problem is often perceived to be an outdated way of life ill-adapted to 'modern' contingencies" (2008: 588).

As was discussed earlier, an important means of coping with drought is to maximize herd growth. Evidence from northern Kenya confirms that the larger the herd size, the better the chances for recovery after a drought (McPeak and Gebru 2004). By contrast, households, such as Lewatachum's, with relatively small herds frequently are pushed permanently out of pastoralism during a serve drought and forced to seek alternative livelihoods in towns or farming areas.

A second and critically important means of coping with drought and its effects is mobility. When a drought strikes, herders move their animals to areas of available grazing and water. One herder of Kargi, Kenya, explains how he coped with the 1999–2000 drought by "migrating the animals from one watering point to another. . . . I left the wife and the children and migrated alone with the animals to the *fora* [herd camp]" (field notes, February 2002). Despite the critical role of mobility, most indicators of poverty discussed in the previous section assume a sedentary livelihood with strong interactions with market towns. As was argued earlier, herders avoid activities that constrain mobility and herd growth, which means minimizing interactions with fixed locations, such as market towns. Moreover, many development investments in dryland areas advocate irrigated agriculture and permanent settlements that discourage herder mobility. The contradictions between the livelihood strategies of mobile pastoralists, such as the Kargi herder mentioned above, and development policies that advocate pastoralist sedentarization are glaring.

To illustrate the importance of mobility, table 6.4 shows its effects on herd sizes during the 1999–2000 drought. The analysis employs two measures of mobility: (1) average number of water points used by herders and (2) the community's reliance on mobile herd camps.[6] The findings in the table are informative. For example, Kargi, which is the most mobile and wealthiest of the sites, experienced virtually no herd losses during the first quarter of 2000, when most drought-induced animal losses occurred. This outcome cannot be explained by variations in the drought itself, since rainfall amounts were very low at all sites and especially low at Kargi (see McPeak et al. 2011). In contrast to Kargi, the drought's effects were devastating at Ngambo and Dirib Gumbo, the two least-mobile communities in the study region. Households there incurred massive herd losses of 50 and 79 percent, respectively (see table 6.4). Not surprisingly, they also are the sites with the highest incidences of poverty and stocklessness (see table 6.2). Drought-induced losses at the other three sites ranged from 24 to 46 percent, and the results generally reflected the importance of mobility in the community. As will be shown later, despite its adaptive importance mobility is viewed by the state as an outdated practice, inefficient and even threatening to a country's security.

Government officials also attribute environmental degradation during droughts to herder practices. By this highlighting of ecological conditions when they are most strained during droughts, environmental degradation serves as another symbol of pastoralist poverty that calls for strong action. In northern Kenya the dual narratives of poverty and environmental degradation are coupled in many contemporary assessments of development in the region. Both problems often are blamed on pastoralism itself: degradation is viewed as the result of overstocking, outdated (communal) tenure institutions, and inefficient land-use practices, while pastoralism is assumed to be a cause of poverty. Like poverty itself, the identification of environmental degradation relies on tools that are inappropriate for tropical drylands, such as those typical of northern Kenya. In fact, there is a growing body of theory and empirical research that challenges the association of pas-

Table 6.4. Livestock Holdings and Drought-Induced Changes

Site	Avg per capita livestock (TLUs) (2000–2002)	% decline 0300 to 1200 (due to drought)	Avg # of water points used each quarter (2000–2001)	% of households relying on herd camps (2000–2001)	Mobility Ranking (1–6, with '1' highest)
Kargi	6.98	0	3.3	88%	1
North Horr	3.61	−24%	1.7	45%[1]	2
Logologo	2.49	−46%	2.0	81%	3
Suguta Marmar	1.14	−33%	1.3	28%	4
Dirib Gumbo	0.97	−79%	1.1	46%	5
Ngambo	0.64	−50%	1.5	1%	6

Source: Little et al. (2008: 599)

Notes: 1. A large majority (> 70 percent) of North Horr households migrated with their entire herds and families at least once during the period 1999–2000.

toralism and drought with environmental degradation, but the impact on policy of this body of work unfortunately has been minimal (Behnke et al. 1993; Home-wood 2008).

Consequences and Politics

The ways in which pastoralist poverty is perceived, identified, and measured undergird the design of policies and programs in northern Kenya and elsewhere in Africa. Near to Ngambo community, for example, the Kenyan government has embarked on several major irrigation investments, where the goal has been to transform the area into settled farming, as well as to encourage settled farming communities to colonize pastoral rangelands. Some of these projects date back to the 1950s, but more recent ones were funded in the 1990s and 2000s (see Little 1992a; Little et al. 2008). They disguise the blatant politics behind the interventions by highlighting the project's potential benefits for food security and poverty alleviation. Yet, irrigated agriculture in Ngambo and surrounding areas has done very little to alleviate food insecurity problems in the area, as table 6.2 suggests.

In other river basins of Kenya large parcels of land have been leased to foreign investment companies and governments. One such example is the Tana River valley, where in its lower portion 40,000 hectares already have been leased to the Kenyan Sugar Mumias Company to grow and process sugar cane, and commercial applications are currently under review or being implemented for leases of 40,000 hectares for a Qatar company to grow food crops; 70,000 hectares for a Canadian company to grow biofuels; and 50,000 hectares for a British company to produce oil seed (Nunow 2013). This same area of the Tana delta is critical dry-season grazing and water for Orma pastoralists, a Boran-speaking pastoralist community who live in the riverine area. Without access to the Tana valley's pastures and water points, it is highly unlikely that Orma will be able to sustain their pastoralist livelihood. Large-scale investments in the Tana River valley are supported by the Kenyan state as means to develop the country's irrigation potential and earn foreign exchange. To improve the productivity and profitability of the region's livestock sector, including the Orma's pastoralist economy, never was considered (ibid.).

To the north in Ethiopia, the politics of pastoralist policy is even more blatant than in Kenya. The government's official policy toward pastoralists states: "In the long-term, the government envisions a stable pastoral and agro pastoral community through the facilitation of gradual and voluntary transition towards permanent settlement especially along the perennial river banks" (Ethiopia 2008: 2). Moreover, in a speech on January 25, 2011, the Ethiopian head of state, the late prime minister Meles Zenawi, castigated those who support mobile pastoralism as a viable livelihood as "promoters of backwardness and poverty" who wish to keep pastoralists as tourist attractions. He then announced an ambitious program of irrigation investment in the Omo River valley of southwest Ethiopia that includes 150,000 hectares of sugar cane production by private and state investors (see *Mursi Online* 2011). Several pastoral and agro-pastoral groups live and depend on the Omo River and its annual flood and will be negatively impacted by the proposed investments in the valley (Turton 2010). Since many pastoralist communities in Ethiopia have struggled with successive Ethiopian governments dating back to the imperial government (pre-1974), it is hardly surprising that the state would want to settle, transform, and control populations that they perceive as troublesome citizens. The multiple goals of poverty alleviation, improved food security, and environmental management are convenient and seemingly noble screens for promoting political agendas that actually undermine pastoralist livelihoods.

The Kenyan state has a more progressive approach toward pastoralist development and rights than Ethiopia or some of its other neighbors (for example, Uganda), but as shown in the Ngambo and Tana River cases, it also has done little to protect pastoral resources from outside interests and from nonpastoral uses. In addition, the Kenyan government occasionally still pursues aggressive militarist interventions against pastoralists of northern Kenya that often result in losses of both human life and livestock. As recent as 2007, the Kenyan government forcefully evicted Samburu herders out of Laikipia District, which resulted in the death of several Samburu (see Straight 2009). Less blatant but equally pernicious is the unwillingness of the Kenyan government to protect the lands of pastoralists from tourist, commercial agriculture, and wildlife conservation interests—the latter being a type of "green" land grab (see discussion in chapter 3). These losses undermine pastoralist mobility as well as aggravate the negative effects of droughts and other hardships. Moreover, at present the Kenyan government has several additional planned irrigation investments in the Tana and Uaso Nyiro river basins, both critical dry-season grazing areas for pastoralists of northern and northeastern Kenya, which will effectively eliminate seasonal mobility for many local pastoralists (see Nunow 2013). To date, large parts of critical river and lake basins and highland grazing zones throughout northern Kenya have been lost for pastoral use, and this already undermines the viability of pastoralism in the region.

When attached to pastoralism, the poverty label does little to alleviate the real problems that pastoralists face, such as a lack of basic social services and infrastructure. Instead, it provides an implicit justification to invest in nonpastoral livelihoods and activities in these areas rather than trying to strengthen pastoral livelihoods. These activities, in turn, have contributed to a self-fulfilling prophecy by removing critical lands and resources needed for mobile pastoralism and, in the end, facilitating the poverty and hunger that they originally sought to eliminate. The Kenyan government, like other states in East Africa, remains threatened by mobile pastoralism and, as noted earlier, periodically takes punitive actions against pastoral communities under the guise of improving local security and eliminating livestock raids. As a livelihood, it also is seen as poorly compatible with free market orthodoxy and a constraint to more profitable investments (for example, in tourism and irrigation) that are perceived to be more conducive to economic growth and modernization. Although there is a growing body of literature that counters the economic arguments against pastoralism by showing its significant regional and national economic contributions (see Behnke 2011; Hatfield and Davies 2006; and McPeak et al. 2011), these counternarratives have had limited impact on unreceptive policy makers. Classifying pastoral regions as impoverished and backward allows the government to implement programs, such as settled irrigation and environmental conservation (chapter 3), that undermine mobile pastoralism, food security, and livestock wealth but incorporate pastoralists into, and under the control of, the modern state. These latter outcomes are the ultimate goals that governments are pursuing.

Summary

This chapter has shown how the politics of anti-pastoralism are disguised through technical analyses of poverty and environmental problems that can disempower pastoralist communities.[7] Because pastoralists usually fare poorly vis-à-vis standard economic measurements, they continue to be labeled among the poorest subpopulations on the continent. The politics associated with labeling pastoralists as very poor justifies the actions that African governments take under poverty and food security programs. The recent concern with insecurity and terrorism in remote border areas of northern and northeastern Kenya, especially along the Kenya/Somalia border, only complicates problems for pastoralists and empowers those who want to settle them regardless of the effects on security and the high social, economic, and environmental costs associated with such actions. As the next chapter will show, neoliberal policies of free trade and open markets are challenged by security mandates to increase border controls in the Horn of Africa and restrict movements of people, including pastoralists and goods. Despite their pariah status among the international community, the region's Somali business community ironically has benefited from the neoliberal reforms of neighboring countries, which have helped their trading networks to expand and stateless Somalia to become a "duty free" trade enclave.

7 "A Sort of Free Business"
Hyper-liberalization and Somali Transnationalism

In JANUARY 2011 Somalia attained the unenviable status of being twenty years without a real central government, the longest period of statelessness in the post–World War I era. Less than a year earlier (July 1, 2010) the territory had marked fifty years of independence from colonial administration, an event that might have been a cause for celebration in most former colonies but was hardly noticed by local and international observers and media. Instead, what has brought renewed international attention to the country is the pesky presence of pirates off Somalia's coast and suspected terrorists on its lands.[1] Indeed, Somalia and Somalis, including those in the growing diaspora, have suffered more than most Africans from stereotypes, poorly informed analyses, and the ravages of opportunistic criminals.

Notwithstanding these recent concerns as well as gripping humanitarian issues in the country, Somalia represents a particularly compelling case of what might be called hyper-liberalization, a stateless economy with no formal market regulations and a relatively duty-free trade milieu. One Somali trader explained that despite the presence of militia-controlled check posts and other impediments, "it is a sort of free business" (field notes, July 1998). A country where pastoralism is a key livelihood, it is the cheapest locale in East Africa to place an international phone call or transfer money and has among the highest percentage of mobile phone subscribers in the region (Hesse 2010). Without the presence of the IMF and World Bank, an economic plan, or government, it has attained some of the free market goals of structural adjustment programs (SAPs) that have confounded many other African countries, including those discussed in earlier chapters. Of course, what economic advances have been made in Somalia have occurred with significant human and other horrific costs.

Where does one categorize Somalia in the context of economic reform and restructuring in Africa? How have Somali business networks and Somalia itself been able to take advantage of opportunities afforded by globalization and pro-trade policy reforms? What is it about the Somalia case that is unique, and what is it that is comparable to other parts of Africa?

This chapter tries to answer these questions by arguing that the timely convergence of state collapse in Somalia and neoliberal economic reforms in eastern Africa re-territorialized the Somali economy and promoted an intricate web of trading and financial networks throughout the region and beyond.[2] This re-territorialization of the Somali economy beyond its national borders will be discussed from three related and important vantage points. The first is from the optic of the town of Garissa, Kenya, the key center in northeastern Kenya for investment and cross-border trade, especially in livestock, between nearby Somalia and Kenya (see map 5.1, chapter 5). The latter activity represents a form of export-oriented commerce that while large in economic scope (> $20 million annually in most recent years, Little 2008b) is virtually invisible in Kenya's official statistics. The second is from the perspective of Eastleigh, Nairobi, the vibrant business district of Nairobi that houses many Somali-owned businesses and is economically linked with both regional cross-border trade and international trade and capital. Dubai, the trade and financial capital of the Middle East that serves large parts of eastern Africa, represents the third vantage point. This modern bastion of global capitalism is where many Somali-owned businesses are located and where Eastleigh and regional Somali merchants often source their goods.

From a spatial perspective the three locales of Somali economic activity embody a complex web of finance, remittance, human, and trade flows that traverses national borders and governments. Eastleigh represents the southern hub of the web and Dubai the northern node. Garissa and its nearby borderlands are in between but strongly linked to both centers of commerce (Eastleigh and Dubai). Each of the three locales reflects different but related aspects of Somali transnationalism and each has benefited from the region's neoliberal reforms, even though Somalia itself has been without a government and especially conflict-ridden since 2006. In fact, it is possible that Somali merchants and networks have benefited more from recent economic reforms than other regional businesses. Could stateless Somalia's transnational trading networks actually have been among the "winners" in sub-Saharan Africa during the reform era of the past three decades? The chapter tries to answer this and other questions.

Macro-economic and Institutional Contexts

Even before the state collapsed in 1991, Somalia had an economy where much economic activity was unofficial and where the formal economy represented very little of real economic life (see Little 2003). Unlike the parallel economy of Maputo, Mozambique, discussed in chapter 1, the Somali economy already was strongly "off the books" (unofficial) in the 1980s. It had been the recipient of an IMF/World Bank–imposed reform package in the 1980s that reduced government expenditures and public sector salaries, which forced many government employees to take on additional work in the informal sector just to survive (Samatar 2007). During that time unofficial trade (including illegal exports of ivory), livestock exports, unrecorded pastoral production and exchange, and remittances from Somalis working abroad in the Middle East accounted for the bulk of domestic economic value. The Somali state maintained control of most key industries and economic activities, including banking and the livestock export trade, but the real economy was out of its limits.

The collapse of the Somali state in 1991 coincided with market reform programs in neighboring Kenya, where more than 300,000 Somali refugees fled during 1991–93 (Campbell 2006). The vast majority of, but not all, the refugees were poor, and many of the better-off individuals ended up in cities, especially Nairobi. Some were wealthy businessmen from Somalia's cities, especially Mogadishu, with capital and strong business networks. They often ended up in Eastleigh, a bustling business and residential section of Nairobi. Kenyan reforms, such as reduced trade barriers and liberalized foreign exchange markets, were especially beneficial to the Somali community. The changes fueled a massive growth in the informal sector ("second economy") and rewarded those, such as Somalis, with strong trading networks and capital.[3] As Campbell points out, "Trade liberalization in Kenya coincided with the influx of Somali refugees in the early 1990s, offering them an edge in already established yet more covert business transactions. With their businesses deeply entrenched in the informal economy in Eastleigh, they benefited from trade liberalization because they were able to move goods across the borders more easily and sell them openly (ibid.: 403)." In short, those with capital and informal businesses were able to take advantage of Kenya's neoliberal reform program, and the Somali business community fit this bill.

Somalia had no internationally recognized government throughout the 1990s and much of the 2000s, but it was not completely off the radar of multilateral development organizations during this period, including the World Bank and United Nations Development Programme (UNDP). The fact that the Somali economy had not completely died off, but instead had experienced growth in certain service and trade sectors, could not be denied by the international community. In fact, until the political turmoil and destructive civil war that tragically erupted again in 2006, the World Bank had planned an economic mission to the country supported by an economic development strategy (see World Bank 2005b).[4] In 2003 Somalia was admitted by the World Bank and UNDP to the LICUS (Least Developed Country and Low-Income Country) group for some of the world's poorest and most conflict-ridden countries, and their staff had begun to seriously reengage with Somalia (Ruggieri 2006; World Bank 2003).[5] By 2005 these two international organizations had made a visit to Dubai to speak to key Somali businessmen about Somalia's political and economic rehabilitation. As will be discussed later in the chapter, many Somali businessmen and businesses, including airline companies and financial services, have operated from Dubai since the state's implosion. Enough economic and political stability had been reached by 2004–2005 that international plans for development assistance, rather than just humanitarian aid, were envisioned for the country. In 2005 the Mogadishu-based Union of Islamic Courts (UIC) movement, in conjunction with the business sector who frequently hired them for security purposes, had brought a degree of peace to Mogadishu and even reopened the main Mogadishu port, which had been closed for more than ten years.

As has been well documented elsewhere, this all changed when the U.S. government supported an alliance of very unpopular warlords, the Alliance for the Restoration of Peace and Counter-Terrorism (ARPCT), against the UIC in 2006 and then later that year provided the green light for an Ethiopian invasion of Somalia (see Marchal 2009; Menkhaus 2007). Both events contributed to a violent eruption of an already difficult situation. The tipping point occurred in 2006 following the U.S.-approved invasion by Ethiopia, which resulted in strong resistance by local communities, changes in local political alliances, and massive conflict and population displacement. This unfortunate event hastened the spread of a militant Islamist youth insurgency, Al-Shabaab, that now controls large parts of southern Somalia and is noted to have ties to international terrorist networks, including Al-Qaeda with its foreign jihadists in the country (see Le Sage 2010). Since the withdrawal of Ethiopian troops in 2008, Mogadishu has been occupied by a small force of African Union (AU) troops to help the Transitional Federal Government (TFG) maintain sovereignty over the small part of the city and country that the TFG controls. Economic activities go on in the country, but there has been massive social upheaval, a new exodus of Somalis leaving the country, and widespread human suffering and rights abuse. Later in the chapter the topic of Somalia's current political and war situations will be addressed in more detail.

Despite failing to reestablish a central government, Somalia had some success in reestablishing a national monetary union and market system after the state's implosion.[6] These have formed an important enabling environment for international trade, including along its borders with neighboring countries, and partially ameliorated what would have been an even greater humanitarian crisis in the area (see Little 2008b). According to Marchal, there initially was so much conflict and poor communications between different regions of the country in 1991–92 that wide discrepancies in exchange rates and prices existed (2002: 28–29). However, by early 1993 a national monetary market based on the Somali shilling and supplemented by aid and remittance-based U.S. dollars had been reestablished, helping to restore confidence in the market and currency. Somali traders involved with regional cross-border trade claim their businesses were aided by the continued convertibility of the Somali shilling (field notes, June 2001).

Informal Finance and Telecommunications

An important reason why the country has been able to maintain a national monetary system is the dynamic and competitive nature of the informal finance system. Its presence and effects are widespread in Eastleigh (Nairobi), Garissa (including the Somalia borderlands), and Dubai. Although already in place prior to 1991, these informal money transfer companies grew rapidly in the 1990s and 2000s. They are referred to as *Hawalidaad* (or more commonly *hawala*—Arabic for "transfer") and are used by individuals, traders, and businesses to receive remittance income from the 1+ million Somalis living outside the country, as well as to transfer money throughout the country, the East African region, and the world. These informal finance enterprises operate with incredible efficiency, a point that has been noted by many observers (Lindley 2009), and they annually transfer into the country up to an estimated $1 billion in remittances from the diaspora (Lindley 2010). What they also do is to help integrate the national monetary system and maintain exchange rate stability within and between different regions and towns. This enormous injection of dollars into the country shores up the value of the Somali shilling and supplements the incomes of thousands of poor and food-insecure Somali households.

This institutional innovation in finance has been developed in tandem with an increasingly sophisticated network of telecommunications, including mobile phone networks and Internet services. The growth of the telecommunication sector in Somalia was strongly influenced by the need to facilitate financial transactions in the remittance and trade sectors. In fact, many of the larger money transfer companies also have considerable investments in the telecommunication system since it requires these technologies to operate efficiently (see Little 2003). Again, this development has helped to better integrate currency markets in the country and improve market information, as well as commodity markets generally. Thus, a secondary outcome of the country's growth in money transfer companies has been an increase in communication technologies and, consequently, an easier platform to maintain business networks and transactions both in the region and around the world.

Commerce

Another macro development in southern Somalia and its borderlands has been the rapid growth in the commercial trade sector since 1991. Somalia has effectively become an entrepôt economy for large parts of the Horn of Africa (Eritrea, Sudan, Ethiopia, and Kenya), taking advantage of its geography (i.e., proximity to the Middle East and especially Dubai) and its stateless, unregulated environment. It imports duty free rice, sugar, electronics, textiles, and other goods, which are then re-exported through southern Somalia's large and porous borders into neighboring Kenya (primarily) and Ethiopia (secondarily) with few if any border taxes—albeit there are transit fees that are charged to move goods across different militia-controlled borders. Few Somali experts would argue that trade and certain segments of the private sector have not done reasonably well since the collapse of the government. In fact, available data indicate that the values of exports and imports were actually higher in the mid-2000s than in 1990 before the state collapsed (World Bank 2005b).

The commercial trade sector of Somalia generally has shown steady growth and resilience. To quote Hagmann, Somalia effectively has become the world's "largest duty free port" (2005: 535). Trucks with consumer goods and foods move between the different regions and travel to countries as distant as Democratic Republic of Congo (DRC), even when there are ongoing conflicts. This large growth in trade-based activities, including an increased import business with Dubai, has helped to integrate markets and keep supply chains operating much better than one would expect given the area's amount of conflict (see Little 2008b).

As indicated earlier, Somali business activities across the Horn of Africa already operated at the margins of the state, so neoliberal reforms in neighboring countries actually made it easier to trade and conduct business. The reduced presence of the state in neighboring economies, especially in Kenya, and the elimination of tariff and other trade barriers allowed informal traders to operate more openly. The border economies of Somalia increasingly became globalized, with links throughout the Horn and beyond, and the borders themselves became opportunities for accumulation and survival. Free trade and borderless economies nicely fit the discourse of neoliberal economic policies, at least until the fear of international terrorism emerged. Concerns about terrorism led neighboring states and the international community generally to rethink border policies with Somalia. For example, the Kenyan state, which historically has had very porous borders with Somalia, closed its borders in 2009 because of fears of terrorist-linked militias in the country, only to reopen them to trade within two months (Chau 2010). As will be shown later in the chapter, cross-border trade confronted greater constraints following the invasion of southern Somalia by the Kenyan army in October 2011.

Garissa Town and the Cross-Border Trade

Just across the border in northeastern Kenya is Garissa town, the designated "capital" of Kenya's Somali region and the center for cross-border trade with stateless Somalia. On the other side of the border is the Lower Jubba Region, a former administrative unit of southern Somalia that straddles the Kenya border and is bounded on the east by the Jubba River and on the south by the Indian Ocean and Kismayo, a key city and port. The concentration of cattle in the Lower Jubba Region is the highest in Somalia, which explains why the Garissa market is Kenya's largest cattle market outside Nairobi (see Little 2003). Because of its livestock resources, including large herds of camels and goats, and configuration of Somali clans and subclans along both sides of the border, the Lower Jubba has always been well integrated with northeastern Kenya and Garissa.

Contrary to common assumptions about the region's steep decline after 1991, the pastoral and commerce sectors of southern Somalia have done surprisingly well in a stateless environment. The beneficiaries increasingly include women who have been able to engage in a growing commerce along Somalia's borders and with Dubai (see Umar 2007; Kantai 2009). With inconsistent and minimal international assistance, there were few options for Somali women and men but to develop a "second economy" based on cross-border trade and smuggling, informal finances, and a global system of remittances that until the mid-2000s allowed the territory to maintain a level of economic and social welfare comparable to some of its neighbors (see Little 2003). With the collapse of the state, some traders were able to redirect business to the growing cross-border commerce with Kenya, while others who were more dependent on alternative livelihoods (for example, rain-fed agriculture) suffered terribly (see Besteman 1999).

As was noted earlier, market liberalization began in Kenya in the early 1990s and, importantly, for the cattle-rich borderlands it included the liberalization of meat processing and trade. The government marketing authority, the Livestock Marketing Department (LMD), which was charged with controlling trade in the pastoral areas, was dismantled, as were many of the state-owned holding grounds for marketing. From 1989 to 2002, cattle sold annually at Garissa market increased from about 24,500 to more than 130,000. These figures do not include unofficial transactions that took place outside the formal market away from tax collectors and veterinary officers, which would have made the numbers considerably higher (Gedi et al. 2008). By the early 2000s, the pastoralist areas of stateless Somalia were supplying more than 65 percent of the cattle sold at Garissa market and about 16 percent of the beef consumed in Nairobi, Kenya, a city of 3.5+ million people (Little 2003). Not surprisingly, the vast growth in informal exports to Kenya kept urban meat prices in Nairobi relatively low and stable during 1996–2005.

With the collapse of the Somalia state, the population of Garissa rapidly grew due to the immigration of Somalis and the town's growing economy and business opportunities. Between 1999 and 2009 it grew from a population of 65,881 to an estimated 155,765, an increase of more than 110 percent (Kenya 2010b; Arid Lands Resource Management Project /Price Waterhouse Coopers 2005).[7] Based on the 2009 census Garissa, a one-time remote backwater of Kenya, is the fastest growing city in the country (Kenya 2010b).

The growth in Garissa's population and its commercial activities also relates to its key role in the livestock trade with Somalia. An examination of the town's business sector supports this observation and demonstrates its strong ties

Figure 7.1. Urban expansion in Garissa, northeastern Kenya. Photo by author.

Figure 7.2. Garissa livestock market, northeastern Kenya. Photo by author.

to regional livestock trade. Many Garissa business owners first started in live-stock trade and then used the profits to invest in other activities. And many still maintain an active engagement in some aspect of the livestock business. For ex-ample, Abdinoor, the owner of one of the largest hotels in Garissa, used profits from livestock trade to finance the establishment's construction. Despite his hotel and other investments, including in the Eastleigh neighborhood of Nairobi, he remained active in livestock trade during the 2000s (field notes, June 2001 and September 2008). Abdullah, another prominent businessman and hotel owner in Garissa town, also amassed his initial capital through livestock trade and trans-port, and he also has investments and businesses in Eastleigh (field notes, Septem-ber 2008). Although it is difficult to estimate the number of businesses in Garissa owned by members of the Somali diaspora itself, it is widely acknowledged that many traders who left southern Somalia in 1991 and 1992 established businesses in Garissa town. "This whole section [of wholesalers] in town did not exist before the Somalis came," remarked Mohamed, an Arab trader whose family has resided in Garissa since colonial times (field notes, June 2001). Following the turmoil of 2006 there was another wave of merchants from southern Somalia who moved to Kenya, including to Garissa, to avoid the conflict back home.[8] The movement of traders from southern Somalia to Garissa facilitates cross-border trade, because these merchants often maintain their market linkages to suppliers in Somalia. In addition to livestock, other products imported through southern Somalia, such as rice, pasta, sugar, and electronics, find their way into Garissa's retail sector.

Evidence of the importance of livestock and cross-border trade in Garissa also is glaringly apparent whenever cross-border trade is halted. For example, most merchants made it very clear to me that their businesses suffer terribly dur-ing the occasional border closures, which can occur with little warning (field notes, September 2008). In fact, it was reported that an estimated one hundred Kenyan merchants were trapped inside Somalia once when the border was closed in 1999, a strong indication of the area's dependence on transborder trade (*Africa News Service* 1999).

A new development that has occurred in the cross-border livestock trade since 2005 is the supply of immature livestock to Somali-leased or Somali-owned ranches in the Voi area of southeastern Kenya, near Mombasa. With pressure from the World Bank and other funders to reduce subsidies to cooperative- and company-owned ranching units, the Kenyan government withdrew financial and other support to cooperatives and ranches. Lacking financial viability, a number of them subsequently were leased to Somali traders, who used them to fatten ani-mals for the Mombasa and export markets (see Mahmoud 2006). A number of these cattle ranches originally were started as cooperatives in the 1970s under a World Bank–financed national livestock development program, but most failed and were taken over by the state or sold to private individuals. A fenced-off area of the busy Garissa market is now used by the veterinary department to inspect and clear young (mainly male) immature cattle from Somalia destined to coastal ranches (field notes, February 2011). One of the largest cattle traders in Garissa town, who even keeps a buying agent in southern Somalia, is the owner of one of these ranches.

These "Somali traders-cum-ranchers," to use Mahmoud's term (2006), also benefited from the state's push to increase exports and foreign exchange earnings. Because they were using the ranches to fatten animals for export from Mombasa port, the state encouraged their activities and provided extension and technical support to them. During 2008 four thousand cattle were exported to Mauritius from Mombasa, and most of these were fattened on coastal ranches operated by Somali traders (Aklilu and Catley 2009: 21).

In a study of these ranches Mahmoud (2006) discusses how many of their animals are sourced from southern Somalia:

> In September 2004, I met a trader in Garissa, who had brought 170 head of cattle from Bardhere, southern Somalia, and sold all of them to a single trader for Kenya Shillings (KSh) 12,000 each (about US$150). The buyer was a Somali TCR [trader-cum-rancher] in Taita Taveta District. Another trader whom I met in Mariakani [near Mombasa] was expecting to purchase 2,100 head of cattle from the Mogadishu area of southern Somalia. The animals were to be trekked to ranches in Taita Taveta and Kwale Districts for fattening. (133)

More recent observations of the Garissa market reveal that this trade from southern Somalia to ranches near the Kenyan coast remains very strong (field notes, September 2008 and February 2011).

The growth in the private meat processing sector in Mombasa that followed the liberalization of the Kenyan meat market in the early 1990s also has aided Somali traders/ranchers. They fatten their animals on leased government or co-operative ranches and supply the private abattoirs and exporters near Mombasa. At least one of these traders, who also owns a large hotel in Garissa town, has established his own abattoir outside Mombasa with an investment of about US $900,000 (personal communication, Hussein Mahmoud). Like the animals destined for overseas export, most of these livestock also come from southern Somalia through elaborate trade networks, demonstrating again how Somalia's borderlands have benefited from trade liberalization policies in Kenya.

In terms of the importance of southern Somalia for the Garissa livestock market, it has grown in significance since the late 1990s, in part because Garissa District's own livestock herds have been damaged by recent droughts and disease outbreaks. They need the Somali animals to restock Kenyan herds. The Kenyan market particularly favors the Daura breed of cattle from southern Somalia, which is a local cross between the Boran and local Somali breeds (also see

Negassa et al. 2008; field notes, February 2011). The Boran breed is especially favored in both domestic and international markets because of their body structure and capacity to quickly gain weight with additional feed and fodder. As a result of increased livestock trade, the number of traders and businesses operating at or near the Garissa market has increased considerably during the past fifteen years (field notes, September 2008). On a weekly market day in late September 2008, more than one hundred livestock traders or brokers (*dilaal*) and more than one hundred different vendors (mainly women) were present selling everything from bottled water and khat (the popular narcotic plant) to cell phone cards and Somali music CDs. Additionally, there were more than thirty trucks waiting to transport cattle to their market destinations, when there might have been twelve to fifteen trucks on a very good market day in 1996–98 (see Little 2003). According to the municipal council representative whom I interviewed in 2008, "the market alone nets 1.2 million Ksh [US$17,150] per month for the council's coffers, which covers most of the monthly salaries for council employees. It is the single most important revenue generator for the town" (field notes, September 2008). Is it surprising then that the town municipality is fighting to keep the market in the city even though urban expansion surrounds it and there is great pressure to move it outside the municipality's jurisdiction? The latter action would increase the income stream of the Garissa District government, but reduce market revenues for the town municipality by about 65 percent (field notes, February 2011).

On the other side of the border numerous consumer products from Dubai are imported through Somali ports and find their way to Garissa and other Kenyan markets via transit points, such as Mandera (300 km north of Garissa) and Libooye, Kenya (140 km east of Garissa). As many Kenyans will acknowledge, the country's cheapest prices for sugar, fuel, and consumer electronics (televisions, stereos, and satellite dishes) are found in Kenyan towns near the Somalia border. In one recent news account, for example, it was reported that Mandera town depends so much on cheap imports smuggled in from Somalia that "many Mandera residents say they cannot survive without their neighbours" (Karanja and Huka 2011: 1). Large-scale traders in Somalia have partners in Eastleigh and Dubai to facilitate cross-border trade at Mandera and at other centers in the region. Discussions with traders and NGO personnel reveal that while this commerce is very important, it also suffers from banditry and, similar to the livestock trade, from sporadic border closures. The occasional government confiscation and impoundment of a truck in Kenya laden with goods from Somalia attests to the significance of this trade (*[The Nairobi] People* 2001: 3; Karanja and Huka 2011).

During the 1970s and 1980s, the Somali state's blinkered focus on overseas export markets and its investments in water and transport infrastructure to support the trade had important consequences for transborder commerce. For many Somali pastoralists, the state was nothing more than an additional source of risk in an environment that already contained many hazards and problems. Herders simply resisted the prescribed market options, which were reinforced through state investments in market and animal trekking routes, water infrastructure, and a ban on informal exports to Kenya. The actions by the government were an attempt to force animals into the export trade based out of Kismayo and Mogadishu ports. The government desired the foreign exchange that could be earned from this trade. Thus, the Somali state, with support from bilateral and international donors, pursued a strategy that encouraged overseas exports of livestock and investments in modern market infrastructure, while discouraging exports to neighboring countries and domestic trade. Despite a marked decline in cattle exports from Somalia during 1985–89, large-scale market infrastructure projects involving millions of dollars of foreign aid were being constructed in Mogadishu and Kismayo up until the end of 1990, when rebel forces were advancing on these cities (see Little 2003).

In the post-1991 period, pastoralists and traders of the border areas who relied on unofficial trade with Kenya weathered the initial era of statelessness better than other groups. Rather than pursue official livestock exports through government channels, they sold their animals across the border to the Garissa market. On paper this activity also was considered illegal by the Kenyan state, but the administration did little to control it. Kenyan businesses and consumers, as well as the government, which derives market taxes from it, simply benefit too much from the trade. Although the official border between Kenya and Somalia has been closed to most trade and population movements since 2008 due to increases in terrorist threats and insecurity, the cross-border livestock trade continues. As one Kenyan civil servant remarked in a recent interview, "the Kenyan government never has wanted to stop the Somali livestock trade and we still favor it" (field notes, February 2011).

Jama, a merchant who resisted official government controls on livestock trade during the 1980s, is an example of a trader who has benefited from the collapse of the Somali state and the subsequent growth in informal cross-border trade.

Jama was 40 years old in 1988, and his trading activities were based in Afmadow, Somalia about 110 km from Kenya. At the time he sold animals for Somalia's domestic markets of Kismayo and Mogadishu and for the Garissa market in Kenya. He had never bought animals for the overseas export trade. He worked with three other middlemen based in the Afmadow area and with traders based in Kenya and Mogadishu. He had been active in livestock trade since 1977, focusing first on camels that he brought in from Kenya. When the unofficial cattle trade to Kenya became lucrative in the mid-1980s, he was ideally located. His sales to Kenya grew steadily and eventually he became one of the largest traders in Afmadow. He and his associates frequently bought directly from nomads along the Kenya border and sold to traders on the Kenya side. Like so many other traders and herders in the area, Jama simply resisted the push to sell animals to overseas markets and, instead, trekked his animals across to Kenya to sell at higher prices there. When the state collapsed, he continued to engage in cross-border trade at least through 1998.

Although the transborder trade remains very important in the region, there have been changes to it. One development worker who works in southern Somalia notes that the presence of the Al-Shabaab militia has altered the clan-based relations of the trade and eliminated clan-based transit fees. However, they have introduced other kinds of fees on the trade (also see Mahmoud 2010). I quote from the interview:

> It is now easier to move goods in the region because the militias and the road taxes have been removed. The livestock trade continues and Afmadow, Somalia, is still an important cattle area and market. Animals are still moving to Kenya. They must now pay *Zakat* taxes—the militia take a certain number of animals from the herd so they can be distributed to the poor. That is how they tax the traders and large herders. Last month I saw about 2,000 animals collected through *Zakat* and then redistributed to the poor in Lower Shebelli [Somalia]. The Zakat tax can be as much as 2–3 percent of the trader's herds or cash earnings, and it is resented by most. (Field notes, February 2011)[9]

Another Somali trader, whom I interviewed underneath a dilapidated metal roof at the Garissa market, also remarked that "now there are no clan-based/ warlord transit taxes for people moving animals between different territories. Islam now provides the common identity for traders not the different clans" (interview, February 17, 2011). Here again we see that the reduction in the costs of trading through the elimination of clan-based militias and their taxes is viewed as a positive development. The interviewee works in the livestock business with his father and brother, with the sibling based in Dinsoor, Somalia, about 350 kilometers from Garissa. In Somalia the brother acts as a buyer for the family business and concentrates on procuring the prized Daura breed of Somali cattle, which as noted earlier fetches a premium price on the Kenyan market, and immature bulls for the family ranch near the Kenya coast. He has money wired to him in Somalia through the hawala system, so he can purchase the animals. The family trading operation is very large. They own trucks for transporting livestock and have businesses in Garissa and Mombasa, including a ranch about 80 kilometers outside the coastal city. During the Barre period, the father would buy cattle for export, and he had a pass that allowed animals to be exported from Kismayo port, but many times he would take the animals across the border to sell at Garissa. He has been trading in southern Somalia since the 1970s. At the time of the interview, the family business had just purchased cattle from Dinsoor and Kismayo, and the animals were being trekked from the Somalia border to Garissa. Since it was so dry in February 2011 and cattle were in very poor condition, they were forced to buy fodder (grass) and water and hire a truck to transport the provisions more than 45 kilometers to the herd. Even with this very costly strategy, it is likely some of their livestock died. Of course, only a large and wealthy trading enterprise, such as the one described here, can afford the expense of trucking water (at a cost of about $320 per water tanker) and fodder ($100 per truck) to their animals.

In contrast to the 1980s and 1990s, it now is common for a livestock trader, such as any of those discussed above, to receive price quotes by mobile phone and to adjust marketing strategies accordingly. Traders who trek animals long distances to border markets often are forced to sell quickly or, as was shown in the case of the Garissa family of traders, spend considerable cash on feed and water. Without adequate holding grounds at Garissa or even at Nairobi, they must time their sales just right or expend considerable cash on provisions. If not, they must watch their animals lose weight and market value while waiting to sell them. Under these risky conditions, the use of mobile phones is essential for obtaining marketing and production information, but their use mainly is near large settlements where cell phone coverage is good.

Not surprisingly, kinship and clan-based relations are prevalent in the cross-border trade, as well as in international trade and remittance networks. As in other parts of the world, they aid traders in gaining access to markets, finance, and information during periods of both boom and bust. Somali traders and transporters are found throughout East Africa and into central Africa, the Middle East, Europe, and the United States, and these networks have grown in significance with the implosion of the Somali state. Therefore, although a pan-Somalia state probably is more unrealistic now than at any point during the past fifty years, a "greater Somalia" based on trade, finance, and migration largely has been achieved.

Eastleigh, an Openly Illegal Economy

Recent newspaper accounts claim that Somalis have come to dominate lucrative parts of the Kenyan economy and may soon own a large segment of the high-valued real estate in Nairobi (Kantai 2009 and 2011). These stories clearly are hyperbole, but nonetheless the impressive growth in Somali business activity and investment in Kenya is a noticeable irritation to Kenya's entrenched elite. Much of it is centered on real estate and businesses in Nairobi's Eastleigh neighborhood. Eastleigh is a dilapidated urban district with poor roads, miserable security, and few government services, but it houses a vibrant commercial sector with several modern shopping malls and hotels. Abdulsamed, for example, describes one recent Eastleigh mall as "sophisticated" with shops of high-quality clothing, electronic goods, and other retail products on one floor and a clinic, money transfer companies, and travel agencies on another (2011: 7). Initially Eastleigh was an

Asian business and residential area in the 1940s and 1950s, but it became a center for Ethiopian refugees in the 1970s following the collapse of the Haile Selassie regime, and for Somali and other East African refugees in the 1990s and 2000s. Asian Kenyans began to move out of this part of town after independence in 1963.

Eastleigh is now the East African hub of Somali trade and capital, a global space where one can buy anything from designer clothes and shoes to the latest consumer electronics and communication technologies (see Abdulsamed 2011; Campbell 2006). Sophisticated weapons, such as the ubiquitous Kalashnikov (AK-47), also are found there for both purchase and rent. Recently, several successful Eastleigh merchants have expanded into the more prosperous central business district of Nairobi. Somali entrepreneurs often quickly turn over their inventories by offering prices well below those of other retailers in town, including well-established Asian-owned businesses. Their concern is more with rapid turnover and volume than with profit per item sold (personal communication, Hussein A. Mahmoud). The shopping area of Eastleigh, which is widely noted to have the busiest commercial street in Nairobi, attracts middle-class shoppers from around the city and other parts of Kenya. They come to shop for upscale brands of fashion, electronics, and other consumer items at steep discounts. On a much smaller scale, similar shopping scenarios play out in border towns, such as Garissa and Mandera, where duty free goods imported from Somalia are widely found.

Eastleigh's links to Garissa are pronounced, with considerable movements of goods, finances, and people between the two areas. Multiple daily bus connections link them and several of the largest livestock merchants who work the Somalia/Kenya cross-border trade also own businesses and residences in the Eastleigh area (also see Campbell 2005: 25–26). Campbell tells the story of a Garissa cattle trader: "During the dry season when the movement of animals is slow, he runs a small retail shop [in Eastleigh] selling the latest imported ladies fashions, including dresses, scarves, long skirts, and blouses" (ibid.: 24–25). The narrative goes on to indicate how the trader moves both types of products, cattle and women's fashionable clothes, often simultaneously between Eastleigh and Garissa (ibid.) and, I might add, probably between Kenya and Somalia itself. Such is the perplexing world of Somali businesses in Eastleigh, where a male Muslim trader imports and sells women's fashionable clothes, but also operates a cattle business with ties deep inside Somalia's rangelands.

In Eastleigh one of the major centers of commerce is an establishment called Garissa Lodge, where dozens of businesses are housed. The establishment's name appropriately captures Garissa town's influence in Eastleigh and vice versa. Moreover, the commercial parts of both Eastleigh and Garissa town are referred to locally as "Little Mogadishu," which indicates the strong ties between the locations and Somalia itself. The Mogadishu analogy also reverberates with a strong sense of nostalgia for stateless Somalia. More pragmatically, it highlights the growing importance of Eastleigh, primarily, and Garissa, secondarily, as centers of Somali business activity and diaspora investment that reach well beyond their borders.

Similar to the livestock trade in Garissa, the daily practice of engaging in what often is illegal commerce serves to legitimize illegality in Eastleigh. In fact, minimal effort is made to halt illegal businesses operating in Eastleigh without licenses and/or selling smuggled goods, in part because many officials who are supposed to control illegal commerce earn rents (bribes) from it. Like the cross-border trade in livestock where everybody openly knows most cattle illegally come from Somalia, Eastleigh trade also is increasingly out in the open. It effectively can be described as "openly informal," neither hidden from authorities nor entirely consistent with an official, public place of business. At the same time it is a vital part of the service economy of Kenya's largest city, Nairobi, whose residents depend on it for low-cost products and services (Little 2003: 166).

Initially when Somali refugees were establishing businesses in Kenya their merchandise often was imported from Dubai through Somali ports. The products were then smuggled across the border to Kenya and eventually ended up in Nairobi. Since the early 2000s at least some successful Kenya-based Somali traders have begun to import their goods directly from Dubai and other locations, such as Malaysia and China. The ties between Eastleigh and Dubai have become so strong that "the importer need not even be present in Dubai to make the actual purchases, as the whole process can be orchestrated by the Eastleigh office" (Campbell 2005: 23). Because of high levels of corruption in the Kenya government, merchants soon learned that it was possible to legally import merchandise without transiting Somalia, by paying off Kenyan customs officials and police officers (see Karanja and Huka 2010). As one Somali businessman indicated to me in a recent interview, "Somalis are importing their Dubai purchases (clothes, electronics, etc.) via Eldoret Airport but now even JKIA [Jomo Kenyatta International Airport, Nairobi]—they just pay some fees to get their goods through customs" (field notes, February 2011). In fact, by 2003 corruption at Eldoret Airport was so endemic that all cargo flights were temporarily halted there. Campbell, for example, discusses "how the majority of the goods targeted for cancellation were imported by Somali traders or by freight companies owned by Somali networks operating largely out of Nairobi's Eastleigh area and coming mostly from the port of Dubai" (2005: 22).

Wealthy Somali businessmen effectively learned that they could bribe their way into making their imports legal and avoid the risky practice of transiting their goods through conflict-ridden Somalia. Once in Nairobi the goods are "then distributed from Eastleigh to the Kenyan market or to wholesalers from Rwanda, South Sudan, Burundi and further afield" (Abdulsamed 2011: 9). Over time Somali traders in Kenya have taken control of the country's electronics and textile trade with Dubai, businesses that until recently were dominated by the Kenyan Indian community (Kantai 2011: 1).

Along with the use of official import channels, a number of Somali-owned businesses have become formally registered in Nairobi and expanded into the city's prominent commercial districts. Much of this expansion has been spurred by (1) Somali refugees within Eastleigh and (2) the Somali diaspora of the Middle East, Europe, and the United States. In a recent study of Somali investment and business activities in Eastleigh, Abdulsamed (2011) describes the importance of the refugees in Kenya and the Somali diaspora outside of East Africa:

> Somalis, refugees in particular, have invested and transformed the suburb [Eastleigh] into a bustling commercial centre. They have bought up residential blocks and rapidly converted them into modern retail outlets. Indeed, many Somalis in Western and Middle Eastern countries have been attracted by the business opportunities in Kenya. Most of the investment centres on family-owned businesses but it also extends to real estate. This funding from the wider Somali Diaspora has been crucial to the expansion of Eastleigh. The capital investments for small enterprises vary but typically involve sums of US$3–5 million. Commercial-mall companies such as Amal, Baraka Bazaar, Garissa Lodge and Sunshine Plaza are in this category, with annual turnover of no more than $7 million. (7)

This growth in investment has led to considerable resentment among rival Kenyan Asian– and Kenyan African–owned businesses in the city. Until recently, they have dominated Nairobi's business sector, and expectedly they are resentful that successful Somali entrepreneurs are now investing in Nairobi real estate and businesses. They still own most real estate property in Nairobi, but are upset that Somalis have been buying up real estate and boosting up local prices (Abdulsamed 2011). In June 2009 there was an incident where Somalis purchased a shopping center and the Kenyan business tenants refused to move out after it was taken over. They protested that Somalis were using funds from piracy ransoms to purchase real estate and start businesses in Nairobi, a common complaint of Kenyan investors (see Mugambi 2009; Okwembah 2009). One journalist, who interviewed a Nairobi police spokesperson, quoted the officer as saying, "We have no hard proof that piracy money is circulating in the economy." However, the reporter goes on to say that the officer raises "concerns that the money could be hot" (Parselelo 2009: 1).

Fears of Somalian money laundering and business dominance resulted in a crackdown in 2009 on Somali-owned businesses and on Kenyan and Somali refugees generally (Wabala 2009). Kenyan officials estimated that about 3 billion Kenyan shillings (US$38 million) annually were flowing through Nairobi's foreign exchange bureaus and realty investments that were unaccounted by banks and government. Officials quickly pointed to Somali refugees and their unregistered businesses as culprits. They assumed that most of the untracked cash stems from informal Somali trade and finance networks that link together Nairobi/Eastleigh, stateless Somalia, the Middle East (especially Dubai), and the United States and Europe (see United States State Department 2010: 148–150).

Under pressure from its constituents the Kenyan government took action against Somali refugees and immigrants, and many were arrested and deported back to Somalia. This policy raised a strong protest from the Somali community, many of whom are legal Kenyan citizens (Amnesty International 2010; *Daily Nation* 2010a; Shiundu 2010).[10] Prominent non-Somali MPs also called for a requirement that Somali investors had to verify their sources of investment capital for properties and businesses already purchased or about to be purchased, with the assumption that laundered money was the source of their capital. However, these politicians retracted this demand when Kenya's Somali leaders, including MPs, protested that their community was being discriminated against and that investors from other ethnic groups also should be made to divulge the sources of their investment capital (*Daily Nation* 2010a and b). Kenyan Somalis have contested the claims of piracy investment funds and money laundering in Nairobi (see Abdulsamed 2011), but many Kenyans on the street still believe the growing prominence of the Somali business sector in Kenya is due to illegal means (field notes, February 2011).

Global Networks and the Dubai Factor

As discussed earlier, connections between Eastleigh and the rest of the world are increasingly pronounced, especially to Dubai. I pointed to the Dubai connection in my earlier work, but its importance to Eastleigh and the Kenyan business sector generally has grown even more since the early 2000s (Little 2003). Not only do Eastleigh-based merchants continue to receive goods from Dubai via Somalia but, as indicated earlier, they also frequently import directly from the emirate. In 2003 stateless Somalia was one of Dubai's largest trading partners in sub-Saharan Africa. In that year the value of non-oil exports and re-exports[11] to Somalia from Dubai was the highest among all sub-Saharan African countries and ninth among all countries in the world, excluding the United States, European countries, China, and Japan. About 3 percent of all Dubai's non-oil exports and re-exports were to Somalia in 2003, a percentage that was even higher than Dubai's re-exports to the continent's wealthiest country, South Africa (Dubai Chamber of Commerce 2003: 6).

Trade between Somalia and Dubai continued to grow in the early 2000s. During 2001 and 2007 annual exports/re-exports to Somalia from the United Arab Emirates (UAE) (including Dubai) reached almost $300 million per annum, slightly more than the value of UAE's exports/re-exports to Kenya in 2006. Figures are based on UAE statistics because it was not possible to obtain Dubai export figures for Somalia after 2003 (see United Arab Emirates [UAE] 2011). Export trade figures for Dubai Emirate generally are hard to obtain by specific country market, except for trade with large markets like the United States, China, India, or the United Kingdom. Dubai trade with sub-Saharan African countries, including to Somalia, is minuscule compared to exports to these middle- and high-income countries. For the UAE figures a common estimate is that Dubai accounts for 75 percent of its total non-oil trade, although I would suggest it is more in the order of 90–95 percent in the case of Somalia and Kenya (see *Dubai Direct Trade* 2010). By 2008 and 2009 the value of the UAE-to-Somalia export/re-export trade had declined to $193.9 and $250.5 million, respectively, probably due to a combination of factors (UAE 2011). These include the global recession, which resulted in several Somali businesses relocating to other locations, such as Kuwait, Malaysia, or even South Sudan (personal communication, Roland Marchal); increased piracy along the Somali coast (see *Gulf News* 2010); and the growth in UAE's exports/re-exports directly to Kenya. With many Somali-owned businesses in Kenya and other Kenyan businesses increasingly importing products directly from Dubai, rather than via Somalia, UAE exports/re-exports to Kenya increased by more than 500 percent during the 2000s. They reached a value of $470.3 million in 2009, or more than $220 million greater than UAE's exports to Somalia in that year. Yet, only three years earlier (2006) UAE trade to Somalia greatly exceeded the country's exports to Kenya (UAE 2011).

An examination of the value and composition of imports to Somalia from all trading partners, including UAE, also is informative. In 2009 the total value of recorded imports to Somalia was $769.3 million, of which UAE accounted for approximately 32 percent of the amount (International Trade Centre 2009). With a current population of about 7 million people that equates to imports of slightly more than US$100 per person or about $600 for a household of six, which is a sizable amount for a low-income country. Combined food commodities, such as cereals, flour, vegetables, and cooking oil, make up about 35 percent of total imports to Somalia from UAE, while sugar and electronics products are 10 and 6.5 percent of imports, respectively (ibid.). Both of the latter items are key transborder trade products that often are re-exported throughout eastern Africa. Other key transborder trade products are pharmaceuticals, textiles and clothes (including footwear), and tobacco products (cigarettes), and in aggregate they account for approximately 8 percent of total imports (ibid.). As noted earlier, textiles and clothes seem to be products that Somali businessmen based in Kenya increasingly import directly from UAE (Dubai), Indonesia, Malaysia, and China.

In Dubai itself, Somali entrepreneurs operate businesses that are linked to eastern Africa, but also to other parts of the Middle East, Europe, Asia, and the United States. Dubai is home to an important segment of the Somali diaspora, especially prominent businessmen who fled Mogadishu almost immediately after the government collapse. Similar to Garissa and Eastleigh, the part of Dubai city where Somali tea shops and businesses are concentrated is referred to as "Little Mogadishu" (Dickinson 2005: 1). As noted earlier, even goods purchased in Dubai for re-export to Kenya often pass through Somalia first because of well-established trade channels from Dubai to Somalia, and also to avoid taxes and import tariffs. An Eastleigh importer can work with a Somali business partner in Dubai and place an order via mobile phone without having to travel to Dubai. The mobile phone, whose use has grown exponentially both in Somalia itself and in Eastleigh, facilitates this trade and its growth in association with regional and international trade. Most airlines that serve Somalia and Somaliland have flights between Dubai and key cities in Somalia, and at least three Somali-owned private airlines are based in the emirate (ibid.).

Indeed, Dubai has become the financial and trading center for Eastleigh and Somalia generally, as well as for the rest of eastern Africa. In a recent study of twenty firms in Somalia, for example, it was observed that 75 percent of them were dependent on trade with the UAE (Hansen 2007: 55). In another study but this time based in Somaliland, Haga shows that Somali women traders also have emerged as key actors in the Dubai import trade, making frequent trips to the region to purchase textiles and clothes, and then reselling the merchandise in Somaliland or re-exporting it to central and southern Somalia and neighboring countries (see Haga 2009).

Somali-based business networks in Dubai also reach diaspora populations in Europe, North America, and southeast Asia. Ram et al., for instance, gives an example of a Somali-owned business in Leicester, England, that started with loans from Somali contacts in Dubai and in Canada (2008: 435). The entrepreneur needed these funds to start his UK-based business. In another study Farah discusses the importance of Dubai for Somali businesses in the diaspora and Somalia itself: "Somalis from all over the world generally use Dubai as their financial and trade centre for their businesses with Somalia itself" (2009: 13).

However, for a Somali to participate and be successful in financial and commercial dealings with Dubai/UAE, one needs to have well-established networks that are geographically diverse. A strategic outcome of the Somali crisis has been the creation of a large, geographically dispersed diaspora that is well integrated through complex financial and other material flows and well suited to an increasingly globalized economy. Today there are more than 1 million, or about one out of eight, Somalis living outside the country, including about 25,000 or more residing in UAE (Hassan and Healy 2009: 8). The remittance economy strengthens these global networks to Somalia itself, where up to an estimated $1 billion of annual remittances is received by families and businesses in the country from Somalis living around the world, especially from those in high-income countries of North America, Europe, and the Middle East (Lindley 2010). One observer estimates that up to 80 percent of start-up capital for small and medium-sized businesses in Somalia comes from these remittances (Sheikh and Healy 2009: 5). While a significant trade diaspora existed prior to 1991, the collapse of the state and its ensuing problems accelerated the growth of a Somali diaspora and the massive remittance flows associated with it.

Somalia Update

As this book goes to press, the situation in Somalia and its borderlands with Kenya is in even more flux than the normal volatility that has characterized the country since 1991. Three events have occurred since 2011 that have impacted the country and Somali business networks, but how and in what ways still are not well understood. First, as mentioned earlier, the Kenyan army actually went into Somalia in large force in October 2011, in order to secure its borders and engage the Al-Shabaab militia. An important rationale was the well-publicized kidnappings of two foreign aid workers in northeastern Kenya and two tourists—of whom one died in captivity in southern Somalia—on the northern Kenya coast by Somali-based militia. Another is speculated to be to support the creation of a regional state in southern Somalia, called Azania or Jubbaland, to buffer Kenya from the terroristic and other threats from Somalia itself (see Keating 2011). What the impact of this invasion by the Kenyan army has been on cross-border trade is not well known at present (July 2012), although there are indications that the trade in livestock continues but with periodic interruptions (interview with NGO official, December 14, 2011). For example, livestock market data for the period January–March 2012 show that cattle sales in Garissa were still the highest in the country among different markets and supplied the largest number of cattle to Nairobi and Mombasa, the country's two largest consumption markets. About 14,000 cattle were sold in an approximate two-month period between January 1 and March 5, 2012 (Farmer and Mbwika 2012: 20–21), which is only about 20 percent below what normally would be sold at the market during those months (Little 2008b). At least some of the decline in sales probably is related to drought-induced losses from the massive climate and humanitarian disaster of 2010–11, which would have affected the number of marketed animals in early 2012. Since livestock are trekked on foot to Kenya from Somalia, cross-border trade in this commodity is less likely to be affected by the ongoing conflict than other types of commerce (for example, food and electronics) dependent on truck transport and easily monitored roads.

Second, since Kenya's invasion in October 2011 the security of Garissa town itself is problematic and subject to continued threats from Somali-based factions. In the first half of 2012 there already have been two horrific incidences of armed attacks in town, including grenade explosions in local churches and public spaces with loss of life. Al-Shabaab claims credit for these atrocities, which they say are in retaliation for Kenya's military involvement in Somalia and its attacks on Al-Shabaab forces. The Islamist group continues to threaten Kenya with additional terrorist attacks, including in Nairobi. The terrorist incidences in Garissa have forced the Kenya army to enforce a dusk-to-dawn curfew and have multiplied the number of security checks going into/out of the town. The heightened insecurity in Garissa and the borderlands obviously affects the economy and trade in the region, although as noted earlier the cross-border livestock trade seems to continue.

Finally, the security situation in certain parts of Somalia itself, especially in and around Mogadishu, has improved as of July 2012. There have been and continue to be a series of successful military campaigns by Kenyan, AU, Ethiopian, and Somali government forces against Al-Shabaab that have forced the insurgents to retreat from Mogadishu and other key areas of central and southern Somalia. These victories and the tentative peace that they have brought to certain cities have spurred some minimal business investment and a return of about 60,000 displaced people to Mogadishu (United Nations Integrated Regional Information Network [IRIN] 2012). Even Turkish Airlines, the national carrier of Turkey, recently has started scheduled flights to Mogadishu, a very important symbolic gesture to the region and world that the Somali situation has improved at least for now. Turkey itself has taken a lead in negotiating a political settlement in Somalia and sponsored a critical international summit on Somalia in Istanbul in April 2012. The concern for Turkey and other countries, including the United States and the UK, is to minimize the political volatility and additional violence that might occur with the scheduled end in August 2012 of the mandated eight-year term of the Western- and UN-supported Transitional Federal Government (TFG) of Somalia and its leaders. Although Al-Shabaab remains a very significant threat with popular support in certain parts of the country (Marchal 2012; Mosley 2012), the TFG's term ended in August 2012 with the election of a new parliament and president, U.S.-educated Hassan Sheikh Mohamud, and the security situation in and around Mogadishu has progressed to the point that the kinds of national and international networks of finance and trade described in this chapter could benefit from the improved environment. While there are grounds to be optimistic, many political issues need to be resolved and past grievances addressed before one can claim with confidence that the new state and improved security will be sustained.

Summary

As this chapter has shown, Somali trader and finance networks became increasingly globalized with the implosion of the Somali state in 1991. The Somali business community has been able to take advantage of reduced trade barriers and currency controls in Kenya and, to a lesser extent, Ethiopia because of established economic linkages within and outside the region. And these connections are not dependent on the existence of a state. If neoliberal globalization is about networks and relationships beyond the nation-state, then few communities in sub-Saharan Africa are better suited for this new globalized environment than are Somalis (also see Healey 2010). The complex web of transactions among the three nodes of Eastleigh, Garissa, and Dubai discussed in this chapter supports this point, with Dubai and its glitzy skyscrapers and affluence being among the quintessential symbols of globalization in the world today. Somalis clearly have taken advantage of the emirate's global position as a center of finance and trade by strategically establishing strong economic and social relationships to it.

As a transnational society with a hyper-liberalized economy, Somalis have done relatively well in adapting to an increasingly connected world, but fared poorly in rebuilding their own country and state. A large part of the problem is that so much of the Somali economy and the revenues it generates are beyond the state's controls and/or borders, which strongly challenges the taxation and revenue-generating capacities of a new government. Economic success spurred by more liberal trade policies in the region does not equip a community to rebuild a nation that despite recent progress remains riveted with conflict, competing ideologies, and well-armed political factions. Somalia is a political and humanitarian drama that continues to unfold, and the violence and human suffering of 2010–11 is unparalleled in its history, with the possible exception of the immediate period (1991–92) following the state's collapse. In 2012 the security situation in Somalia has improved, Al-Shabaab is in retreat from some of its strongholds in the south, and the country's first elections in more than twenty-five years were held in August that saw a new president elected, Hassan Sheikh Mohamud. Even with this relatively optimistic scenario, the government still holds sovereignty over only a fraction of the nation's territory and economy, and an assassination attempt on the new president already has occurred. In short, the country's future and its political order remain very uncertain.

Conclusions

Rethinking Encounters and Reformist Narratives

This book has been about social and economic changes in several African countries that can be traced to economic and political reform programs first introduced in the early 1980s. It has used the twin platforms of neoliberalism, with its emphases on individualism and economic growth, and globalization, with its focus on global flows of goods, technologies, and ideas, to explain a series of ethnographic encounters across a broad set of sectors and issues. The book suggests that these cases represent a more general trend in Africa and elsewhere in low-income countries, as evidenced, for example, by the widespread imposition of such models as contract farming (chapter 1) and community-based conservation (chapter 3). Borrowing from Foucault's concept of governmentality and James Scott's notion of legibility, the book also has highlighted a set of powerful narratives about economy, society, and development that often have been hijacked and misrepresented by neoliberal reformists, and thus miss what actually is happening in rural and urban Africa, as well as potential opportunities for local development. Similar to earlier works by Ferguson (1990) in Lesotho, Mitchell (2002) in Egypt, and Li (2009) in Indonesia, the book argues that particular development narratives and polices are used to disguise underlying politico-economic agendas that are intended to place greater controls on local populations or, in some cases, transfer lands and other resources to state and/or private investors. It explains how these narratives and reforms often discredit local markets, tenure systems, livelihoods, and organizations in favor of a technology of audit, corporate business management, export-based growth, and support for large private companies that often are foreign owned. All of these take place under the pretense of increased economic and political freedoms for the individual.

With the support of international financial institutions and development agencies, African governments pursued a reform agenda during the past almost three decades that favored export over local markets, large farms and agribusiness firms over small-scale farmers and traders, and external definitions of welfare and poverty over local realities and perceptions. In principle, the state and government regulations assumed smaller roles in the economy and free markets and private investments were encouraged, with minimal protections for local communities or redistributive mechanisms to ensure that local populations also benefited from economic growth. In the meantime the gap between rich and poor and the incidence of poverty in most rural areas of Africa has grown (Stein 2011). As the book has shown, in reality the state and its donor supporters maintained active roles in providing subsidies, infrastructure, tariff reductions, and security to investors and the private sector, even while insisting that it was private-sector-led development without government assistance. And some governments adopted certain characteristics of neoliberalism, such as expanding markets and increasing food production, in order to increase their controls on local populations, especially those in remote locations. What emerged in this context was a veneer of reforms and official structures that masked the real economy of risk-taking herders and farmers, tranborder traders and migrants, and entrepreneurial market women. As the book has shown, the outputs of these economic actors often do not show up in the official statistics of governments and development agencies that are used to inform policy and investment programs.

However, in political terms some of the reforms that were initiated clearly opened up spaces for underrepresented groups to improve their rights and, consequently, their share of development resources and benefits. The rolling back of the state and the push for democratic elections ignited an explosion in the number of NGOs and civil society organizations, which for some marginal groups provided new opportunities for beneficial alliances, including with international groups. Small, indigenous groups, such as the Maasai-related Il Chamus discussed in chapters 3 and 4, drew on democratic discourses and new minority and human rights initiatives to build key alliances with national and international actors that advanced their own political struggles. In a very positive sense, the opening up of a relatively free press in Kenya following the end of the repressive Moi era also allowed groups such as Il Chamus to use the media to publicize their political cause and eventually become "renowned for legal battles in defence of their rights" (Thuku 2012). Other marginalized groups have followed similar strategies, even though most of them—including Il Chamus—have yet to reap significant political and economic dividends. These public tactics, however, would have been difficult without democratic reforms and Moi's departure from office.

The corporate neoliberalism that has been discussed in this book is sterile, calculated, and neatly ordered. It can be counted, audited, and monitored and requires uniformly produced outputs, factory-like work conditions, and specialization. Recall the discussion in chapter 1 of farm workers on horticultural schemes with company shirts, supermarkets demanding exact-sized produce, pineapple workers with chemical sprayers on their backs, and women vegetable packers whose hands are periodically swabbed for pathogens. In this squeaky-clean environment there is little room for unkempt pastoralists with their hardy, well-adapted, but small cattle, or small-scale farmers growing produce on irregularly shaped fields without modern inputs, such as fertilizers and pesticides. Indeed, the colorfully dressed pastoralist with her/his mobile herds strongly clashes with the modernist view of cattle ranching with fenced pastures and manufactured feed supplements. Similarly, the image of the small-scale, female vegetable producer and trader in West Africa contrasts with the agribusiness portrait of sprinkler-fed, fertilized fields and packing sheds, whose corporate owners benefit from re-duced tariffs and government subsidies and dump surplus produce on the local market. The proponents of neoliberalism espouse a singular vision of develop-ment and modernity that excludes alternative narratives and livelihoods, even though they often are more economically and environmentally sustainable than the resource-intensive and costly investments being offered.

As the book has shown, markets reflect power relations and social constructs that are never fair to all parties, whether in Africa, Asia, or the United States. Power is what markets are about, and it is what distorts them in favor of the po-litically connected rather than the most efficient resource users. As I have tried to show, this book is not anti-market, anti–private sector, or even anti–foreign in-vestment, since many African countries badly require investment capital. To the contrary, the farmers, herders, and traders discussed in the different case studies are all market-savvy, private-sector actors, and could benefit from investments that build on their economic contributions and livelihoods. Only a few of them work in the public sector, and none are able to exist without interactions with the market. The private-sector programs that have been encouraged by policies and programs during the past three decades mainly encompass large businesses (of-ten foreign) and large-scale farmers and agribusinesses, especially those focused on export/international markets. As this book has shown, it is a private sector that is heavily intertwined with the public sector, from the politicians who sit on the boards of community conservancies in Kenya (chapter 3), to the exports farms in Ghana and The Gambia that benefit from government extension and reduced tar-iffs (chapter 1), to the ecotourist firms that draw on donor agency funds and pub-lic infrastructure while serving as "models" of private-sector partnerships (chap-ter 3). There also are the foreign agribusiness firms and conservation groups that increasingly are provided land free or at rates well below market prices (chapters 3 and 6). What are excluded from this definition of the private sector are petty traders, pastoralists, and small-scale farmers who tragically often find their lands and livelihoods threatened by public assistance for private-sector investments mo-tivated by imposed development models.

Ironically, despite the strong pro-market rhetoric of neoliberalism, several of the cases discussed here reflect anti-market tendencies, defined as actions that reduce market competition and increase barriers to market entry. Note the case of contract farming in chapter 1, the ultimate symbol of advanced agrarian capi-talism, which attempts to control product and labor markets from the point of production to final sale, even enforcing penalties on contracted farmers who try to sell their produce on the free (open) market. Or large ecotourist firms that can draw on subsidized loans or grants from development agencies and INGOs to promote biodiversity conservation, but end up limiting opportunities for local enterprises to compete for lucrative tourist markets. Finally, there are the recent cases where large foreign firms have been granted massive land concessions that unfairly put them at an advantage over local livestock and crop producers, even when the facts and research demonstrate that the latter actors make significant economic impacts without subsidies and preferential tax benefits. Note the strong contributions to national exports and GDP that East African pastoralists make through animal production and trade, although these contributions rarely are officially acknowledged (chapter 6). As the book highlights in the cases of Ghana and The Gambia, subsidized export firms and investors who are expected to produce solely for the export market compete with local traders and farmers for lucrative domestic trade options, including local hotel markets where small-scale women traders vie for business. Governments and development agencies seem naively unaware of the domestic aspect of these export-oriented enterprises, but the impacts of their behavior are painfully felt by the low-income producers and traders with whom they unfairly compete (see chapter 1).

Anthropologists often are very adroit at uncovering the hidden transcripts and invented traditions and histories that lie below the surface of everyday social and political realities. Many of the examples presented in this book, including those cases mentioned above, are about these hidden transcripts and histories that contradict official narratives about development and its beneficiaries. However, not all of these transcripts and practices are well hidden; instead, some are easily accessible to those who wish to acknowledge them. For example, it would not be too difficult to assess available evidence about food aid dependency, the nature of pastoralist poverty, or subsidies to private-sector investors, in order to counter accepted wisdoms. However, this information is either discarded or just not acknowledged. Here is where hegemonic political agendas figure in the calculations about which evidence to recognize and which to neglect. As the book has argued, there are strong reasons why it is politically expedient to categorize whole subpopulations as food aid dependent and/or poor, since it allows governments to pursue pilot experiments like resettlement and large-scale sedentarization that serve important political purposes.

Thus, in the different reform initiatives that are discussed in the book, particular narratives and facts are privileged and others are discouraged or even silenced. As the book suggests, those accepted as fact can become the basis for major policy and investment programs. The case studies in this book take on a range of these policy-based narratives, especially those centered on the so-called private sector, trade and markets, and the causes of poverty. Despite their differences, all these discourses invoke a type of pro-business, or more accurately, pro-corporate-business, solution whether in the context of social safety nets or environmental conservation. Therefore, better environmental conservation is achieved through private enterprise development ("nature as business") (chapter 3); poverty is eliminated by pro-poor trade policies (chapter 6); and food insecurity is overcome through increased commercialization (chapter 5).

For a strong centrist state the technique of neoliberalism, with its concern for auditing and measurement, can empower administrators and policy makers to further control local populations through development programs and investments, while at the same time espousing free markets and democracy. The book has shown this to be the case for pastoralists and for remote, food-insecure populations of Ethiopia's highlands that in some cases have been resettled and/or have lost lands in the name of development and food security, as well as have been encouraged to volunteer labor for local development. The insistence of many safety net programs, including those based on food and/or cash transfers, on making poverty legible through a sophisticated arsenal of methods and statistical techniques provides the fodder for states to reinforce their political agendas against populations that they consider politically troublesome and/or barriers to large-scale investment agendas. In the quest for economic growth and modernization, these populations, who mainly produce for local and regional markets, do not fit the modern vision of commercial, export-oriented agriculture, and therefore are in need of reform.

Implicit in the reform programs described in the book is also a cultural model that depicts a particular image of a modern, responsible citizenry. The individual in this model does not practice mobile pastoralism, wear customary clothing, plant crops in oddly shaped fields with intercropped rows, engage in informal trade, or depend on government health services. Instead, the culturally ideal person is settled, works for a large farm as a laborer or works his/her own farm with modern inputs, sells produce only through licensed markets no matter how inconvenient and costly this action is, and is responsible for her/his own health care costs.

Like most grand narratives, neoliberalism and its effects in Africa are chock full of contradictions, and this book has uncovered many of them. Consider the case of Somali pastoralists of northeastern Kenya. In one narrative they are impoverished herders in need of alternative livelihoods, but in another they are successful, technologically sophisticated entrepreneurs whose business achievements now are the subject of government suspicion and inquiry and public outcry (chapter 7). Remove the poor Somali pastoralist from the "bush" and transform her/him into a Nairobi-based businessperson with global business contacts, and instantly the individual is a source of suspicion and potential criminality from which private investors and the public require protection! The fact that the Somali pastoralists and traders annually export from the region an astounding 1.6 million animals to Middle Eastern markets without any development or public assistance is a market achievement that should be applauded, rather than resisted by most governments in the region. As the book points out, Somali business networks, many of which maintain strong linkages to pastoralism, have been some of the winners of reform programs but in unanticipated ways, and they continue to attract considerable disdain from regional governments and their citizenry. For the most part, they also are perceived as inconsistent with the international community's vision of modernity and market-based achievement, which has little room for merchants who operate on the geographic and political margins and whose ethnic and religious (Islam) statuses make them even more problematic.

Consider also the Maasai community's use of participation and empowerment language to pursue political agendas and lands lost to national parks, and the strong protests that these actions invoked from the international conservation community (chapter 3). Ironically, the aggrieved international groups often themselves were strong advocates and funders of highly participatory, community-based conservation schemes. However, for these parties empowerment and participation meant local engagement in biodiversity programs to the benefit of wildlife rather than involvement in politically charged issues, such as land rights and democratic representation.

Other contradictions associated with reform programs can be found in the different ways in which pastoralists themselves and their livelihoods are portrayed even within the same country. Consider the case of Kenya, for example. In its poverty alleviation programs, herders are depicted as impoverished abusers of the environment in need of radical social transformation (chapter 6). By contrast, the country's community-based conservation (CBC) initiatives present them as natural conservationists whose culture and open-range production system sustain rather than damage valuable biodiversity (i.e., wildlife). One set of narratives proposes to eliminate pastoralist livelihoods, the other to maintain them.

Development narratives can be powerful enough to silence these kinds of contradictions even when the very foundation of the development paradigm itself is challenged. For example, the African realities of increased poverty, hunger, and stagnant economic growth in the 1980s and 1990s were glossed over by blaming poor governance and corruption rather than structural adjustment programs. When the pesky problems of poverty and hunger persisted into the late 1990s and 2000s, a new form of conditionality called the Poverty Reduction Strategy Plan (PRSP) was implemented, but the general fixation on economic growth models was maintained. Safety net programs, in turn, were introduced, or in some cases reintroduced, to help poor farmers and workers attain minimum asset and food security protections, but the general development approach of the era remained unchanged. From this perspective, market and political reforms were working just fine, but the problem was that most Africans were too poor and hungry to benefit from them. Welfare-based programs in the 2000s, such as the Productive Safety Net Programme (PSNP) in Ethiopia, were initiated to address this problem, but they did not challenge the basic narrative about the merits of export-led growth models.

This book has tried to go beyond a strict focus on discourses and narratives by also addressing the material realities of local economic and political struggles. Africa and Africans do not need externally prescribed solutions and discourses or imposed models to address their own problems of poverty, food insecurity, and conflict. As we saw in the case of small-scale horticultural traders in The Gambia and a pineapple-growing cooperative in Ghana, they need a more equitable playing field that encourages their participation in development programs rather than policies and programs that disadvantage them. They do not need to be reformed in the likeness of the corporate, responsible individual or on the basis of market ideologies that mask unfair market relations and skew economic and social benefits. Nor do they need to be assaulted with policies and programs that undermine their own future livelihoods by transferring some of the best agricultural lands and richest mineral deposits to foreign investors and corporations. Current estimates are that African governments, desperate for foreign investment, already have leased (primarily) or sold off more than 40 million hectares to foreign agribusiness and mining firms (Provost 2012). In one case in South Sudan, a Norwegian company has signed an agreement with the new government for a ninety-nine-year lease on 179,000 hectares at the ridiculous rate of US$0.07 per hectare (ibid.). While African states advertise these investment lands as "vacant," most of the time a local farming, or more likely mobile herding, group uses them, as was demonstrated in the case of the Tana delta, Kenya (chapter 6).

The book has been critical of certain development and reform models, but it has tried to restrain from general castigations against development, which can be counter to the interests of African communities and institutions. As noted in the introduction, the book is not anti-development. There are no African families that I know of who do not want improved health systems, clean and safe water, secure environments, and efficient schools for their children. Is that not development, and is development not more than just the presence of foreign aid? Many valuable efforts have been made and successes gained, funded both locally and from external funds, for reducing child mortality rates, improving basic education, and lessening rates of HIV/AIDS infection (see Vitoria et al. 2009). Indeed, efforts to improve formal education and public health in Africa in the 1990s and 2000s, especially regarding HIV/AIDS and malaria, required effective public institutions and funding, which had been ravaged by SAPs. Increases in donor funding for government programs and institutions in the 2000s can be linked to concerns with public health issues, which often meant bringing the state back into the development process, counter to many of the reform agendas. Effective lobby groups and citizen organizations in Africa and the West, as well as the emergence of major philanthropist institutions, such as the Bill and Melinda Gates Foundation, ensured that the anti-government, pro-private-sector rhetoric did not counter widespread public health efforts. For example, large funding earmarks in the U.S. Congress in the late 1990s and 2000s have been reserved for HIV/AIDS and malaria eradication programs, and many of these development programs worked (work) closely with African governments (see Attwood et al. 2008).

There also are very few Africans, including those whose stories are told in this book, who are not quick to take advantage of new technologies, practices, and markets that improve their lives and livelihoods. The instances of informal cross-border trade and livestock export activities discussed in the book are good examples of this, as is the very rapid adoption of information and communication technologies (ICTs), especially mobile phones. The latter phenomenon really could be a "game changer" for development and democracy in Africa, because they allow communications, connections, and the fostering of networks that were not possible until very recently and they hold great promise among so many different economic and social sectors. Is there any development idea or technology that has been so widely and rapidly adopted in Africa as mobile phones? The well-known, mobile-phone-based banking company in Kenya, called M-Pesa, is a good example of a positive ICT development that is widely used by both urban and rural populations (Morawczynski 2009). Other beneficial or potentially beneficial outcomes of ICTs relate to improved dissemination of market and health information, timely remittances from the diaspora, and opportunities for long-distance education. There obviously can be a downside to ICT technology, as witnessed in the ways that text messaging from mobile phones in Kenya incited violence after the disputed 2007 elections in that country, but the potentially positive aspects of ICTs are many.

Several of these and other success stories in Africa mainly occurred without outside development assistance. The massive growth in a remittance-based economy in Africa, for example, has developed independent of official development assistance, and its annual value, estimated at about $40 billion per year (including North Africa), now exceeds official foreign aid figures in several African countries (see Ratha and Plaza 2012). In a development context these funds have financed rural schools, health clinics, housing construction, and business start-ups (chapter 7). At a family or individual level, remittance flows assist large numbers of poor and middle-income families to finance school fees, health costs, and food and other consumption purchases. The remittance industry clearly is a positive development that allows African economies to reduce their own dependence on external development assistance. Its growth also has been facilitated by the increased use of ICTs in Africa.

What of the large development agencies and international financial institutions (IFIs) who supported the structural adjustment programs (SAPs) and many of the policies discussed in the book? At the very least their large sizes and politically driven mandates limit their capacity to work locally and respond to development opportunities afforded by the positive changes mentioned above, especially when compared to smaller, more nimble local development organizations and NGOs. Their size, bureaucratic clumsiness, and political mandates makes them easy targets for critics, including myself. As the book has suggested, large development agencies and their personnel are constrained by their inability to understand the nuances of local histories and politics, since their mode of operation is to homogenize social and political realities, in order to make them legible for development planners. Nonetheless, there is a growing recognition even among most of these institutions, including the large IFIs, that unfettered markets are not always the best means for distributing benefits and basic services to low-income populations. In the words of the noted Africanist historian, Anthony Hopkins: "The World Bank is oscillating between 'getting the prices right' and bringing the state back in, which is proof of how complex issues of poverty in Africa are" (2005: 515). Moreover, the development arena clearly has changed in the past decade with the emergence of China as a key financier of infrastructure and other development investments throughout Africa, which challenges the hegemony of IFIs as well as Western development agencies operating in Africa. This trend is likely only to grow as evidenced by China's recent and very large development aid commitments to Africa and by the current domestic budget crises in Europe and the United States. Chinese state companies are key actors in the large-scale mining and land-grab activities that were mentioned earlier, and their emphasis on economic growth at all costs, using massive agribusiness operations while violating the rights of smallholders, makes them little different from other foreign enterprises and investments discussed in the book.

Perhaps most troubling for the rural poor in Africa is governments' wholesale leasing of valuable land and water rights to foreign investors, including the Chinese, in the hopes of attracting foreign investment. Notwithstanding the human rights and legal issues involved with such large-scale injustices, the pattern strongly contradicts a development model based on productivity gains in small-scale agriculture, which many economists suggest is the most viable, sustainable, and equitable option for Africa (see Ravallion 2009; Lipton and Hunt 2011). In the words of Hunt and Lipton: "There is evidence, including from Asia's Green Revolution, that they [small-scale farmers] come to use yield-enhancing inputs and practices—if profitable and accessible—more intensively and successfully than large farms. . . . There has been a recent acceleration in large-scale acquisitions of land in Africa, usually by foreign investors, but many of these large holdings do not catalyse the development of small farms" (2011:7–8). Although information on these land deals remains difficult to obtain, most evidence indicates that this process is going on with some World Bank assistance in certain countries but without much assistance from bilateral development organizations (see Vidal and Provost 2012). If these large-scale land and resource transfers continue, their cumulative effects will further marginalize many rural Africans and undermine their incomes and expenditures, which are essential ingredients for sustained economic growth and development. A more equitable form of development that includes regulations, programs, and policy measures to ensure fairness and dampen excessive wealth disparities and market risks has been shown to be critical for both a sustainable economy and healthy democracy (Stiglitz 2012).

Another troubling trend that is addressed in the book is the increased and intricate relationship between post-9/11 security concerns and international development. The Somalia case (chapter 7) probably is the most obvious example of the development/security nexus, but regional trade and finance flows and institutions throughout the Horn of Africa have provoked interest among the global security community. As the book points out, the misplaced foreign interventions in Somalia during 2006–2008 contributed to a self-fulfilling prophecy by turning it into a haven for foreign jihadists and Al-Qaeda-linked movements, such as Al-Shabaab, which had minimal presence in the country pre-2006. Moreover, state projects to settle populations against their will and unfairly take over large parcels of their land and resources have been shown to have politically destabilizing and security impacts, as demonstrated by the collapse of Somalia in 1991 (Little 2003), but also the Gambian coup of 1994 (chapter 1) and the Democratic Republic of the Congo's prolonged war.

Despite many obstacles and challenges, there is reason to hold out optimism for Africa. The book's cases of resilience and success in the face of misplaced policies and considerable hardship attest to this. Many of the positive outcomes have occurred without much development or even government assistance, and change on the continent will continue and probably accelerate in the future. These changes, including the role of China in domestic development programs, could make the development agendas of many large Western agencies increasingly irrelevant or, at best, limit them to observer roles unless they themselves are reformed. The youthful and sustained population growth of the continent at a time when most advanced economies are experiencing an increasingly aged population and a decline in the working-age population (21–60 years), are other trends that could bode well for youthful Africa's future. In short, if a new set of narratives with policy prescriptions and programs for the equitable and sustainable extraction of the continent's rich natural resources that build on local markets, institutions, and farmer practices, replace the tired "pro-growth at any cost" initiatives of the past thirty years, then the twenty-first century indeed could be very bright for Africa and its residents.

Notes

Introduction

1. The book uses the geographic terms "sub-Saharan Africa" and "Africa" interchangeably, but the places and discussions are centered on sub-Saharan Africa and little reference is made to North Africa.

2. The current economic downturn in the West and the startling specter of IMF loans to Greece and its monitoring of national budgets in Italy and Spain have not gone unnoticed in Africa, especially among intellectuals and activists. An Ethiopian academic recently joked to me that when Greece agrees to reform conditions imposed by the IMF it is bailed out with $100+ billion in loans. However, when an African country does the same it receives only a small fraction of this amount, usually less than $1–2 billion. My colleague is sadly correct!

3. This relies on a measurement of poverty based on the United Nations (UN) human development index (UNDP 2011).

4. Counter to most popular critiques of SAPs, most African governments approached the IMF and World Bank for financial assistance prior to agreeing to a set of loan conditions.

5. Whether they acknowledge his contribution or not, many authors who write about the use of labels and categories to classify populations and simplify complex realties in development owe a large intellectual debt to James Scott (1998), particularly his concept of legibility. As Scott demonstrates so well, states make complex local realities and practices legible to them, so that they can control, govern, and tax them.

1. "They Think We Can Manufacture Crops"

1. A recent World Bank report also cautions against too optimistic a future for NTCs in Africa: "An expansion of developing-country nontraditional exports could create an adding up problem if several countries rapidly expand production, perhaps so much that export revenues decline. . . . The Food and Agriculture Organization of the United Nations estimates that an increase in China's exports of green beans is likely to reduce world market prices, with adverse effects on the export revenues of other developing countries" (World Bank 2007a:133).

2. Parts of this section are based on Little and Dolan (2000).

3. The terms "large farms" and "firms" are used interchangeably in the chapter, since most export firms considered here also operate their own large farms.

4. In most CF ventures in sub-Saharan Africa informal verbal agreements, rather than written contracts, are the norm (Little and Dolan 2000; Little 1994). In these cases, the buyer can enforce informal contracts by cutting off inputs, refusing to buy in subsequent seasons, and/or seeking assistance from local chiefs and government officials.

5. Similar preferences for large-scale farms and firms were demonstrated in a USAID-financed horticultural export program in Kenya that attempted to attract foreign investment by arguing that agricultural labor in the horticultural zones was cheap, unorganized (i.e., no worker organizations or unions), and mainly made up of women (i.e., a docile labor force) (Mannon 2005:19).

6. In the Gambia a large horticultural export farm is 10 or more hectares, but in Ghana it is 50+ hectares (Agro-Ind 2002; Little and Dolan 2000; Trienekens et al. 2004). Land is cheaper and more abundant in Ghana's pineapple belt where, unlike in The Gambia, irrigation is not normally used.

7. European consumers have come to prefer the variety of pineapples that is produced in Costa Rica. Attempts by Ghanaian farmers to produce this same variety of fruit generally have failed, which is why some market analysts question the future sustainability of the country's pineapple export business to Europe (Wageningen University/Michigan State University 2007).

8. This practice also is very common in Kenya, where export firms often dump their produce on local markets for tourist hotels. In Kenya the establishment of roadside "pineapple stands" by the U.S. transnational firm Dole Fruit Inc. is evidence of the value of the domestic market to large export enterprises.

2. "Everybody Is a Petty Trader"

1. Most wholesalers and transporters in the study were male.

3. "We Now Milk Elephants"

1. Group ranches were started in the 1970s under a World Bank–funded development program for commercializing pastoral production in the communal areas of Kenya. The program promoted group land titles and the organization of communities into group landholding entities as a compromise between strictly private and communal land tenure systems. With group land titles, it was anticipated that more members could qualify for credit and begin to produce for the beef market than was the case in the 1970s. Most studies of group ranches show that these outcomes never happened (see Galaty 1992).

2. The Dorobo are a Maa-speaking hunting and gathering community closely allied with the Maasai who customarily occupied forested, highland areas like Enoosupukia, dispersed throughout Maasai territories. Depending on the context and one's definition, it is sometimes accurate to consider the Dorobo as part of Maasai ethnicity, but in other circumstances it is better to treat them as a separate identity (see Spear and Waller 1993; Galaty 1982; Matter 2010). In the case of this dispute, they clearly are more closely allied with Maasai than with Bantu-speaking Kikuyu, with whom they share no linguistic and few cultural characteristics.

3. For example, Dr. Mukhisa Kituyi, with a PhD degree in anthropology, worked for a Kenyan-based environmental NGO, African Centre for Technology (ACT), immediately prior to becoming an MP and assistant minister in the Kenyan government. He has since left politics. In Tanzania Maasai politicians frequently also were (are) involved with environmental NGOs (Hodgson 2011).

4. Land trusts, "comprised of representatives from local communities, act as a player in the private marketplace, creating economic incentives and brokering agreements to encourage the conservation-friendly use of private lands. Through a land trust, communities can negotiate easements on private land for wildlife, compensate individual landowners for the opportunity costs, and even purchase land outright" (African Wildlife Foundation [AWF] 2008).

5. In the Maasai area of Loliondo in neighboring Tanzania, Galaty (2013) also documents how returns to pastoralist livestock production per km^2 far exceeded revenues per km^2 from wildlife-based activities, including licensed game hunting and tourism.

6. Many of the private ranches in Laikipia and nearby Isiolo District are as large as 4,000

or more hectares, and date to the early colonial period when the government removed Maasai from Laikipia to make way for European settlement.

7. Endorois, a small Kalenjin-speaking community, successfully brought an international case before the African Human Rights Commission based in The Gambia on the basis that the Kenyan government unfairly evicted them from their Bogoria lands without adequate compensation. The government took the action in order to create the Lake Bogoria National Reserve. In its 2010 ruling the commission "ordered Kenya to restore the Endorois to their historic land and to compensate them" (Human Rights Watch 2010). Despite the victory, the government still has not restored the protected land to the Endorois nor paid them fair compensation.

8. The southern part of Baringo District was part of Koibetak District, and thus the southern half of Lake Bogoria National Reserve was in this new district until 2010, when the two districts were recombined into Baringo County under the new Kenyan constitution.

4. "They Are Beating Us Over the Head with Democracy"

1. A plethora of highly publicized court cases over corruption in Kenya, including the so-called Goldenberg scandal that resulted in the disappearance of over US$1 billion in public funds, drew national and international attention.

2. By contrast, when I first carried out anthropological research in Kenya in 1980 discussions of ethnicity ("tribalism"), in both popular and academic venues, were strongly discouraged and rarely published. To do so would open oneself to accusations of being a colonial tribalist. However, beginning with the period of multiparty politics in the 1990s, ethnic-based ("tribal") references became prevalent in media, government, and even academic exchanges.

3. Good histories of the Baringo basin can be found in Anderson (2002) and Spear and Waller (1993).

4. This section draws on some of the work in Little (1998).

5. Kibaki held a cabinet post during the Kenyatta era and was vice president for a short period during the Moi era.

6. This lawsuit became well known to the Kenyan public and media because one of the key pieces of evidence Il Chamus claimants submitted in court was a toothless goat. They took this action to show the extent of damage to their key economic asset, livestock, caused by the spread of *Prosopus spp.* The presence of the goat before a white-wigged Kenyan judge brought on more than a little ridicule by the press, as well as strong reaction among the Kenyan public. Different newspaper reporters in Kenya picked up on the story of the toothless goat in court, as did several international news services (Kadida 2006; Masibo 2008). Based on the court's ruling in favor of the Il Chamus, the government is supposed to assist the community in utilizing and/or eliminating *Prosopus* and to provide compensation for damages. However, so far very little compensation has been paid, nor have major project initiatives been funded (field notes, June 2009). Nonetheless, the case highlighted the plight of Il Chamus and brought national attention to a community that most Kenyans had never heard of prior to the media accounts.

7. As noted earlier, pseudonyms are used throughout the book except in cases where the identity of the individual is obvious (for example, President Daniel arap Moi).

8. Postelection violence in 2007–2008 was minimal in central Baringo, especially since there were few Kikuyu and Luo residing in the district. Those Kikuyu who had businesses in Marigat, the main Il Chamus town, were not seriously harassed by locals as was the case elsewhere in the Rift Valley. Nonetheless, on January 15, 2008, Kikuyu residents of the area who wished to leave were escorted out of the district by the Kenyan army. A few of them returned

to Marigat after the situation calmed down, but others had yet to return as of June 2009 (field notes, June 2009).

5. "The Government Is Always Telling Us What to Think"

1. For example, Lentz et al. note, "Discussions on food aid and dependency often draw on what appears to be a broad body of evidence but upon closer inspection reveals that much of this . . . are supported only by unverified anecdotes rather than detailed ethnographic or econometric research" (Lentz et al. 2005: 10).

2. Parts of this section are based on Little (2008a).

3. In 1972, only 52 percent of peasants in Dessie Zurie, South Wollo, cultivated their own land, and another 23 percent were part-time tenants and part land owners. The rest were landless tenant farmers, sharecroppers, or farm workers (Kiros and Mehretu 1977: 5).

4. He currently lives in exile on a farm in Zimbabwe.

5. *Mekenajo* refers to a practice whereby owners of a single ox combine their animals, so they have the required number of oxen (2) to plow their fields. It is a widespread institution in South Wollo.

6. The material in this section draws in part from Little (2008a).

7. PA stands for Peasant Association, and farmers often use it interchangeably with the term "kebele" to refer to the local administrative unit. After the 1991 revolution the term "kebele" increasingly was used to describe these local administrative units, since PA mainly is associated with the previous socialist government of the Derg.

8. The government made it clear that all participants had to contribute labor for public works projects to receive food or cash unless they were disabled or elderly. This tactic was very much in line with the goals of reducing dependency-like behavior and increasing individual accountability.

9. The highest months of food aid distribution during the 1999–2000 drought in Ethiopia were from July to September 2000, when distribution exceeded 100,000 metric tons per month (Hammond and Maxwell 2002: 272). Unfortunately, by this time almost all of the drought-induced damage to assets and livelihoods in South Wollo had already taken place.

6. "Counting the Poor"

1. The Government of Kenya currently is pursuing a long-term policy strategy titled "Vision 2030," which hopes to transform Kenya into a "modern" middle-income country by the year 2030. Its first five-year development plan under "Vision 2030" still highlights growth and poverty reduction as key foci. I quote from the recent plan: "Other than high growth, the MTP places a premium on faster job creation, poverty reduction, improved income distribution and gender equity while also ensuring that balance is attained in development across all regions of the country" (Kenya 2008: 2).

2. This section also draws on materials presented in Little et al. (2008).

3. This and the next two examples are drawn from the author's written contributions to McPeak et al. (2011).

4. A TLU is defined as one head of cattle, 0.7 camel, or 10 goats or sheep.

5. The reascendance of growth-oriented development models in the 1980s and 1990s and the subsequent decline of the Marxist and dependency schools in development studies probably accounts for this relative lack of attention to inequality and class-based analyses.

6. This discussion draws heavily on materials in Little et al. (2008) and McPeak and Little (2004).

7. A similar point was made by Ferguson more than twenty years ago, when he referred to a rural development project in Lesotho as the "anti-politics" machine (Ferguson 1990).

7. "A Sort of Free Business"

1. I am not counting the current five years (2007–2012) that the Transitional Federal Government (TFG) has been in Mogadishu as a period when there has been a functioning state. Its highly contested government controlled no more than a few square blocks of the capital city of Mogadishu until 2012, and the rest of the country remains without government control. In the north there is the Republic of Somaliland, which is not recognized internationally except by a few rogue states, such as Libya, although it has made some significant progress toward achieving political stability. The country, or at least the southern and central parts that once formed the Italian colony of Somalia, still is for all practical purposes stateless despite renewed optimism in 2012 that conflict and social conditions are beginning to markedly improve.

2. I credit Tobias Hagmann for helping me think through this argument.

3. Somali culture always has had a distinctly transnational flavor. In fact, few populations in sub-Saharan Africa were more affected by colonial partition than the Somali community and it was forced to develop expansive networks across international boundaries. In the late nineteenth century they were split among five different colonial territories in the Horn of Africa under the control of three competing European powers—Britain, Italy, and France—and an expansionist regional empire, Abyssinia (Ethiopia). Somali trading networks also had reached parts of the Middle East and south Asia as early as the sixteenth century (see Cassanelli 1982).

4. It is not the intention here to rehash the history of civil conflict and violence in Somalia since the country's collapse in 1991 (for the early period of the conflict, see Mubarak 1997; Clarke and Herbst 1997; and for more recent assessments, see Menkhaus 2007; Verhoeven 2009). However, it should be noted that with the exception of the first half of 2012, the situation in Somalia greatly deteriorated since the bulk of data for this chapter (pre-2006) were gathered.

5. In 2005 I attended a joint UNDP/World Bank–sponsored seminar in Washington, D.C., on the Somali remittance economy, where discussions about a development program for the war-torn country were openly held.

6. This discussion excludes Somaliland in the northwest, which has its own functioning government, currency, and monetary system.

7. The 2009 population census results are not yet disaggregated by individual towns, so the figure for Garissa town is derived from the Garissa District figure for 2009, which is 623,060. The estimate for Garissa town is based on a percentage (25%) of the district's total population in 1999. If anything, the 2009 figure for the town (155,765) based on this method of calculation probably is well below the actual population, since it is highly likely Garissa town grew much faster than the rest of the district. In the country as a whole, urban population now accounts for 32.3 percent of total population (Kenya 2010b: 3), which is an urban ratio about 30 percent higher than was used to estimate Garissa town's population.

8. Of course, the nearby presence of the Dadaab refugee settlement, the largest refugee camp in the world with a population over 500,000, contributes to the general growth in population and service and supply businesses in Garissa. Dadaab is about 80 kilometers northeast of Garissa town.

9. Zakat is a charitable contribution of cash and/or other resources given by Muslims to the

poor. Under Al-Shabaab rule in southern Somalia it is seen by some traders as a tax on their businesses.

10. The harassment of Somali refugees in Eastleigh and their forced deportation from Kenya actually began earlier than 2009 (Rutten and Muli 2008)

11. Many products, such as textiles from Indonesia or electronics from China, come to Dubai and then are re-exported to Somalia or to Somali-owned businesses in Kenya. As a recent newspaper account from Indonesia indicates, the country exports 20 million Indonesian sarongs to Somalia but all of these first go to Dubai. The same story goes on to explain that "most trade with Somalia has been routed via Dubai because of security concerns related to the ongoing civil war in Somalia and rampant piracy in its coastal waters" (Tisnabudi 2010: 1).

References

Aalen, Lovise. 2006. "Ethnic Federalism and Self-Determination for Nationalities in a Semi-Authoritarian State: The Case of Ethiopia." *International Journal on Minority and Group Rights* 13: 243–261.

Abdulsamed, Farah. 2011. *Somali Investment in Kenya.* Briefing Paper AFP BP 2011/02. London: Chatham House.

Abraham, Korir S. 2012. *Kenya at 50: Unrealised Rights of Minority and Indigenous Peoples.* London: Minority Rights Group International.

Abrahamsen, R. 2000. *Disciplining Democracy: Development Discourse and Good Government in Africa.* London: Zed Press.

———. 2004. "Poverty Reduction or Adjustment by Another Name." *Review of African Political Economy* 31 (99): 184–187.

Africa News Service. 1999. "100 Kenyans Trapped in Somalia." http://www.comtexnews.com.

African Commission on Human and Peoples' Rights (ACHPR). 2007. *Advisory of the African Commission on Human and Peoples' Rights of the United Nations: Declaration on the Rights of Indigenous Peoples.* Banjul, The Gambia: ACHPR.

African Union. 2008. *Report of the Chairperson of the Commission on the Situation in Somalia.* Peace and Security Council 105th Meeting. Addis Ababa: African Union.

African Wildlife Foundation (AWF). 2008. "Land Trusts." http://www.awf.org/Section /Land/Landtrusts.

———. 2011. "Adopt African Acres Today." http://shop.awf.org/Acre/Default.Aspx.

African Wildlife Fund (AWF)/KWS (Kenya Wildlife Services). 2007. "Draft Memorandum of Understanding: Collaboration in the Conservation and Management of Wildlife and Habitat in Kenya." http://www.Kws.org/Images/AWF-KWS %20mou%207%20Nov%202007).Pdf.

Agadjanian, Victor. 2002. "Men Doing 'Women's Work': Masculinity and Gender Relations among Street Vendors in Maputo, Mozambique." *Journal of Men's Studies* 10 (3): 329–342.

Agro-Ind. 2002. "European Union–West Africa Agro-Business Sector Meeting." November 4–7. Dakar, Senegal. http://www.Proinvest-Eu.org/Files/Files/AGROIND /Html_En/Gambia.Html.

Ahmed, Mohamed. 2008. "The Marginalized Communities." *Daily Nation,* February 2. http://www.nationmedia.com/dailynation/printpage.asp?newsid=115932.

Akinyi, Nancy. 2007. "ECK to Decide on Il Chamus Community." *Kenya Broadcasting Corporation.* July 30. http://www.kbc.co.ke/story.asp?Id=38865.

Akinyi, Nancy, and Walter Dzuya. 2008. "Battle Rages for Parliamentary Nominations." *Kenya Broadcasting Corporation,* February 14. http://www.kbc.co.ke/story.asp.

Aklilu, Yacoub, and Andy Catley. 2009. *Livestock Exports from the Horn of Africa: An Analysis of Benefits by Pastoralist Wealth Group and Policy Implications.* Medford, Mass.: Feinstein International Center, Tufts University.

Amnesty International. 2010. *From Life without Peace to Peace without Life: The Treat-*

ment of Somali Refugees and Asylum-Seekers in Kenya. London: Amnesty International.

Anderson, David. 2002. *Eroding the Commons: The Politics of Ecology in Baringo, Kenya, 1890–1963*. Oxford: James Currey.

———. 2005. "'Yours in Struggle for Majimbo': Nationalism and the Party Politics of Decolonisation in Kenya, 1955–1964." *Journal of Contemporary History* 40 (3): 547–64.

———. 2010. "Majimboism: The Troubled History of an Idea." In *Our Turn to Eat: Politics in Kenya Since 1950*, ed. Daniel Branch, Nicholas Cheeseman, and Leigh Gardner. Berlin: Lit Verlag.

Anderson, Jens A. 2006. "Informal Moves, Informal Markets: International Migrants and Traders from Mzimba District, Malawi." *African Affairs* 105 (420): 375–397.

Arid Lands Resource Management Project /Price Waterhouse Coopers. 2005. *Garissa District Vision and Strategy: 2005–2015*. Nairobi: Arid Lands Resource Management Project.

Arrighi, G. 2002. "The African Crisis: World Systems and Regional Aspects." *New Left Review* 15: 5–36.

Aryeetey, Ernest, and Ravi Kanbur, eds. 2008. *The Economy of Ghana: Analytical Perspectives on Stability, Growth and Poverty*. Oxford: James Currey.

Aryeetey, Jane Harrigan, and Machiko Nissanke, eds. 2000. *Economic Reforms in Ghana: The Miracle and the Mirage*. Oxford: James Currey.

Ashley, C. 2000. "Applying Livelihood Approaches to Natural Resource Management Initiatives: Experiences in Namibia and Kenya." ODI Working Paper 134. Overseas Development Institute, London.

Ashley, C., and K. Hussein. 2000. *Developing Methodologies for Livelihood Impact Assessment: Experience of the African Wildlife Foundation in East Africa*. London: Overseas Development Institute.

Attwood, Brian, M. Peter Mcpherson, and Andrew Natsios. 2008. "Arrested Development: Making Foreign Aid a More Effective Tool." *Foreign Affairs* 87 (6): 122–132.

Avramoski, Oliver. 2004. "The Role of Public Participation and Citizen Involvement in Lake Basin Management." Unpublished Paper. Department of Environmental Sciences and Policy Central European University Nádor U. 9, 1051. Budapest, Hungary.

Babiker, Mustafa. 2013. "Mobile Pastoralism and Land-Grabbing in Sudan: Impacts and Responses." In *Development at the Margins: Pathways of Change in the Horn of Africa*, ed. Andy Catley, Jeremy Lind, and Ian Scoones, 177–185. London: Routledge.

Barham, B., M. Clark, E. Katz, and R. Schurman. 1992. "Nontraditional Agricultural Exports in Latin America." *Latin American Research Review* 27 (2): 43–82.

Baringo County Council and Koibetak County Council/World Wildlife Fund. 2007. *Lake Bogoria National Reserve: Integrated Management Plan, 2007–2012*. Nairobi: WWF Eastern Africa Regional Programme Office.

Barrett, C. B., and D. G. Maxwell. 2005. *Food Aid after Fifty Years: Recasting Its Role*. London: Routledge.

Barrett, H. R., A. W. Browne, and B. W. Ilbery. 2004. "The Trade in Fresh Horticultural Produce from Sub-Saharan Africa to the United Kingdom." In *Geographies of Commodity Chains*, ed. A. Hughes, 19–38. London: Routledge.

Barrow, Edmund, Helen Gichohi, and Mark Infield. 2000. *Summary and Key Lessons from a Comparative Review and Analysis of Community Conservation in East Africa.* Nairobi: IUCN Eastern Africa Regional Office.

Baulch, Bob. 1987. "Entitlements and the Wollo Famine of 1982–1985." *Disasters* 11 (2): 195–204.

Bayart, Jean-Francois, Stephen Ellis, and Beatrice Hibou, eds. 1999. *The Criminalization of the State in Africa.* Oxford: James Currey.

BBC (British Broadcasting Corporation). 2006. "Landmark Ruling for Kenya Nomads." *BBC News,* December 19. http://news.bbc.co.uk/go/pr/fr/-/1/hi/world/africa /6194373.stm.

Behnke, R. 2011. *Livestock's Contribution to Kenya's Economy: 150% Higher than Previously Thought.* Livestock Brief. IGAD Livestock Policy Initiative. Addis Ababa: Livestock Policy Initiative Program.

Behnke, R., I. Scoones, and C. Kerven, eds. 1993. *Range Ecology at Disequilibrium: New Models of Natural Variability and Pastoral Adaptation in African Savannas.* London: Overseas Development Institute.

Bekele, Eshetu. 2008. "Status of Extreme Poverty and Hunger in Pastoral Areas of Ethiopia: Looking Inward and Forward." In *Proceedings of the Fourth National Conference on Pastoral Development in Ethiopia, 2007,* ed. S. Adi and T. Getahun, 92–108. Addis Ababa: Pastoralist Forum Ethiopia.

Berry, Sara. 2007. "Marginal Gains, Market Values, and History." *African Studies Review* 50 (2): 57–70.

Besteman, Catherine. 1999. *Unraveling Somalia: Race, Violence, and the Legacy of Slavery.* Philadelphia: University of Pennsylvania Press.

Bird, K., K. Moore, D. Hulme, and A. Shepherd. 2002. "Chronic Poverty and Remote Rural Areas." CPRC Working Paper 13. Institute for Development Policy and Management, University of Manchester, Manchester, UK.

Boafo-Arthur, Kwame. 2007. *Ghana: One Decade of the Liberal State.* Dakar: Codesria Book.

Bond, Patrick, and George Dor. 2007. "Uneven Health Outcomes and Political Resistance under Residual Neoliberalism in Africa." In *Neoliberalism, Globalization, and Inequalities: Consequences for Health and Quality of Life,* ed. Vicente Navarro, 345–367. Amityville, N.Y: Baywood Publishing.

Boyd, Charlotte, with Roger Blench, David Bourn, Liz Drake, and Peter Stevenson. 1999. "Reconciling Interests among Wildlife, Livestock and People in Eastern Africa: A Sustainable Livelihoods Approach." Natural Resources Perspectives 45. London: Overseas Development Institute.

Branch, Daniel, and Nic Cheeseman. 2009. "Democratization, Sequencing, and State Failure in Africa: Lessons from Kenya." *African Affairs* 108 (430): 1–26.

Bratton, Michael. 1997. *Democratic Experiments in Africa: Regime Transitions in Comparative Perspective.* Cambridge: Cambridge University Press.

Broch-Due, Vigdis. 1990. "'Livestock Speak Louder Than Sweet Words': Changing Property and Gender Relations among the Turkana." In *Property, Poverty and People: Changing Rights in Property and Problems of Pastoral Development,* ed. P. Baxter and R. Hogg, 147–163. Manchester, UK: Dept. of Soc. Anthro., University of Manchester.

———. 1999. "Remembered Cattle, Forgotten People: The Morality of Exchange and the

Exclusion of the Turkana Poor." In *The Poor Are Not Us: Poverty and Pastoralists*, ed. D. Anderson and V. Broch-Due, 50–88. Oxford: James Currey Publishers.

Brockington, Daniel. 2002. *Fortress Conservation: The Preservation of the Mkomazi Game Reserve, Tanzania*. Oxford: James Currey Publishers.

Brosius, P. 1999. "On the Practice of Transnational Cultural Critique." *Identities* 6 (2–3): 179–200.

Brown, Alison, ed. 2006. *Contested Space: Street Trading, Public Space, and Livelihoods in Developing Countries*. Warwickshire, UK: Practical Action Publishing.

Brown, Alison, Michal Lyons, and Ibrahima Dankoco. 2010. "Street Traders and the Emerging Spaces for Urban Voice and Citizenship in African Cities." *Urban Studies* 47 (3): 666–683.

Brown, O., and C. Sander. 2007. *Supermarket Buying Power: Global Supply Chains and Smallholder Farmers*. Winnipeg: International Institute for Sustainable Development.

Brown, Stephen. 2001. "Authoritarian Rules and Multi-party Elections in Africa: How Foreign Donors Help to Keep Daniel Arap Moi in Power." *Third World Quarterly* 22 (5): 725–739.

———. 2007. "From Demiurge to Midwife: The Changing Donor Roles in Kenya's Democratisation Process." In *Kenya: The Struggle for Democracy*, ed. G. Murunga and S. Nasong'o, 300–330. London: Zed Press.

Brown, Taylor, and Amdissa Teshome. 2007. "Implementing Policies for Chronic Poverty in Ethiopia." Background Paper for the Chronic Poverty Report 2008–09. University of Manchester Chronic Poverty Research Centre, Manchester, UK.

Bruck, Tilman, and Kathleen van den Broeck. 2006. *Growth, Employment and Poverty in Mozambique*. Pretoria: Southern African Regional Poverty Network.

Bryceson, Deborah, and Deborah Potts. 2006. *African Urban Economies: Viability, Vitality, or Vitiation*. London: Palgave Macmillan.

Bulte, Erwin H., Randall B. Boone, Randy Stringer, and Philip K. Thornton. 2008. "Elephants or Onions? Paying for Nature in Amboseli, Kenya." *Environment and Development Economics* 13 (May): 395–414.

Burchell, Graham, C. Gordon, and P. Miller, eds. 1991. *The Foucault Effect: Studies in Governmentality with Two Lectures by and an Interview with Michel Foucault*. Chicago: University of Chicago Press.

Business Daily. 2010. "New Laws Bolster Court to Make Landmark Ruling." Nairobi, November 8. http://www.businessdailyafrica.com/corporate+news/-/539550 /1049622/-/view/printversion/-/h3pc7ez/-/index.html.

Campbell, David J., Helen Gichohi, Robin Reid, Albert Mwangi, Lucy Chege, and Thor Sawin. 2003. "Interactions between People and Wildlife in Southeastern Kajiado District." LUCID Working Paper Series no. 18. Land Use Change Impacts and Dynamics (LUCID) Project, Michigan State University, East Lansing.

Campbell, Elizabeth H. 2005. *Formalizing the Informal Economy: Somali Refugee and Migrant Trade Networks in Nairobi*. Report no. 47. Geneva: Global Commission on International Migration.

———. 2006. "Urban Refugees in Nairobi: Problems of Protection, Mechanisms of Survival, and Possibilities for Integration." *Journal of Refugee Studies* 19 (3): 396–413.

Carrier, Neil. 2011. "Reviving Yaaku: Identity and indigeneity in Northern Kenya." *African Studies* 70 (2): 246–263.

Carter, M., B. Barham, and D. Mesbah. 1996. "Agroexport Booms and the Rural Resource Poor in Chile, Guatemala, and Paraguay." *Latin American Research Review* 31 (1): 33–65.

Cassanelli, Lee. 1982. *The Shaping of Somali Society: Reconstructing the History of a Pastoral People, 1600–1900.* Philadelphia: University of Pennsylvania Press.

Castro, A. Peter, and Kassahun Kebede. 2003. "Detailed Field Notes from Interviews in Oromiya and South Wello Zones, Amhara Region, Ethiopia, July 2003." BASIS South Wollo Research Program.

Castro, A. Peter, and D. Mengistu. 2002. "Detailed Field Notes from Interviews in Oromiya and South Wello Zones, Amhara Region, Ethiopia, June 2002." BASIS South Wollo Research Program.

Castro, A. Peter, Alula Pankhurst, and Yigremew Adal. 2001. "Detailed Field Notes from Interviews in Oromiya and South Wello Zones, Amhara Region, Ethiopia, May 2001." BASIS South Wollo Research Program.

Catley, Andy, Jeremy Lind, and Ian Scoones. 2013. "Development at the Margins: Pastoralism in the Horn of Africa." In *Development at the Margins: Pathways of Change in the Horn of Africa,* ed. Andy Catley, Jeremy Lind, and Ian Scoones. London: Routledge.

CBS (Central Bureau of Statistics). 2003. *Geographic Dimensions of Well-Being in Kenya: Where Are the Poor?* Nairobi: Ministry of Planning and National Development in Collaboration with International Livestock Research Institute.

Centre for Minority Rights Development (CEMIRIDE). 2006. *Annual Report 2005/2006.* Nairobi: CEMIRIDE.

Chau, Donovan C. 2010. "The Fourth Point: An Examination of the Influence of Kenyan Somalis in Somalia." *Journal of Contemporary African Studies* 28 (3): 297–312.

Chilcote, Ronald H., ed. 1983. *Theories of Development: Mode of Production or Dependency.* Beverly Hills, Calif.: Sage Publications.

Clarke, John. 2004. "Dissolving the Public Realm? The Logics and Limits of Neo-Liberalism." *Journal of Social Policy* 33(1): 27–48.

———. 2008. "Living with/in and without Neo-Liberalism." *Focaal* 51 (1):135–147.

Clarke, Walter, and Jeffrey Herbst. 1997. *Learning from Somalia: The Lessons of Armed Humanitarian Intervention.* Boulder: Westview Press.

Coalition of European Lobbies for Eastern African Pastoralism. 2011. "Fact Sheet: Eastern African Pastoralism." http://www.Celep.info/?Cat=4.

Collier, Paul. 2008. *The Bottom Billion: Why the Poorest Countries Are Failing and What Can Be Done about It.* Oxford: Oxford University Press.

Comaroff, Jean, and John L. Comaroff. 2001. *Millennial Capitalism and the Culture of Neoliberalism.* Durham, N.C: Duke University Press.

Commonwealth Secretariat and National Investment Board (The Gambia). N.d. *Cut Flowers, The Gambia: An Opportunity to Invest.* London: Commonwealth Secretariat; Banjul, The Gambia: National Investment Board.

Conley, T., and C. Udry. 2004. *Learning about a New Technology: Pineapple in Ghana.* New Haven, Conn.: Center for Economic Growth, Yale University.

Cooke, D., and A. Hughes. 1997. "The Politics of Economic Recovery: The Gambia's Experience of Structural Adjustment, 1985–94." *Commonwealth and Comparative Politics* 35 (1): 93–117.

Cotula, L., S. Vermeulen, R. Leonard, and J. Keeley. 2009. *Land Grab or Development*

Opportunity: Agricultural Investment and International Land Deals in Africa. Rome: International Fund for Agricultural Development.

Craig, David, and Doug Porter (2003). "Poverty Reduction Strategy Papers: A New Convergence." *World Development* 31 (1): 53–69.

Cultural Survival. 2005. "Maasai Wary of Draft Constitution Backed by Government." *Cultural Survival,* November 4. http://www.culturalsurvival.org/print/7793.

———. 2006. "Maasai-Led Grassroots Education Efforts Prove Essential to Referendum Defeat." *Cultural Survival,* February 8. http://www.culturalsurvival.org/print /7820.

Daddieh, C., and P. D. Little, with K. Arhin. 1995. *Pineapple Production and Labor Relations in the Peri-Urban Area of Accra, Ghana.* Binghamton, N.Y.: Institute for Development Anthropology.

Daily Nation. 2004. "Commentary Calls for More 'Effective Structures' to Conserve Wildlife." Nairobi. December 4, 12.

———. 2010a. "Eastleigh Traders Protest over Crackdown." January 22. http://www .nation.co.ke/news/-/1056/847724/-/vpengl/-/index.html.

———. 2010b. "Ilchamus Back in Court to Stop Nominations." November 24. http:// allafrica.com.proxy.library.emory.edu/stories/201011250606.html.

———. 2010c. "PM Assures Somalis over Crackdown." January 26. http://www.nation .co.ke/news/politics/-/1064/850330/-/wruhx9z/-/index.html.

Daily Observer. 1994. "Editorial: Control the Land before It's Lost Forever." Banjul, The Gambia. May 9, 6.

Daniels, Lisa. 1988. "The Economics of Staggered Production and Storage for Selected Horticultural Crops in The Gambia." Master's thesis, Economics Department, University of Wisconsin at Madison.

Dejene, Alemneh. 1990. *Environment, Famine, and Politics in Ethiopia: A View from the Village.* Boulder, Colo.: Lynne Rienner Publishers.

De Soto, Hernando. 2000. *The Mystery of Capital: Why Capitalism Triumphs in the West and Fails Everywhere Else.* New York: Basic Books.

Deveau, Vanessa, and Maria I. Marshall. 2008. "How Beneficial Is Tourism? An Analysis of the Economic Impact of Tourism in Il N'gwesi, Kenya." Paper prepared for presentation at the American Agricultural Economics Association Annual Meeting, Orlando, Fla., July 27–29.

Devereux, Stephen. 2010. "Better Marginalized Than Incorporated? Political Livelihoods in Somali Region, Ethiopia." *European Journal of Development Research* 22 (5): 678–695.

Devereux, Stephen, Rachel Sabates-Wheeler, Mulugeta Tefera, and Hailemichael Taye. 2006. *Ethiopia's Productive Safety Net Programme (PSNP): Trends in PSNP Transfers within Targeted Households.* Sussex, UK: Institute of Development Studies.

De Waal, Alex. 1997. *Famine Crimes: Politics and the Disaster Relief Industry in Africa.* Bloomington: Indiana University Press.

De Wilde, John C. 1967. *Experiences with Agricultural Development in Tropical Africa.* Vol. 1. Baltimore: Johns Hopkins University Press.

Dickinson, Daniel. 2005. "Somalis Cash in on Dubai Boom." *BBC News.* Dec 19. http://newsvote.bbc.co.uk/mpapps/pagetools/print/news.bbc.co.uk/2/hi/africa /4535642.stm.

Dietz, T. 1996. *Entitlements to Natural Resources: Contours of Political Environmental Geography.* Utrecht, Netherlands: International Books.

Dolan, Catherine S. 1997. "TESCO Is King: Gender and Labor Dynamics in Horticultural Exporting, Meru District, Kenya." PhD diss., State University of New York, Binghamton.

———. 2001. "The Good Wife: Struggles over Land and Labour in the Kenyan Horticultural Sector." *Journal of Development Studies* 27 (3): 39–70.

Dolan, Catherine, and J. Humphrey. 2000. "Governance and Trade in Fresh Vegetables: The Impact of UK Supermarkets on the African Horticulture Industry." *Journal of Development Studies* 37 (2): 147–176.

———. 2004. "Changing Governance Patterns in the Trade in Fresh Vegetables between Africa and the United Kingdom." *Environment and Planning* 36 (3): 491–509.

Dove, Michael. 2006. "Indigenous People and Environmental Politics." *Annual Review of Anthropology* 35:191–208.

Dowie, Mark. 2006. "Conservation Refugees: When Protecting Nature Means Kicking People Out." *Seedling*, January, 6–12.

Dubai Chamber of Commerce. 2003. "Trade Statistics." *Economic Bulletin* 3 (19): 1–12.

Dubai Direct Trade. 2010. "Dubai Trade Launches New Digital Edition of Dubai External Trade Statistics." June 29. http://www.dubaidirecttrade.com/dubai-trade -launches-new-digital-edition-of-dubai-external- trade-statistics.

Economist. 2001a. "The Berbers Rise." Vol. 359, no. 8220 (May 5): 39.

———. 2001b. "Protest Gathers on the Borders." Vol. 361, no. 8244 (October 2): 48.

———. 2004. "People Aren't Cattle." Vol. 372, no. 8384 (July 17): 50.

———. 2011. "Africa Rising." Vol. 401, no. 8762 (December 3): 15.

Entreplan. 2005. *The Gambia: Impact Assessment Final Report.* Programme for Capacity Building in Support of Preparation of Economic Partnership Agreement (8 ACP TPS 110). Reading, UK: Entreplan.

Equator Initiative. 2003. *Namunyak Wildlife Conservation Trust: Samburu District, Kenya.* Nairobi: Equator Initiative.

———. 2011. "Report 2 (of 6): People of the Wildlife—Kenya." http://www.equatorinitiative .org/images/stories/equatorknowledge/publications/peopleofthewildlife_tve.pdf.

Escobar, Arturo. 1995. *Encountering Development: The Making and Unmaking of the Third World.* Princeton, N.J.: Princeton University Press.

Eshetu, Bekele. 2008. "Status of Extreme Poverty and Hunger in Pastoral Areas of Ethiopia: Looking Inward and Forward." In *Proceedings of the Fourth National Conference: Pastoral Development in Ethiopia,* August 29–30, 2007, ed. Adi Sora and Daniel Temesgen, 92–108. Addis Ababa: Pastoralist Forum Ethiopia.

Ethiopia [Federal Democratic Republic of]. 2002. *Food Security Strategy.* Addis Ababa: Ministry of Rural Development.

———. 2005. *Ethiopia: Building on Progress: A Plan for Accelerated and Sustained Development to End Poverty (PASDEP). 2005/06–2009/10.* Addis Ababa: Ministry of Finance and Economic Development (Mofed).

———. 2008. *Policy Statement for the Sustainable Development of Pastoral and Agropastoral Areas of Ethiopia.* Addis Ababa: Ministry of Federal Affairs.

———. 2009. *Food Security Programme: 2010–2014.* Addis Ababa: Ministry of Agriculture.

Ethiopia Sanitary and Phytosanitary Standards and Livestock and Meat Marketing Program. 2011. "Ethiopian Meat and Live Animal Exports Register Dramatic Increase." *Focus on Ethiopia's Meat and Live Animal Export Trade Bulletin* 5 (July): 1–3.

Ethiopian Network on Food Security. 2002. "Monthly Report," no.12/02. Dec. 13.

FAO (Food and Agricultural Organization). 1967. *Survey of Njemps Territory, Baringo District.* Nairobi: FAO.

———. 1989–2002. "Trade Statistics." http://Faostat.Fao.org

———. 1992. *Horticultural Improvement Project: Project Findings and Recommendations, The Gambia.* Report prepared for the Government of The Gambia by FAO/UNDP. Rome: FAO.

FAO (Food and Agriculture Organization)/WFP (World Food Programme). 2002. *Special Report: FAO/WFP Crop and Food Supply Assessment Mission to Ethiopia.* FAO Global Information and Early Warning System on Food and Agriculture, World Food Programme. Rome, Italy: FAO/WFP.

Farah, Abdulkadir Osman. 2009. "Diaspora Involvement in the Development of Somalia." Development, Innovation and International Political Economy Research (DIIPER), Research Series, Working Paper no. 13. Aalborg University, Denmark.

Farmer, Elizabeth, and James Mbwika. 2012. *End Market Analysis of Livestock and Meat: A Desk Study.* Microreport no. 84. Washington, D.C.: USAID.

Ferguson, James. 1990. *The Anti-Politics Machine: "Development," Depoliticization, and Bureaucratic Power in Lesotho.* Cambridge: Cambridge University Press.

———. 2006. *Global Shadows: Africa in the Neoliberal World Order.* Durham, N.C.: Duke University Press.

———. 2007. Formalities of Poverty: Thinking about Social Assistance in Neoliberal South Africa. *African Studies Review* 50 (2): 71–86.

———. 2009. The Uses of Neoliberalism. *Antipode* 41 (S1): 166–184.

Fletcher, John, and Yeganeh Morakabati. 2008. "Tourism Activity, Terrorism and Political Instability within the Commonwealth: The Cases of Fiji and Kenya." *International Journal of Tourism Research* 10 (6): 537–556.

Food Security Analysis Unit (FSAU)/Somalia. 2008. Press release. "More Than a Quarter of the Population of Somalia Are in Humanitarian Crisis." Nairobi: FSAU/Somalia.

Foucault, Michel. 1991a. "Politics and the Study of Discourse." In *The Foucault Effect: Studies in Governmentality with Two Lectures by and an Interview with Michel Foucault,* ed. G. Burchell, C. Gordon, and P. Miller, 53–72. Chicago: University of Chicago Press.

———. 1991b. "Governmentality." In *The Foucault Effect: Studies in Governmentality with Two Lectures by and an Interview with Michel Foucault,* ed. G. Burchell, C. Gordon, and P. Miller, 87–104. Chicago: University of Chicago Press.

Friedberg, Judith. 2004. *French Beans and Food Scares: Culture and Commerce in an Anxious Era.* Oxford: Oxford University Press.

Galaty, John G. 1982. "Being 'Maasai'; Being 'People-Of-the-Cattle': Ethnic Shifters in East Africa." *American Ethnologist* 9:1–20.

———. 1992. "'The Land Is Yours': Social and Economic Factors in the Privatization, Sub-Division and Sale of Maasai Ranches." *Nomadic Peoples* 30: 26–40.

———. 2013. "Land-Grabbing in Eastern African Rangelands." In *Pastoralism and Development in Africa: Dynamic Change at the Margins,* ed. Andy Catley, Jeremy Lind, and Ian Scoones, 143–153. London: Routledge.

Gambia [The]. 1993. *Task Force on the Formulation of a National industrial Policy.* Banjul, The Gambia: Ministry of Trade, Industry, and Employment.

Gamewatchers Safaris. 2012. "Shompole Lodge." http://www.porini.com/kenya.html ?sub=shompole-lodge.

Gebre-Egziabher, Tegegne, and Mulat Demeke. 2004. *Small Businesses in Small Towns of the Eastern Amhara Region: Nature and Economic Performance.* Madison, Wisc.: BASIS CRSP.

Geda, Alemayehu. 2008. *Scoping Study on the Chinese Relation with Sub Saharan Africa: The Case of Ethiopia.* Nairobi: African Economic Research Consortium (AERC).

Gedi, Abdi, Omar Salah, Ndambo Charles, Ahmed M. Mohamed, Abdi M. Ali, W. Kabaka, and Ahmed M. Farah. 2008. "The Garissa Cattle Market." Presentation to the COMESA Workshop on Pastoral Livelihoods, Garissa, Kenya, September 22–26.

Ghana Private-Public Partnership Food Industry Development Program. 2003. *Mission Report: Analysis of the Ghanaian Fresh Fruits and Vegetables Industry (March 1–8, 2003).* Accra: USAID/Ghana; East Lansing: Michigan State University.

Gibbon, Peter, ed. 1995. *Markets, Civil Society, and Democracy in Kenya.* Uppsala: Nordiska Afrikainstitutet.

Gibson-Graham, J.-K. 2008. "Diverse Economies: Performative Practices for 'Other Worlds.'" *Progress in Human Geography* 32 (5):613–632.

Gilligan, Daniel, John Hoddinott, and Alemayehu Seyoum Taffesse. 2008. *An Analysis of Ethiopia's Productive Safety Nets Programme and Its Linkages.* Washington, D.C.: International Food Policy Research Institute.

Githongo, G. 2003. "Those Magnificent Somalis and Their Flying Informal Networks." *East African Standard,* July 28.

Global Humanitarian Assistance. 2011. "Ethiopia." http://www.globalhumanitarianassistance.org/countryprofile/ethiopia.

Glover, David, and Ken Kusterer. 1990. *Small Farmers, Big Business: Contract Farming and Rural Development.* New York: Palgrave Macmillan.

Gould, Jeremy. 2005. *The New Conditionality. The Politics of Poverty Reduction Strategies.* London: Zed Books.

Graham, Douglas, I. De Coloane, A. Francisco, W. Nall, M. Walker, and P. Jenkins. 1991. *Peri-urban Baseline Research Results: Maputo, Mozambique.* Columbus: Ohio State University Rural Finance Program.

Green, Maia. 2006. "Representing Poverty and Attacking Representations: Perspectives on Poverty from Social Anthropology." *Journal of Development Studies* 42 (7): 1108–1129.

Gulf News. 2010. "Dhow Owners Boycott Somalia Trade." April 10. http://www.gulfnews.com/business/shipping/dhow-owners-boycott-somalia-trade-1.610261.

Hadjmichael, M. T., T. Rumbaugh, and E. Verreydt. 1992. *The Gambia: Economic Adjustment in a Small Open Economy.* IMF Occasional Paper 100. Washington, D.C.: International Monetary Fund.

Haga, Rannveig Jetne. 2009. "Tradition as Resource: Transnational Somali Women Traders Facing the Realities of Civil War." PhD thesis, Uppsala University, Uppsala, Sweden.

Hagmann, Tobias. 2005. "From State Collapse to Duty Free Shop: Somalia's Path to Modernity." *African Affairs* 104 (416): 525–535.

Hammond, Laura. 2008. "Strategies of Invisibilization: How Ethiopia's Resettlement Programme Hides the Poorest of the Poor." *Journal of Refugee Studies* 21 (4): 517–536.

Hammond, Laura, and Walter Eggenberger. 1999. *Food Aid Deliveries to South Welo Increased but Targeting Remains a Problem.* Addis Ababa: United Nations Development Programme–Emergencies Unit for Ethiopia.

Hammond, Laura, and Daniel Maxwell. 2002. "The Ethiopian Crisis of 1999–2000: Lessons Learned, Questions Unanswered." *Disasters* 26 (3): 262–279.

Hanlon, Joseph. 1986. *Apartheid's Second Front: South Africa's War against Its Neighbours.* Hammondswort, UK: Penguin.

———. 1991. *Mozambique: Who Calls the Shots.* Oxford: James Currey.

———. 1996. *Peace without Profit: How the IMF Blocks Rebuilding in Mozambique.* Oxford: James Currey.

Hanmer, Lucia, Gerrishon Ikiara, Walter Eberlei, and Carolyn Abong. 2003. "Kenya." *Development Policy Review* 21 (2): 179–196.

Hansen, Karen, and Mariken Vaa, eds. 2004. *Reconsidering Informality: Perspectives from Urban Africa.* Uppsala: Nordiska Afrikainstitutet.

Hansen, Stig. 2007. *"Civil War Economies, the Hunt for Profit and the Incentives for Peace (the Case of Somalia)."* AE Working Paper no. 1. Department of Economics and International Development, University of Bath, UK.

Harrison, Elizabeth. 2002. "The Problem with the 'Locals': Partnership and Participation in Ethiopia." *Development and Change* 33 (4): 587–610.

Harrison, Graham. 2004. *The World Bank and African Governance: The Construction of Governance States.* London: Routledge.

———. 2005. "Economic Faith, Social Project and a Misreading of African Society: The Travails of Neoliberalism in Africa." *Third World Quarterly* 26 (8): 1303–1320.

———. 2010a. "Editorial: Post-Neoliberalism?" *Review of African Political Economy* 37 (123): 1–5.

———. 2010b. *Neoliberal Africa: The Impact of Global Social Engineering.* London: Zed Press.

Harvey, David. 2005. A *Brief History of Neoliberalism.* Oxford: Oxford University Press.

Harvey, P., and J. Lind. 2005. *Dependency and Humanitarian Relief: A Critical Analysis.* Humanitarian Policy Group (HPG) Report 19. London: Overseas Development Institute.

Hassan, Sheikh, and Sally Healy. 2009. *Somalia's Missing Million: The Somali Diaspora and Its Role in Development.* Nairobi: UNDP.

Hatfield, Richard, and Jonathan Davies. 2006. *Global Review of the Economics of Pastoralism.* Nairobi: World Initiative for Sustainable Pastoralism.

Haugerud, Angelique. 1995. *The Culture of Politics in Modern Kenya.* Cambridge: Cambridge University Press.

Healy, Sally. 2010. "Reflections on the Somali State: What Went Wrong and Why It Might Not Matter." In *Milk and Peace, Drought and War: Somali Culture, Society and Politics,* ed. Markus Hoehne and Virginia Luling, 367–384. New York: Columbia University Press.

Helleiner, G. K., ed. 2002. *Non-traditional Export Promotion in Africa: Experience and Issues.* New York: Palgrave.

Heintz, James B., Carlos Oya, and Eduardo Zepeda. 2008. "Towards an Employment-Centered Development Strategy for Poverty Reduction in The Gambia: Macro-Economic and Labour Market Characteristics." Country Study no. 16. New York: International Poverty Centre, UNDP.

Hesse, Brian. 2010. "Where Somalia Works." *Journal of Contemporary African Studies* 28 (3): 343–362.

Hibou, Beatrice. 2004. *Privatizing the State* (English translation). New York: Columbia University Press.

Hodgson, Dorothy. 2002. "Precarious Alliances: The Cultural Politics and Structural Predicaments of the Indigenous Rights Movement in Tanzania." *American Anthropologist* 104 (4):1086–1096.

———. 2011. *Becoming Maasai, Becoming Indigenous: Politics and Identity in a Neoliberal Age.* Bloomington: Indiana University Press.

Holden, Constance. 2005. "Kenyan Edict Threatens Famed Park." *Science* 310 (October 14): 215.

Homewood, K. 2008. *Ecology of African Pastoralist Systems.* Oxford: James Currey Publishers.

Hopkins, A. G. 2005. "Making Poverty History: Review Essay." *International Journal of African Historical Studies* 38 (3): 513–531.

Hubl, Klaus. 1986. "The Nomadic Livestock Production Systems of Somalia." In *Agriculture in the Winds of Change,* ed. P. Conze and T. Labahn, 55–72. Saarbrucken-Schafbrucke, Germany: Epi Verlag Gmb.

Hulme, David, and Marshall Murphree. 2001. "Community Conservation as Policy Promise and Performance." In *African Wildlife and Livelihoods: The Promise and Performance of Community Conservation,* ed. David Hulme and Marshall Murphree, 280–297. Portsmouth, N.H.: Heinemann.

Hulme, David, and A. Shepherd. 2003. "Conceptualizing Chronic Poverty." *World Development* 31 (3): 403–422.

Human Rights Watch. 2010. "Kenya: Landmark Ruling on Indigenous Land Rights— African Human Rights Commission Condemns Expulsion of Endorois People for Tourism." News release. February 10. http://www.hrw.org/en/news/2010/02/04/kenya-landmark-ruling-Indigenous-land-rights.

Humphrey, J. 2004. "Commodities, Diversification and Poverty Reduction." Paper presented at FAO Symposium on the State of Agricultural Commodity Market Research, Rome, December 5–16, 2003.

Hunt, Diana, and Michael Lipton. 2011. *Green Revolutions for Sub-Saharan Africa.* Chatham House Briefing Paper, Africa Programme, AFP BP 2011/01. London: Chatham House.

Hyatt, Susan B. 2011. "What Was Neoliberalism and What Comes Next?" In *Policy Worlds: Anthropology and the Analysis of Contemporary Power,* ed. C. Shore, S. Wright, and D. Pero, 105–123. Oxford: Berghan Books.

IDL Group. 2007. *Building Consensus for Social Protection: Insights from Ethiopia's Productive Safety Net Programme (PSNP).* Bristol, UK: IDL Group.

Igoe, James. 2006. "Becoming Indigenous Peoples: Difference, Inequality, and the Globalization of East African Identity Politics." *African Affairs* 105 (420): 399–420.

Igoe, James, and Dan Brockington. 2007. "Neoliberal Conservation: A Brief Introduction." *Conservation and Society* 5 (4): 432–449.

ILO (International Labor Organization). 2002. *Women and Men in the Informal Economy: A Statistical Picture.* Geneva: ILO.

IMF (International Monetary Fund). 2005. *Kenya: Poverty Reduction Strategy Paper.* IMF Country Report no. 05/11. Washington, D.C.: IMF.

IMF/World Bank. 2002. *Poverty Reduction Strategy Papers: Implementation Progress.* Washington, D.C.: IMF.

Infoplease. 2008. *World Atlas and Map Library.* http://www.infoplease.com/atlas.

International Trade Centre. 2009. "Trade Competitiveness Map." http://legacy.intracen.org/appli1/tradecom/tp_ip_ci.aspx?RP=706&YR=2009.

International Work Group for Indigenous Affairs (IWGIA). 2007. "Kenya: A Landmark Ruling for the Indigenous People in Kenya." News Archive. http://www.iwgia.org /sw8127.asp.

Issacson, Allen. 1988. "Preface." In *Dumba Nengue, Run for Your Life: Peasant Tales of Tragedy in Mozambique,* by Lina Magaia, 1–2. Trenton, N.J.: Africa World Press.

ISSER (Institute of Statistical, Social and Economic Research).1992. *The State of the Ghanaian Economy in 1991.* Legon, Ghana: ISSER, University of Ghana.

Jallow, Mathew K. 1994. "Sukuta Clan Fight to Regain Property." *Daily Observer* (Banjul, The Gambia), May 9, 1, 14.

Jenkins, Paul. 2004. "Beyond the Formal/Informal Dichotomy: Access to Land in Maputo, Mozambique." In *Reconsidering Informality: Perspectives from Urban Africa,* ed. Karen Hansen and Mariken Vaa, 210–226. Uppsala: Nordiska Afrikainstitutet.

Juma, Celastus, H. Krugman, and A. Ayako. 1993. *The Unsteady State: Structural Adjustment and Sustainable Development in Kenya.* Nairobi: ACTS.

Kadida, Jillo. 2006. "Toothless Goat in Court in Case over Harmful Weed." *Daily Nation* (Nairobi), July 12. http://allafrica.com.proxy.library.emory.edu/stories /200607110218.html.

Kahata, Jane, and Judy Imbanga. 2002. "Sustainable Tourism: A Report on the Civil Society Review of the Implementation of Agenda 21 in Kenya." Prepared for the Kenya NGO Earth Summit Forum 2002, Nairobi.

Kantai, Parselelo. 2009. "Real Estate: Somali Factor Drives Up Price of Property." *Financial Times,* October 29. http://www.ft.com.

———. 2011. "Inside Garissa Lodge, Nairobi's Somali Trading Hub." *Africa Report,* January 31. http://www.theafricareport.com/archives2/frontlines/5136196.

Karanja, Muchiri, and Hassan Huka. 2010. "Border Where Anything Gets In, for Just Sh1,000." *Daily Nation,* July 19. http://www.nation.co.ke/news/border+where +anything+gets+in++for+just+sh1+000+/-/1056/960748/-/view/printversion /-/n541q/-/index.html.

———. 2011. "Here Gunfire and Trade in Contraband Go Hand in Hand." *Daily Nation,* May 25. http://www.nation.co.ke/counties/here+gunfire+and+trade+in+contraband +go+hand+in+hand+/-/1107872/1169462/-/k591p4/-/index.html.

Kates, Robert W., and Partha Dasgupta. 2007. "African Poverty: A Grand Challenge for Sustainability." *Proceedings of the National Academy of Sciences of the United States of America* 104 (43): 16747–16750.

Keating, Joshua. 2011. "Welcome to Azania/Jubbaland: The World's Newest Pseudo-state." *Foreign Policy,* April 6. http://blog.foreignpolicy.com/posts/2011/04/06 /welcome_to_azania_somalias_newest_pseudostate.

Kebede, Emebet. 2006. "Moving from Emergency Food Aid to Predictable Cash Transfers: Recent Experience in Ethiopia." *Development Policy Review* 24 (5): 579–599.

Keenan, Jeremy. 2004. *The Lesser Gods of the Sahara: Social Change and Contested Terrain amongst the Tuareg of Algeria.* London: Frank Cass.

Kenya [Government of]. 1996. *Wildlife Policy.* Nairobi: Government Printers.

———. 2004. *Economic Recovery Strategy for Wealth and Employment Creation 2003–2007.* Nairobi: Ministry of Finance.

———. 2006. "In the Matter of Il Chamus and the Constitution of Kenya: Judgement." Misc. Civil Application no. 305 of 2004. High Court of Kenya, Nairobi.

———. 2008. *Kenya Vision 2030: First Medium Term Plan (MTP) 2008–2012.* Nairobi: Government Printers.

———. 2010a. *The Constitution of Kenya.* Nairobi: National Council for Law Reporting with the Authority of the Attorney General.

———. 2010b. *2009 Census Population and Housing Highlights.* Nairobi: Kenya National Bureau of Statistics.

Kenya Agricultural Research Institute (KARI). 2007. *Environmental and Social Management Framework: Kenya Agricultural Productivity and Sustainable Land Management Project (KAPSLM).* Nairobi: KARI.

Kenya Land [Carter] Commission. 1934. *Evidence and Memoranda.* 2 vols. Nairobi: Government Printer.

Kingfisher, Catherine, and Jeff Maskovsky. 2008. "Introduction: The Limits of Neoliberalism." *Critique of Anthropology* 28: 115–126.

Kipsang, Wycliff, and Noah Cheploen. 2012. "Tension as Il Chamus, Endorois Arm Their Morans." *Daily Nation,* February 14. http://allafrica.com.proxy.library.emory.edu/stories/201202150132.html.

Kiros, F. G., and A. Mehretu. 1977. *Survey of Socio-Economic Characteristics of Rural Ethiopia.* Research Bulletin 15: Comparative Review and Analysis. Addis Ababa: Institute for Development Research, Addis Ababa University.

Klopp, Jacqueline M. 2000. "Pilfering the Public: The Problem of Land Grabbing in Contemporary Kenya." *Africa Today* 47 (1): 7–26.

———. 2001. "Ethnic Clashes and Winning Elections: The Case of Kenya's Electoral Despotism." *Canadian Journal African Studies* 35 (3): 473–517.

———. 2002. "Can Moral Ethnicity Trump Political Tribalism: The Struggle for Land and Nation in Kenya." *African Studies* 61(2): 269–294.

Konadu-Agyemang, Kwadwo, ed. 2001. *IMF and World Bank Sponsored Structural Adjustment Programs in Africa: Ghana's Experience, 1983–1999.* Surrey, UK: Ashgate.

Koteen, Sarah. 2004. "Financing Species Conservation: A Menu of Options." Washington, D.C.: Center for Conservation Finance, World Wildlife Fund.

Kristjanson, Patricia, Maren Radeny, Isabelle Baltenweck, Joseph Ogutu, and An Notenbaert. 2005. "Livelihood Mapping and Poverty Correlates at a Meso-Level in Kenya." *Food Policy* 30: 568–583.

KWS (Kenya Wildlife Services). 1993. *A Policy Framework and Development Progamme, 1991–1996: Annex 6, Community Conservation and Wildlife Management outside Parks and Reserves.* Nairobi: KWS.

———. 1994. *Policy Statement and Operational Summary for Revenue-Sharing and the Wildlife for Development Fund (WDF).* Nairobi: KWS.

———. 1995. *Report on Game Scout Reporting for Laikipia/Samburu Districts.* Nairobi: KWS.

———. 1997a. "Parks beyond Parks: Celebrating 50 Years of National Parks in Kenya, 1946–1996." In *Annual Report 1996.* Nairobi: KWS.

———. 1997b. *Partnership News,* no. 1. Newsletter of the Partnership Department of the Kenya Wildlife Services.

———. 2007. *Conservation and Management Strategy for Grevy's Zebra (Equus grevyi) in Kenya: 2007–2011.* Nairobi: KWS.

Laikipia Wildlife Forum. 2004. *Laikipia Wildlife Forum Newsletter* (May).

———. 2006. *Laikipia Wildlife Forum Newsletter* (July).

———. 2008. "Naibunga Sanctuary." http://www.laikipia.org/hotel_naibunga.htm.

Lamphear, John. 1992. *The Scattering Time: Turkana Responses to the Imposition of Colonial Rule*. Oxford: Oxford University Press.

Lamprey, Richard H., and Robin S. Reid. 2004. "Expansion of Human Settlement in Kenya's Maasai Mara: What Future for Pastoralism and Wildlife?" *Journal of Biogeography* 31 (6): 997–1032.

Landell Mills Associates. 1989. *A Market Survey for Gambian Horticultural Crops in the UK, Sweden, the Netherlands and the Federal Republic of Germany: Final Report*. Commissioned by the Export Market Development Division of the Commonwealth Secretariat. Bath, UK: Landell Mills Associates.

Leach, Melissa, and Robin Mearns, eds. 1996. *The Lie of the Land: Challenging Received Wisdom on the African Environment*. Oxford: James Currey Publishers.

Lent, D., M. Fox, S. Njuguna, and J. Wahome. 2002. *Conservation of Resources through Enterprise (CORE): Mid-Term Evaluation Final Report*. Nairobi: Management Systems International.

Lentz, Eric, C. Barrett, and J. Hoddinott. 2005. *Food Aid Dependency: Implications for Emergency Food Security Assessments*. Rome: World Food Programme.

Le Sage, Andre. 2010. *Somalia's Endless Transition: Breaking the Deadlock*. Strategic Forum no. 257. Washington, D.C.: Institute for National Strategic Studies, National Defense University.

Lesamuti, Joshua. 2005. "Create a Constituency for the Ilchamus Community." *Standard* (Kenya), September 20. http://www.eastandard.net/archives/cl/print/news.php?articleid=29159.

Leys, Colin. 1974. *Underdevelopment in Kenya: The Political Economy of Neo-Colonialism, 1964–1971*. Berkeley: University of California Press.

Li, Tanya M. 2009. *The Will to Improve: Governmentality, Development and the Practice of Politics*. Durham, N.C.: Duke University Press.

Lind, Jeremy, and Teriessa Jalleta. 2005. *Poverty, Power, and Relief Assistance: Meanings and Perceptions of "Dependency" in Ethiopia*. HPG Background Paper. London: Overseas Development Institute.

Lindley, Anna. 2009. "Between 'Dirty Money' and 'Development Capital': Somali Money Transfer Infrastructure under Global Scrutiny." *African Affairs* 108 (433): 519–539.

———. 2010. *The Early Morning Phone Call: Somali Refugees' Remittances*. Oxford: Berghahn Books.

Lindsay, W. K. 1987. "Integrating Parks and Pastoralists: Image and Reality in Kenya Maasailand." In *The Scramble for Resources: Conservation Policies in Africa, 1884–1984*, ed. D. Anderson and A. Grove, 149–167. Cambridge: Cambridge University Press.

Little, Peter D. 1992a. *The Elusive Granary: Herder, Farmer, and State in Northern Kenya*. Cambridge: Cambridge University Press.

———. 1992b. "Traders, Brokers, and Market 'Crisis' in Southern Somalia." *Africa* 62 (1): 94–124.

———. 1994. "Contract Farming and the Development Question." In *Living under Contract: Contract Farming and Agrarian Transformation in Africa*, ed. P. Little and M. Watts, 217–250. Madison: University of Wisconsin Press.

———. 1998. "Maasai Identity on the Periphery." *American Anthropologist* 100 (2): 444–468.

———. 2003. *Somalia: Economy without State.* Bloomington: Indiana University Press.

———. 2006. "Working across Borders: Methodological and Policy Challenges of Cross-Border Livestock Trade in the Horn of Africa." In *Pastoral Livestock Marketing in Eastern Africa: Research and Policy Challenges,* ed. John McPeak and Peter D. Little, 169–185. Warwickshire, UK: ITDG Publications.

———. 2008a. "Food Aid Dependency in Northeast Ethiopia: Myth or Reality?" *World Development* 36 (5): 860–874.

———. 2008b. "Livelihoods, Assets and Food Security in a Protracted Political Crisis: The Case of the Jubba Region, Southern Somalia." In *Beyond Relief: Food Security in Protracted Crises,* ed. L. Alinovi, G. Heimrich, and L. Russo, 107–126. Warwickshire, UK: ITDG Publications/Practical Action Publishing.

Little, Peter D., and Catherine S. Dolan. 2000. "What It Means to Be Restructured: 'Non-Traditional' Commodities and Structural Adjustment in Sub-Saharan Africa." In *Commodities and Globalization: Anthropological Perspectives,* ed. A. Haugerud, P. Stone, and P. Little, 59–78. Boulder, Colo.: Rowman and Littlefield.

Little, Peter D., and Catherine S. Dolan, with I. Jack. 1993. *Labor Relations and Trading in the Peri-urban Areas of Banjul, The Gambia.* Binghamton, N.Y.: Institute for Development Anthropology.

Little, Peter D., and Irae Baptista Lundin de Coloane. 1993. "Trading to Eat: Petty Trade and Income Strategies in the Peri-urban Areas of Maputo, Mozambique." *Development Anthropology Network* 11 (2): 1–8.

Little, Peter D., John G. McPeak, C. Barrett, and P. Kristjanson. 2008. "Challenging Orthodoxies: Understanding Pastoral Poverty in East Africa." *Development and Change* 39 (4): 585–609.

Little, Peter D., John G. McPeak, Roy Behnke, and Getachew Gebru. 2010. *Future Scenarios for Pastoral Development in Ethiopia, 2010–2025.* Report no. 2, Pastoral Economic Growth and Development Policy Assessment. Addis Ababa: Department for International Development.

Little, Peter D., M. P. Stone, T. Mogues, A. P. Castro, and W. Negatu. 2006. "'Moving in Place:' Drought and Poverty Dynamics in South Wollo, Ethiopia." *Journal of Development Studies* 42 (2):200–225.

Little, Peter D., and M. J. Watts, eds. 1994. *Living under Contract: Contract Farming and Agrarian Transformation in Sub-Saharan Africa.* Madison: University of Wisconsin Press.

Littlejohn, Gary. 2010. "Briefings Reloaded: Tell Us about It." *Review of African Political Economy* 37 (123): 87–88.

Loum, M. 2002. "Bad Governance and Democratic Failure: A Look at Gambia's 1994 Coup." *Civil Wars* 5 (1): 145–174.

Lusigi, Walter. 1984. "Future Directions for the Afrotropical Realm." In *National Parks, Conservation and Development,* ed. J. McNeely and K. Miller, 137–146. Washington, D.C.: Smithsonian Institution Press.

Lynch, G. 2006. "Negotiating Ethnicity: Identity Politics in Contemporary Kenya." *Review of African Political Economy* 107: 49–65.

Lyons, Michael, Alison Brown, and Zhigang Li. 2008. "The 'Third Tier' of Globalization: African Traders in Guangzhou." *City* 12 (2): 196–206.

MAA Pastoralists Council (MPC). 2002. "A Memorandum by the Maa Pastoralists Council to the Constitution of Kenya Review Commission." Constitution of

Kenya Review Commission, Nairobi. http://www.kenyaconstitution.org/docs /11d122.htm.

MAA Speaking Communities of Kenya. 2004. "A Memorandum on the Anglo-Maasai Agreements: A Case of Historical and Contemporary Injustices and the Dispossession of the Maasai Land." Presented to the Office of the President; Ministries of Justice & Constitutional Affairs; Lands, Settlement & Housing; the Office of the Attorney General; the British High Commission—Nairobi; the District Commissioners' Offices of Laikipiak, Baringo, Marsabit, Isiolo, Narok, Nakuru, Samburu and Kajiado Districts, Kenya.

MacGaffey, Janet, and Remy Bazenquissa-Ganga. 2000. *Congo-Paris: Transnational Traders on the Margins of the Law.* Bloomington: Indiana University Press.

Magaia, Lina. 1988. *Dumba Nengue, Run for Your Life: Peasant Tales of Tragedy in Mozambique.* Trenton, N.J.: Africa World Press.

Mahmoud, Hussein A. 2006. "Innovations in Pastoral Livestock Marketing: The Emergence and the Role of 'Somali Cattle Traders-Cum-Ranchers' in Kenya." In *Pastoral Livestock Marketing in Eastern Africa: Research and Policy Challenges,* ed. J. McPeak and P. Little, 129–144. Warwickshire, UK: ITDG Publishing.

———. 2010. *Livestock Trade in the Kenyan, Somali and Ethiopian Borderlands.* Chatham House Briefing Paper, Africa Programme, AFP BP 2010/02. London: Chatham House.

Mainyoito Pastoralist Integrated Development Organization (MPIDO). 2007. "Our Programmes." http://www.mpido.org/prog.html.

Makoloo, Maurice Odhiambo. 2005. *Kenya: Minorities, Indigenous Peoples, and Ethnic Diversity.* Report of Minority Rights Group International and CEMIRIDE. London: Minority Rights Group International.

Mamdani, Mahmood. 1990. "Uganda: Contradictions of the IMF Programme and Perspective." *Development and Change* 21 (3): 427–467.

Mannon, Susan E. 2005. "Risk Takers, Risk Makers: Small Farmers and Non-Traditional Agro-Exports in Kenya and Costa Rica." *Human Organization* 64 (1): 16–27.

Marchal, Roland. 2002. *A Survey of Mogadishu's Economy.* Nairobi: European Commission.

———. 2009. "A Tentative Assessment of the Somali *Harakat Al-Shabaab.*" *Journal of Eastern African Studies* 3 (3): 381–404.

———. 2012. "Somalia on Hold." *Focus on the Horn.* http://focusonthehorn.files .wordpress.com/2012/05/somalia-on-hold.pdf.

Masibo, Kennedy. 2008. "Lawyer to File New Case over Noxious Weed." *Daily Nation,* August 17. http://allafrica.com.proxy.library.emory.edu/stories/200808180073.html

Matter, Scott. 2009. "Clashing Claims: Conflict and Violence as Unintended Consequences of Tenure Transformation at Enoosupukia, Kenya." Workshop in Political Theory and Policy Analysis, Indiana University, Bloomington, Indiana.

———. 2010. "Clashing Claims: Neopatrimonial Governance, Land Tenure Transformation, and Violence at Enoosupukia, Kenya." *PoLAR: Political and Legal Anthropology Review* 33 (1): 67–88.

Mbaria, John. 2004. "Ex-KWS Boss Criticizes Sale Plans." *Daily Nation* (Nairobi), August 15.

———. 2007. "The Myth of Ecotourism." *East African,* November 19. http://www .nationmedia.com/eastafrican.

Mbatia, Benjamin. 2006. "Indigenous and Displaced Persons and Parliamentary Repre-

sentation: Rangal Memeiguran and Others versus Attorney-General and Others."
Kenyalaw.org. December 18. http://www.kenyalaw.org/articles/print.php?view=
249&cat=7.

Mbembe, J.-A. 2001. *On the Postcolony.* Berkeley: University of California Press.

Mbitiru, Chege. 1997. "Wildlife Body Backs Hunting." *Daily Nation* (Nairobi), March
26, 1–2.

Mburu, J., R. Birner, and M. Zeller. 2003. "Relative Importance and Determinants of
Landowners' Transaction Costs in Collaborative Wildlife Management in Kenya:
An Empirical Analysis." *Ecological Economics* 45 (1): 59–73.

McCann, James. 1995. *People of the Plow: An Agricultural History of Ethiopia, 1800–1900.*
Madison: University of Wisconsin Press.

McKay, Andrew. 2005. "Trade Policy Issues in a Small African Economy: The Trade
Policy Review of The Gambia 2004." *World Economy* 28 (9): 1197–1209.

McPeak, John, and Getachew Gebru.2004. *Herd Accumulation: A Pastoral Strategy to
Reduce Risk Exposure.* PARIMA Research Brief 2004–05. Davis, Calif.: Global
Livestock-CRSP, University of California.

McPeak, John, and Peter D. Little. 2004. "'Cursed If You Do, Cursed If You Don't': The
Contradictory Processes of Sedentarization in Northern Kenya." In *As Nomads
Settle: Social, Health, and Ecological Consequences of Pastoral Sedentarization in
Northern Kenya,* ed. E. Fratkin and E. Roth, 87–104. New York: Kluwer Academic/
Plenum Publishers.

———, eds. 2006. *Pastoral Livestock Marketing in Eastern Africa: Research and Policy
Challenges.* Warwickshire, UK: ITDG Publishing.

McPeak, John, Peter D. Little, and Cheryl Doss. 2011. *Risk and Social Change in an African Rural Economy: Livelihoods in Pastoralist Communities.* London: Routledge.

McRae, Michael. 1998. "Survival Test for Kenya's Wildife." *Science* 280 (April 24):
510–512.

Meagher, Kate. 2003. "A Back Door to Globalisation? Structural Adjustment, Globalisation and Transborder Trade in West Africa." *Review of African Political Economy*
95: 57–75.

———. 2009. "Trading on Faith: Religious Movements and Informal Economic Governance in Nigeria." *Journal of Modern African Studies* 47 (3): 397–423.

———. 2010. *Identity Economics: Social Networks and the Informal Economy in Nigeria.*
Oxford: James Currey Publishers.

Meguro, Toshio. 2008. "How Can Local People Work in Wildlife Conservation?" Research Seminar, African Studies Centre, Kyoto University, Kyoto, Japan, June 10.

Menkhaus, Kenneth. 2007. "The Crisis in Somalia: Tragedy in Five Acts." *African Affairs*
106 (424): 357–390.

Menkhaus, Kenneth, and Kathryn Craven.1996. "Land Alienation and the Imposition of
State Farms in the Lower Jubba Valley." In *The Struggle for Land in Southern Somalia: The War behind the War,* ed. Catherine Besteman and L. Cassanelli, 133–
153. Boulder, Colo.: Westview Press.

Minority Rights Group (MRG) International. 2005. *Kenya Delivers Constitutional Be-
trayal of Minority and Indigenous Peoples.* Report of June 9, 2005. London: MRG
International.

———. 2008. *Kenya One Year On: New Beginning or Business as Usual.* London: MRG
International.

Minot, N., and M. Ngigi. 2004. *Building on Successes in African Agriculture: Are Kenya's Horticultural Exports a Replicable Success Story?* Focus 12/Brief 7, 2020 Vision for Food, Agriculture, and the Environment. Washington, D.C.: International Food Policy Research Institute.

Mitchell, Timothy. 2002. *Rule of Experts: Egypt, Techno-Politics, Modernity.* Berkeley: University of California Press.

Moncrieffe, Joy, and Rosalind Eyben, eds. 2007. *The Power of Labeling.* London: Earthscan.

Moore, David. 1999. "'Sail on O Ship of State': Neo-Liberalism, Globalisation, and the Governance of Africa." *Journal of Peasant Studies* 27 (1): 61–97.

Morawczynski, Olga. 2009. "Exploring the Usage and Impact of 'Transformational' Mobile Financial Services: The Case of M-PESA in Kenya." *Journal of Eastern African Studies* 3 (3): 509–525.

Mosley, Jason. 2012. *End of the Road Map: Somalia after the London and Istanbul Conferences.* Africa Programme Paper, AFP PP2012/04. London: Chatham House.

Mosley, William G., Judith Carney, and Laurence Becker. 2010. "Neoliberal Policy, Rural Livelihoods, and Urban Food Security in West Africa: A Comparative Study of The Gambia, Cote d'Ivioire, and Mali." *Proceedings of the National Academy of Sciences (PNAS)* 107 (13): 5774–5779.

Mubarak, Jamil A. 1997. "The 'Hidden Hand' behind the Resilience of the Stateless Economy of Somalia." *World Development* 25: 2027–2041.

Mugambi, Kaburu. 2009. "Piracy Money Distorting Property Prices." *Daily Nation,* November 18. http://www.nation.co.ke/business/news/-/1006/687864/-/iekgm7z/-/index.html.

Mugonyi, David, and Jeff Otieno. 2005. "State Hands Back Amboseli to the Maasai." *Daily Nation,* October 1. http://infoweb.newsbank.com.proxy.library.emory.edu.

Muiruri, Peter. 2011. "Conservancies Magnet to Tycoons, but Who Benefits." *East African Standard,* December 29. http://m.standardmedia.co.ke/homeaway.php?Id=2000049072.

Munoz, Heraldo. 1981. *From Dependency to Development: Strategies to Overcome Underdevelopment and Inequality.* Boulder, Colo.: Westview Press.

Mursi Online. 2011. "Speech by Meles Zenawi during the 13th Annual Pastoralists' Day Celebrations, Jinka, South Omo, 25/1/2011." Department for International Development, Oxford University. http://www.mursi.org/pdf/meles%20jinka%20speech.pdf.

Murunga, Godwin. 2007. "Governance and the Politics of Structural Adjustment in Kenya." In *Kenya: The Struggle for Democracy,* ed. G. Murunga and S. Nasong'o, 263–299. London: Zed Press.

Murunga, Godwin, and S. Nasong'o, eds. 2007. *Kenya: The Struggle for Democracy.* London: Zed Press.

Mutai, Edwin. 2005. "Council Warns of Chaos over Amboseli N. Park." *Kenya Times,* November 11. http://www.timesnews.co.ke/11nov05/nwsstory/news5.html.

Mynott, Adam. 2005. "Kenya Wildlife Haven Downgraded." *BBC News,* October 11. http://news.bbc.co.uk/1/hi/world/africa/4331002.stm.

Nair, Mohan, and Claire Coote. 2007. *Mozambique: Trends in Growth of Modern Retail and Wholesale Chains and Related Agribusiness.* Information Sheet. Regoverning Markets: Small-Scale Producers in Modern Agrifood Markets Project. April. http://www.regoverningmarkets.org/en/filemanager/active?fid=438.

Narayan, Deepa. 2000. *Voices of the Poor.* Vol. 1: *Can Anyone Hear Us?* World Bank Publication. Washington, D.C.: World Bank.

Nasong'o, S., and G. Murunga. 2007. "Prospects for Democracy in Kenya." In *Kenya: The Struggle for Democracy,* ed. G. Murunga and S. Nasong'o, 3–16. London: Zed Books.

Ndegwa, S. 2001. A *Decade of Democracy in Africa.* Leiden: Brill.

Ndung'u, Margaret. 1997. *Knowledge, Attitude, Practices Follow Up Survey, Amboseli Park.* Nairobi: KWS.

Negassa, Asfaw, Riccardo Costagli, George Matete, Mohammad Jabbar, Samuel Okuthe Oyieke, Mohamed Hassan Abdulle, and Amos Omore. 2008. *Towards Improving Livestock Export Marketing Support Services in the Somali Context: Survey Findings and Implications.* Discussion Paper no. 13. Nairobi: International Livestock Research Institute.

Neumann, Roderick P. 1995. "Local Challenges to Global Agendas: Conservation, Economic Liberalization and the Pastoralists' Rights Movement in Tanzania." *Antipode* 27 (4): 363–382.

New York Times. 2008. "U.S. Forces Fire Missiles into Somalia at a Kenyan." March 4. http://www.nytimes.com/2008/03/04/world/africa/04somalia.html.

Ngowi, Rodrique. 2006. "People vs. Wildlife in Parched Kenya: Plan to Give Maasai Control of Sanctuary Raises Concerns among Conservationists." *Washington Post,* March 5. http://www.washingtonpost.com/wp-dyn/content/article/2006/03/04/AR2006030400336.html.

Njeru, Mugo. 1998. "Leaders Condemn Evictions." *Sunday Nation* (Nairobi), April 12, 23.

Nordstrom, Carolyn. 2007. *Global Outlaws: Crime, Money, and Power in the Contemporary World.* Berkeley: University of California Press.

Northern Rangelands Trust (NRT). 2008. "About Northern Rangelands Trust." http://www.nrt-kenya.org/home.html.

———. 2011. "Breaking News—Giraffes Boat Home to Kenya Sanctuary." February 11. http://www.nrt-kenya.org/news/giraffetranslocation.html.

Nsehe, Mfonobong. 2011. "Who Were Africa's Richest Dictators?" *Forbes,* November 8. http://www.forbes.com/sites/mfonobongnsehe/2011/11/08/who-were-africas-richest-dictators/2/.

Nunow, Abdirizak A. 2013. "Land Deals and the Changing Political Economy of Livelihoods in the Tana Delta, Kenya." In *Pastoralism and Development in Africa: Dynamic Change at the Margins,* ed. Andy Catley, Jeremy Lind, and Ian Scoones, 154–163. London: Routledge.

Nyborg, I., I. Jack, and J. Manneh. 1990. "Evaluation of the Bakau and Lamin Horticultural Societies, The Gambia." Paper prepared for the Royal Norwegian Society for Development, Skedsmo, Norway.

Oakland Institute. 2011. *Understanding Land Investment Deals in Africa: Country Report: Ethiopia.* Oakland, Calif.: Oakland Institute.

Oba, Gufu. 1996. "Shifting Identities along Resource Borders: Becoming and Continuing to Be Boorana Oromo." In *Being and Becoming Oromo: Historical and Anthropological Enquiries,* ed. P. Baxter, J. Hultin, and A. Triulizi, 117–131. Uppsala: Nordiska Afrikainstitutet.

Odada, Eric O., Japheth O. Onyando, and Peninah A. Obudho. 2006. "Lake Baringo: Addressing Threatened Biodiversity and Livelihoods." *Lakes and Reservoirs: Research and Management* 11: 287–299.

Ogachi, Oanda. 1999. "Economic Reform, Political Liberalization, and Economic Ethnic Conflict in Kenya." *Africa Development* 24 (1–2): 83–108.

Okello, J. J., C. Narrod, and D. Roy. 2007. *Food Safety Requirements in African Green Bean Exports and Their Impact on Small Farmers.* IFPRI Discussion Paper 00737. Washington, D.C.: International Food Policy Research Institute (IFPRI).

Okello, Rosemary. 2003. "A Giant Step towards a New Constitution." *Yawezekana Newsletter* (Nairobi), June 5, 1, 4.

Okwembah, David. 2009. "Kenya's New Property Kings." *Daily Nation,* March 14. http://www.nation.co.ke/news/-/1056/545998/-/item/1/-/50gqijz/-/index.html.

Okwi, Paul O., Godfrey Ndeng'e, Patti Kristjanson, Mike Arunga, An Notenbaert, Abisalom Omolo, Norbert Henninger, Todd Benson, Patrick Kariuki, and John Owuor. 2007. "Spatial Determinants of Poverty in Rural Kenya." *Proceedings of the National Academy of Sciences of the United States of America* 104 (43): 16769–16774.

Omwega, Asaneth, and Segbedzi Norgbey. 2004. *Lake Baringo Community-Based Land and Water Management Project: Evaluation Report on Project GF/3010-00-03.* Nairobi: UNEP.

Overa, Ranghild. 2007. "When Men Do Women's Work: Structural Adjustment, Unemployment and Changing Gender Relations in the Informal Economy of Accra, Ghana." *Journal of Modern African Studies* 45 (4): 539–563.

Parselelo, Kantai. 2009. "Real Estate: Somali Factor Drives Up Price of Property." *Financial Times Reports,* December 11. http://www.ft.com/cms/s/700e33ba-c28c-11de-be3a-00144feab49a,dwp_uuid=b78f2aa4-c.

———. 2011. "Inside Garissa Lodge, Nairobi's Somali Trading Hub." *Africa Report,* January 31. http://www.theafricareport.com/archives2/frontlines/5136196-inside-lodge-nairobi's-somali-trading-hub.

Pastoralists and Hunter-Gatherers Ethnic Minority (PHGEM) Network. 2002. "The Case for the Recognition and Protection of the Rights of Kenya's Indigenous Peoples: Memorandum to the Constitution of Kenya Review Commission." Constitution of Kenya Review Commission, Nairobi. http://www.ogiek.org/sitemap/case-memorandum.htm.

Peberdy, S. A. 2000. "Border Crossings: Small Entrepreneurs and Cross-Border Trade between South Africa and Mozambique." *Tijdschrift Voor Economische en Sociale Geografie* 91 (4): 361–378.

Peberdy, S. A., and J. Crush. 2006. "Histories, Realities, and Negotiating Movement in Southern Africa." In *Migration without Borders: Essays on the Free Movement of People,* ed. Antoine Pecoud and Paul De Guchteneire, 175–197. Oxford: Berghahn Books.

Peck, Jamie, Nik Theodore, and Neil Brenner. 2010. "Postneoliberalism and Its Malcontents." *Antipode* 41 (S1): 94–116.

[*The Nairobi*] *People.* 2001. "Police Impound Lorries," June 25, 5.

Pflanz, Mike. 2008. "Elephants Killed by Spear Attacks in Kenya." *Telegraph,* March 17. http://www.telegraph.co.uk/earth/main.jhtml?xml=/earth/2008/03/17/eaeleph117.xml.

Pitcher, M. Anne. 2002. *Transforming Mozambique: The Politics of Privatization, 1975–2000.* Cambridge: Cambridge University Press.

Planas, T. 1990. "Proceedings of National Policy Planning Conference for Horticulture."

Paper presented at the National Horticultural Policy Planning Workshop, Karaiba Beach Hotel, Banjul, The Gambia, December 3–5.

Pricewaterhouse Coopers. 2005. *Baringo District Vision and Strategy: 2005–2015.* Nairobi: Arid Lands Resource Management Project.

Provost, Claire. 2012. "New International Land Deals Database Reveals Rush to Buy Up Africa." *Guardian,* April 27. http://www.guardian.co.uk/global-development/2012/apr/27/international-land-deals-database-africa?intcmp=239.

Qingfen, Ding. 2011. "Ethiopia Seeks More Investment." *China Daily,* May 5. http://www.chinadaily.com.cn/cndy/2011-05/05/content_12447121.htm.

Quisumbing, A. R. 2003. "Food Aid and Child Nutrition in Rural Ethiopia." *World Development* 31 (7): 1309–1324.

Radalet, S., and M. McPherson, eds. 1995. *Economic Recovery in The Gambia: Insights for Adjustment in Sub-Saharan Africa.* Cambridge, Mass.: Harvard University Press.

Raeymaekers, Timothy, and Luca Jourdan. 2009. "Economic Opportunities and Local Governance on an African Frontier: The Case of the Semliki Basin (Congo-Uganda)." *Journal of Eastern African Studies* 3 (2): 317–332.

Ram, Monder, Nicholas Theodorakopoulos, and Trevor Jones. 2008. "Forms of Capital, Mixed Embeddedness and Somali Enterprise." *Work Employment Society* 22: 427–446.

Rass, Nikola. 2006. "Policies and Strategies to Address the Vulnerability of Pastoralists in Sub-Saharan Africa." Pro-Poor Livestock Policy Initiative (PPLPI) Working Paper no. 37. Rome: FAO.

Ratha, Dilip, and Sonia Plaza. 2012. "Harnessing Diasporas: Africa Can Tap Some of Its Millions of Emigrants to Help Development Efforts." *Finance and Development,* September, 48–51.

Ravallion, Martin. 2009. "Are There Lessons for Africa from China's Success against Poverty?" *World Development* 37 (2): 303–313.

Resource Management and Research. 1984. *Southern Rangelands Survey.* Mogadishu: National Range Agency.

Rhamato, Dessalegn. 1991. *Famine and Survival Strategies: A Case Study of Northeast Ethiopia.* Uppsala: Scandinavian Institute of African Studies.

Ribot, J., and A. Larson. 2004. "Democratic Decentralization through a Natural Resources Lens: An Introduction." *European Journal of Development Research* 16 (1):1–25.

Richardson, Julie. 1996. *Structural Adjustment and Environmental Linkages: A Case Study of Kenya.* London: Overseas Development Institute.

Roitman, Janet L. 2005. *Fiscal Disobedience: An Anthropology of Economic Regulation in Central Africa.* Princeton, N.J.: Princeton University Press.

Roth, Michael, Ben Carr, and Jeff Cochrane. 1994. *Land Rights and Intra-household Employment and Resource Use in the Peri-urban Area of Banjul, The Gambia.* Madison, Wisc.: Land Tenure Center.

Roth, Michael, and Tewodaj Mogues,. 2003. "Food Self-Sufficiency or Income Security? Managing Human and Physical Assets to Secure Livelihoods and Food Security in South Wello, Ethiopia." Paper prepared for the BASIS Workshop, Bahir Dar, Ethiopia, June 2003.

Ruggieri, Clarissa. 2006. "State Reconstruction and Economic Recovery in Somalia: An Alternative Option between Central-State and Clan-Based Systems of Gover-

nance." *Journal of Middle Eastern Geopolitics* 1 (1): 25–37. http://padis2.uniroma1
.it:81/ojs/index.php/jmeg/index.

Rutten, Marcel. 2002. "Parks beyond Parks: Genuine Community-Based Eco-Tourism or Just Another Land Loss for Maasai Pastoralists in Kenya?" Issue Paper no. 111, African Studies Centre, Leiden, Netherlands.

———. 2003. "Linking Western Tour Operators with Community-Based Protected Areas in Kenya: Globalising Paradise for Whom?" Unpublished paper. African Studies Centre, Leiden, Netherlands.

———. 2004. "Partnerships in Community-Based Ecotourism Projects: Experiences from the Maasai Region, Kenya." ASC Working Paper 57/2004, African Studies Centre, Leiden, Netherlands.

Rutten, Marcel, A. Leliveld, and D. Foeken. 2008. *Inside Poverty and Development in Africa: Critical Reflections on Pro-poor Policies.* Leiden: Brill.

Rutten, Marcel, A. Mazrui, and F. Grignon, eds. 2001. *Out for the Count: The 1997 General Elections and Prospects for Democracy in Kenya.* Kampala, Uganda: Fountain Publishers.

Rutten, Marcel, and Koki Muli. 2008. "The Migration Debate in Kenya." In *International Migration and National Development in Sub-Saharan Africa: Viewpoints and Policy Initiatives in the Countries of Origin,* ed. A. Adepoju, T. Van Naerssen, and A. Zoomers, 182–203. Leiden: Brill Publishers.

Sachs, Jeffery. 2006. *The End of Poverty: Economic Possibilities for Our Time.* New York: Penguin Press.

Sahn, D. E., ed. 1996. *Economic Reform and the Poor in Africa.* Oxford: Oxford University Press.

Salomon, Michael J. 2000. *Evaluating Community Conservation in Kenya.* MSc thesis, University of Alberta, Canada.

Samatar, Abdi. 2007. "Somalia's Post-conflict Economy: A Political Economy Approach." *Bildhaan: An International Journal of Somali Studies* 7: 126–168.

Samburu County Council. 2008. *Samburu County Council, Kenya.* http://www .samburucouncil.com/.reserves.htm.

Sato, Shun. 1998. "The Rendille and the Adaptive Strategies of East African Pastoralists." In *Conflict, Age and Power in North East Africa,* ed. E. Kurimoto and S. Simonse, 206–226. Oxford: James Currey Publishers.

Sautier, D., H. Vermeulen, M. Fok, and E. Biénabe. 2006. "Case Studies of Agri-Processing and Contract Agriculture in Africa." Series of Contributions for the Preparation of the World Development Report 2008, World Bank, Washington, D.C.

Schmidt-Soltau, Kai. 2006. *Indigenous Peoples Plan (Ilchamus, Ogiek and Sengwer) of the Kenya Agricultural Productivity–Sustainable Land Management Project.* Nairobi: Kenya Agricultural Research Institute.

Segers, Kaatje, Joost Dessein, Stein Hagberg, Patrick Develtere, Mitiku Haile, and Jozef Deckers. 2008. "Be Like Bees: The Politics of Mobilizing Farmers for Development in Tigray, Ethiopia." *African Affairs* 108 (430): 91–109.

Scott, James. 1998. *Seeing Like a State: How Certain Schemes to Improve the Human Condition Have Failed.* New Haven, Conn.: Yale University Press.

Scott-Villiers, Patta. 2011. "We Are Not Poor! Dominant and Subaltern Discourses of Pastoralist Development in the Horn of Africa." *Journal of International Development* 23: 771–781.

Sen, A. K. 1981. *Poverty and Famines: An Essay on Entitlement and Deprivation.* Oxford: Oxford University Press.

Seymour, Frances J., and John Mugabe. 2000. "Kenya." In *The Right Conditions: The World Bank, Structural Adjustment, and Forest Policy Reform,* ed. Frances J. Seymour and Navroz R. Dubash, 113–132. Washington, D.C.: World Resources Institute.

Shah, Rajiv. 2011. "Insights." *USAID Frontlines,* June/July. http://www.usaid.gov/press /frontlines/fl_jun11/fl_jun11_insights.html.

Sharp, Kay, Taylor Brown, and Amdissa Teshome. 2006. *Targeting Ethiopia's Productive Safety Net Programme (PSNP).* London: Overseas Development Institute.

Shiundu, Alphonce. 2010. "Police Harass Somali Refugees-Amnesty." *Daily Nation,* December 8. http://www.nation.co.ke/news/-/1056/1068328/-/item/1/-/r32xw1/-/index .html.

Smith, Kevin, and Peter D. Little. 2002. *Understanding Community Perceptions of Livelihoods, Assets, and Recovery Strategies: Preliminary Findings from Northern Kenya.* Madison: BASIS Research Program, Department of Agricultural and Applied Economics, University of Wisconsin-Madison.

Sobania, Neil. 1979. *Background History of the Mt. Kulal Region of Kenya.* IPAL Technical Report Number A-2. Nairobi: UNESCO.

Spear, Thomas, and Richard Waller, eds. 1993. *Being Maasai: Ethnicity and Identity in East Africa.* Oxford: James Currey Publishers.

Stein, Howard. 2011. "World Bank Agricultural Policies, Poverty, and Income Inequality in Sub-Saharan Africa." *Cambridge Journal of Regions, Economy and Society* 4: 79–90.

Stevenhagen, R. 2007. *Report of the Special Rapporteur on the Situation of Human Rights and Fundamental Freedoms of Indigenous People.* Implementation of General Assembly Resolution 60/251 of 15 March 2006 Entitled "Human Rights Council." New York: United Nations.

Stiglitz, Joseph E. 2012. *The Price of Inequality: How Today's Divided Society Endangers Our Future.* New York: W. W. Norton.

Stone, M. Priscilla, and Kassahun Kebede. 2003. "Interview Notes, South Wollo and Oromiya Zones, June 2003." BASIS South Wollo Research Program.

Straight, Belinda. 2009. "Making Sense of Violence in the 'Badlands' of Kenya." *Anthropology and Humanism* 34 (1): 21–30.

Survival International. 2012. "German Tourist Firm Warns Samburu Eviction Could Harm Kenyan Tourism." January 25. http://www.survivalinternational.org /news/8041.

Takane, Tsutomu. 2004. "Smallholders and Nontraditional Exports under Economic Liberalization: The Case of Pineapples in Ghana." *African Study Monographs* 25 (1): 29–43.

Thompson, Michael, and Katherine M. Homewood. 2002. "Entrepreneurs, Elites and Exclusion in Maasailand: Trends in Wildlife Conservation and Pastoralist Development." *Human Ecology* 30 (1): 107–138.

Thomson, Joseph. 1887. *Through Masai Land: A Journey of Exploration among the Snow-Clad Mountains and Exotic Tribes of Eastern Equatorial Africa.* London: Sampson Low, Marston, Searle, and Rivington.

Thuku, Wahome. 2012. "Il Chamus Fault IEBC for Not Giving them a Home." *Standard,*

February 12. http://www.standardmedia.co.ke/commentaries/insidepage.php?id
= 2000051981&cid=15&currentpage=3.

Thurlow, James, Jane Kiringai, and Madhur Gautam. 2007. *Rural Investments to Accelerate Growth and Poverty Reduction in Kenya.* IFPRI Discussion Paper 00723. Washington, D.C.: International Food Policy Research Institute (IFPRI).

Tisnabudi, Ivan. 2010. "Trade Deal with Somalia to Help Rebuild, Clothe Ailing Nation." *Jakarta Globe.* http://www.thejakartaglobe.com/business/trade-deal-with -somalia-to-help-rebuild-cloth-ailing-nation/353437.

Trienekens, J. H., J. M.Hagen, and S. Willems. 2004. "Innovation through International Supply Chain Development: A Case Study." Paper presented at the IAMA (International Agribusiness Management Association) Symposium, Montreux, Switzerland, June 11–12.

Trienekens, J. H., and S. Willems. 2007. "Innovation and Governance in International Food Supply Chains: The Cases of Ghanaian Pineapples and South African Grapes." *International Food and Agribusiness Management Review* 10 (4): 42–63.

Turk, Joyce. 1995. "An Assessment of Animal Health Projects: U.S. Agency for International Development." *Agriculture and Human Values* 12 (2): 81–89.

Turton, David. 2010. "The Downstream Impact." Paper presented at the Royal Africa Society Meeting on the Gibe 3 Dam, School of Oriental and African Studies (SOAS), London, October 11.

Umar, A., with B. Baluch. 2007. *Risk Taking for a Living: Trade and Marketing in the Somali Region, Ethiopia.* Addis Ababa: UN-OCHA/Pastoral Communication Initiative Project.

United Arab Emirates (UAE). 2011. *Foreign Trade Information Service Provider, Ministry of Foreign Trade.* April 14. http://tradeexchange.ae/.

UNDP (United Nations Development Programme). 2006a. *The Gambia: National Human Development Report 2001.* New York: UNDP.

———. 2006b. *Mozambique: National Human Development Report 2005.* New York: UNDP.

———. 2011. *Human Development Report 2010—The Real Wealth of Nations: Pathways to Human Development.* New York: Palgrave Macmillan.

United Nations Environment Programme (UNEP). 2002. *Protecting the Environment from Land Degradation: UNEP's Action in the Framework of the Global Environment Facility.* Nairobi: UNEP.

United Nations Human Rights Council (UNHRC). 2007. *Report of the Special Rapporteur on the Situation of Human Rights and Fundamental Freedoms of Indigenous People.* Implementation of General Assembly Resolution 60/251 of 15 March 2006. New York: United Nations.

United Nations Integrated Regional information Network (IRIN). 2012. "Somalia: Return to Mogadishu." July 19. http://allafrica.com.proxy.library.emory.edu/stories /201207200668.html.

USAID (United States Agency for International Development). 1997. *New Partnerships Initiative (NPI) Final Report.* Nairobi: USAID.

———. 2003. "American Food Aid Pledges Top One Million Tons for the Ethiopian Humanitarian Crisis." http://www.usaid.gov/press/releases/2003/pr030702.html.

———. 2006. "Success Story, Il Ngwesi Lodge: Linking Business with Nature." http:// www.usaid.gov/ke/ke.naremgnt/success_ilngwei.htm.

United States State Department. 2010. *International Narcotics Control Strategy Report.*

Vol. 2: *Money Laundering and Financial Crimes*. Washington, D.C.: U.S. State Department.

Van Binsbergen, Wim, and Rijk Van Dijk, eds. 2005. *Situating Globality: African Agency in the Appropriation of Global Culture*. Leiden, Netherlands: Brill.

Van der Veen, Albertien. 2000. "Report on the Food and Nutrition Situation in South Wollo, Amhara Region, Ethiopia." Unpublished report. World Health Organization, Geneva, Switzerland.

Verhoeven, Harry. 2009. "The Self-Fulfilling Prophecy of Failed States: Somalia, State Collapse and the Global War on Terror." *Journal of Eastern African Studies* 3 (3): 405–425.

Victor, A. 2007. "The Dynamics of Horticultural Export Value Chains on the Livelihood of Small Farm Households in Southern Ghana." *African Journal of Agricultural Research* 2 (9): 435–440.

Vidal, John. 2008. "The Great Green Land Grab." *Guardian*, February 13. http://rebic .com/library/world/2008/021308%20gcu%20the%20great.pdf.

Vidal, John, and Claire Provost. 2012. "Campaigners Claim World Bank Helps Facilitate Land Grabs in Africa." *Guardian*, April 23. http://www.guardian.co.uk/global -development/2012/apr/23/world-bank-land-grabs-africa.

Vitoria, M., R. Granich, and C. F. Gilks, C. Gunneber, M. Hosseini, W. Were, M. Raviglione, and K. M. De Cock. 2009. "The Global Fight against HIV/AIDS, Tuberculosis, and Malaria: Current Status and Future Perspectives." *American Journal of Clinical Pathology* 131: 844–848.

Von Braun, Joachim, and Ruth Meinzen-Dick. 2009. "'Land Grabbing' by Foreign Investors in Developing Countries: Risks and Opportunities." Policy Brief 13, International Food Policy Research Institute (IFPRI). Washington, D.C.: IFPRI.

Wabala, Dominic. 2009. "Police Round Up Foreigners in City." *Daily Nation*, December 6. http://www.nation.co.ke/news/-/1056/818484/-/vnknvr/-/index.html.

Wadda, Rohey, and Russell Craig. 1993. *Social Dimensions of Adjustment: 1992 Priority Survey Report*. Banjul, The Gambia: Central Statistics Department, Ministry of Finance and Economic Affairs.

Wageningen University/Michigan State University. 2007. *Ghana: Sustainable Horticultural Export Chain*. Study commissioned by AHOLD, Albert Heijn, Bakker Barendrecht, the Agro Chain Science Foundation (AKK) and KLM. Wageningen, Netherlands: Agricultural Economics Research Institute (LEI), Wageningen University; East Lansing: Michigan State University.

Waki, Justice Philip, Gavin McFadyen, and Pascal Kambale. 2008. *Commission of Inquiry into Post-election Violence (CIPEV) ("Waki Report")*. Nairobi: Special Commission on Post-Election Violence (CIPEV).

Wallerstein, Immanuel. 2008. "The Demise of Neoliberal Globalization." *Mrzine* (online publication of *Monthly Review*), February 1. http://mrzine.monthlyreview.org /2008/wallerstein010208.html.

Watson, Andrew. 1999. *Conservation of Biodiverse Resource Areas (COBRA) Project: Kenya (1992–1998)*. Summary Report. Bethesda, Md.: DAI.

Watts, Michael J. 1999. "Contested Communities, Malignant Markets, and Gilded Governance: Justice, Resource Extraction, and Conservation in the Tropics." In *People, Plants, and Justice: The Politics of Nature Conservation*, ed. Charles Zerner, 21–51. New York: Columbia University Press.

Weber, H. 2004. "Reconstituting the 'Third World'? Poverty Reduction and Territoriality in the Global Politics of Development." *Third World Quarterly* 25 (1): 187–206.

Were, Edmond M. 2005. "The Domain of Authority and Sphere of Influence of Wildlife Conservation and Management Policy in Kenya." *Journal of Third World Studies* (Fall): 227–248.

Western, David, and Helen Gichoi. 1993. "Segregation Effects and the Impoverishment of Savanna Parks: The Case for Ecosystem Viability Analysis." *Journal of African Ecology* 31 (4): 269–281.

Western, David, Michael Wright, and Shirley Strum, eds. 1994. *Natural Connections: Perspectives in Community-Based Conservation.* Washington, D.C.: Island Press.

White, Howard, and Tony Killick. 2001. *African Poverty at the Millennium: Causes, Complexities, and Challenges.* Washington, D.C.: World Bank.

Williamson, John. 2000. "What Should the World Bank Think about the Washington Consensus?" *World Bank Research Observer* 15 (2): 251–264.

WISP (World Initiative for Sustainable Pastoralism). 2010. "Description of WISP." http://www.iucn.org/wisp/.

Wolde-Mariam, Mesfin.1984. *Rural Vulnerability to Famine in Ethiopia, 1958–1977.* New Delhi: Vikas Publishing House.

Wolf, Eric.1982. *Europe and the People without History.* Berkeley: University of California Press.

World Agroforestry Centre/NEPAD. 2007. *Contract Farming Offers Fresh Hope for Africa's Declining Agriculture.* East Africa Policy Brief no. 2. Nairobi: World Agroforestry Centre; Midrand, South Africa: NEPAD (National Economic Partnership for Africa's Development).

World Bank. 1981. *Accelerated Development in Sub-Saharan Africa: An Agenda for Action.* Washington, D.C.: World Bank.

——. 1983. *Project Report: Somalia-Trans-Juba Livestock Project.* Washington, D.C.: World Bank.

——. 1984. *Toward Sustained Development in Africa: A Joint Programme for Action.* Washington, D.C.: World Bank.

——. 1989. *Sub-Saharan Africa: From Crisis to Sustainable Growth.* Washington, D.C.: World Bank.

——. 1994. *Adjustment in Africa: Reforms Results and the Road Ahead.* Washington, D.C.: World Bank.

——. 2002. *World Development Indicators.* Washington, D.C.: World Bank.

——. 2003. *Country Re-engagement Note: Somalia.* Washington, D.C.: World Bank.

——. 2005a. *Agricultural Productivity and Sustainable Land Management (KAPSLM) Project.* Washington, D.C.: World Bank.

——. 2005b. *Somalia: From Resilience towards Recovery and Development.* Poverty Reduction and Economic Management 2, Country Department for Somalia. Washington, D.C.: World Bank.

——. 2006. *Ethiopia Productive Safety Net Appraisal Mission.* Aide memoire. Washington, D.C.: World Bank.

——. 2007a.*World Development Report 2008: Agriculture for Development.* Washington, D.C.: World Bank.

——. 2007b. "The Gambia: From Entrepot to Exporter and Ecotourism." Diagnostic

Trade Integration Study for the Integrated Framework for Trade-Related Technical Assistance to Least Developed Countries. Washington, D.C.: World Bank.

———. 2009. *World Development Report 2010: Development and Climate Change.* Washington, D.C.: World Bank.

———. 2011. "Voices of the Poor Project Team." http://web.Worldbank.org/WBSITE /EXTERNAL/TOPICS/EXTPOVERTY/0,,contentmdk:20621435~menupk:336998 ~pagepk:148956~pipk:216618~thesitepk:336992~iscurl:y,00.html.

World Trade Organisation (WTO). 2004. *Trade Policy Review: The Gambia, 2004.* Geneva: WTO.

World Wildlife Fund (WWF). 1997. *Measuring the Conservation Impact of ICDPs, Final Report.* Gland, Switzerland: WWF.

———. 2008. "Lake Bogoria Integrated Catchment Management Programme." WWF. http://www.panda.org/about_wwf/where_we_work/project/projects/index.cfm ?uprojectid=keo066.

Yeboah, Godfred. 2005. "The Farmapine Model: A Cooperative Marketing Strategy and a Market-Based Development Approach in Sub-Saharan Africa." *Choices: A Publication of the American Agricultural Economics Association* 20 (1): 81–86.

Zewde, Bahru. 2001. *A History of Modern Ethiopia, 1855–1991.* Athens: Ohio University Press.

Zoomers, Annelies. 2010. "Globalisation and the Foreignisation of Space: Seven Processes Driving the Current Land Grab." *Journal of Peasant Studies* 37 (2): 429–447.

Index

Page references in italics refer to figures or tables.

Shudder

OTHER BOOKS AND AUDIO BOOKS
BY JENNIE HANSEN:

Abandoned

All I Hold Dear

Beyond Summer Dreams

The Bracelet

The Emerald

The Topaz

The Ruby

Breaking Point

Chance Encounter

Code Red

Coming Home

High Stakes

Macady

Some Sweet Day

Wild Card

High Country

Shudder

a novel

Jennie Hansen

Covenant Communications, Inc.

Acknowledgments

AS WITH EVERY NOVEL I write, I owe a great deal to my husband, Boyd, who is patient and helpful through each phase. Another thank-you goes to my children, especially Lezlie and Janice, who are my critique team. Thanks also goes to a special circle of writing friends who are my unfailing cheerleaders. And it is a given that Kirk Shaw and all of the staff at Covenant deserve my gratitude for all they do.

This time, I also wish to thank Ida Nelson for her firsthand knowledge of Boise and her unflagging assistance in finding locations and establishing distances. There are several law officers who wish to remain anonymous who deserve thanks also.

Shudder is a book I knew I would write one day. During the years I worked as a reporter, served in Relief Society, and even while being employed as a librarian, I heard stories from isolated, lonely women. I witnessed the bruises, the broken bones, and the haunting fear in their eyes. I became the confidant and only friend of one such woman. I was a visiting teacher to another. My daughter befriended a young woman who suffered a devastating loss and was attempting to fight her way back. I've talked with police officers and social workers about abuse. During general conference, I have heard General Authorities and prophets denounce those men who would inflict pain on their spouses and children, declaring them unworthy of holding the priesthood. The truth is that no woman deserves to be abused by the man to whom she has given her trust fully, and every woman is in need of true and lasting friendship.

This story is dedicated to the women who have shared their stories with me over the years, trusting in my friendship. May God bless you, wherever you are.

Chapter 1

"IT WAS A DARK AND stormy night." Darcy wished she could get the stupid phrase out of her head. True, there was a storm raging, and technically it was still night. But not all of the darkness came from the black clouds; some were the product of her fearful thoughts. It had been a night just like this when DeLana died. Darcy had been alone that night, too, studying for a chemistry exam, when the officers came to her door. Blue-and-red lights had flashed intermittently from a police cruiser parked at the edge of the front lawn, blurred by a torrential rainstorm. The older of the two policemen had asked for her parents and mumbled something about a drunk driver and slippery roads. It all became a painful blur with only one stark fact standing out above everything else: Darcy's older sister was dead.

She attempted to shake off memories of the past and focused on the present as she worried about her roommate, Clare, who was out later than usual. Clare had never had a serious boyfriend before now, though. "I'm not her mother," Darcy reminded herself as she moved one slat of the blind again so she could peer out at the swaying trees and the rain lashing at the window. She wouldn't worry so much if Clare were with anyone other than Blaine Prescott. There was just something about Blaine that set Darcy's teeth on edge.

The building creaked, but Darcy immediately dismissed the sound. The apartment building was old, and being alone in their apartment wasn't new to her. For the past two months, Clare had spent almost every evening with Blaine, while their former roommate, Ellen, had seldom been around in the months leading up to her wedding. Her roommates' popularity regrettably made Darcy doubly aware of her

own infrequent dates. She had never claimed a large entourage of young men seeking her time and attention, but she'd never been as completely without male friends as she'd found herself during the past few months. Of course, working long hours and a full slate of college classes precluded a busy social life.

It had been two weeks since Ellen had moved out, and Darcy and Clare would have to find another roommate soon or move to a smaller apartment. Discussing the problem with Clare had proved to be impossible between her boyfriend's constant presence and the two young women's conflicting schedules. She'd have to go ahead on her own with making the arrangements. Tomorrow she'd prepare an ad to go in the paper, and on Sunday she'd put a message on the singles ward bulletin board. Clare's new job paid well, and she could easily afford to pay her share of the rent, but Darcy was hard pressed to pay a third of the rent; she certainly couldn't pay half. She turned back to the window.

Car lights cut through the blackness, coming much too quickly. She held her breath as the lights swept into the driveway and disappeared behind the four-story apartment building. Releasing the blind, she slipped back into bed where she lay still, listening for the faint swish of the elevator, a key in the lock, and the careful steps of her roommate.

As expected, the sounds came, though they seemed slower than usual, and Clare didn't seem to be taking her usual care not to disturb Darcy's sleep. Several times she seemed to stumble, and once, Darcy thought she heard mumbled words. The sound of running water came from the bathroom the girls shared followed by the closing of Clare's door. Silence followed, and Darcy had almost drifted to sleep when a faint sound reached her. Clare was crying.

Darcy sat up then hesitated. She wasn't certain whether she should go to her friend or respect her privacy. Moving hesitantly, she left her room and took the few short steps to Clare's room.

"Clare?" Darcy tapped softly on the door. A muffled sound came from the other side. Darcy wasn't sure if it was an invitation to enter, but she assumed it was. Pushing the door open, she hurried to Clare's bedside. Dropping to her knees, she reached out to touch her friend. "Are you all right? Are you sick?"

She couldn't understand Clare's muffled reply, but she felt the wetness on her friend's cheek. "Did you have a fight with Blaine?"

"No!" The answer came too quickly and sounded defensive. Darcy had given up sharing her reservations about Blaine with Clare. They'd been best friends as long as either could remember. They were the rare childhood friends who had grown up almost next door to each other and had still been there for each other through high-school trials and triumphs, college, the death of Darcy's older sister, Clare's mother's illness and subsequent passing, and now their first full-time jobs. It wasn't worth messing up their friendship over Blaine.

"It's nothing." Clare gulped noisily. "I fell on the rain-slick steps and hurt my wrist."

"Let me see." Darcy clicked the switch on Clare's bedside lamp. "Whoa! That doesn't look good." Darcy gingerly touched Clare's arm above her red and swollen wrist. "You need to see a doctor."

"I'm sure it will be all right in a little while. I don't have to work tomorrow . . ."

"Today!" Darcy interrupted. "It's already almost four o'clock, and that wrist needs to be x-rayed and wrapped. Come on, I'm taking you to St. Luke's emergency room."

Clare continued to protest, but Darcy refused to listen. She pulled back Clare's quilt and paused before adding in a dry voice, "At least you won't have to get dressed."

"I couldn't unbutton my shirt or take off my jeans with one hand." Clare sniffled.

"And it didn't occur to you to ask me to help you?" Darcy found her friend's shoes and slipped them on her feet. Putting an arm around Clare, she helped her to the front room and then found rain slickers for each of them before grabbing her purse and car keys.

When Clare was settled in the front passenger seat with her seat belt fastened, Darcy hurried around the front of the car to take her place behind the wheel. They didn't talk much on the drive to the hospital. Between the rapid beat of the windshield wipers and frequent puddles that seemed to want to change the direction they traveled each time she struck one, it didn't seem like the right time to ask why Blaine hadn't seen Clare fall or noticed that she needed to have her wrist checked.

The emergency room was busy when they arrived. The storm was being blamed for two car accidents plus the usual weekend stream of patients which were keeping the doctors busy, resulting in almost an hour's wait before Clare was taken to an examination cubicle. She was no longer crying, but she was either numb or half asleep by the time a doctor stepped into the room.

Without ceremony, the doctor picked up the clipboard Darcy had filled out, briefly scanned it, then stepped to the gurney where Clare sat. Picking up Clare's arm, she probed the swollen tissue. From where Darcy stood, she saw the doctor's attention focus on a single bruise on one side of Clare's right wrist then turn back to study a row of bruises on the other. The doctor glanced at Darcy and shook her head before scribbling something on the clipboard.

"Were you drinking?" The doctor sounded almost bored.

"No, of course not," Clare protested. She turned to Darcy. "You know Blaine and I don't drink."

"She said she slipped on wet stairs. There was no alcohol involved," Darcy assured the doctor. Blaine might be a jerk, but he didn't drink. She was pretty sure of that, and she knew Clare never touched alcohol.

"Someone will be here to take you to X-ray in a few minutes," the doctor said, walking away with hurried, deliberate steps. She seemed annoyed, but Darcy figured it might just be that she'd had a long shift and was anxious to go home.

Another hour passed before the X-rays were complete and the doctor returned to announce that one of Clare's wrist bones was cracked and that it would be necessary to place a brace on it to hold the bone immobile. When she finished, the doctor scribbled a prescription and handed it to Darcy. "Have her take one tablet every four hours and see her personal physician in two weeks." She started to leave then looked back at Clare. "The hospital provides counseling services if you'd like to meet with someone. The receptionist at the front desk can make an appointment for you." She disappeared into a cubicle farther down the long room.

Clare's face turned red, and Darcy hurried to assure her she'd filled out all of the correct insurance information and that the receptionist at the front desk had made a copy of Clare's insurance card. Putting her arm around Clare, Darcy continued. "Dr. What's-her-

name obviously doesn't have the best bedside manner, but don't worry about it. I'll drive you home, and once you're settled in bed, I'll go to the pharmacy to fill your prescription."

The rain had stopped, and the sun was shining through vivid patches of blue when Darcy and Clare emerged from the hospital. Clare sat silently huddled in her seat all the way to their apartment. Darcy helped her up the stairs and into a pair of pajamas.

"Would you like a glass of juice or something to eat before I go to the pharmacy?" Darcy asked when Clare was settled in her bed.

"No, I just want to sleep." Clare turned on her side, taking care to rest her arm with its bulky brace on top of her quilt.

"I'll be back as soon as I can," Darcy promised, looking down at Clare's blond curls spread across her pillow. Even pale and feeling miserable, Clare was beautiful in a way Darcy knew she would never be. Not that she was ugly or anything like that. It was just that her dishwater-blond shade of hair and hazel eyes were no match for Clare's pale, almost-white hair and china-blue eyes. Darcy had always envied Clare's tiny, delicate nose too.

"Don't rush." Clare's words were slurred. "You didn't get much sleep last night either, and I'm not hurting as much now as I was earlier. A nurse gave me a shot before the doctor put the brace on my wrist, and you've already done so m . . ." Her words trailed off as she closed her eyes.

Stepping back into the hall, Darcy glanced longingly at her bedroom door then picked up her purse again. She'd sleep better once she'd picked up the prescription.

* * *

When she returned to the apartment, she was surprised to hear Clare's voice. She'd been sure her roommate would still be asleep. As she approached the bedroom door, it became clear that Clare was talking on her cell phone.

Not wishing to eavesdrop or interrupt, Darcy carried the small bag from the pharmacy into the bathroom and left it on a shelf above the sink.

"I haven't had a chance to ask her yet." Clare's voice carried clearly through the thin wall.

"I will. I promise, but I don't think she'll agree." Darcy wondered if she was the subject of Clare's telephone call. If she was talking to Blaine, and if they were planning to line her up with one of Blaine's dorky friends, she wouldn't agree to it. Blaine's family was rich and prominent in Boise, but Darcy didn't want anything to do with anyone who might bring her into closer contact with Clare's chauvinistic, know-it-all boyfriend. Even though he was an attorney, employed by his father in one of the city's most prestigious law firms, there was something about him that grated on Darcy's nerves, and she suspected his ethics didn't match his father's firm's sterling reputation.

"I'll try." Clare's voice sounded strained. "But I don't think this is a good time. I'm really tired . . . I know, but the doctor gave me a shot . . . No, of course not. I know it was my own fault . . . Darcy will be back any minute . . . Yes, I will . . . I love you too . . . Good-bye."

Darcy wasn't certain which was the stronger emotion: guilt for listening to Clare's conversation or annoyance that Blaine had stayed on the line to badger Clare about something after she explained that she'd fallen and needed to sleep. Actually, now that she had time to think about it, she again thought it strange that Blaine hadn't seen Clare fall and been the one to take her to the hospital.

Darcy yawned. She'd just peek in on Clare to be certain she was comfortable before crawling back into bed for a few hours. She usually ran several mornings a week and had planned an extra long run, but sleep held more appeal than running this morning.

When she eased the door open, Darcy saw Clare curled up like a kitten on her bed. Her cell phone lay inches from her fingers as though she'd dropped it the moment she'd finished talking to Blaine. Darcy stepped forward to pick up the phone. As she began to set it on the nightstand beside Clare, she impulsively turned it off. Clare didn't need any more disturbances.

Returning to her own room, Darcy stripped off her jeans and shoes before sliding under the comforter. She fell asleep almost instantly.

The sound of the phone ringing awakened her long before she felt prepared to face the world again. She staggered into the kitchen, hoping to stop the persistent noise before it disturbed Clare. She and Clare had discussed discontinuing the hardwired telephone after Ellen left. Darcy planned to purchase a cell phone like Clare's with her next

paycheck so they wouldn't have to worry about missed calls when one or both were out of the apartment or sleeping.

"Hello," she muttered as she put the receiver to her ear.

"Clare isn't answering her phone. Where is she?"

"She's sleeping." Darcy struggled to be polite. If she'd had any idea Blaine would call back on the apartment phone, she would have turned it off too. She'd go shopping for a cell phone of her own soon and make certain the apartment phone was turned off on Monday.

"Go get her. I need to talk to her."

"I'm sorry, Blaine, but she really needs to sleep, and I have no intention of disturbing her until that pain shot wears off." Darcy spoke with firmness as she glanced at the nearby wall clock. She'd been asleep barely thirty minutes and Clare only about five minutes more.

"This'll only take a minute," Blaine wheedled.

"No. Clare was seriously injured this morning and is now sedated. She can't come to the phone."

"She'll want to talk to me."

"I don't care how much she might want to talk to you. I'm not waking her." Darcy struggled to hang on to her temper. "Don't you understand plain English? She was up all night with you, then injured, and her doctor gave her a shot to put her to sleep so she can rest. You can call her later this afternoon."

"I'm coming by to take her to lunch."

"No, you're not! She's in no condition to go anywhere, and if you show up here before four o'clock, I'll call the police and have you charged with trespassing!" Darcy slammed the phone back on its receiver. She hesitated a moment then shut off the ringer and switched on the answering machine. "How can Clare stand that creep?" she muttered as she staggered back to her bed.

* * *

Clare awoke feeling as though her head was stuffed with cotton. Her mouth was dry, and she felt disoriented. A glimpse of her alarm clock indicated it was after three. *Blaine!* He was going to pick her up for lunch. She hoped he'd understand that she couldn't help

falling into such a deep sleep after her trip to the hospital. Surely he must have called.

She sat up too abruptly and grimaced with pain when she accidentally leaned her weight on her injured wrist. After just a moment's pause to get her bearings and allow the worst of the pain to fade, she swung her legs off the side of the bed and groped for her robe. Darcy would be leaving for work soon, and she needed to talk with her before she left the apartment.

She could only get one arm through a sleeve of her robe and had to settle for draping the other side over her shoulder. As she turned, she noticed her cell phone sitting on her nightstand. Picking it up, she was about to drop it in her pocket when she noticed it wasn't on. *I must have accidentally turned it off after I talked to Blaine this morning. I shouldn't have done that. I promised him I'd always leave it on.* She quickly turned it on and noticed she had several messages waiting. Perhaps she should call him back. No, he'd want her to talk with Darcy first.

She entered the living room as Darcy emerged from her bedroom wearing her uniform. There were dark circles under her eyes, and she looked tired. Her light brown hair wasn't as carefully brushed as usual. Clare knew this the sixth night in a row Darcy had worked and that being on her feet so many hours, along with spending the early part of the day in a classroom, left her friend exhausted. Fortunately, this was Darcy's last semester, and after she did her student teaching, she'd be able to get a better-paying job and would no longer need to wait tables.

"Darcy?"

"Oh, Clare, are you feeling better? I left your prescription in the bathroom. I'm sorry to leave you alone this evening, but it's too late to get someone to fill my shift."

Clare knew that Darcy received more tips on Saturday nights than other nights and that she couldn't afford to pass up working her usual Saturday shift. "I'll be all right. Blaine will probably come over and stay with me until you get off."

Darcy frowned. "You really need to rest."

"I won't do anything strenuous. He'll probably bring a pizza and we'll watch TV."

"If you get tired, send him home."

"I will." She watched Darcy put on her coat and knew she had to say something quickly. "You know we haven't talked much about getting another roommate."

"I'll see if I can get an ad ready during my break," Darcy promised.

"No, I mean . . . I've already found us another roommate." Clare scuffed a toe across the carpet, unable to meet Darcy's eyes.

"You have? What's she like? Is she LDS? How soon will she be moving in?"

"It's Blaine. He wants to move into our vacant room. That room has its own bathroom, and it's clear across the apartment from our rooms. You know he can afford to pay his share of the rent, and we'll be much safer with a man living here—"

"Blaine? No way!"

Clare caught a glimpse of Darcy's incredulous expression. She'd been skeptical too when Blaine first proposed becoming their new roommate, but he'd convinced her it was the perfect solution. Now she just needed to overcome Darcy's skepticism.

"You know his moral standards are the same as ours. He's a returned missionary, and we can trust him not to do anything inappropriate," Clare pointed out.

"Uh-uh. Ever hear of avoiding even the appearance of evil? We're getting a female roommate." Darcy was adamant. "I can't believe you would even *suggest* allowing Blaine to move in with us!"

"Our apartment is nice, but this really isn't the best neighborhood. I'd feel much safer with Blaine living here." Clare wasn't ready to give up.

"If my dad heard we were even considering letting your boyfriend move in, he would totally explode. If this neighborhood makes you nervous, we can find another apartment in a better neighborhood."

"You know that if we move, we'll have to settle for a smaller apartment, and all the work we put into fixing this one up will be for nothing." Clare was beginning to feel desperate. She had to persuade Darcy that Blaine's plan would work.

"Clare, I've got to get to work. Having Blaine as a roommate isn't an option I'm willing to even consider. Why would he want to live with us anyway? He can afford any apartment he wants. His daddy is

Mr. Big Bucks, and he's always telling us what a great job he has and how much money he makes."

"He worries about me and wants to be sure I'm safe."

"If he's so worried about you, why didn't he make certain you were safely inside our building before leaving this morning?" Darcy opened the door and closed it quickly behind her.

Clare blinked back tears. She'd handled it all wrong. Blaine would be disappointed, and she hated disappointing him. But honesty compelled her to admit that every one of Darcy's objections were the same ones she'd given Blaine.

* * *

Darcy's burst of temper cooled as she drove toward the restaurant where she worked. She shouldn't have let Clare's proposal upset her so much. She was tired, but that was no excuse for losing her temper. Clare was still in pain and wasn't thinking clearly. Tomorrow they wouldn't be so rushed or tired, and they could discuss the matter more rationally. Clare would see reason, and if Darcy couldn't convince her that allowing Blaine to live with them wasn't a good idea, she'd suggest they discuss the matter with Bishop Gregston, their singles ward bishop.

Pulling her ten-year-old Escort into the parking lot, she headed for the back row where employees were allowed to park. Even though the area was clearly marked EMPLOYEES ONLY, there were some vehicles that obviously didn't belong in the few allotted spaces. Finally, at the far end of the row, she was able to maneuver her little car between two large SUVs.

The restaurant was full, and a line of people waited to be seated. There was no time to catch her breath before beginning work.

By nine o'clock her legs ached, and she was looking forward to the break she should have gotten two hours earlier. With just an hour until the restaurant closed, she debated even taking a break, but sitting down for fifteen minutes was too tempting. She hurried toward the staff area.

"Excuse me, miss." A man seated at a corner table caught her attention. He wasn't at one of her tables, but she'd noticed him and

the tall blond woman with him when they'd entered the restaurant. She wasn't sure why she'd noticed him. There wasn't anything particularly unusual about him. His brown hair was an ordinary color, and he wore glasses with a narrow, gold metal rim that gave him a studious look. Maybe it was the way he walked. Not many men as tall as this one walked with the smooth assurance she'd noticed as he'd made his way to his table.

"Could we see the dessert menu?" he asked, and she noticed an appraising twinkle in his eyes.

"And I'd like my glass refilled." The sleek blond indicated her empty glass. Darcy noticed something vaguely familiar about the woman. It might just be that she was a regular customer, but she suspected it was more than that. Seeing that the couple's waitress was busy with a large party, Darcy quietly left dessert menus with the couple and refilled the woman's glass before leaving for her break.

When Darcy returned from her break, she was surprised to see the couple still seated at the corner table, deeply involved in conversation. Turning her attention to her own area, she took dessert orders from a table of theater goers who had been in earlier for dinner. Several regulars sat at tables, and she exchanged pleasantries or joked with them, but the restaurant was thinning out. Tips had been good, and even though she was tired, she felt optimistic that she'd have enough money to pay her share of the rent when it came due.

Feeling a tug on her apron, she turned to see a man who frequented the restaurant and who had gained a reputation for bothering the waitresses. He didn't appear to be more than forty and wasn't bad looking, but he always drank more than he ate. And he seldom left a tip. She'd been dismayed to find him in her section that night. Though the restaurant offered wine on its menu, the waitresses all knew the wine steward didn't deliver to any patron the amount of liquor the man consumed whenever he was in the restaurant. Clearly he kept a flask in his pocket. As the evening progressed, he invariably changed from an unassuming businessman to an aggressive would-be lady's man.

"What time do you get off, darlin'?" She ignored the question and tugged her apron free of his grasp.

"Here's your check, sir." She set the paper on his table.

"I'd like another drink." He thrust his glass toward her.

"The restaurant is closing. If you want another drink, you'll need to move to the bar next door." She turned away, and he grabbed at her again, catching her arm.

"You ain't very friendly," he whined in a slurred voice.

"Let go of me, or I'll call the manager," she spoke slowly and distinctly in a cold, no-nonsense voice. He released his grip but sent her a reproachful glare. Seeing no new customers at any of her tables, she returned to the kitchen, where she fumed to one of the other waitresses.

"Management should refuse to serve Mr. Carlson. People like him should be in the bar, not the restaurant."

"I'm glad you got him tonight instead of me," the other waitress said. "He never leaves a tip, and other customers don't want to sit near him. I'm sick of him always trying to touch me when I walk by."

"That's it," another waitress said. "The place is empty and we can go home." One waitress bent down to rub the calves of her legs while the other one removed a roll of bills from her apron pocket. "The only thing that makes Saturdays survivable is the number of good tips, and I got lucky tonight. Pauline Prescott was in tonight with some guy. She said if he insisted on paying for dinner, she'd get the tip. She left a fifty on their table."

No wonder that woman looked familiar. Darcy groaned, remembering the blond who had looked familiar. She was Blaine's sister! She'd seen her picture in the paper when she had been named as the attorney representing the accused in a recent high-profile case.

She quickly gathered up her coat and handbag, suddenly anxious to get home to check on Clare. She hoped her roommate would be alone and peacefully sleeping. She didn't want to argue with her anymore over her absurd suggestion that Blaine move into the third bedroom in their apartment, and she certainly didn't want to have to be polite to the irritating man her friend had fallen for.

She was disappointed to see that the two large SUVs were still on either side of her little car. It always made her nervous to back out of a parking spot when she didn't have good visuals on either side. Pulling her keys from her pocket, she promised herself, as she did every night she worked, that her next car would have a wireless door opener.

She leaned forward to unlock the door and felt an arm circle her waist. A hand cut off her scream. She took a step back and slammed her heel down on her attacker's foot. She pressed hard and heard him mutter several expletives. The hand holding her keys was pressed tightly to her side, but with her other hand she clawed at the hand covering her mouth. She managed to move it far enough to call for help before her voice was muffled again.

She heard a loud smack and felt a jolt behind her. Suddenly she was free, her attacker sprawled on the pavement. She sagged against her car door.

"Are you all right?" asked the tall man who had asked for the dessert menu earlier that night. Pauline Prescott's boyfriend was her rescuer. She wasn't surprised to see that irritating drunk out cold on the pavement.

"I called the police, David," Pauline said as she walked up to him.

Darcy leaned against her car, feeling weak and exhausted. All of the waitresses complained about Mr. Carlson, but they all considered him pretty harmless. *Why had he chosen to come after her?*

"Here, I think you need to sit down." David took Darcy's keys from her shaking hand and unlocked her car door. Relieved, she sank into the car seat and leaned her head against the steering wheel.

"Did he hurt you?" David asked.

"No. I'm not hurt. I was just scared. Thank you." She paused, remembering she had to get home to Clare. "I really appreciate your help, but I need to go now."

"You can't leave yet. The police are on their way." Pauline frowned and tapped her foot. The sound of sirens filled the air.

It was more than an hour later that the officers who responded to Pauline's call finished their questions and Darcy was allowed to leave. Pauline and David had stayed with her, and she'd learned that David's last name was Schoenfeld and that he was a coach at Boise High School. She thanked them both for rescuing her and for their consideration in staying with her.

It was approaching midnight when Darcy finally pulled into her parking space behind the apartment building and locked her car before hurrying inside. She heard the television as soon as she stepped inside the apartment and felt a stab of disappointment when she saw

Blaine seated beside Clare on the sofa. Remembering his sister's kindness to her earlier, she determined to be gracious to him.

"Hello, Blaine," she said, then turned to Clare. "Are you feeling better? I'm not sure you should be up."

"I'm fine," Clare attempted to reassure her, but the dark circles under her eyes and her slumped shoulders suggested otherwise. "You look more frazzled than I feel," Clare added, eyeing Darcy critically. "Did the restaurant stay open later than usual?" Darcy's hand went to her hair, and she realized she must look a mess after her scuffle with Mr. Carlson.

"No, the problem was after I left work. If Blaine's sister and her date hadn't parked next to me, I could have been badly hurt." Darcy went on to tell them about the evening's events.

"Oh, Darcy, I'm glad they were there to help you." Clare struggled to her feet to give Darcy an awkward one-armed hug.

"I'm not surprised that Pauline involved herself in something dangerous," Blaine said. "It does surprise me, though, that David exerted himself to do anything. He's usually a big wimp."

"I wouldn't think a high-school coach would deserve being described as a wimp," Darcy said.

"He's a little older than me," Blaine elaborated. "He and Pauline were classmates. He'd never stand up for himself when any guy threw a punch his way. He never even went out for any of the tough sports—only for golf, tennis, track, swimming, and sissy stuff like that. He played volleyball too—on the coed team. He qualified to compete in some big golf tournament once and chose to sing in a choir festival that was being held the same day instead."

"I don't think that makes him a wimp, and he didn't hesitate to knock this guy's lights out."

"He was probably just trying to impress Pauline. I thought that after she finished law school and started to make a name for herself, she'd dump him, but she's never been any good at attracting men and probably figures she'd better hang onto David until she finds something better."

Darcy bit her tongue to keep from commenting on Blaine's insensitive remarks concerning his sister and her friend. "Well, I'm going to bed. Church starts at nine, and I didn't get much sleep last night." She added the last as a pointed reminder that Clare needed to rest too.

Exhausted, Darcy fell into bed, but as she drifted to sleep, she could still hear the murmur of Blaine's voice coming from the front room.

* * *

Darcy tacked the small notice announcing that she and Clare were looking for a roommate to the singles ward bulletin board the next morning before slipping inside the chapel for sacrament meeting. She found a seat beside a couple of young women she'd gotten to know in the little more than two months that she and Clare had been living in Boise. They both smiled and whispered a greeting. When they looked past her, obviously looking for Clare, she explained. "Clare broke her wrist and didn't feel like coming today."

"What happened?" Elaine asked.

"Her wet shoes slipped in the entryway to our building when she was coming back from a date on Friday."

"Oh, how awful! I'd be so embarrassed to fall like that in front of my boyfriend." Elaine looked sympathetic.

"If you had a boyfriend," the other girl, Tammy, said, giggling. Suddenly her smile disappeared, and she looked thoughtful. "Clare's been dating Blaine Prescott, hasn't she?"

Darcy nodded.

"Where was *he* when Clare *happened* to fall?" Something in her voice caused little alarm bells to ring in Darcy's head, and she remembered she'd heard rumors that Tammy and Blaine had been an item before Darcy and Clare moved into the ward.

"Shhh! The meeting's about to start," Elaine whispered.

Darcy reached for a hymn book then settled back against the bench. She mouthed the words to the opening song, but her mind was otherwise engaged. *Where* was *Blaine when Clare fell? Why did the doctor at the hospital suggest counseling to Clare? Was it possible she hadn't meant financial counseling?* Her mind filled with a picture of Clare's wrist with four long narrow bruises on one side and one larger one on the other. She didn't like the ugly picture her thoughts were suggesting.

Darcy struggled to keep her mind focused on the sacrament meeting speakers, then on the lessons taught in Sunday School and

Relief Society, but at unexpected moments, she found her thoughts drifting back to Clare and her injury. She found herself wondering if she should have stayed home with Clare instead of coming to church.

"Darcy? Darcy Olsen?" She was leaving the Relief Society room at the end of the three-hour block when someone called her name.

"Yes?" She turned to see a young woman with long, straight hair who looked barely eighteen. There was something about the girl's beaming smile that brought a smile to Darcy's face.

"I was afraid I'd missed you," the girl gasped. "My name is Stacy Moore. I saw your note on the bulletin board and wanted to tell you I'm interested. Is there a time when I could meet with you and your roommate to see the apartment and answer any questions you have about me?"

"Clare works weekdays, but she might take tomorrow off since she has a broken wrist. Why don't you come over about eleven tomorrow morning? If she isn't there, I can show you the apartment."

"That would be great. I have a job, but I don't start until next Monday, and I would like to be settled in an apartment by then. I'm staying with my sister and her family, but it's awfully crowded."

"Great! I'll see you tomorrow then."

Darcy began the walk back to the apartment with a lighter step. Stacy had impressed her as friendly and congenial. Stacy was a little younger than her and Clare, who had both graduated from Washington State last spring, but she was a member of the Church and had a job, so there shouldn't be any problem. Darcy just hoped Clare was ready to forget her silly idea of having Blaine move in with them.

For a moment she regretted that she hadn't found a good job like Clare had when they'd first arrived in Boise so that she could afford to pay half the rent instead of only a third. But she wasn't sorry she'd enrolled at Boise State to take a few more classes and do a semester of student teaching. An English degree hadn't been terribly useful for finding a job, and she'd quickly regretted not getting an English teaching degree in the first place, so she'd taken the waitress position and applied at Boise State. She'd been taking classes all summer in addition to working. Anyway, she was far more interested in teaching than in finding some low-level business position. By the time she finished her student teaching and found a job, she'd be able to afford a bigger share of the rent.

Twisting her key in the lock, Darcy pushed the door open and stared in dismay at the mess that greeted her. Boxes were scattered across the front room and down the hall leading to the third bedroom. Clare stood frozen beneath the arch that separated the kitchen and living room.

"What's going on?" Darcy asked. Clare's face told her she wasn't going to like the answer.

Clare turned a bright, phony smile toward her. "We have a new roommate," she announced.

"But we haven't . . ."

"Hi, roomie." Blaine stepped from the hall to place an arm around Clare.

Chapter 2

"WHAT DO YOU MEAN?" DARCY hoped Blaine wasn't referring to himself as their new roommate, but a sick feeling in her stomach told her he was.

"Didn't Clare tell you I was arriving today?" Blaine gave her a faux innocent smile.

"Clare told me you had asked to move into our apartment. I thought she was joking." Darcy struggled to stay calm.

"No joke. I'm here."

"This better be a joke." Darcy thrust out her chin. "Clare and I never agreed to your moving in, and when we find a roommate, *she* will be someone we both want to live here. I set up an appointment with a girl in our ward to look at the apartment tomorrow and meet Clare."

"Now, now, don't be like that. Clare wants me to live here, and you know you'll both be much safer with me here."

"How safe was Clare the other morning when you dumped her off and let her break her wrist?"

"Darcy!" Clare gasped. "You know Blaine always walks me to the door like a gentleman."

"Oh, really? Then why didn't he offer to drive you to the hospital when you fell and broke your wrist? And how do you explain those bruises on your arm? It doesn't appear he was watching out for your safety when you got those!" Darcy knew from the white color of Clare's face that she'd gone too far.

"She said she was fine." Blaine stepped forward, anger blazing in his eyes. "I don't know why you've taken a dislike to me, but I suspect

it has little to do with me and more to do with your jealousy of Clare. You can't stand that she has a good job and makes more money than you do, or that she's popular and pretty. You've always lived in her shadow and would resent anyone who makes her happier than you ever can."

"Of all the stupidity!" Darcy shook her head. "If we're going to indulge in a little psychobabble, may I suggest there might be something wrong with a man who chooses to leave his very upscale apartment to move into the low-rent district with two women."

"I'm willing to make the sacrifice." Blaine grinned snidely.

"Please, Darcy." Clare sounded nervous. "Can't we just give it a try?"

"No!" Darcy wasn't willing to give an inch. "You know coed housing isn't approved by our church leaders. That point was made perfectly clear in our institute classes at Washington State."

"We were students then," Clare protested. "We're adults now."

"The Church has never had one set of moral standards for minors and another for adults." She gave Clare a lopsided smile. "Besides, you know very well that the moment my dad learns we agreed to a male roommate, he'll be here to move us back home."

"Oh, really adult!" Blaine mocked.

"You need to leave so Clare and I can discuss this," Darcy said to Blaine.

"I'm not going anywhere." He folded his arms and glared at her with a superior smirk.

"You can go quietly, or I can call the police." Darcy stood her ground. "I have a signed contract that says you can't move in without both my consent and Clare's. And you *definitely* don't have my consent."

"You wouldn't!" Clare gasped and stepped forward to appeal to Darcy. "He's already moved out of his old apartment and turned in the keys. Let him stay tonight, and we can talk more tomorrow."

"This is ridiculous," Darcy fumed. "Blaine can go stay with his father or his sister. He's not exactly homeless."

"Be reasonable," Clare continued to plead.

"I am. You're the ones being unreasonable. Blaine goes now!" She flung open the apartment door and began pushing Blaine's boxes out into the hall.

"Stop! Don't do this!" Clare was in tears.

"I have to." Darcy paused to place an arm around Clare's shoulder. "You know letting him stay would be wrong."

Blaine gripped Clare's shoulder and thrust her away from Darcy. She struggled to regain her feet before falling onto the sofa. Putting his nose almost in Darcy's face, he shouted, "All right, I'll leave for now. But I'll be back!"

"Take your boxes with you!"

"I'll send someone for them!" He stepped into the hall, where he nearly tripped over a box Darcy had pushed through the door. Picking it up, he flung it forcefully toward her.

A corner of the box struck Darcy's thigh, then dropped to the floor. Ignoring the pain, she shoved the door shut and slid the dead-bolt into place before slowly turning around to face Clare. Slowly she walked toward the sofa where her friend was huddled with tears streaming down her face.

"I'm sorry. That wasn't very diplomatic, but surely you must see that it just wouldn't work for Blaine to live with us. Not only would it be wrong to allow your boyfriend to live with us, but he and I don't get along." She sank to her knees beside Clare, wincing when the spot where the box had struck her brushed against the sofa.

"Why did you have to make him so angry?" Clare lifted her damp face toward Darcy. "I'll just die if he doesn't come back."

"I should have controlled my temper better," Darcy admitted. Her eyes widened as she noticed several new bruises on Clare's arms and a suspicious red mark on her cheek. "But to be perfectly honest, I think you'd be better off if he didn't come back."

"That's a cruel thing to say."

"Is Blaine responsible for those bruises on your arm? And for your broken wrist?"

"I bruise easy. You know that." Clare frowned and drew back from Darcy. "Blaine is a big man and strong. He'd never hurt me on purpose."

"I don't buy that. I think he knows very well that his rough tactics hurt you just like he meant to hurt me when he threw that box at me. There was nothing accidental about that."

"You threatened him, and he lost his temper. You can't blame him for that," Clare protested.

"I *can* blame him. I've had a terrible temper all my life, and I work hard to control it. Even when I fail to curb it, I never hurt anyone. Having a temper doesn't make anyone less responsible for their actions," Darcy tried to reason with Clare.

"I don't see why you're so opposed to Blaine living here. It would save me money since I could ride to work with him. He works in the same building I do. Ellen was always late with her share of the rent, and Blaine wouldn't ever be late. It would be good to have a priesthood holder in our apartment, too. I always envied you that. My dad died before I was old enough to really appreciate priesthood blessings and counsel."

"Moving in with us and hurting someone every time he doesn't get his way aren't indications Blaine honors his priesthood." Darcy shook her head, refusing to accept Clare's argument.

"Blaine is a returned missionary!" Clare sat up straight and folded her arms. "I don't understand why you're doing this to me. I thought we were friends and that you'd be happy for me. Instead all you're doing is finding fault with the man I love. Accusing him of not honoring the priesthood is going too far."

"No, a priesthood holder who attempts to move in with two single women is going too far. And agreeing to let him live here is going too far." Darcy stood up. She took several steps toward her bedroom then stopped. She turned back to Clare. "I don't want to fight with you. I care deeply about you, and if you take some time to think about this without Blaine around to influence you, you'll know I'm right."

"Maybe you're the one who should leave!" Clare rushed past her, slamming her door as she disappeared into her bedroom.

* * *

Clare threw herself on her bed to cry. How could Darcy be so unreasonable? While growing up, they'd seldom disagreed or been angry with each other for more than a few minutes. Maybe Blaine was right, and Darcy didn't want Clare to have a close relationship with anyone other than her. She couldn't believe Darcy would be so selfish. She had her mom and dad and four younger siblings. She had more cousins than Clare could count, as well, while Clare had only had her mom, and she

didn't even have her anymore. She'd dated a few times while in high school, but her mother's needs had left her with little time for boys. Later, at the university, she'd been intent on getting her degree and recovering from the loss of her mother. Few of her dates had resulted in a second date. Blaine was her first real boyfriend, and she was finding there was something satisfying about being part of a couple.

Clare told herself that she needed someone strong and decisive like Blaine. He made her feel loved and that she belonged somewhere. With him she found relief from the load of responsibility she'd carried since her childhood. The first time she'd met him, which happened to be in the elevator of the building where she'd just been hired to work in the accounting department of a large architectural firm, she'd been in awe of his self-confidence and flattered by his flirting. When she'd seem him again at stake conference and he'd stopped to speak with her, she'd been amazed that he remembered her. The very next day he'd shown up at her office to take her to lunch. Over lunch he told her he believed their meeting was no accident and that God had brought them together.

Soon she'd been spending every spare minute with Blaine. He'd even bought her a cell phone so that they'd never be more than a push of a button apart. He'd bought it for her right after she'd walked across the street with one of the young men from her office to meet Blaine for their luncheon date.

Clare reached for a tissue and winced at the pain in her arm. It really wasn't Blaine's fault she'd broken her wrist. After a late dinner Friday night, they'd lingered at the table until the restaurant was about to close then went to a movie. She thought he'd take her home right after the movie, but instead he'd driven to a spot above the capitol and broached the subject of moving into their apartment.

She'd known at once that Darcy wouldn't like the idea. Darcy didn't approve of Blaine, which was silly since Blaine was a returned missionary, had a good job, and came from a family of some prominence. She'd expressed her reservations about Blaine's suggestion, mentioning that such an arrangement might become a source for gossip.

"I'll have to discuss it with Darcy," she'd said.

"You don't have to get Darcy's approval for every decision you make," he'd said. "You can help me pack tomorrow, then we'll go

someplace nice for lunch. I'll call someone to deliver my things to the apartment the next day."

"I think you should wait . . ."

"There's no reason to wait. I've already committed to being out of my apartment this weekend."

"Give me time to talk to Darcy," Clare had pleaded when they stopped behind the apartment building.

"What's there to talk about?"

"It's terribly late. I need to go." She'd reached for the door handle.

"We're not through here!" Blaine had grasped her wrist, jerking her back onto the car seat.

A white hot pain had shot through her arm, and little black dots swam before her eyes when she fell against the car console. She'd lowered her head, fighting nausea.

Eventually she'd become aware that rain was falling in torrents, and though she was inside Blaine's car, her cheeks were wet. "I'll pick you up at ten," she heard Blaine say in a disgusted tone before he reached across her to push her car door open.

"I need more time," she'd mumbled. "My wrist hurts bad, and I'm afraid I won't be able to do much."

"You're just sulking because I won't let Darcy run our lives."

"No, when . . . I fell against the gearshift, I hurt my wrist."

"Come on, I'll walk you to the door. It'll feel better after a few hours' sleep."

He'd pulled his jacket over both their heads as they ran for the back door to the apartment building. Before dashing back out into the rain, he'd pulled her close and kissed her sweetly on the lips. "It'll be all right," he'd whispered. "Trust me."

Now, several hours later, Clare was still anxiously waiting for Blaine to call. She'd never been so angry with Darcy. It was unfair of her to insult Blaine when he was only trying to be helpful. She'd never forgive Darcy if Blaine decided he wanted nothing more to do with her.

Chapter 3

CLARE SLOSHED MILK ON THE counter while pouring some on her cereal. She'd found making her bed nearly impossible, and getting dressed by herself had been difficult too, but she persisted. She had no intention of missing a day of work. Blaine hadn't called, but she was still in hopes of meeting him at their usual place for lunch.

"Are you going to work this morning?" Darcy stood in the doorway, wearing a robe and looking half asleep.

Clare nodded without speaking.

"I can drive you if you feel sure you're well enough to work," Darcy offered.

"I'll take the bus." Clare turned her back to Darcy.

"I was hoping you'd be here when Stacy comes."

"I'm not agreeing to her or anyone other than Blaine."

"All right, I'll cancel the appointment, but I'll never agree to a male roommate. I'd hoped a good night's sleep would help you see how inappropriate it would be to have your boyfriend live with us."

Clare picked up the vial of pain pills she'd carried from the bathroom. Shaking one from the small bottle onto the countertop, she swallowed it with some orange juice. Leaving her uneaten bowl of cereal, she returned to her room, averting her face as she walked past Darcy. Moments later, with her handbag on her arm, she left the apartment.

Darcy moved to the front window, where she watched for Clare to emerge from the building and begin the four-block hike to the nearest bus stop. Her heart felt heavy, and she wondered what to do. It wasn't like Clare to remain angry, particularly over such a silly issue.

Or was she, Darcy, the one being unreasonable? Choosing a female roommate over Blaine seemed like a no-brainer to her, but out of fairness, she supposed she should at least examine Clare's argument.

She returned to her room to dress in jogging shorts for her morning run. Looking down at the huge bruise that extended below the hem of her shorts, she ground her teeth together then switched to sweat pants. She didn't run every morning but usually managed long runs on Mondays and Saturdays, the two days she didn't have classes, and she made shorter runs at least a couple other days during the week.

While she ran, Darcy thought over every argument Clare and Blaine had produced. Though their apartment wasn't in one of the more highbrow neighborhoods, it wasn't in a slum either, and Boise really wasn't a high-crime city, nor did it have scary neighborhoods like she'd heard about in larger cities. So that argument didn't wash.

Was she resentful of Clare's success in finding a good job or of the interest men paid her? Not really, she concluded. If she'd found a better job, she wouldn't have committed herself to expanding her English degree to a teaching degree, and she had really always wanted to teach. It was only her eagerness to graduate sooner that had kept her from pursuing teaching credentials in the first place. As for Clare's blond prettiness, who wouldn't be a little envious? But she honestly didn't think it was something she obsessed about.

Over and over she examined each point of her argument with Clare and Blaine as her feet pounded first on pavement then along a trail that ran beside the Boise River. The changing color of the leaves, the crystal clear air, and the rhythmic motion calmed her irritation over the situation, and as she recalled Clare's desire for the priesthood in their apartment, her conviction grew that having Blaine for a roommate was not the answer.

Gradually, she turned from considering Clare's argument to ways she might convince Clare to seek a female roommate. Her steps slowed as she approached the apartment building. She didn't have a plan yet, but she felt confident that one would come to her.

As she entered the apartment, she frowned over the boxes still strewn across the front room. The mail had arrived, and she eagerly opened a lavender envelope from her mother and laughed at the

descriptions of her younger siblings' antics. She also felt some amusement that her mother didn't write to her via e-mail like her dad and at least two of her siblings did almost every day. Even her youngest brother, thirteen-year-old Terry, sent her an occasional Internet joke. It was nice to have the letters, though. They were something she could keep and treasure.

She tossed the rest of the mail on the table to wait until after her shower. She struggled to keep her annoyance with Blaine and Clare in check as she made her way around Blaine's boxes. After showering and dressing for work, she returned to the mail. Leafing through it, she noticed an envelope stuck between the pages of a grocery store flier. Picking it up, she saw the university's logo in the corner. She opened it with shaking fingers and scanned the single page hurriedly before letting out a little squeal. She'd be doing her student teaching at Boise High School beginning in just two weeks!

After dancing around the room with the letter pressed to her chest, she ran to the phone. She couldn't wait to tell Clare. With her hand on the receiver, she paused. It might not be a good idea to call Clare at work. As angry as she was when she left that morning, Clare might not appreciate being interrupted. She dialed her mother instead.

* * *

Only a small lamp lit the front room when Darcy stepped into the apartment late the following night. It was enough to reveal that Blaine's boxes were gone. She noted their absence with satisfaction and turned toward her bedroom. She switched the lamp off on her way. Seconds later, light flooded the small hall that separated her room from Clare's.

"Look!" Clare held up her left hand for Darcy to see. A huge diamond rested on her ring finger.

"Wow!" Darcy stepped closer for a better look. "It's huge. Congratulations." Her arms went around Clare to give her a gentle hug, taking care not to bump her friend's injury. Inside she felt an ache. She knew she should be excited and happy for Clare, and she would be if Clare weren't marrying Blaine. No matter how hard Darcy tried, and she had tried when Clare first began seeing him, she couldn't

like Blaine. At first it was just annoyance that he seemed to think he knew more than anyone else about everything, but lately she'd become concerned that he might be both emotionally and physically abusive to Clare. His fit of temper the other day had certainly left Darcy with a painful, ugly bruise, and the large number of bruises she'd observed on Clare the past few weeks were reason for suspicion as far as Darcy was concerned.

"He took me to dinner then to the temple grounds where he proposed. It was so romantic." Clare seemed to glow with happiness in spite of the gray pallor of her skin and the dark circles of fatigue under her eyes.

"Have you set a date yet?" Darcy led Clare into the bedroom where they could sit for a chat. Clare sat on the edge of the bed, looking ill at ease.

"No, Blaine says we can't set a date until his father's secretary finds out which dates his brother, who is running for state attorney general, has free, and checks with hotels and orchestras for availability. She'll set up an appointment for us to pick out my gown too." Her fingers traced the pattern in Darcy's bedspread.

"Will you be married in the Boise Temple? You probably should make appointments as soon as possible with your bishops."

"We haven't talked about that yet or made any detailed plans." Clare looked sad for a moment. "I wish Mom were still alive and could help me plan my wedding."

"You know I'll give you any help I can."

Clare smiled and seemed to brighten.

"Come on. Let's go back out to the kitchen and open a bottle of sparkling cider," Darcy suggested. "It's not every day a girl gets engaged— or is given a diamond the size of Plymouth Rock."

"No, we both need to get some rest." Clare stood and made a hurried move toward the door. "We can celebrate later." She quickly crossed the hall to her own room.

Darcy stared after Clare, startled by her hasty departure, and wondered if she'd said something wrong. She didn't like Blaine, but if Clare loved him, she'd do her best to be supportive. She'd better start saving money, too, for an apartment of her own. She hoped that as soon as she finished her student teaching, she'd be able to find a

teaching position nearby that paid well enough for her to afford an apartment. If she didn't, she'd have to move back home.

Darcy lay awake thinking about Clare and her engagement. Marriage to Blaine would change their friendship. She suspected Blaine would do everything possible to drive the two friends apart. Already he sulked if Clare chose to go shopping or to a fireside with Darcy or any of the friends they'd made in their ward instead of with him. He nearly always found some excuse to keep Clare from spending time with anyone other than him. Darcy wondered why Clare didn't feel smothered by Blaine's constant attention.

She couldn't shake the suspicion that Blaine had something to do with Clare's broken wrist and the frequent bruises Darcy had noticed on her friend. Eventually she drifted into a restless slumber. Some vague premonition seemed to be telling her all wasn't right, and several times she awakened when unfamiliar sounds disrupted her sleep.

She was up at five and out the door forty-five minutes later. Her day followed the usual mad dash to classes followed by a shift at the restaurant, but she took time before leaving campus to visit with her counselor and learn more details about the teacher she'd be working with at the high school and the classes she'd be teaching. She learned she'd be working with Sarah Becker, who taught four English classes and one creative writing class. While driving to work after the interview, her mind continued to whirl with possibilities and questions she should have asked.

Finding a parking space was always easier on weekdays than on the weekend. She parked as close to the restaurant as she could and hurried inside. The restaurant wasn't busy that evening, which left her time to consider her counselor's advice. It would be difficult to keep working while student teaching, but if she quit her job, how would she pay her share of expenses? And if Clare married and moved out before Darcy finished her student teaching, she'd have to find new roommates because she couldn't afford an apartment by herself. Even though her mind was filled with plans for the future, when she left the restaurant she took care to walk with another waitress to her car.

As Darcy pulled into the apartment parking area, she noticed a vaguely familiar car parked in the space that had been her old roommate Ellen's. Perhaps one of their neighbors who knew Ellen was gone

had decided to allow a guest to park there. Gathering up her heavy backpack, she trudged toward the building.

All was dark and quiet when she entered the apartment and made her way to her room. As she knelt to pray before crawling into bed, the same uneasy feeling that had disturbed her sleep the night before left her feeling on edge. Though she was tired, she had trouble falling asleep.

When Darcy awoke the next morning, she pulled on shorts and scraped her hair back into a ponytail. The clock said morning, but it was still dark out, so she picked up her windbreaker with its glow-in-the-dark stripes. She'd eat breakfast and shower after her run. From the front of the apartment she could hear voices. It was unusual for Clare to turn on the television while getting ready for work. She usually took great care on the mornings Darcy didn't have classes to avoid awakening her if she chose to sleep in.

"Good morning," she called as she stepped into the kitchen. She stopped abruptly, seeing that Clare wasn't alone. Blaine sat across from her at the kitchen table. Behind him, she caught a glimpse of an unmade bed and scattered clothing in the room that had been Ellen's. Clare didn't turn to face her, and Blaine's expression could only be described as smugly triumphant.

Chapter 4

WITHOUT SAYING A WORD, DARCY turned toward the door. Taking the stairs two at a time, she hit the street running. *Why? Why is Clare doing this? She knows how I feel and she knows the Church's view on men and women living together outside of marriage. I always thought her testimony was as strong as mine and that our friendship mattered to her.*

Instead of turning toward the park and the river, she turned toward the high school where she would soon be spending her days student teaching. But she wasn't thinking about her assignment with the school. The unobstructed high-school track appealed to her need to run fast and hard.

Having Blaine as a roommate wasn't an option for her, and it appeared Clare wouldn't change her mind and agree to find another woman to share expenses. Their contract with the apartment's agent was meaningless since Clare wouldn't agree to a different roommate and Darcy couldn't afford to pay half of the rent for the large apartment.

Hurt and disappointment hit her in waves as she ran. She and Clare had been best friends since preschool. They had always been there for each other. Darcy had known that when they married, the relationship between the friends would change, but she hadn't expected Clare to do something so hateful as secretly moving her boyfriend into their apartment behind Darcy's back, knowing how Darcy felt about it. *Being engaged makes no difference; it's still wrong and under-handed!*

Her steps slowed as she approached the large, three-story building that had recently been renovated to keep Boise High School's presence in the older part of the city. Moving past the building, she made her

way to the track, where she picked up speed again as she began her first lap. She was vaguely conscious of how much more comfortable it was to run on the track rather than on the concrete sidewalks. It was safer, too, when the tears she struggled to keep at bay dimmed her vision. She passed several other runners but paid them no attention.

She continued to run until she became aware of an ache in her legs and that she was much too warm in her nylon jacket. She slowed to a walk to finish the lap then found herself limping as she made her way to the bleachers to sit on the bottom tier and catch her breath.

Resting her elbows on her knees, she cupped her chin in her hands. Her face was wet, and she wasn't sure how much dampness was perspiration and how much was due to tears. *What am I going to do?* she asked herself as she'd been doing ever since she'd left the apartment. She didn't want to go back, but knew she'd eventually have to. *But then what?*

"Are you all right?" She looked up to see a tall man in running shorts standing over her. He was too old to be a student. *David Schoenfeld!* She recognized the man who had come to her rescue the night Mr. Carlson had attempted to assault her. She remembered, too, that Pauline Prescott had mentioned he was a coach at Boise High School.

"I'm fine, David," she stammered, searching her jacket pocket for a tissue.

He looked startled for a moment. "You're not one of my students, are you?"

"No." She tried to laugh, but the sound came out closer to a sob. "We met last week when you rescued me from an attack by a drunken customer behind the restaurant where I work."

"Sorry, I didn't recognize . . ."

"That's okay."

"I remember you now. Is that where you got that bruise?" He sat down beside her, and she followed his glance to where her shorts had ridden up, revealing part of the dark mark on her thigh.

"No, my roommate's boyfriend threw a box at me." Too late she remembered his connection to Blaine through Blaine's sister, Pauline.

"He *what?*" David's face showed his astonishment. "He sounds like a jerk."

"He has a temper." She was glad he didn't know to whom she referred. There was no reason he should recognize her as the friend of Blaine's fiancée.

"I guess I should have asked for permission to run here," she said to change the subject. "I used to run on the high-school track back home and never considered the rules might be different here."

"It's no problem. You can run here mornings, evenings, or weekends—whenever the track isn't in use by a class. Do you live near here?"

"Not extremely close. I'm supposed to start student teaching here in a couple of weeks, and I'm thinking of looking for an apartment within walking distance of the school. My counselor said I shouldn't try to keep my waitress job while student teaching, so I'm looking for a less-expensive apartment. I'll have to sell my car to pay rent, which limits me even more." Even if she sold her car, it was doubtful she could afford a new apartment. All morning, she'd been edging toward the conclusion that the only way she could avoid the messy situation she'd run away from was to go home. She dreaded telling her parents she'd failed at her attempt at independence. She also dreaded telling her counselor she wouldn't be accepting the assignment to train at the beautiful old school.

"I don't know of any apartments nearby, but I know a lady who is looking for someone to live in while she recuperates from a bad fall." David spoke slowly as though considering his words with care.

"I don't have any nursing skills."

"She's not looking for a nurse. In fact, she's pretty independent as far as feeding herself and things like that. A home health nurse stops by every morning to get her up, bathe her, and look after her medical needs, and her daughter stops by every afternoon. It's just that there are a half dozen stairs leading up to both her front and back porches, and though she gets around in a wheelchair, she finds transferring from her bed to the chair difficult. At night she's nervous about being alone for fear she'd be unable to get out of her house should there be a fire or some kind of emergency. She'd like someone to be there to assist her if she has trouble."

"Is she a relative? You seem to know quite a bit about her."

"She's in my ward, uh, congregation."

Darcy laughed. "I'm LDS too, so I know what you mean. You must attend a family ward."

"I do. I was thinking of attending one of the singles wards at the institute, but then I was called to be a counselor in the elders quorum of the ward I live in, and, well, I like being in a family ward." He grinned, and she noticed a slight dimple in his left cheek. "Well, what do you think? Are you interested?"

"I might be. Could you give me her address?"

"Sure. Be right back." He loped over to where a pile of jackets and water bottles rested on a bleacher step to pick up a clipboard. When he returned, he scribbled a name and address on a piece of paper, tore off the sheet, and handed it to her. "It might be best to call ahead and arrange to go over there when her daughter is there to answer the door."

"All right. Thanks." She folded the paper and tucked it in the pocket of her jacket as she rose to her feet. "I'd better go."

"Maybe I'll see you around—if you come to run again or when you start your student teaching. I run every morning." His friendly invitation went a long way toward easing the weight that seemed to be bearing down on her heart.

"I have early classes on Tuesdays and Thursdays so I don't run those days." She shifted her weight from one foot to the other, feeling reluctant to leave but knowing she must. "See ya." She waved and headed toward the sidewalk.

* * *

Clare loaded the dishwasher. She should be on her way to work, but Blaine thought if she weren't there when Darcy returned to the apartment, Darcy would throw his belongings out on the street. He'd gone to his job, leaving her with instructions to stand up to Darcy. She paced the floor, both hoping Darcy would soon return and dreading the confrontation she knew was coming. Catching a glimpse of Blaine's unmade bed, she hurried to make it for him. She didn't want Darcy to have any excuse for complaint.

As Clare straightened the sheets and fluffed the pillows with one hand, heaviness settled in her heart. A nice dinner and strolling hand-in-hand through the temple grounds had led to Blaine's romantic proposal. The evening had been perfect until they'd returned to the apartment. Together

they'd unpacked Blaine's boxes, and she'd helped him decide where to put his stereo and CDs. While he hooked up his computer, she'd moved his clothes to drawers and hung his shirts in the closet. She'd been making up his bed just as she was doing now when he'd tossed a pillow at her. She'd lost her balance and tumbled onto the bed. Contrite, he'd settled beside her then drew her into his arms for a long kiss. She was ashamed to admit that it had been Blaine who remembered Darcy would soon arrive and that they needed to be in their separate rooms with everything appearing normal when Darcy walked through the door.

Arranging the heavy comforter on the bed was difficult with one hand this morning, but she managed, then turned her attention to picking up several items of clothing from the floor. When she carried them to the hamper in the bathroom, she saw that the sink needed cleaning and the mirror shining. While she worked, she thought about the argument she and Blaine had had when she'd tried to talk to him about staying temple worthy.

He'd laughed and said she was obsessing about nothing. "We're practically married and completely committed to each other. Even the most straightlaced Church leaders allow engaged couples a little slack," he'd teased. Still, the incident had dimmed the glow surrounding that special night, and she wasn't convinced they had nothing to worry about.

She supposed Blaine was right and that she'd overreacted. Just to prove she trusted him, she'd invited him to fasten the little buttons that ran down the back of her favorite blouse this morning. Heat rose in her cheeks as she remembered that incident, and a voice in the back of her head questioned whether her offer had been wise.

He'd chuckled while slowly buttoning her blouse, reminding her that he'd spent two nights in the apartment without Darcy even knowing he was there. Clare had joined in his laughter but hadn't felt at ease over the situation. She and Darcy had always been honest with each other, and deceiving her longtime friend didn't feel right. If Darcy would get to know Blaine better, Clare was sure everything would work out. Darcy had a father and brothers; she shouldn't begrudge Clare finally having a man of her own.

Hearing a key in the lock, Clare hurried back to the living room to sit in a chair and pick up a magazine. "Hi!" She looked up as Darcy stepped into the apartment.

"Hi, yourself." Darcy spoke cautiously while looking around as if trying to determine whether Blaine was there. The gesture annoyed Clare.

"He went to work. I stayed home so we could talk."

Both of Darcy's eyebrows went up. "It's a little late for that, isn't it? I assume Blaine hasn't packed up and moved back out."

"No, he hasn't. Blaine is staying."

"Clare," Darcy tossed her jacket on a chair and sat on the sofa a few feet from Clare. "I haven't been running all this time. I stopped at Bishop Gregston's office. I asked him what he thought of two women having a male roommate."

"You had no right . . ."

"Yes, I do have a right to ask that question. Ordinarily, if you and Blaine chose to live together, that would be none of my business, except that in this case, your choice puts me in the position of living with Blaine too, which I'm not willing to do. Bishop Gregston strongly advised against accepting the situation."

"I won't agree to anyone else moving in here." Clare's voice trembled, but she remained adamant. "And I know you can't afford to pay half of the rent on this apartment. With your student teaching about to start, you'll have to cut back on the hours you work, and your finances are already stretched." She'd promised Blaine she'd be firm no matter what argument Darcy used. Blaine said her friend would eventually accept the situation, and all this silliness would be forgotten, with she and Darcy continuing as friends just as they always had.

"I was afraid you'd say that." Darcy took a deep breath.

"Then you're ready to stop insulting Blaine and accept that he's our roommate now? You'll see he's really a lot of fun."

"No," Darcy said. "Bishop Gregston isn't the only one I talked to. I called my dad and told him everything. He said Blaine isn't honoring his priesthood or showing proper respect to you by moving into our apartment. He said that if I can't persuade you to do the right thing, then I'll have to leave. He transferred enough money to my account so that I can stay at a motel while I look for another apartment."

"You can't move out!" Clare protested. "How will it look for Blaine and me to live here alone?"

"The same way it looks with me here. I'm not your chaperone."

"You said you'd never ask your dad for money." Clare felt rising panic. She didn't want Darcy to leave, but Blaine would be angry if she gave in—and everything went better when she avoided making Blaine angry.

"I never asked. He said this issue is too important to let my pride stand in the way of doing what's right. I promised I'd pay him back after I finish my student teaching and find a job."

"He thinks Blaine and I are immoral!" She stood up, her face red with anger. "We haven't done anything wrong. You and your dad have dirty minds. Just because we live in the same apartment doesn't mean we've lowered our standards."

"Clare, maybe you're strong enough to live together and stay morally clean, but do you really think it's wise to put yourself in a position where it will be harder to resist the temptation to become intimate? Don't you remember any of the lessons from Young Women about avoiding even the appearance of evil?"

"You're the one who is putting me in a difficult position," Clare accused. "Everything will be fine if you stay." Darcy was stubborn, but she'd never known her to be unreasonable before. How could she even consider moving out and leaving Clare to become the subject of gossip?

"You know that's not true. You and Blaine are the ones who have put *me* in an impossible situation." Darcy rose to her feet. After taking a couple of steps, she turned back to Clare. "Even if you and Blaine weren't romantically involved, I could never live in the same household as Blaine, and you know it. He's domineering, rude, and he treats you like a servant." She continued on her way to her bedroom, closing the door behind her.

Clare crumpled in one corner of the sofa. She'd never forgive Darcy for the cruel things she'd said. Darcy just didn't understand how lonely Clare had always been. It wasn't easy for her to make friends, and she'd been grateful when she'd met Darcy her first day of preschool and Darcy had announced that she was going to be her friend. They'd joined the same clubs, slept over at each other's houses, and applied to the same college. Darcy hadn't seemed to mind that Clare's mother was an invalid and that Clare was needed at home when other children had time to play. She'd made a game of helping Clare with her chores.

Clare had done her best to console Darcy when Darcy's sister had been killed by a drunk driver. And she'd believed Darcy had her best interests at heart when she'd advised her and helped her choose a nursing home and then make funeral arrangements when Clare's mother passed away. Until Blaine identified the many decisions Darcy had made that should have been Clare's, she'd never doubted the relationship between her and her best friend or considered that Darcy had taken advantage of her situation to keep Clare dependent on her. Now she didn't know what to think. She'd never expected her best friend and the man she loved to dislike each other so intensely.

She listened to the sound of drawers opening and closing and knew Darcy was serious about leaving. She clung to the arm of the sofa to keep from running to Darcy's room to beg her to stay. As Darcy walked past her with her arms loaded with boxes and bags, Clare reached for the small phone in her pocket.

"Darcy's moving out," she blurted when Blaine answered after the sixth ring. "She's carrying her things to her car right now."

"Who cares!"

"But we can't share an apartment by ourselves."

"I'm busy right now, so don't worry about it. I'll take care of everything, and we'll talk about it tonight." He hung up.

* * *

Darcy made a last check of the apartment, removing her pictures, CDs, a lamp, and her dishes. She'd paid for half of the groceries that sat in the refrigerator and on cupboard shelves, but she decided to only take her new box of cereal. At least she'd be able to have breakfast in the morning, and she usually ate dinner at work anyway. She picked up the cereal box and discovered it was empty. Knowing Clare never ate Wheat Chex, she knew who had emptied it. Rather than point out one more indication of Blaine's lack of consideration, she tossed the box in the trash and made one last trip to deliver her belongings to her car.

Praying for strength to leave Clare without another confrontation, Darcy returned to the apartment. Clare sat stony-faced on the sofa where she'd remained while Darcy packed.

"My key," she said softly as she set her key on the end table beside Clare. "I'm not sure where I'll be after the next few days, but as soon as I get a phone, I'll call to let you know where you can reach me."

"Don't bother," Clare said.

"I'll call anyway, and if you don't accept my call, I'll keep calling until you do. You don't think so now, but I really do love you."

"I thought you were my friend." Clare began to cry, and Darcy sat beside her to pull her into her arms.

"I am your friend and I always will be."

"If you were my friend, you wouldn't leave like this and you wouldn't insult and tear down the man I love. After all the plans we made, how can you just leave?"

"Come with me and we can start over together. You don't have to stay here."

"I love Blaine, and he's counting on me to stand by him. I won't let him down."

"Oh, Clare." Darcy was crying now too. "Can't you see you're letting yourself down? I tried to like Blaine for your sake, but I can't. Your life hasn't been easy, and you deserve someone so much better than Blaine. Promise me, please, that if you ever need help, you'll call me."

Clare drew back from Darcy. "I'll miss you, but I'll never go to you for help. Blaine is all I need now."

Chapter 5

WHEN DARCY REACHED THE MOTEL where her father had made reservations for her, she had little time to unload her car before leaving for work. She donned her uniform then made a hasty call to the number David Schoenfeld had given her. Though she was dubious about a live-in arrangement, she felt a need to act quickly.

"Roper residence," a child's voice answered.

"May I speak to Karlene Roper?" she asked.

"She's sleeping. Do you want to talk to my mom?"

"Yes, please."

It was only moments before a woman's voice came on the line. "Who's calling, please?"

Darcy gave her name and explained that David Schoenfeld had suggested she call. They talked for a few minutes and made an appointment for the next afternoon.

Darcy hung up the phone, feeling she'd just glimpsed the first light at the end of a long tunnel. Anne Wilson, Mrs. Roper's daughter, had sounded nice over the phone, though under a great deal of pressure. The woman had explained that she had five young children and was anxious to be able to spend evenings at home with them and her husband without worrying about her mother's safety.

Later that evening, Darcy's shift at the restaurant seemed to drag, and though Darcy tried to smile and be pleasant to the customers, she kept thinking of Clare. She couldn't help feeling like she'd abandoned her best friend—or like her best friend had abandoned her. After struggling with feelings of loss, self-pity, and anger all evening, she experienced a rare bout of homesickness which prompted her to call

her parents as soon as she returned to her room at the motel. She was pleased to hear her mother's voice.

She expected her mother to sympathize with her over the loss of her dear friend, but instead her mother reminded her that Clare had a strong need to feel loved and that her friend's biggest dream had always been to be part of a family.

"She faced so much responsibility at such a young age," Darcy's mother said. "I suspect this young man makes her feel that it's her turn to be looked after. Added to that is the promise of the family she's yearned for. And she's in love. Whether she loves wisely or not, a woman in love is likely to overlook a lot of faults."

"What did I do wrong, Mom?" she asked.

"I don't know that you did anything wrong. At any rate, it will do no good to blame yourself. Clare is an adult and has the right to choose her personal standard of behavior."

"I know she has a testimony and that her faith is important to her. And I keep thinking that if I'd stayed, I could have helped her prepare for a temple marriage. My presence alone might have discouraged inappropriate behavior."

"If you'd stayed, you'd have been placing yourself in a compromising situation and weakening your own testimony. You and Clare have been inseparable companions since you were small children, and I know this situation grieves you, but now all you can do for her is pray. Heavenly Father will never give up on her, and you needn't either. Stay in touch, and let her know she still matters to you."

After bidding her mother good night and preparing herself for bed, Darcy lay awake for a long time mulling over her mother's words. A powerful conviction grew in her heart. Someday Clare would need her, and she knew she had to be prepared to be there for her. She'd still be Clare's friend even if Clare no longer reciprocated their friendship.

* * *

Darcy parked in front of a small, tidy house and noted the numerous trees and shrubs on a large lot. The peaked roof of a two-story garage was just visible behind the white-frame house. She checked the address on the piece of paper she clutched in her hand then slowly

opened her door. The walkway from the street to the high front porch was chipped and cracked; a tree root had lifted a whole section. She could see it would be daunting for anyone confined to a wheelchair.

She rang the doorbell, which was answered promptly. She found herself facing a pretty young woman only a few years older than herself. A toddler tugged at her jeans, and she cradled an infant in her arms. "Hello, I'm Anne," the young woman said as she smiled and invited Darcy inside.

Darcy's meeting with Karlene Roper's daughter went well, and when she met the older woman, she was delighted to find she wasn't as old as she'd assumed she might be. She estimated the other woman was in her early fifties, though her modern hairstyle and slender figure made her appear younger. As they conversed in the living room, Darcy found Karlene to be well-educated with an enjoyable sense of humor as well. An automobile accident had left her with multiple fractures in both legs, necessitating the use of a wheelchair.

"I talked to Brother Schoenfeld about you," Karlene said. "He seemed to think we could be of assistance to each other."

"He suggested the same to me," Darcy said. "I'm in need of a place to live while I student teach at the high school."

"And I need a responsible adult in the house at night, according to my doctor. Anne does her best. She brings the younger children here each afternoon. She vacuums and straightens up the kitchen too, but she needs to be in her own home after the older children return from school and her husband gets off work. I can offer you your own bedroom and bathroom and the use of the kitchen and laundry facilities. I'm sure Anne or one of the sisters from the ward would be happy to come over to give you an occasional free evening if you think you'd be interested in living here."

"Yes, I'm interested," Darcy said. It wouldn't be the same as having a place of her own, but it would only be for a few months, and it would make it possible to remain independent and get her teaching degree.

"Well, Darcy, if we're going to become roommates, I suggest you start calling me Karlene." Karlene's welcoming smile revealed the hint of a dimple in one cheek.

"Agreed, Karlene!" Darcy smiled, pleased that the other woman wanted their relationship to be informal.

"There is one thing you should know." Karlene lowered her voice and glanced pointedly toward the open door where her daughter was running the vacuum. "My 'accident' was no accident. Anne, my doctor, and even the police think I imagined the attack, but I know what happened and that my memories of that night are not hallucinations. I'm not crazy. Someone really did try to kill me. If you want to change your mind about living in my home, you still can."

Darcy hesitated just a moment. Whether Karlene had imagined someone tried to kill her or if someone really had attempted to take the woman's life, she shouldn't be left alone, but was Darcy the person Karlene needed at this time? She felt drawn to Karlene, but was that enough?

She really didn't have a choice. She needed an affordable place to live within walking distance of the high school, and she'd never find a better arrangement than what Karlene had offered her.

* * *

"Thanks for the tip about Karlene Roper," Darcy said to David as he caught up to her on the track Saturday morning. "I moved into her house yesterday."

"She's a great lady. I think you'll like her," David responded.

"I already do. I enjoy talking to her, and she amazes me with all she does from a wheelchair. She spends hours at her computer and does an amazing amount of housework, like dusting and cooking."

"She's not the sort to let an unfortunate experience slow her down too much. I suppose she told you she supports herself doing budget analysis and online research for a major marketing firm."

"Yes. She also told me that she was widowed at a young age and was left to support herself and her daughter alone."

They continued to run, and it seemed to Darcy that their strides were quite evenly matched, even though he topped her five-feet-ten height by five or six inches. She usually preferred to run alone because she hated holding back to accommodate another person, but running beside David felt comfortable.

"Do you run marathons?" David asked after a few minutes. "You seem to be pretty good at both speed and endurance."

"I ran a couple of marathons a few years ago, but I'm more comfortable with the half-marathons. I don't really like setting a training regimen, and I'm not into competitive running. I just like to run for the exercise and the emotional release it gives me."

"I should have you speak to some of my P.E. classes. I'm committed to the lifelong sports concept, but too many of my students view sports as strictly competitive or something they have to endure to get a P.E. credit."

Darcy chuckled. "It's not so different in my field. There are plenty of people who never pick up a book, attend a concert, or visit an art gallery once they finish school and are no longer required to do so."

"I guess you're right. I know plenty of jocks who fall into that category."

"It's not just the jocks. I had a professor back at Washington State who said our nation's biggest handicap is obesity—fat bods and fat heads. He had plenty to say about people who never exercise their minds or their bodies."

They shared a chuckle, then Darcy pointed to the bleachers where she'd left her jacket. "I think I'm about ready to call it quits for today. This is my first run since Tuesday, and if I do another mile, I'm afraid I'll be too stiff to do anything else today."

"I'm finished for today too." David slowed his pace. "I promised to help one of the elders in the ward move a set of bunk beds his sons have outgrown to his brother's house, and I usually treat myself to a big breakfast at IHOP on Saturday mornings. Why don't you join me? My treat."

Darcy hesitated. Karlene had made it clear Darcy didn't need to hurry back. An old friend was coming to visit, and her son-in-law had plans to spend the day making some needed repairs on her house.

"If you want to shower and change first, I can pick you up in thirty minutes. Since I have keys to the school's athletic facilities, I usually shower and change here."

"All right," Darcy agreed.

During the short walk to Karlene's house and while taking a quick shower, she questioned whether she should have accepted David's offer. She had no idea whether his relationship with Pauline Prescott was serious or not, but she'd gotten the impression they knew each

other well. And though she felt comfortable around David, she didn't want to encourage anything more than a professional relationship if he was involved with someone else.

Pulling her wet hair back into a ponytail, Darcy pulled on tan cargo pants and a sweatshirt. She dropped her keys and wallet into a side pocket before stepping from her room.

"Darcy," Karlene called to her as she hurried toward the front door. "I'd like you to meet my friend." Darcy was surprised to see that Karlene's friend wasn't the expected older lady but a gentleman with silver hair. He was dressed in khakis and a golf shirt and looked remarkably fit. He rose to his feet as she entered the room.

"Darcy is the young lady I told you about," Karlene said to her friend. "She's going to be living here while she does her student teaching in the English department at the high school. Darcy, this is Evan Swim. We went to school together years ago. He recently retired from the police department in Salt Lake City and is thinking of moving back to Boise, where he grew up."

"It's nice to meet you, Mr. Swim." She extended a hand, which he took, giving it a firm shake.

"I'm pleased to meet you too." He seemed to be looking her over carefully. "Are you from this area?"

"No, I grew up in Tacoma. A friend and I arrived here in June." Through the window she saw a newer model pickup truck pull up to the curb, and David jumped out.

"There's my ride," she said, turning to Karlene. "Have a good day, and I'll see you later."

She met David on the sidewalk and was surprised when he walked her around to the passenger side of the truck and held the door for her. This wasn't a date, just two friends having breakfast together.

There were no uncomfortable lapses in conversation as David drove to the restaurant. In fact, it amazed Darcy how easy it was to talk and laugh with David. She hoped he wouldn't think her a glutton when she ordered a Spanish omelet, hash browns, and toast, but when their orders were delivered, she marveled at the size of the stack of pancakes the waitress set in front of him. She enjoyed food and was grateful for a metabolism that made it unnecessary for her to count calories, but she knew she could never manage a breakfast the size of

the one he ordered. She suspected that his job as a high school track and volleyball coach plus some long, lean genes accounted for his almost beanpole frame.

Over breakfast, she learned he'd served a mission to South Korea and had completed a year at Ricks College before his mission, transferring to Boise State after his return. She told him about her four younger siblings, and he described the dairy farm near Twin Falls where he and two older sisters and a younger brother had grown up. She was shocked when she caught a glimpse of her watch and saw how much time had passed while they'd talked and laughed.

"I better get going," she said, folding her napkin. "My father was adamant that I go shopping for a cell phone today."

"You don't have a cell phone?" David seemed surprised.

"I've never been one to chat on the phone a lot, and it just seemed to be an expense I could avoid, but now Dad thinks I should have one for emergencies and so that he and Mom won't disturb Karlene when they call."

As they left the restaurant, Darcy thanked David for buying her breakfast. She'd protested his paying, but he'd been adamant that she was his guest.

"If you'll drop me off at a mall, I'll shop for a cell phone then catch a bus back to Karlene's house," Darcy suggested.

"All right, on one condition." He started the engine and pulled out of the parking lot.

"What condition is that?"

"That you add this number to your contact list." He handed her a slip of paper on which he'd written his phone number. She tucked the paper in a pocket, still wondering if it was a good idea to become too friendly with David considering his ties to Blaine's sister.

David drove them to a shopping center and pulled up in front of an electronics store. Before leaving Darcy at the store, he told her, "Don't worry about church tomorrow. Brother Keely, the high priest group leader, will be stopping by in his van to pick up Sister Roper. He and his wife said to tell you they have plenty of room for you too." With a lighter heart than she'd felt for several days, Darcy entered the store.

* * *

The first time Darcy attempted to call Clare, Blaine answered, so Darcy promptly hung up. She didn't trust herself to be civil in speaking to him. She tried three more times during the week after purchasing her small, flip-top phone, but each call was met with a recording inviting her to leave a message. Finally, on the third try, she left a brief message, leaving her number and asking Clare to return her call. Each night as she drifted to sleep, Darcy felt a pang of regret that Clare hadn't called her back, and she vowed to try to get through to her again the next day. Soon, in all the excitement of her new responsibilities as a student teacher, she didn't find the time to call.

Her first month of student teaching was filled with challenges, but Darcy found the faculty welcoming and appreciated David's attempts to ease her way as he introduced her to his colleagues. Sarah Becker, her mentor, was friendly, and the two women established a comfortable relationship almost at once. Since Sarah didn't have any classes the last period of the day, this became their time to go over lesson plans and for Sarah to give Darcy pointers for improving her classroom instruction techniques and for dealing with a few rowdy students who were more interested in creating chaos than in studying the works of Victor Hugo or learning the finer points of sentence structure.

Her mornings started early, with a dozen laps around the track then a dash back to her room to shower and dress. Most mornings, David appeared to run laps with her, and breakfast together on Saturdays became an anticipated ritual. Often he sat beside her during sacrament meeting or Sunday School, but he never asked her out, leaving her to assume his romantic interests were with someone else—most likely the rich, beautiful Pauline Prescott.

Pauline had been in the news a lot lately for leaving her father's law firm and going to work in the county attorney's office. Darcy had been tempted to ask David why she'd given up private practice for what was surely much lower pay in the public prosecutor's office, but she felt reluctant to bring up a subject which might lead to admitting her acquaintance with Pauline's brother.

* * *

"Hi, Karlene," Darcy greeted the older woman one afternoon as she returned from school, her backpack laden with exams she needed to correct before morning. She was surprised to see Karlene in the front room instead of in her office, where she usually spent the afternoons while her daughter performed those household tasks the injured woman couldn't reach from her chair.

"Are you all right?" Darcy asked. The older woman appeared agitated.

"I think he's found me," Karlene said.

"Who—?"

"The man who forced me over that bridge." Karlene sounded impatient with the need to explain.

"Did someone threaten you in any way?" Darcy couldn't imagine who would want to harm Karlene Roper. She was one of the kindest, most thoughtful people she knew. She laid her backpack down and took a seat near the other woman.

"A man called. He seemed to be trying to disguise his voice and sounded very dark."

"You don't think it might have been merely a wrong number?" Darcy moved closer to Karlene.

"No, he called me Mrs. Roper."

"You never told me why someone might want to harm you," she reminded Karlene. "Why do you think the accident was a deliberate attempt on your life? And why would anyone be so determined to kill you that he would make a second attempt?"

Darcy saw Karlene's hand tremble. The woman hadn't referred again to her belief that someone had deliberately tried to kill her since that first interview. The woman was clearly frightened, and whether someone was actually trying to kill her or not, Karlene believed her life was in danger. Karlene's fear transferred to Darcy, and she felt an urge to rush to the window and close the drapes. She didn't move but found herself periodically glancing toward the street visible through the large bay window.

"I was returning from a conference in Sun Valley and decided to drive over the mountains instead of taking the freeway. With only a short distance to go, I impulsively turned off on a road that took me to one of my favorite picnic spots when my husband was alive. It was

a beautiful day, and I decided to take a short hike. I took my camera along as I've always loved that area, and photography is a hobby I enjoy. I didn't take many shots, but I enjoyed the springtime stroll. When I returned to my car, I continued the drive, anxious to reach home before dark. A large pickup truck came up behind me going very fast on the narrow road. I slowed down to let him pass, but instead of passing, he bumped the back of my car. I sped up, and he did too. His higher bumper struck the side of my car, forcing it against the rail. I was struggling to return to my lane, but he kept pushing until the rail broke and my car went over."

Darcy swallowed. "That certainly sounds deliberate."

"The investigating officer seemed to think I was merely struck by a speeding driver who failed to stop. He even hinted that I might have been speeding too and that there wasn't another vehicle involved."

"Surely the crash site and your car were examined. There should have been tracks and paint scrapes."

"A group of teenagers who admitted to racing in pickup trucks were chasing each other around those hills when they saw my car lights before they flickered out. They decided to investigate. They parked on the bridge, and between their trucks and the footsteps of nearly a dozen teenagers, they destroyed any evidence that might have been found on the bridge. My car rolled several times and was totaled. No paint scrapings from another vehicle were found." The only sign of Karlene's agitation now was how she continuously twisted the rings on her fingers. "Those kids probably saved my life. They called the police and paramedics and stayed with me until the rescue vehicles arrived."

"Did you see the driver of the truck? Could he have been one of the teenagers?" Darcy somehow felt the events Karlene described were not a figment of her imagination.

"Yes, I saw him clearly in the rearview mirror on the right side of my car. He wasn't a boy, and the determined look on his face said he knew what he was doing."

"And you'd never seen him before?" Darcy couldn't help a nervous glance toward the large picture window.

"I don't think so, yet there was something familiar about him. I've tried and tried to remember why I thought he was familiar, but it's no

use. But I'm sure he's the man who called me minutes after Anne and the children left today to say he wasn't through with me yet."

"You called the police, didn't you?"

"I called Evan Swim."

"But what can he do? You said he lives in Salt Lake." This time Darcy gave in to the urge to close the blinds. "I don't understand why someone wants to kill you." It made no sense to Darcy. Karlene wasn't the sort of person who made enemies. She seemed well-liked and respected by her neighbors, and Darcy found her friendly and pleasant.

"I don't know either," the older woman admitted with a brief shake of her head. "That's the part that has me questioning my sanity and why I asked my friend, Lieutenant Swim, his opinion several weeks ago."

"Does he think you're in danger?" Darcy shuddered.

"He suggested I have an alarm system installed and that I have my telephone number changed to an unlisted number. He also said I should warn you to be on the lookout for anything unusual in the neighborhood."

Darcy felt certain that if a former police lieutenant thought Karlene Roper needed to take precautions, then there was real danger. What had Darcy done? Had she left a morally dangerous situation just to find herself in a physically dangerous one?

Chapter 6

CLARE LOOKED AT BLAINE'S ROOM with dismay. She wasn't sure why she still referred to the room as Blaine's when she spent almost as much time in it as he did, though most of her clothes and her makeup were still in the room on the other side of the apartment she'd originally called hers. Blaine's clothing, along with mounds of paper, covered every surface and cluttered the floor. It was impossible to walk through the room without stepping on snack wrappers or CDs. She stooped to pick up a shirt that lay crumpled behind Blaine's briefcase. The case was wide open, and a small silver object caught her eye. She reached for it.

My cell phone! She almost shouted her discovery aloud, but some sense of self-preservation kept her silent. Blaine had been angry when she reported that she'd lost the little phone, but she suspected he'd be even angrier if she told him it had been in his briefcase all along. She must have dropped it there, instead of into her purse one of the mornings he'd driven her to work. She'd been so upset about Darcy leaving, that right after her departure she'd made a number of mistakes. She still couldn't believe she and Blaine had gotten so carried away when he attempted to comfort her.

Blaine said it didn't matter—they could still be married in the temple because they hadn't been unfaithful to each other, or they could have the kind of grand wedding his mother wanted for them and go to the temple on their first anniversary. It would be better for the family law firm to have a big, splashy wedding anyway to which they could invite their biggest clients and the influential people from whom his brother, Brett, needed to gain support for his campaign.

Clare didn't accept Blaine's argument that they could still go to the temple. She had been taught too well in church to rationalize that. And Darcy's mother, who had been her Laurel leader, had explained that lying to a bishop about serious transgressions was an infraction of God's trust. She'd angered Blaine when she'd tried to explain that the temple was no longer an option and had collected more bruises for it. She hoped he'd soon realize how easily she bruised.

The first Sunday after Blaine moved into the apartment, he'd insisted they attend his family's ward. Neither of his parents was there, but they were greeted warmly by a number of people after sacrament meeting, and several sisters invited Clare to attend Relief Society. She was surprised when Blaine said they couldn't stay for Relief Society and priesthood meetings. She'd soon learned that she'd embarrassed him by not partaking of the sacrament. He'd accused her of making a spectacle of them and inviting gossip. That was the last time they'd gone to church. Between her accumulation of bruises and her guilty conscience, she was too embarrassed to go to church anymore anyway, so she supposed the big wedding Mrs. Prescott wanted to stage was her only option.

She flipped open the small phone and pressed the power button. There was only one bar showing, but she thumbed through her missed calls. At least a dozen were from the same unfamiliar number. Turning to her voice mail, she found just one message. Unexpected tears filled her eyes as she learned Darcy had kept her promise to call. The message was from the same number as the one with the many missed calls. She found herself locking the number away in her mind.

With a quick glance toward the bedroom door, she turned off the phone and dropped it back in the briefcase. She'd say nothing until Blaine discovered the cell phone himself.

"Come on, Clare, we're going to be late," Blaine said from the front room.

"I'm ready," she called back. She quickly snatched the tie he'd asked for from the tie rack.

"Here it is." She smiled as she handed the tie to him.

"Do I look all right?" she asked. They'd been dating for three months and had been engaged for one, and yet she hadn't met Blaine's family, but today that would change. Blaine's father had invited them to attend a

luncheon and made it clear he expected the whole family, including Blaine's fiancée, to be present. She'd dressed with care in the white lace dress she'd bought for her institute graduation a few months earlier.

"You need to wear something a little more mature." Blaine eyed her critically. "That thing looks like something a high-school kid might wear. Put on that navy suit with the silver pin stripes."

Clare looked down at her dress in dismay. She'd felt feminine and pretty in the dress, thinking its simple lines and slightly flared skirt perfect for a midday luncheon. Without a word, she turned to her room, where she pulled the dress off. Sliding it onto a hanger, she hung it at the very back of her closet. She tried not to think of the day she and Darcy had driven to Seattle to shop for their graduation dresses. It had been an unusually bright and sunny day. Even the elusive Mt. Ranier had peeked through its usual cloud cover to smile benevolently at them. The friends had laughed and made plans for the great adventure of moving to Boise, and they'd discovered a delightful little sidewalk café that served the most luscious French silk pie.

Moving quickly, she donned the severe business suit with a gray satin blouse and found her navy pumps. In less than five minutes, she rejoined Blaine, who merely looked at his watch and frowned.

When they reached the hotel, they were quickly escorted to a banquet room, and Clare was taken aback to see such a large gathering. She'd assumed the luncheon would be more intimate, giving her an opportunity to get to know Blaine's family. Instead, at least fifty people milled around the table, loudly discussing Brett's political campaign.

"It's about time you got here," an older, silver-haired man said as he approached them. He was handsome in his impeccably designed suit, and carried with him an unmistakable air of confidence. "You and the girl need to go over there for pictures." He nodded his head toward the knot of people gathered around a man she could only assume was Blaine's brother.

"Sure, Dad." Blaine touched her elbow to guide her into the melee of confusion surrounding his brother.

Dad? Why hadn't Blaine introduced her? Surely he knew her name, even if they hadn't been formally introduced. Clare swallowed her instinctive protest and let Blaine lead her to the side of a slightly taller, leaner version of her fiancé.

"Just smile and keep your mouth shut," Blaine hissed in her ear as he held out his hand and plastered a huge smile across his own face. Once again introductions were lost in a flurry of questions, and she was pushed one way then the other as the various photographers flashed their lights in her eyes and bombarded Brett with questions. *Thank goodness Blaine is keeping his arm firmly around my waist.* She was glad, too, that she'd finally discarded the bulky brace she'd worn on her arm for what seemed like forever. Blaine was right; she really didn't need it anymore.

One reporter zeroed in on Clare. "What a fabulous ring," she gushed. "Aren't you the lucky one to capture Southern Idaho's most eligible bachelor! Come sit with me and fill me in on all the juicy details."

"Sorry, Lucille." Blaine pulled Clare snugly to his side. "No interview today."

"But I will get an exclusive, won't I? I know my readers are dying to know who is designing her dress. You can tell me the date, can't you? So I can circle it in red on my calendar?"

"All right." Blaine laughed. "But then you have to promise to go away."

"Oh, all right." She practically drooled as she held her thumb poised over a tiny recorder.

Blaine leaned forward then whispered loudly, "December twenty-fourth. We've decided to be married Christmas Eve."

Clare felt as stunned as she had the first time Blaine had struck her. He hadn't once mentioned that he wanted to be married on Christmas Eve. She felt a thrill of happiness. She'd be Mrs. Blaine Prescott when she woke up Christmas morning. Instead of waking up in Darcy's bedroom and sharing Christmas with the Olsen family, she'd be Blaine's wife and would begin a family of her own.

When Clare finally found herself seated at the family table after the reporters had been ushered from the room, she looked around shyly. At this point, she decided introductions were unnecessary. She'd figured out who everyone was, and they couldn't help knowing she was Blaine's fiancée.

Brett's wife wasn't at all what she had expected. Penny Prescott's hair was white blond, almost the same shade as her own hair, and

cropped extremely short. She was almost anorexic thin and appeared bored with everything around her. She wore a skinny, backless black dress that highlighted her thinness. Diamond studs glinted in her ears, and a huge diamond adorned her left hand.

Clare found Brett's mother intimidating. She hadn't realized she'd been hoping for a warm surrogate mother until she met the sleek, businesslike Danielle Prescott. Dressed in a severe drab olive-green suit matched with four-inch heels, Danielle jumped up to consult with various members of Brett's team and scribbled notes as often as did her husband.

Clare was aware that Blaine's parents didn't live together, though they weren't divorced. They'd sold the family home while Blaine was on his mission. Garrett had invested in a trendy penthouse apartment while Danielle had purchased a condo in the suburbs. When Blaine returned from his mission, he'd enrolled at the local college, and when he later graduated from an eastern law school, his father had paid the first year's lease on a fashionable downtown apartment where Blaine had lived until last month.

Clare had seen a newspaper photo of Pauline several months ago and had no trouble recognizing her. To Clare's amusement, Blaine's sister wore a cream lace dress almost identical to the white one Clare had originally planned to wear to the luncheon. Her blond hair was caught up in a sleek bun atop her head with bright red chopsticks skewered through it. She smiled at Clare, and Clare found herself returning the smile.

"I'm Pauline." She held out her hand to Clare, and Clare took it. Releasing it, Pauline said, "I'd like you to meet my friend, David Schoenfeld. We've known each other forever. He's a high-school coach."

"Pleased to meet you," Clare said. Outwardly she maintained a calm poise, but inside she breathed a sigh of relief. There was at least one member of Blaine's family with whom she might develop a real friendship. Thinking of friends, she felt a stab of pain for the lost friendship with Darcy.

* * *

Darcy came awake with a start. She lay still, listening, but didn't hear anything out of the ordinary and wondered what had awakened her.

After a few minutes of hearing nothing, she decided that since she was awake, she might as well check on Karlene. She'd noticed increasing nervousness in the older woman and wondered if she might have fallen or tried to get up and knocked something over. Slipping out of bed, she reached for her robe.

Her footsteps made no sound as she hurried down the hall, treading on thick carpet. At Karlene's door she paused to listen. Hearing nothing, she eased the door open a couple of inches. Her landlady appeared to be sleeping peacefully.

She was almost back to her room when she heard a faint scraping sound coming from the kitchen. Changing directions, she cautiously made her way to the kitchen. With her heart pounding so loudly, she wasn't sure if she could hear someone attempting to break in or not, so she stood still, straining to hear. A metallic scratching sound came again. This time she was certain someone was trying to gain access through the back door. *Thank goodness Karlene had followed her friend's advice to have dead bolts installed.*

Though only a few feet from the kitchen wall phone, Darcy turned to flee back to her own room. Her hands shook as she flipped open the small phone that lay on her bedside table to dial 911. She held the phone to her ear, hardly daring to breathe until a voice asked her to state her emergency.

"Someone is trying to break into this house," she whispered. When asked, she rattled off the address and identified herself. "Please hurry," she added. "An invalid woman and I are the only people in the house," she added, hoping the information would bring a speedier response from the police department.

A loud crash caused her to nearly drop the phone. "He broke a window!" she practically screamed.

"Stay on the line. Officers will be there in minutes," a calm voice said in her ear. Ignoring the voice, she dropped the cell phone in her pocket and hurried to Karlene's room. Bursting through the door, she stopped short, seeing the shadowy form of the other woman sitting up in bed.

"Karlene, someone is trying to break in," Darcy gasped.

"Come inside and lock the door!" Karlene yelled.

Darcy not only pressed the lock on the door but pushed a bulky dresser in front of the entrance.

"The police are on their way!" She hurried to Karlene's bedside.

"Help me get up and bring me my robe," Karlene said as she clicked on a bedside lamp.

"The light . . ." Darcy feared the light shining under the door would lead the intruder straight to them. She stopped abruptly. Karlene held a gun in her hand.

"If anyone has managed to get inside, they've already heard our voices, and if he breaks into this room, I want to see who I'm shooting."

Darcy swallowed and felt her eyes widen. She remembered barging into the room moments earlier. Her abrupt arrival might have been met with a bullet. Shaking off the unpleasant speculation, she hurried to help Karlene into her chair then handed her a robe.

"Police! Open the door!" Pounding accompanied the voices.

"Go ahead before they break my door." Karlene motioned her toward the door. "If an intruder made his way inside the house, I'm sure he left the same way he got in as soon as he saw police lights."

Darcy found moving the dresser away from the door more difficult than putting it there had been. But once it was out of the way, she hurried toward the front door, clicking light switches as she went. Spotting a uniform through the narrow sidelight window, she unbolted the door.

"Are you all right, miss?" the officer asked as she invited him inside. She noticed two police cruisers parked at the curb before closing the door behind the officer.

"Just frightened," she admitted.

"If you don't mind, we'd like to do a walkthrough."

She nodded her head, and he moved toward the kitchen.

Darcy and Karlene both waited in the front room. When the officer returned twenty minutes later, he reported that the intruder was not found and that the only damage to their home seemed to be a broken window in the kitchen. Both women answered the questions directed at them for the police report, but Darcy noticed that Karlene never mentioned her belief that someone wanted to kill her. She also noticed that the gun Karlene had held earlier was nowhere in sight.

Chapter 7

BLAINE PULLED INTO HIS PARKING space and shut off the engine. "Don't forget you're to meet Mother at the bridal shop at 12:10. Ten minutes should be plenty of time to get from your office to the shop. She's very busy and can't wait if you're late."

"Won't you be driving me there?" Clare was startled to discover she would be on her own to meet Mrs. Prescott.

"I have an appointment with a client who can only meet me at noon." Blaine climbed out of the car and hurried around to her side to hold the door for her. She smiled her thanks. He'd always held her door when they first started dating but had stopped doing so when he started driving her to work each day.

"I should have brought my own car."

"I'd hate to have Mother see you driving that wreck." Blaine made an exaggerated shudder.

"I like my car," Clare protested. She'd used the small amount of money left from her mother's insurance policy to buy the used Saturn after she and Darcy arrived in Boise.

"I know you do, sweetie, but you need to remember you're about to become a Prescott, and you have an image to keep up." He gave her a quick kiss before turning toward the stairs that led to his family's law firm. Clare watched him go before turning toward the courtyard she needed to cross to reach her own office.

The morning passed quickly. For once, no one brought her a last-minute project, and she was able to grab her jacket and be out of the office right at noon. She turned south and walked as rapidly as possible, but a glance at her watch warned her she would be late. Not by

much—just a few minutes—but if Danielle Prescott was as precise about time as Blaine, Clare wouldn't be making a favorable impression on her soon-to-be mother-in-law.

Clare's side was aching and she was out of breath when she reached the shop. She gasped for breath while trying to compose herself before entering the fashionable shop. She momentarily regretted that she hadn't continued running with Darcy as she had in high school. By the time they'd reached college, their schedules were different, and she had admitted to herself that she really wasn't as enthused about running as Darcy. Besides, she couldn't begin to keep up with her friend and felt guilty for slowing her down.

When Clare stepped inside the shop, she looked around for Blaine's mother but didn't see her. A wave of panic hit her. How would she explain to Blaine that she'd hurried as fast as she could, but his mother had left before she arrived?

"May I help you?" A saleswoman bustled toward her.

"I was to meet Danielle Prescott here."

"You're Miss Reynolds?"

Clare nodded her head.

"Mrs. Prescott had a change in her schedule. She stopped by earlier this morning and selected several gowns for you to choose from. If you'll follow me, the fitting room is ready for you."

Clare felt a brief annoyance that Blaine's mother hadn't called to let her know she wouldn't be able to keep the appointment. Had she known Danielle wouldn't be there, she could have avoided arriving panting, disheveled, and feeling a little ill.

She followed the saleswoman to a large room lined with mirrors. A thick carpet covered the floor. Small graceful tables held huge floral bouquets, and soft romantic music played in the background. A seamstress knelt beside a young woman in a gorgeous gown, marking and pinning a hem. Another woman, obviously the young bride-to-be's mother, acted as a cheerleader, telling her daughter how lovely she looked and how perfect the dress was for her. Clare felt a twinge of envy. She missed her mother—and Darcy. They should have both been there to share her excitement and help her choose. A series of small rooms with white doors trimmed in gold opened off of the larger room. The saleswoman led Clare to one of these rooms.

"I'll be assisting you today. Please remove your outer clothing," the woman instructed as she lifted one of three gowns that hung on a rail.

Clare set her handbag on a small table and prepared to try on the dress. The dress wasn't even fastened before Clare knew it wasn't what she wanted. Instead of the tiers of ruffles and lace she'd always dreamed of, the dress was sleek and without trim, cut straight with a long slit up the skirt almost to her thigh, and the bodice, what there was of it, was hopelessly immodest.

"I'd like to try a different gown." She put her hand over the saleswoman's hand to stop her from zipping the dress.

"But miss, you haven't seen yourself in the mirrors. The elegant simplicity of this gown will accent your own considerable beauty."

"I really prefer a more traditional gown." Clare didn't wish to hurt the woman's feelings, but she knew she'd be uncomfortable in the dress.

"Perhaps it's for the best." The woman sighed with a pointed look at a series of bruises at the top of each of Clare's arms. She returned the dress to its hanger and drew the second dress from the overhead rod. She quickly slipped it over Clare's head.

This dress was better but not quite what Clare had dreamed of wearing at her wedding. She was a romantic and all through her teens had dreamed of marrying in a *Gone with the Wind*–style Southern ball gown. Though tight in the front, this dress poufed out in the back, forming a cascading bustle. It was sleeveless and the scoop neckline showed more than Clare wished to display.

"Incredible! You look sensational," the saleswoman gushed as she held the door for Clare to precede her into the larger area. After a short promenade before the mirrors in the larger room, Clare retreated to the fitting room once more. The dress was beautiful and sophisticated, but she scarcely recognized herself in it.

There was just one gown left on the rod. It was a soft, pale cream silk, and Clare's fantasies had always included white, but then her fantasies had included the temple too. Her lip quivered, and she struggled to appear poised as the saleswoman slipped the dress over her head and zipped up the side fasteners before reaching for streamers that tied in a bow at the back of the princess waistline, leaving some ribbon to trail down her back to the hemline. *At least this gown is more modest than the*

others, she told herself, *even if it is the wrong color.* The skirt wasn't exactly full, but it draped in soft folds to the floor and swirled about her ankles as she walked. The sleeves weren't long but were puffy and full, ending just above her elbows.

She studied the dress in the mirrors. It really was lovely even if it wasn't the dress she would have chosen if she'd been shopping on her own. She had a small trust and her salary, but she couldn't afford the exclusive shop she found herself in or the designer labels in which the boutique specialized, which Blaine and his mother considered essential. She should be grateful Danielle had offered to pay for their wedding as her gift to them instead of finding fault with her soon-to-be mother-in-law's selections.

With a sigh of resignation, she chose the cream silk, and the saleswoman scurried about, summoning a seamstress to take care of the fitting details.

"The fit must be perfect. Mrs. Prescott scheduled fittings for you each week until the wedding. Please try not to gain or lose weight." The seamstress seemed about to say something more then frowned before glancing at the saleswoman, who shook her head. Clare caught the two women staring at a dark bruise on her shoulder and felt herself blush.

As soon as she finished dressing in her own clothes, she hurried from the shop. Her manager had been understanding when she'd requested permission to return late to the office, so she'd just have time to grab a sandwich. Spotting a fast food restaurant, she hurried inside to order a value meal to go.

Carrying her lunch in a paper bag, she hurried to the company staff break room. She hadn't eaten there since her first few weeks at her job. Seating herself at a small table, she opened her lunch and took a hearty bite of her hamburger. As she ate, she looked around. The room was empty. Either everyone else had gone out to lunch, as she usually did, or they'd finished and returned to their desks. She thought about her disappointing visit to the bridal shop and found herself wishing Darcy had been there with her. She smiled, remembering some of the shopping excursions she and Darcy had shared.

A ringing telephone shattered the quiet, and she looked around until she spotted a phone hanging on the wall near a microwave and a

coffee pot. She hesitated a moment, wondering if she should answer, but unable to resist, she hurried across the room to pick up the receiver.

"Hello?" She spoke in a tentative voice.

"Is Jarrod Baumgartner in the staff room?" She recognized the company receptionist's voice.

"No, I haven't seen him."

"Okay, thanks." The call disconnected.

Clare returned the phone to its cradle almost reluctantly. She wished she could tell Darcy about her wedding dress. Surely they'd been friends too long for them to still be angry with each other. Besides, she and Darcy had made a pact when they were just thirteen that they would each be the other's maid of honor when their momentous days arrived. She remembered the telephone number she'd found in her cell phone. Impulsively she dialed the number.

* * *

Her ringing cell phone brought Darcy's head up with a flush of embarrassment. "Sorry, I forgot to set it on vibrate." She reached for the phone to shut it off.

"No, go ahead and take your call," Sarah told her. "I was just going to suggest a break. We're really all set with next week's lesson plans anyway."

Darcy smiled in gratitude. Ever since someone had tried to break into Karlene's house, she'd been nervous about any gaps between when the nurse left and Karlene's daughter Anne arrived to be with her.

"Hello," she said into her phone without checking the caller ID.

"Darcy?" Clare's voice sounded tentative and unsure.

"Clare, is that you? Wow, I've missed you so much."

"I've missed you too," Clare admitted, still sounding subdued. "I lost my cell phone, so I didn't know you had called, then I found it, and I wasn't sure you'd want to hear from me."

"Clare, you're my best friend. Of course I want to hear from you. Are you all right? Are you happy? Can we get together for lunch?"

Clare laughed, and the sound was like music to Darcy. Their estrangement had felt like a deep wound to her.

"We've set a date for the wedding. We're getting married Christmas Eve at four o'clock in the afternoon. I know you've planned since we got here to go home for Christmas, but I really want you to be at my wedding and to be my maid of honor."

"Isn't the temple closed?"

"The ceremony will be at the Grove Hotel, followed by dinner and a reception."

Darcy choked back the words that rose to her lips. She didn't want to risk alienating Clare again by saying anything that might hurt her or that she might take as criticism. "Pretty swanky!" she drawled instead.

"Blaine's mother is paying for the wedding . . . which reminds me, the bridal shop needs your measurements. Do you think you could drop in there for a fitting sometime next week?" She gave Darcy the address, and they talked for a few minutes about plans for the wedding and about Darcy's student teaching.

"I need to get back to work. I'll call you again next week. I've lost my cell phone again, and we had the apartment phone removed since we both have cell phones."

After Clare hung up, Darcy closed her phone and sat for several minutes staring into space. She was grateful and relieved to finally hear from Clare, but something about the call seemed to be setting off tiny alarms in her head. She was disappointed that Clare wasn't getting sealed in the temple, but she wasn't really surprised.

"Is something wrong? Was your call bad news?" Sarah returned to the chair she'd vacated a few minutes earlier.

"No, it wasn't bad news in the sense you probably mean," Darcy mused. "My best friend is getting married the day before Christmas, and she picked out her dress today, but she didn't sound excited. It's probably just my imagination and the fact that I don't think much of her fiancé, but I thought she didn't sound as happy as a woman should be who is getting married in five weeks."

"Probably pre-wedding jitters. I almost backed out when I got that close to my wedding." Sarah laughed.

* * *

"Are you sure you don't mind if I run this morning?" Darcy hadn't run since the attempted break-in. She'd been concerned about leaving Karlene alone in the house. Though the other woman was getting around better and could now move herself from her bed to her chair and back, she still couldn't leave the house without assistance.

"You go ahead. I'll be fine," Karlene assured her.

Making certain the door was locked behind her, Darcy set off for the track. The air was cold, and her breath came out in puffs of white, but by the time she reached the high school, she felt much warmer. Only one runner was on the track, and even though he was at the far end, she recognized David's long, easy stride.

Gradually, she closed the gap between them until she overtook him by her fifth lap. She suspected he had slowed his pace to give her a chance to catch up.

"Good morning. Have you been sleeping in lately?" He grinned as he greeted her.

"No, someone tried to break into the house a few nights ago, and I've been nervous about leaving Karlene alone."

"Is she okay?"

"Yes. We were both scared, but the police came quickly enough to scare the intruder. Whoever tried to break in smashed the kitchen window. The next morning Karlene had it replaced with shatterproof glass."

"You should have called me."

"I thought of calling you. I called the police."

"Do the police have any suspects?"

"I don't think so. The intruder left when the police came. All the police found were the broken window and scratch marks on the outside of the kitchen door lock. They seemed to think the person responsible was probably someone looking for easy drug money."

"You sound skeptical." David looked at her quizzically. "Do you have reason to think there was another motive?"

"I'm not sure," Darcy admitted. "Karlene feels it was connected to her accident. She maintains her accident was a deliberate attempt to kill her and that the killer has now discovered where she lives and has come to finish the job."

"She was pretty vocal right after the accident about it being a deliberate attack. The police seemed to dismiss her explanation of the events that occurred that night, and she hasn't mentioned it for some time, so I thought she'd changed her mind."

"Drug addicts are everywhere, and theft seems to be their usual method of supporting their habits, so if it weren't for the threatening call she got last week, I'd dismiss the attempted break-in as just bad luck."

"She got a call? I hope she reported it to the police." David had increased his speed, seeming to reveal his agitation over the events Darcy reported.

"She didn't tell the police, but she called her friend in Salt Lake, the one who is a retired police lieutenant."

They ran a lap in silence. David seemed deep in thought, but at length he said, "I think I'll cut my run short so I can make a few calls. The ward leaders and the neighborhood watch captain need to be alerted to keep a closer watch on Sister Roper's house."

"I had planned to keep this run shorter too. I'm anxious to check on Karlene." They both slowed to a walk.

"Thanks for filling me in," David said before jogging toward the building. "See ya tomorrow."

"Bye! Hopefully I'll be here."

She turned toward Karlene's house just as the sun appeared over the horizon. She'd reached the corner when the wail of sirens reached her. Seeing two patrol cars squeal to a stop in front of Karlene's house, she began to run. A fire truck passed her before she reached the front lawn.

Chapter 8

"YOU CAN'T GO IN THERE." A policeman held out his arm, barring Darcy from entering the Roper house.

"Karlene," she gasped, trying to push past him. "She's in a wheelchair and . . ."

"It's okay. She's unharmed. The EMTs are transporting her to the hospital to be checked, but she's adamant that she's just fine."

Turning to the ambulance parked at the curb, Darcy ran toward it. "Karlene—" she began.

"I don't think she's injured, but she was choking from the smoke. I want her to be checked by a doctor." Darcy recognized Anne standing beside the ambulance.

"Darcy?" She heard Karlene speak her name and hurried to peer inside the ambulance, where the woman lay on a gurney. She was leaning up on one elbow. "It's all nonsense. I don't need to go to the hospital, but Anne insists. Try to keep the firemen from making too much of a mess of my house."

"I'll check on everything," was all she had time to promise before Anne scurried inside and an EMT closed the double doors at the back of the ambulance. She turned back to face the officer who had barred her way earlier.

"I live here. Can you tell me what happened?" She showed the officer her ID.

"It appears it wasn't anything too serious, though it might have been if Mrs. Roper's daughter hadn't arrived when she did. The fire department is through here, so there's no harm in going inside now."

Darcy stepped through the doorway and was immediately assailed by the acrid odor of smoke. She walked through the various rooms one by one, finding no evidence of what might have happened other than the stench of a fire. Puzzled, she stepped back outside, where she found a couple of firemen poking piles of leaves that had accumulated in the shrubs and flower beds next to the house. She approached them.

"Where was the fire?" she asked. "I've gone all through the house."

"The fire didn't reach the house," one of the firemen explained. "Mrs. Roper's daughter smelled the smoke and called us. We arrived before it spread that far, though in a few more minutes it would have spread from the rose trellis to the eaves and onto the roof."

"You mean the fire was actually *outside* the house?"

"Yes. Fortunately it started near the clothes dryer vent, which gave the smoke a conduit into the house and drew attention to it more quickly than it might have otherwise."

"It seems strange that a fire would start in a trellis, especially this time of year," Darcy said. She caught the exchange of looks between the two firemen and suspected they didn't believe the fire was an accident.

"Do you or Mrs. Roper smoke?" one of the firemen asked. "I found traces of cigarettes among the ashes from the leaves."

"No, neither of us smokes and neither do any of our friends who have been here recently," she assured him. While they talked, she noticed the large piles of blackened leaves beside the wooden trellis that leaned precariously against the house. There was no reason for such an accumulation of leaves in one place. In fact, she remembered that right after she arrived at Karlene's house, the Boy Scout troop sponsored by Karlene's ward had staged a cleanup day during which they removed Karlene's leaves.

"Where did all of these leaves come from?" she asked. "They weren't here yesterday, but there were a dozen or more large bags of leaves beside the trash cans in the alley." She explained about the Scouts and that she had been adding a few of the bags to the weekly trash pickup each week.

"We didn't see any bags in the alley," the younger fireman said. A shiver ran down Darcy's spine. Someone had emptied those bags next to the house and staged the fire to make it look like an accident.

"There you are!" Darcy turned to see David loping across the lawn toward her. "One of my students said he saw police cars and fire trucks here, so I came by to check. Is Karlene injured?"

"No, she's fine. Anne insisted on having her checked at the hospital." She glanced at her watch and felt panicked. "I'm late for school, and I haven't even showered yet."

"I saw Sarah when I let the principal know I was leaving. She said not to worry if you miss class, but she'd appreciate knowing if you're all right. I'll call the principal and have him pass the message on to her."

"Do you live here?" the older fireman asked David. "I understood the only occupants were two women."

David blushed. "No, I don't live here, but both women who do are close friends," he said. He turned back to Darcy. "Why don't you go shower and change? I'll stay out here until you finish, then I'll take you to breakfast, and you can tell me all about it."

Darcy filled David in on the little she knew about the fire over pancakes and sausage. When they finished eating, they decided to go to the hospital to check on Karlene. They found her sitting up in bed arguing with Anne. Karlene was determined to check herself out of the hospital, and Anne was equally determined that her mother should stay overnight then spend the Thanksgiving weekend at Anne's home.

"That would leave Darcy alone," Karlene protested.

"I could go to my parents' for Thanksgiving," Darcy suggested. "I gave up on the idea after the break-in, but if you go to Anne's . . ."

"Well, of course you should spend Thanksgiving with your family. I'll be just fine with Anne." Anne smiled her gratitude at Darcy over her mother's head.

"I doubt you can get a ticket this late," David pointed out as they walked down the hall a few minutes later.

"I'm not planning to fly," Darcy said. "Since you found me a place to live where I don't have to pay rent, I didn't have to sell my car, so I'll drive."

"That's a pretty long drive for your old car."

"It got me here, and I haven't had any problems with it."

"How recently did you have the fluids checked or get a tune-up?"

"Dad took care of all that before I left home."

"Last June?"

"Well, yes, but I haven't driven it much the past two months since I started student teaching."

"What if I take a look at it when we get back to your house?" David offered.

It didn't take long for David to point out that her car was leaking oil and needed some major attention. Darcy sat down on the back step to stare sadly at her car. She knew she should have found a garage and had her car checked regularly, but she'd been busy and short on money.

David joined her on the step. "I could drive you home," he offered.

"No, David. It's a little more than 450 miles one way."

"I know how far it is. We could leave right after school tomorrow and be there around ten—that is, if you think your mom will invite me to stay for Thanksgiving dinner."

"Of course she would invite you, but . . ."

"It's settled, then. We'll leave as soon as school is out tomorrow. That just leaves tonight. You can't stay alone in Karlene's house."

"I don't think I have a choice."

"Don't you have a girlfriend you could stay with for one night?"

"I did. We came to Boise together, but when her boyfriend moved in, I moved out. We attended a singles ward all summer, but I really never got to know anyone well enough to call them up now and say I'm coming to spend the night."

"What about Sarah? The two of you seem to have hit it off pretty well."

"I like Sarah, but she has a husband and a one-room apartment. They plan to move to a house during Christmas break, which would be too late for me."

"Okay, that settles it. Why don't you go inside and pack while I see if I can fix that oil leak enough to get you through until you can get it to a garage."

"I'd better call my mom, too, and let her know to plan on an extra place setting at the table Thursday."

Darcy was almost finished packing the items she would need for a weekend at her parents' house when the doorbell rang. She peeked

through the window and was surprised to see Karlene's friend, Evan Swim. Swinging the door open, she greeted him.

"Karlene isn't here," she reported.

"I know. She called me from the hospital. In fact, I just came from there. She's concerned about you being alone in her house tonight."

"She won't be alone." Darcy wasn't surprised to see David hurrying around the side of the house, but she was more surprised to see Brother Keely's shorter and more rotund figure hurrying to keep pace with him.

"Lieutenant Swim, these are two of Karlene's friends. Brother Keely is the high priest group leader in Karlene's ward, and David Schoenfeld is her home teacher." Turning to them, she added, "Lieutenant Swim is a retired police officer."

"They'll be perfectly safe," David said after introductions. "Anne's husband and brother-in-law will watch the Wilson house, where Karlene is staying, while Ted and I will be sleeping in Ted's van in the driveway of Karlene's house where we can keep an eye on things and ensure Darcy's safety."

"I hope there's room for three in that van." Evan made it clear he intended to be part of the effort, and Darcy wondered if there was perhaps more than a long standing friendship between Karlene and the former lieutenant.

* * *

Darcy's last class the following day was cancelled, and she and David were on their way by three o'clock. Traffic was heavy heading west, and they speculated on how many people were heading out of town for the holiday. Darcy felt a twinge of sadness that Clare wasn't traveling home with her. Since her mother died, Clare had spent every holiday with Darcy and her family.

"You're not worrying about Karlene, are you?" David seemed to sense her pensive mood.

"No, I think we left her in good hands." Darcy laughed. Brother Keely had been a whirlwind of activity since he learned of the two attempts against Karlene's home. He had men from the ward lined up in four-hour shifts through the weekend to guard the house, and he'd

recruited several women from the Relief Society to stop in to visit with Karlene and assist her if she needed help with dressing or with preparing meals. She'd be with her daughter's family over Thanksgiving weekend, and they'd left Evan busy cleaning out a long-unused room over the garage where he intended to stay until he was satisfied that his old friend was out of danger.

"All right, if it's not Karlene you're worrying about, what brought that look of sadness to your face that I've noticed ever since we left Boise?"

She considered evading the question, but David was levelheaded, and she'd come to respect his opinions. She didn't need to name Pauline's brother as the source of her concern.

"It's my former roommate," she admitted after a slight hesitation. "We've been best friends since we were five years old, and I worry about her."

"This is the one who let her boyfriend move into her apartment?"

"Yes. She and I had made plans months ago to go home together for Thanksgiving. Her parents are deceased, and she has no brothers or sisters, so we've spent holidays together for a long time. I miss her."

"It seems she's made her choice."

"I'm not sure she did." Darcy stared out the window. "She's shy and not very self-confident. She spent most of her growing-up years looking after her mother who wasn't well and who demanded a lot of attention. She hates being alone, and she's always dreamed of being part of a large family like mine, and though we've always included her, I think she never really felt she was one of us. I think she was attracted to her boyfriend because she needs someone to lean on and make her feel she belongs. He's kind of domineering and bossy. He insists on knowing where she is every minute."

"Uh-oh, that doesn't sound good."

"He's rough too. She's constantly covered with bruises, and recently I think he might have been responsible for her broken wrist."

"I assume you've tried convincing her this guy isn't good for her?"

"I've tried, but she accused me of being jealous because I don't have a boyfriend. She's convinced he's everything she's ever dreamed of. He's a returned missionary, a college graduate with a good job, and attractive. When she let him move into the vacant room in our apartment, I

decided it was time for me to move out." She struggled not to give in to tears. Ever since she was a child, she'd found that tears came easily when she was angry.

"He's a returned missionary? Since when does a returned missionary think it's all right to move into his girlfriend's apartment? And as far as that physical abuse goes—and it is physical abuse—she shouldn't put up with that . . . She ought to run as far and as fast as she can."

"I've tried to tell her that, but she's in love, and they're getting married soon." The miles of sagebrush were giving way to mountains. "I'm surprised you don't have any meets this weekend." She successfully changed the subject as they started talking about the upcoming competitions his teams faced. Eventually, the conversation turned to his family.

"Won't your family be expecting you for Thanksgiving?" she asked, fearing his chivalrous offer to drive her to Tacoma might cause disappointment for his family.

"I have two older sisters, both married with families of their own. My oldest sister invited Mom and Dad to spend Thanksgiving with them in Logan. Pace, my younger brother, is going with them, then they're going down to Salt Lake to shop for suits for his mission. He's headed for Brazil in a few weeks. I really didn't relish driving to Logan and back by myself. My other sister lives in Twin Falls and will be spending the holiday with her in-laws."

She couldn't think of a tactful way to ask if he'd been invited to spend Thanksgiving with Pauline's family, so she let the subject drop.

As they neared the top of the pass, they encountered snow that had been scraped to the sides of the road, and she was glad she hadn't attempted the drive in her little car, especially alone. She enjoyed the scenic drive through the Columbia Gorge and even drifted to sleep for a short time. When she awoke, David was pulling off the highway.

"Hungry?" he asked. She nodded her head, and they were soon parked near a fast food restaurant enjoying hamburgers and the view of the river.

"I think I should drive now," she offered. "I'm familiar with the freeway exchange in Portland."

"Are you comfortable driving a truck?" David asked.

"Yes," she assured him. "Dad trusted me with his pickup long before Mom let me drive her car."

David soon relaxed and drifted to sleep once they started on the road again. She glanced over at him several times. Darcy liked him. *More than a little,* she thought with a twinge of sadness because of David's involvement with Pauline. *He's as nice as he is good-looking.* She considered asking about Pauline then conceded she was too much of a coward to broach the subject.

Turning the truck onto the quiet street where she'd grown up, she wondered for a moment if her parents had waited up for her. It even crossed her mind that her scatteredbrained little sister might not have even passed on the information that she was coming and bringing David. She wished she'd been able to talk to her mom, but Tracy had said that mom was shopping and she was the only one at home. The three-level wood house set in a thick grove of trees came into view, and it looked like every light in the house was on. Either everyone was waiting up for her, or Tracy and Trent were having one of their parties. They were the youngest of her siblings and the most outgoing. The pair had about a million friends, and they thought nothing of casually inviting them all over to watch a show or to just hang out.

David straightened in his seat as she pulled into the driveway. He whistled softly. "Quite a house!"

"It looks fancier than it is," she told him. "Dad's in construction, and he built it. It took about twenty years because he could only afford to finish a little bit at a time. He didn't finish my sister's, DeLana's, and my room until two months before she was killed by a drunk driver, and he's still working on the back deck."

"I didn't know about your sister."

"It was a difficult time. I don't talk about it much." She shut off the engine, and as the sound died away, an explosion of shouts and people surged through the front door of the house.

"She's here! Darcy's here!"

"Take a deep breath and prepare to be mobbed." Darcy opened the door and sped around the truck to greet her family. Several minutes passed before she could untangle herself and present David to her family.

"This is—" she began.

"Your boyfriend!" chorused Terry and Tracy.

Darcy could feel her face grow hot, though when she got brave enough to look at David, he was grinning and exchanging high fives

with Tracy and Terry. She interrupted to introduce him to her parents and other siblings.

"We're glad you two made it here safely. Now come inside and we'll catch up on all of the news. I saved dinner for you." Darcy's mother took charge, ushering them inside. Terry and Cody gathered David's and Darcy's bags from the space behind the seats of David's truck before following the others into the house.

"Nice house." David stood in the entryway looking around at the great room that flowed into a dining area with a large oval table with seating for eight with plenty of space to expand as needed. Beyond the table an island separated an oversized kitchen from the remainder of the room. "Your daughter told me you built it yourself," David said to Darcy's father, Marvin.

"The kids helped. So did Lynette." Marvin put an arm around his wife and gave her a hug. "You might say it's been a family venture."

"Terry, take Darcy's bag up to her room. Cody, the guest room is ready for David; take his bag there and show him around." She turned to Darcy and David. "I'll have plates dished up for both of you in less than ten minutes."

Darcy felt a rush of emotion on entering the room she'd shared first with DeLana then claimed as her own after her sister's death. Clare had shared the room with Darcy more than DeLana had. Remembering all the confidences exchanged with her friend in that room brought a lump to her throat. It had been almost six months since she'd last slept beneath the down comforter that covered her childhood bed. Her mother had bought the comforter and a matching one for the twin bed Clare slept in the first time her friend had come to stay for several weeks during one of Clare's mother's frequent hospitalizations. She and Clare had returned frequently while attending Washington State, and the room contained a multitude of memories that nearly overwhelmed Darcy in Clare's absence.

* * *

Darcy arose early Thanksgiving morning to help her mother get the turkey stuffed and to start on the pies. While they worked, the other family members and David strolled into the kitchen where they were greeted with cold cereal and orange juice for breakfast.

"Mom says we're on our own for breakfast this morning," Terry said apologetically to David.

"My mom does the same thing on Thanksgiving morning," David told the boy. "A light breakfast is perfect. It leaves more room for turkey and pie."

"Right!" Cody agreed. "Besides, if we're going to whip the Second Ward this morning, we need to be a lean, mean fighting machine! My friends and I have been practicing a few new moves to show those guys."

"Do you play basketball?" Terry asked David. "You're pretty tall."

"I play a little bit, though volleyball is my preferred sport."

"Some of the guys from the First and Second Wards get together every Thanksgiving morning for a tournament. Some of the dads play too. Do you want to join us?" Cody's voice held an edge of excitement.

"It gets us out of the women's hair," Marvin added.

"Sure! Sounds like fun," David agreed. His eyes caught Darcy's and he winked.

After the guys left to play ball, Darcy and her sisters worked with their mother to prepare dinner. Though Tracy complained about having to work while Terry got to go play, she didn't appear particularly upset.

"Are you going to marry David?" she asked.

"No, he's just a friend."

"Most girls don't invite their boyfriends home to meet their families unless they're serious."

"Ha!" Danene poked Tracy. "Since when did you get to be an expert on boyfriends?"

"I know lots of things." Tracy tossed her head. "I know you're hoping Bart Dickonson is going to invite you to the Winter Ball, but he'll probably ask Angela Folson."

"You little snoop! You've been reading my journal!"

"No, I haven't." Tracy moved a few discreet steps away from Danene. "Angela has her own cell phone, and she was talking kind of loud when Terry and I sat behind her at the game last Friday."

"It's not polite to eavesdrop," Lynette reminded Tracy.

"Angela was probably talking really loud on purpose just so Tracy would tell me she was going to the dance with Bart." The vegetables

she was chopping for the salad nearly disappeared in a series of swift slices of the knife Danene wielded.

"Here, let me do that while you set the table." Her mother took the knife from Danene's hand.

"So how long have you and David been dating?" Tracy interrogated.

"We're not dating." Darcy laughed, but she was careful to keep her back to her inquisitive little sister. "We met about three months ago when he rescued me from an intoxicated patron at the restaurant where I worked. He and his girlfriend were really nice to me. Then when I started doing my student teaching, I found out he's a coach at the same school. He likes to run, so I often see him at the track where we both run, and when I was looking for a new place to live, he recommended me to the lady who needed someone to help her while she heals from an accident."

"If he already has a girlfriend, why did he come with you for Thanksgiving instead of spending Thanksgiving with her?" Tracy asked. Darcy looked at her mother as though seeking help, but Lynette merely shrugged her shoulders, letting Darcy know she was on her own to deal with her younger sister's questions.

"Her family is awfully busy with preparations for one brother's wedding and the other's political campaign. She's an attorney, and she just started a new job where she's handling a high-profile murder case. She didn't think she could take a day off, and since it looked like I couldn't come home because my car needs some repairs, he offered to drive me home so that neither of us would be alone today."

"Well, I think he likes you." Tracy picked up a bowl to carry to the table.

With both of Darcy's sisters out of the room, Lynette set down the mixer she was using to mash potatoes. "What about Clare?" she asked quietly.

"Mom, I just don't know. She hasn't been herself since she met Blaine. At first I tried to like him, but now I—I guess *hate* is too strong of a word—dislike him an awful lot. Clare is his adoring slave. He runs her whole life, and not only does he boss her around, but I'm sure he abuses her. I know people with fair skin bruise easily, but I've never seen her with so many bruises before."

"What makes you think Blaine is responsible for her bruises? She might just be low in iron or be a little anemic. Have you suggested she see a doctor?"

"It's not just the bruises. Clare is really vague about how she broke her wrist. They both claim he walked her to the door the night she broke it, but if he did, why didn't he take her to the hospital or at least show more concern?"

"Something smells good!" Marvin led the way as the men and boys erupted through the back door.

"David was really awesome!" Terry shouted. "We smoked the Second Ward."

"They didn't know what hit them!" Cody added with a grin. "Our plan worked perfectly. We were tied, then David came in and hit four outside shots in a row. You should have seen him. It was all First Ward the rest of the game."

"You got in some good dunks too." David clapped Cody on the back. "And Terry is an excellent guard."

"Did you play?" Lynette kissed her husband on the cheek.

"Not me. There were plenty of young men there, so I volunteered to keep score."

"There's the doorbell. Danene, get the door." Lynette raised her voice to be heard over the play-by-play and congratulations taking place. "Quick, get washed up." She shooed the men from the room.

By the time the family was seated around the table, they'd been joined not just by David but by nearly a dozen relatives, many of whom arrived carrying pies or salads. Darcy wondered if David might feel a little overwhelmed by her family, but he seemed to be completely at ease—so much at ease that he took Terry's hero worship and the curious questions from her aunts and cousins in stride as they plied him with carefully worded inquiries concerning his and Darcy's relationship.

As usual, Marvin volunteered his and the other men's services as dishwashers, but Lynette chased them out of her kitchen, swearing there was no way she'd let a bunch of clumsy men handle her best china. Tracy and most of the younger cousins ducked out of dishwashing duties too, but Darcy, Danene, and two of their aunts met Lynette's approval.

Darcy enjoyed the time spent with her mother, sister, and aunts, but she found herself wondering how David was faring. She knew she

had no real cause for worry. After all, David was a coach, and she knew the men in her family would all be gathered around the largest television in the house to watch football games.

She was bending down, stacking pans in a lower cupboard, when she heard a sound behind her. Looking up, she saw David watching her with an odd smile on his face. He turned to address her mother. "Would you mind if I stole Darcy for awhile?" he asked. "I've never visited this part of Washington before, and I understand your house is near the Puget Sound. I'd like to see the sound with a local guide."

"You'll need a sweater." Her mother turned to her. The knowing smile on her aunts' faces brought a flush to Darcy's cheeks.

"My jacket is hanging by the back door," Danene whispered with a sympathetic wink.

Grabbing the jacket, Darcy bolted out the door with David right behind her. They walked silently to David's truck, where he held the passenger door for her.

"We're not far from a lookout point and a narrow stretch of beach. I grew up running there," she informed him as he put the truck in reverse.

"I'm too full to run." David flashed her a grin. "Besides, those kids gave me a real workout this morning."

Darcy laughed, and the slight strain she'd felt before leaving the house disappeared. She directed him down a narrow road, and in minutes they emerged to see a dazzling expanse of water spread before them. Several large boulders could be seen poking through the water, but bordering the gentle waves that lapped against the shore was a ribbon of pale sand.

They found a place to park the truck then stripped off their shoes and socks, leaving them behind as they wandered onto the sand.

Darcy enjoyed the cool feel of sand between her toes, but she noticed that David walked a little gingerly.

"It's colder than I expected," he said as a tiny rivulet of water washed over his bare feet.

"Washington isn't exactly in the tropics." Darcy laughed. "Even in the summer beach outings don't include a lot of swimming."

When they reached the end of the strip of beach, they climbed over several large rocks to reach a high point with an unobstructed view of the sound.

"Wow! It's beautiful, and that looks like a ship out there." He pointed toward a vessel moving slowly up the sound.

"Portland, Tacoma, and Seattle are all busy seaports. In addition to cargo ships, we often see cruise ships and ferries. People live on a large number of the islands in the sound as well, and many of them use private small craft to get from the mainland to their islands."

Conversation drifted toward their work at Boise High School, and Darcy shared her hope that after her student teaching was finished she'd be able to stay on. Sarah Becker was expecting her first baby and planning to leave at the end of the semester. By tacit agreement they avoided discussing the strange situation at Karlene's house, though Darcy suspected it would become the topic of conversation on the long drive back to Boise.

They sat on the rock talking for some time, then as the sun began to sink over the water, the sky turned vivid shades of pink and amber. David stood when the colors faded and the first stars began to twinkle. He extended a hand to Darcy. "I suppose we better start back before your family thinks I've kidnapped you."

Darcy took his hand and rose to her feet. To her surprise, he didn't release it but instead helped her climb down the rocks then continued to hold her hand as they made their way across the sand and back to David's truck.

Chapter 9

LIFE IN KARLENE AND DARCY'S household took on its familiar rhythm after both women returned from Thanksgiving except that Evan became a permanent fixture around the place. He turned the room over the garage into a one-room efficiency apartment, though he seldom ate there. He took most of his meals with Karlene.

Darcy wondered if Karlene still had need of her, but the older woman assured her she was much more comfortable knowing that if she needed assistance during the night or with dressing that Darcy was there.

"It seems you and David are getting along awfully well," Karlene remarked one morning as Darcy prepared to rush off to school. She wanted to be a few minutes early because Sarah had been ill the previous day, and Darcy suspected she would have Sarah's classes to herself all day.

"He's a great running partner, and it was awfully kind of him to drive me home for Thanksgiving." She attempted to pass off Karlene's comment in a casual manner.

"Evan and I were just commenting the other day that you made a cute couple." Karlene sipped from her cup and appeared to be concentrating on her breakfast, but Darcy suspected the woman was watching her carefully. She felt heat rushing up the sides of her face and turned away before her flushed face revealed too much.

"He's a nice guy, and I appreciate his friendship." She paused then added, "I'll be a little later than usual getting back this afternoon. I need to stop at the bridal shop for a fitting for the dress I'll be wearing at my friend's wedding."

Karlene smiled in a knowing way, making Darcy want to protest the assumption she knew the other woman was making concerning her relationship with David, but if she said anything, she'd only give credence to that assumption. Some part of her mind mocked her denial that she was romantically interested in David. Ever since their trip to Tacoma, she frequently found David in her thoughts, and it seemed there was often something special in his eyes and in the smile he gave her when they met on the track each morning.

"I have to be going." She reached for the bag that held her lesson plans for the day. She looked around before setting the bag back down. "Evan is usually here by now," she remarked, feeling anxious to be on her way but reluctant to leave Karlene alone.

"I'm here." Evan poked his head around the door that led to Karlene's home office. "I borrowed Karlene's computer to check a few things. You go ahead."

"All right. I'll see you both later." She zipped up her jacket and reached for her bag once more.

On the walk to school, Darcy went over Karlene's comments concerning David. It wasn't the first time the older woman had hinted that she thought there was something romantic happening between Darcy and David or mentioned what a fine person he was and that the young woman who married him would be making a fine catch. Darcy couldn't help smiling at the old-fashioned phrase. She agreed that when it came to David's fine qualities, she couldn't think of one thing in his behavior toward her that wasn't commendable. Unfortunately, there wasn't anything certain about his having romantic feelings toward her. He'd held her hand on the beach in Tacoma, but it had begun to get dark, and he'd merely shown gentlemanly concern about steadying her as they walked. He hadn't asked her out or even hinted that he might. Though they ate breakfast together Saturday mornings, they took turns paying.

Perhaps she should make the first step to take their friendship to the next level. But what if she merely embarrassed him and he began looking for ways to avoid her?

As she approached the school, her gaze went to the track field as a matter of habit. Several students were running warm-up laps, but there was no sign of David.

A movement near the street caught her attention. A man and a woman stood near an SUV. They were both tall and slender. The man had his back to her. He stood with one arm resting atop the vehicle. Something about his stance appeared familiar—as did the SUV. A feeling of dread swept over her, and she paused to watch. The woman whose face had been obscured by her companion's shoulders moved as though preparing to enter the SUV, and Darcy recognized Pauline. She didn't need to see the man to know he was David. She watched as he held the door for Pauline to enter the vehicle, then he stooped, and his head disappeared inside the open door.

Darcy didn't wait for him to withdraw his head and close the door. She resumed walking. So much for her daydreams and Karlene's speculation. Obviously David was still seeing Pauline. She plastered a smile on her face and made her way to the front door of the high school.

* * *

"I can't wear that!" Darcy gasped when she saw the strapless, nearly backless dress the woman in the bridal shop produced for her to try on. "It's indecent."

"But it's the dress the bride selected . . ."

"I doubt that." Darcy stubbornly held her ground. "Someone selected that *thing,* but it wasn't the bride. She's my best friend, and she knows I'd never wear something like that."

"Excuse me a moment." The woman rushed to a telephone that sat on a desk inside a nearby office. She pushed at the door to close it as she entered the office, but it didn't catch. Slowly it swung back. Curious, Darcy moved closer.

"But madam, this impossible girl refuses to even try on the gown." The woman paused as if listening then made a sharp exclamation. "Your daughter? She too dislikes the dress? But it is from Olegini, an original design she made up just for your wedding." Again there was a pause, a longer one this time. "Yes, madam. But of course."

Before the fitter could turn around, Darcy stepped back to her previous position. The woman approached her with her head high and said in stiff tones, "The design will be altered to a less-sophisticated

version. Mrs. Prescott does not wish for the bridesmaids to appear more glamorous than the bride."

Darcy struggled to hide a smile as she left the shop. She'd been right about the style of dresses chosen for her and the other bridesmaids. They weren't Clare's choice. Her smile disappeared. It seemed she and Pauline had more in common than she'd supposed. Apparently the beautiful attorney had scruples about appearing in public half naked too.

Her steps slowed as she approached the bus stop, and a wave of melancholy swept over her. She'd never once imagined that she wouldn't be the one shopping with Clare for her wedding finery or that she wouldn't be hosting a shower for her best friend. She'd spoken with Clare earlier that day, but she'd been in a hurry to get back to her class, and Clare had been rushing to meet Blaine. Clare had only called to say Pauline was hosting a luncheon a week before the wedding and that Darcy was invited to attend. She'd added that it had been decided that she should dispense with any other pre-wedding showers.

She was thrilled to hear from Clare at long last but disappointed that the luncheon was being held on a weekday, a day and a time she'd be unable to attend. The principal had contacted her shortly after she'd arrived at school that morning to inform her that Sarah's baby had come early and to ask Darcy if she would take over Sarah's classes for the few weeks left in the semester. He'd assured her that he had already spoken with her counselor at Boise State. She explained the situation to Clare.

"This could be your chance," Clare said with enthusiasm. "Is she coming back next semester?"

"No, she told me she wants to stay home with the baby for the remainder of the school year and that she would recommend me for the job."

"Darcy, that's wonderful!"

"I don't have the job yet."

"But you will. I'm just sure of it. I was afraid you'd go someplace else to look for a job and we'd lose touch. If you stay in Boise, we can go to lunch and shopping like we used to."

"We haven't done much of that lately," Darcy said with regret.

"I know, but after Blaine and I come back from our honeymoon, I'll have more time."

* * *

"We'd come for Clare's wedding if we could," Lynette said regretfully when Darcy called her mother. "Airline tickets for the whole family are too expensive, and I don't feel good about driving over the pass this time of year. Perhaps if we'd had more notice . . . and we can't leave the kids on their own for Christmas."

"I know, Mom. Besides, I checked the weather report, and it looks like there will be snow in the Cascades that whole week. It's snowing right now. I won't even dare drive home after the wedding."

"You got your car fixed?"

"Yes, but I wouldn't think of driving through those mountain passes even if I had four-wheel drive, which I don't."

"We could buy a ticket for you."

"No, don't spend money on a ticket for me when you need the money for the kids' Christmas. Besides, it's doubtful I could even get reservations this late. Don't worry, I'll be fine." She spoke with her mother for a couple more minutes then closed her cell phone and wandered into the kitchen, where Karlene and Evan were having a late breakfast.

"Sit down and eat with us," Karlene invited.

"I know having breakfast with us won't be nearly as much fun as your usual Saturday morning breakfast with David," Evan teased.

"It's snowing too hard to run this morning." Darcy glanced out the window again as she'd done a dozen times that morning. She sat at the table and accepted the basket of muffins Karlene extended toward her.

"If I were David, I'd nix the run this morning too, but I'd still take a pretty girl to breakfast." She intercepted the wink Evan gave Karlene.

"We're both too busy getting ready for test week." She spread strawberry jam on her muffin and acknowledged that Evan baked a mean muffin. She didn't mention that she was grateful for the snow that had kept her from running with David that morning. She had no one but herself to blame for the silly fantasies she'd entertained since the trip to Tacoma. She'd always known about Pauline. A short break from their daily run would help her put their friendship back in perspective.

Speaking of Pauline, she noticed the woman's picture on the front page of the newspaper Evan was holding up. When Evan set the front page section of the paper down and picked up the sports, Darcy pulled the page with Pauline's picture closer. She was almost through reading the article when Evan noticed her interest.

"Seems there's a new attorney in the county attorney's office," he remarked. "I must say I'm surprised. First time I ever heard of a Prescott working for the taxpayers instead of for the guy with the deepest pockets."

"I was attacked once by a patron at the restaurant where I worked. Pauline Prescott was there at the time, and she and her date came to my aid." Even though Darcy defended Pauline, she wished the woman wasn't quite so commendable or pretty or . . . David's girlfriend.

"I understand her brother is running for state attorney general. I suppose that's one way to keep it all in the family. She and her brother can prosecute them, and the other brother and their father can defend them." Evan's voice revealed more than a little sarcasm.

"Now, Evan, that was a long time ago," Karlene chided before turning to Darcy. "Evan started out on the police force here in Boise. Pauline's father defended a man who shot Evan's partner, and Mr. Prescott got him off even though Evan witnessed the shooting. Later the man killed two other people in another state. Evan has never gotten over his bitterness."

"Those two people wouldn't have died if Garrett Prescott hadn't found a way to keep me from testifying."

"I think David knows Pauline Prescott," Karlene mused. "It seems there was a picture of the two of them together in the newspaper a few years ago. They won some competition together, I believe."

* * *

Light snow was falling when Darcy left the house for Clare's wedding. Making certain the hood of her ski parka protected the hairstyle she'd paid more for than she could afford, she hurried the four blocks to the nearest bus stop. She'd allowed plenty of time since her car was in the shop again, making catching a bus essential. If the storm increased, she might have to consider a cab for the return trip.

She stamped her feet and thought about the rehearsal the previous evening. Blaine's mother had hired a wedding coordinator who kept to a strict timetable, and the dinner that followed was for the wedding party only. The only person she'd recognized at the rehearsal other than Clare and Blaine was Pauline, who had looked at her with a puzzled expression as though she didn't recognize her but thought she should. She'd been disappointed that there had been no opportunity to talk to Clare. Blaine hadn't left her side for a moment.

On reaching the hotel, Darcy hurried to the room that had been reserved for the bridesmaids' use, where she changed quickly into her gown. She was pleased to see that additional fabric had been added to the bodice of the attendants' bright red dresses along with a short faux fur cape to match the muffs the six bridesmaids would each carry. She couldn't help feeling a little sad and hurt because she hadn't been able to help Clare plan the wedding or shop for her trousseau. She hadn't even hosted a shower for her dearest friend, but she had every intention of assisting Clare in dressing for her wedding.

She was almost dressed when the other girls arrived. She'd met them for the first time the previous evening at the rehearsal. She knew which ones were family, friends, or cousins, and which was Blaine's sister-in-law. Penny Prescott was aloof, and Darcy suspected she was miffed that she wouldn't be serving as matron of honor. The other girls seemed to know each other and paid little attention to her. Pauline was the only one to make an attempt at being friendly.

"Don't go far," Pauline whispered when Darcy attempted to leave the room in search of Clare's dressing room. "Mother and Ms. Atkinson will throw fits if we're not all right where they expect us to be when the first note of the wedding march begins."

"I'm just going to help Clare dress," she answered back.

"Mother and the wedding planner have all that under control." There was a hint of sympathy in Pauline's eyes.

"I'm sure they do." Darcy's words were a little sharper than she intended. "Clare has no mother or female relatives here to give her support and encouragement. I'm the closest to family she's got. Besides, isn't it the maid of honor's responsibility to help the bride dress?" She reached for the door.

"Room 216," the other woman whispered back.

Perhaps the short exchange with David's girlfriend put her on the defensive, but it also served as a warning. She wouldn't let anyone keep her from being with Clare. She rapped on the door to 216 and waited impatiently. Finally, the woman who had orchestrated the rehearsal came to the door.

"Good afternoon, Mrs. Prescott." Darcy spoke airily and didn't wait for an invitation before pushing her way inside the room.

"Just wait with the other girls . . ." Danielle began.

"Clare." Darcy brushed past the woman and hurried to her friend.

"Oh, Darcy." Tears sparkled in Clare's eyes. "I thought you might have decided to go home for Christmas after all." She reached out to clasp Darcy's hands.

"You know I wouldn't miss your wedding." Stepping back while retaining Clare's hands, Darcy surveyed Clare. The dress wasn't the fantasy dress Clare had described to Darcy many times through the years, but nothing about this wedding matched those dreams. "Let me get a good look at you."

She was pleased to see no fresh bruises and only one faded dark spot at the top of one of Clare's arms. Her dress was a beautiful creamy silk, cut lower than either she or Clare had ever worn before, but it wasn't nearly as bad as she had feared after her first glimpse of the attendants' dresses. Her friend had lost weight and looked a little tremulous, but she was smiling.

"Are you really happy?" Darcy whispered so that only Clare could hear.

"Oh, yes. Blaine's being so sweet. Everything is going to be wonderful now. His father is giving us a beautiful condo in a great neighborhood as a wedding present and has arranged for a decorator so I don't have to do anything." She giggled, reminding Darcy of all the times they'd giggled together over girlish secrets.

"You can redo it all after the decorator is gone," Darcy whispered. "It looks like you're all dressed."

"Yes. And it's time to begin. An usher should be outside the door by now to escort you to your seat, Danielle. Miss Olsen, you may stay with the bride while I line up the procession, then please take your place."

Clare and Darcy stood looking at each other.

"God's blessings. Be happy." Darcy spoke from her heart.

"Don't be sad," Clare whispered over a lump in her throat. "I will be happy, and we'll always be friends. Blaine and I are only taking a short honeymoon because he has an important case coming up. It'll take a great deal of his attention, so we'll have plenty of time to be together again."

"Good." Darcy struggled to keep her tears back. She didn't want red eyes or smeared mascara to mar Clare's wedding pictures. She squeezed her friend's hand once more. "Call me as soon as you get back, and we'll make plans." She hesitated a moment then added, "If you ever need anything, I'll be there for you."

"All right, girls! Take your places." Ms. Atkinson stood in the doorway.

Chapter 10

WITH HER HAND LIGHTLY RESTING on Blaine's brother's arm, Darcy's halting footsteps followed the music to the front of the room, where they separated and she turned to watch Clare begin her slow march down the aisle on the arm of her soon-to-be father-in-law. Just once, their eyes met, and Darcy knew her friend was experiencing a moment's grief. Whether that grief was for the absence of any family of her own or for the postponed temple wedding or who knows what else, Darcy could only guess.

Flashes from a dozen cameras highlighted the procession, and Darcy expected the evening's news would carry snippets of the wedding at six and ten. Clare's eyes wavered, and her face looked pinched for just a moment. Darcy thought her friend might be ill, but then her chin came up, and she seemed to focus on the man waiting for her beside a makeshift altar. A brilliant smile lit her face, and she moved steadily toward Blaine. Darcy, too, plastered a smile on her face and determined to be cheerful and supportive.

The wedding went off smoothly, but Darcy found the dinner and reception chaotic. Waiters rushed through the crowd carrying trays of fancy glasses, and people gathered in groups, clogging passage between tables. She noticed that more people seemed to gather around Brett and Penny than waited to congratulate the bridal couple.

She felt alone and left out. In all their dreaming and planning for the future, she never once considered that the day would come when she wouldn't share those dreams with Clare or that Clare's friends would be strangers to her. Even if Clare wasn't marrying Blaine, Darcy

reminded herself, she might have married someone from clear across the country, and Clare still wouldn't have a family to support her.

From across the room she recognized a familiar form beside Pauline, his hand resting at the back of her waist. *David!* She should have expected he would attend the wedding, but she hadn't. An odd lump formed in her throat, and she hoped she could avoid his attention. She didn't want to see him and Pauline together. Besides, he had probably put two and two together when he recognized her as Clare's maid-of-honor and knew she'd been speaking of Blaine when she'd complained about her former roommate's abusive boyfriend. He leaned forward to speak to someone, and Darcy began working her way to a table at the far end of the room.

As she attempted to press her way through or around clusters of people, she caught snatches of conversation.

"This should give his campaign a boost. Weddings always appeal to women voters."

"Arranging for clips to be shown on television of him taking time out from the campaign to be his brother's best man should help secure the family values voters."

"It's too bad they couldn't have a formal line, but if they did, the bride's friend would be in the pictures instead of Penny. You'd think she would have had the grace to step aside to allow Brett and Penny as much coverage as possible." Darcy's face felt warm, and she squeezed past the table.

"It's time he came out and made a statement about . . ."

"Beautiful bride." Darcy paused, pleased that someone remembered she was attending a wedding, not a political rally.

"Is she related to the newly elected state senator from Butte County?" the woman added.

"No," one of the other women at the table responded. "She's really a nobody. I heard she was an orphan with no family at all." Darcy ground her teeth but resisted making a scene.

"At least she's pretty, and no family is better than one that would be a political liability."

"We all thought he'd make a match with the Wallace girl, but after her unfortunate accident, I hear she moved back East somewhere."

Darcy was relieved to reach the table in a corner far from the cameras, reporters, and local dignitaries who had attended the wedding. She quickly sat down and set her fur muff on the table, wishing it were large enough to hide behind until she could politely leave. Idly she picked at the single red rose pinned to the white fur.

"You look like you could use a little company." She watched as one of the groomsmen slid onto the vacant chair beside her. She recognized him as the young man who had escorted Penny Prescott down the aisle. She also suspected he'd been drinking something stronger than the sparkling cider that filled the fluted champagne glass she twirled in her own fingers.

"You 'n' me . . . we're just extra baggage now." He grinned. "They don't need us anymore. How 'bout we sneak outta here an' find a place where the music really rocks."

"Sorry." Darcy kept her voice pleasant. "I already have plans."

"Plans that include me." He smiled, showing plenty of straight, white teeth. He'd be cute if he were sober and a little less arrogant.

"No, really. I . . ."

"Levi, the lady said no. Why don't I call a cab to take you home?" Darcy was embarrassed to find David rescuing her once more from an amorous drunk, even one as harmless as the young man beside her appeared to be.

"Go find your own girl," Levi sneered. "Oh, that's right. You've got a girl. The ill-us-ter-ous Miss Prescott, attorney-at-law. I hear she's as mean as that brother of hers . . . couldn't wait to get on the prosecutin' side."

"That's enough." David's voice was sharp. "I know you and Blaine had a disagreement earlier, but you've no call to take your frustration out on Pauline or this young lady."

"Sorry," Levi mumbled. "Wouldna come, but m' sister said I had to."

"It seems to me you've done your duty." David's voice sounded kinder. "Come on, let me help you to a cab." He helped the tipsy young man to his feet, then turning, he smiled at Darcy and whispered, "I'll be right back."

Once the pair was out of sight, Darcy berated herself for not antici- pating that David would attend the wedding. Of course, he'd be at the

wedding. Any woman would expect her boyfriend to attend her brother's wedding. She debated slipping out the door and disappearing before he returned. *He probably thinks I invite attention from drunks.* Casually, she rose to her feet, cast one longing look toward the knot of people surrounding Clare, then hurried out the door to make her way to the dressing room to reclaim the clothes she'd worn to the hotel. She had no intention of standing at a bus stop in a much-too-short, puffy red gown, stiletto red heels, and a fake fur cape.

Darcy stripped off the dress and returned it to a hanger. She'd never wear it again, so there was no good reason to drag it on the bus with her. Ms. Atkinson had explained that the capes and muffs were rented, so she unpinned the red rose, which she tucked in her bag as a memento of her friend's wedding.

Attired once more in jeans, she zipped up her light parka and opened the door. There stood David, leaning against the opposite wall.

"Let's go." He reached out to take her bag.

"What about Pauline?"

"What about Pauline? She has her own car. Besides, she only lives a few blocks from here." He took Darcy's arm and led her toward the elevator. Her mind seemed to slip into slow motion, leaving her unable to speak or reason.

She was seated on the bench seat of his truck before she spoke again. "Won't Pauline be upset when she finds you left the reception?"

He started the engine and pulled the truck from the parking garage onto the slushy street before responding. "She's probably surprised I hung around as long as I did. In fact, she's probably split by now too."

Darcy didn't know what to say. She glanced at him, wondering what kind of relationship he and Pauline had. His eyes met hers for just a second before returning to the road. Snow was no longer falling, but the streets were slick with a thin layer of wet slush, and lawns were covered with a blanket of white. A glimmer of moonlight peeked through thinning clouds to give the city a washed-clean look. Until they left the busier streets, David appeared to be concentrating on the wet streets.

"Um," he said as he pulled onto a side street. He appeared uncomfortable, almost embarrassed. "Pauline and I weren't together tonight. She wasn't my date, if that's what you thought."

"Yes, I assumed you were together." She was careful not to glance his way. "You were together that night at the restaurant, and I've seen you together a few other times."

Silence followed her admission. For several miles, neither spoke. David seemed to totally concentrate on driving. When he pulled into Karlene's driveway, he didn't shut off the engine or move to open his door. Finally, Darcy reached for the door handle.

"Wait." David held out his hand as though to physically prevent her from leaving his truck. She looked askance at him. "I mean . . . I don't know how to say this without sounding vain and arrogant . . . I've never tried to get a girl to like me . . . They just do . . . Even in high school . . . well, sometimes girls got their feelings hurt. There was one girl who didn't even know I existed, though she knew all the answers to every question in any subject. Most of the kids considered her a snob. One day, coach asked me to enter a mixed doubles, two-person volleyball competition. He paired me with that girl, a tall, skinny blond who seemed to have two left feet—until she got on a volleyball court."

"Pauline Prescott," Darcy muttered.

"Yes. Pauline. She wasn't the least bit impressed by me, which oddly enough made me more comfortable around her. She wasn't looking for a date; she just wanted to play ball and win. We did win, and little by little we became friends. I learned she came from a rich, powerful family but was miserable at home. Her parents fought a lot, and she and Blaine were the constant objects of their ridicule, while Brett was their golden child."

"I thought your family lived near Twin Falls."

"My family moved to Twin Falls right after I graduated from high school, but I stayed here to go to college. Pauline and I continued to partner for two-person games and played on the college's coed team for two years, then I left on a mission, and her parents sent her to an eastern Ivy League school then on to law school."

"That must have been hard for you to be apart so long," Darcy said, trying to be sympathetic, but she wished David would spare her the details of his romance with Pauline. She eyed the door handle once more, longing to escape to the house and her room, but David went on.

"We didn't stay in touch during those years, but after she returned, we ran into each other at a city recreation league game and began partnering again. She'd become attractive and poised, and yes, I noticed. We dated a few times, but other than our love for volleyball, we don't share common dreams and goals. We occasionally go out for dinner after a game, and she's asked me a few times to be her escort for social functions when she's needed one." He grinned a crooked self-deprecating smile. "Her parents don't approve of me, my career, or my social standing, which is why she likes to show up at big shindigs with me in tow. She likes to see her father sweat over the possibility that his daughter might end up with a high-school coach, son of a farmer, for a husband." He paused, and Darcy didn't know what to say. *How could anyone* not *approve of David?*

"I've wondered if letting Mr. Prescott think I was interested in his daughter was sort of a lie, but I never considered our little game would turn around and bite me."

"I don't understand," Darcy said, though her heart was beginning to pound as though it knew something that hadn't sunk into her head yet.

"I finally met a girl I do want to impress, and she thinks I'm involved with someone else. I haven't even dared ask her out because her evenings are tied up with looking after her landlady." He gave her a tentative smile.

"Me?" She gulped and wondered if she was jumping to an unwarranted conclusion.

"Yes, you. Surely you must have guessed that though I take my duties as a home teacher seriously, I might have another motive for showing up to check on Karlene as frequently as I've been doing."

Darcy stared at David openmouthed, not quite certain she understood what David was telling her. He reached forward to softly brush his fingers down her cheek. "Is there any chance we might become more than friends?"

"Yes, I'd like to give that a try." She was practically stammering. This couldn't be happening. *Get a grip,* she cautioned herself. She'd tried so hard to turn off the daydreams where David was concerned, now only to discover that her efforts had been unnecessary. She was suddenly afraid her quick response to his question might make her appear too eager. She closed her eyes, counted to three, and opened them again.

Something moved behind the window where David sat with his back to the door. Instinctively, she gripped his hand. "Someone's out there!" she whispered.

David turned slowly to face the side window. "I don't see anything. Maybe it was Evan walking from his apartment to the house."

"Maybe," she drew the word out, "but I don't think so. It looked more like someone sneaking behind bushes and the neighbor's hedge to get a better look at us."

"Probably some teenage voyeur hoping to get an eyeful by spying on parked vehicles," David said. He was probably right. She was just jumpy; there had been no threatening incidents since before Thanksgiving.

"It's starting to snow again. I better get you inside and be on my way." He opened the door and hurried around to her side of the truck. He reached for her small bag first then took her hand to help her down from the high seat. He didn't release it as they walked up the path leading to the house.

When they reached the front porch, she put out her hand to take her bag. Before surrendering it to her, he said, "I'm sorry you won't be able to go home for Christmas."

"Clare's been my best friend since we were small children; I couldn't miss her wedding. This will be my first Christmas away from my family, but it wouldn't have felt like Christmas anyway without her. Every year since her mother died, she has spent all of Christmas break with us, and before that we ran back and forth between our houses on Christmas Day."

"Pauline was a good friend I could count on, but we weren't *that* close," David said. "You were fortunate to have Clare for a friend."

"I never even thought about your being at Clare and Blaine's wedding. I thought you and Pauline were dating, but I guess I was so focused on Clare that I never gave much thought to Blaine's family and friends. Anyway, I assumed you'd be spending Christmas with your family."

"If the snow doesn't turn into a bad storm, I'll drive to Twin Falls for a few hours tomorrow to have dinner with my family and deliver a few presents. Would you like to go with me?" Before she could respond, he added, "I really would like you to go with me."

Even though the invitation was last-minute, she found herself saying, "Yes. I'd like that too. What time should I be ready?"

"Is nine too early? It's only a two-hour drive, so that will put us there in plenty of time to pass out presents to the nieces and nephews before dinner."

"Nine will be great."

"I'll see you in the morning, then." He brushed her cheek with the tips of his fingers, leaving her slightly disappointed when he turned to hurry back to his truck. After only a few steps, he turned around again. "I just remembered something you said when we first started running together. Didn't you say you had to move out of the apartment you shared with a friend because her boyfriend moved in? That friend was Clare, wasn't it?"

Darcy nodded her head and wondered if he'd remember what else she'd said about Clare's boyfriend. But he only said, "You were wise to get out."

David walked back to his truck while Darcy unlocked the door.

Darcy stepped inside the house to be greeted by the aroma of baking bread, cinnamon, and chocolate. "Mmm, smells good." She poked her head into the kitchen, where Karlene and Evan sat at the table with a plate of cinnamon twists and mugs of hot chocolate.

"Come join us. I made plenty," Evan invited. He stood to reach another cup from the cupboard.

Shrugging off her coat and sitting beside Karlene at the table, she accepted the steaming cup of chocolate Evan placed before her.

Karlene slid the plate of warm cinnamon twists closer to Darcy. Picking one up, Darcy bit into it and sighed. "Food for the gods. Karlene, if you don't marry this man, I just might." She looked up to see a smile pass between the two older people, and she swore Karlene was blushing.

"Is there something you want to tell me?" She arched an eyebrow and grinned.

"We've been talking about it," Evan admitted with a sheepish grin.

"We're not making any announcements just yet," Karlene added.

"I keep telling her we're not getting any younger."

"There's something about that man . . ." Karlene's voice trailed off, and Darcy knew she wasn't referring to Evan. She turned to follow the older woman's gaze to the living room, where she caught a glimpse of a man's face on the television before it disappeared.

"Do you know him?" Darcy asked.

"No, I don't think so. This is a repeat of an earlier news program. When I saw it earlier, I thought there was something familiar about the man, and seeing it again . . . I had the same feeling."

"You might have seen a picture of him sometime," Evan offered. "He's pretty well known around the state. Jessop Bernard has a finger in a lot of pies."

"No, I don't think it was a picture, but I can't imagine where I might have seen him. Oh well. It's not important. This is Christmas Eve, and I always watch *Mr. Kruger's Christmas* on Christmas Eve. Do you want to join us, Darcy?"

"No thanks, I have to be up early tomorrow. David invited me to go with him to his parents' home for Christmas tomorrow. But you two go ahead." She didn't miss the knowing smile that passed between the pair as she left the room. As she closed her bedroom door, she remembered she'd meant to ask Evan if he'd arrived at the house while David and Darcy were parked out front.

Chapter 11

"I LANDED A BIG ONE today—the biggest of my career so far." Blaine gave the steering wheel a brisk turn.

"That's wonderful!" Clare fingered the armrest, resisting the urge to cling to it. Blaine didn't like it when she exhibited less-than-complete confidence in his driving ability.

"A guy like that usually goes for a public defender, so I wasn't thrilled when he called my office from the county jail, but a hefty retainer arrived by messenger within an hour. He said he wanted the best, and I was it. Then he said I'd defended him a year ago when he got picked up on a DUI, and he liked my style, so now that he has the cash to pay, he wants me to represent him again."

"Another DUI?" Ever since Darcy's sister had been killed by a drunk driver, Clare had felt little sympathy for anyone who drank then got behind the wheel of a car. She didn't like to think about her husband defending such people.

"Not hardly! Drunks are a dime a dozen, and their cases are usually handled by new and junior level attorneys, usually pro bono, too. I looked him up before agreeing to take his case. It seems this guy said he couldn't afford an attorney for the DUI so Dad volunteered me. He said every law firm has to do a certain amount of pro bono, and I might as well get mine over with. I don't even remember the case, but the guy is rolling in dough now. He's up for murder one and wants me to represent him."

"Is he guilty?"

Blaine rolled his eyes and pulled into the parking garage. After locking the car, he resumed the conversation as though Clare hadn't

spoken. "Get dressed in something slinky, and we'll go out on the town to celebrate." He headed for the elevator ahead of Clare.

Clare followed, but she felt unusually tired, and she really didn't enjoy the clubs Blaine picked when he wanted to entertain clients or wished to be seen. She suspected this would be that kind of occasion. She stepped out of her shoes as she stepped inside their condo.

"Couldn't we just celebrate quietly here at home? We both have to be up early tomorrow for work." *With Blaine in such a good mood, this might be the time to share my news,* she thought silently.

"Dad won't expect me early tomorrow. He knows we'll be celebrating tonight. And there's no reason for you to go in early either. It's time you quit your job."

"Quit my job?" Clare stared at her husband in shock. "I can't just quit. I like my job, and I just got a raise."

"Look, baby, you just don't get it. What you make is peanuts. My fee from just one case is more than you'll earn in a couple years. The new client who walked into my office today wants my full attention, and he's willing to pay for it. I can't concentrate on something this big if I'm never sure where you are or if some jerk engineer is hitting on you. I support us, and I'm the head of this family, so I make the decisions. Turn in your notice tomorrow."

"The engineers don't hit on me!"

"I saw that creep hanging all over you when I picked you up for lunch today."

"He wasn't hanging over me. He was checking the estimates I worked up for him. Jack is married, and his behavior is completely professional toward me and all of the secretaries at the firm." A sudden pain ripped across the side of her head, and she staggered backward. Everything before her seemed to waver. Blaine grasped her shoulders, shaking her fiercely.

"You're a liar. I know what I saw." A stinging slap was followed by a fist crashing into her face, choking off her scream. The room turned dark, and she felt herself falling.

When she came to, she was lying on her bed with a cold cloth held to her cheek. "I didn't mean to hurt you," Blaine apologized, appearing close to tears. "Why do you always have to argue with me? You know it makes me angry, and when I'm angry I forget to be careful."

Feeling confused and disoriented, she couldn't speak. Her head hurt, but some instinct warned her not to say the wrong thing. Blaine went on. "If you'd only trust me to know what's best, this wouldn't happen. I love you, and I don't want to hurt you. You're my wife, and you can't blame me for getting upset when you're unreasonable. You only need to remember you're not alone anymore; I'm looking after you now. Come on, give me a smile, and we'll forget this happened. Tomorrow, you'll turn in your two weeks notice, and this silly quarrel will be forgotten."

Clare wanted to cry, but she knew Blaine couldn't stand it when she cried. *Everything was going so well. Why did I have to spoil it by arguing with him? I planned to quit my job when the baby comes anyway. He was so sweet during our honeymoon and the weeks leading up to our wedding; why did I ruin everything by insisting on having my own way?*

Blaine put his arm around her and helped her to a sitting position. "I didn't mean to hurt you. I promise it won't happen again. Just sit here, and I'll have dinner delivered." He snuggled an afghan around her shoulders and hurried to the telephone. All evening he showered her with solicitous attention, and she fell asleep snuggled in his arms. She couldn't be angry with him when he was so remorseful. Anyway, it was her fault; she knew he became upset when she argued with him.

When morning came, she awoke to a delicious aroma and discovered that Blaine had prepared sausage, cinnamon toast, orange juice, and eggs for her. He brought it on a tray and propped pillows behind her back to make eating more comfortable. He even turned on the stereo and played one of her favorite CDs. She looked down at the plate he set before her, and her stomach began to roil. Gamely she took a forkful of eggs, swallowed, then lifted a sausage to her mouth.

"It's wonderful." She forced a smile. "But I really need to visit the bathroom before I eat. She scrambled off the bed and hurried to the bathroom, where she promptly lost the little she'd eaten.

After flushing the toilet and running water in the sink, she gave the room a quick spray of air freshener before returning to her bed to finish her breakfast. This time she drank the juice and nibbled at the toast before attempting the eggs and sausage. She'd have to tell Blaine

about the baby. She would have told him sooner, but she wasn't certain how he'd feel about their becoming parents so soon.

She'd begun to suspect she was pregnant a week before their wedding but had hoped her slight nausea and the other signs were just nerves, but now, three weeks later, she was convinced her suspicions were correct. If Blaine hadn't sold her car and if she had money, she'd have bought one of those test kits or visited a doctor to confirm it.

She was finishing applying makeup to cover the large bruises on her face when Blaine set a paper in front of her. She glanced at it and winced. Blaine had typed up her letter of resignation for her, effective immediately. She took the pen he handed her and signed her name.

"There. Now go back to bed. It's all taken care of, and I'll drop the letter off for you on my way to the office." He kissed the top of her head, folded the paper, and tucked it inside his coat pocket.

Clare didn't go back to bed. Instead she scrubbed the kitchen floor and cleaned the bathroom. The townhouse was spotless when she finally took two aspirin and sat down to rest. She didn't really want any lunch, but an article she'd read sometime ago had said hunger often led to nausea during the first three months of pregnancy.

While nibbling on crackers and an apple slice, she thumbed through the telephone directory looking for an obstetrician within walking distance of the condo. She found several but didn't call one. Without a job her insurance would be cancelled. If she went to a doctor, she'd have to ask Blaine for the money to pay for an office visit, and she wasn't ready to do that.

It was silly, really. She'd married into a well-to-do family, but she didn't have access to any money. Since before they were married, she'd been giving her checks to Blaine to deposit in the bank. After three months, he still hadn't found time to add her name to the account, and she'd never owned a credit card. He always paid for meals when they ate out and took care of their expenses, but she missed the security of having a small amount of cash. One day they'd have to sit down and talk about money, but so far she'd been reluctant to bring up the subject.

Despite the aspirin, her head continued to ache, and she decided to take a nap.

* * *

After four days of sitting in her apartment with nothing to do, Clare decided to call Darcy. Blaine didn't want her to use her cell phone for anything but emergencies and to talk to him, but she'd noticed a phone in the clubhouse. She decided to call from there.

"I'm so glad you're finally home," Darcy said after answering Clare's call. "Since you didn't return any of my calls, I thought you must be awfully busy or still on your honeymoon."

"No, I'm not busy, but Blaine and I got new phones with private numbers. We promised not to give out the numbers to anyone but each other."

"Blaine's old phone still works," Darcy said. "When you didn't answer yours, I called him a couple of times. I wrote his number down right after the two of you began dating. He said you were busy, but he'd tell you I'd called." Darcy's words shocked Clare. She hadn't known Blaine had kept his old cell phone. She supposed it made sense for him to have a portable phone he could use for business. It was kind of romantic that he'd gotten a second set of phones just so they could always be in touch, but she wondered why he hadn't mentioned that he'd kept his old phone or why he hadn't let her keep hers.

"He must have forgotten. He's handling a big case right now." She didn't want Darcy to know the news had disturbed her. "He's representing Leon Skidmore in the Lauren Tisdale murder trial coming up in a few months. It's taking up all of his time. In fact, he's working today and will probably have to work weekends until the trial is over."

"You're free right now?" Darcy sounded excited.

"Yes, I guess I am."

"Let's go to lunch—my treat. I'm off today for Martin Luther King Day. Give me your address, and I'll be there in thirty minutes. It's been way too long since we had lunch together."

* * *

"Oh, this was a good idea." Clare leaned back in her chair. It was just so good to be with Darcy, to laugh and talk with her best friend again.

"Now for my big news!" Darcy leaned closer. "Drumroll, please— I've been offered a contract for the remainder of the school year at

Boise High School. I'll be teaching all of the classes I student taught last semester."

"That's wonderful! May I be the first to say congratulations and I told you so." Both girls giggled. It really was like old times. "Will you be getting your own apartment now?"

"No, Karlene Roper, the lady I've been living with and helping while she's healing from an accident, invited me to stay until the end of the school year. She doesn't need live-in help anymore, but she likes having someone around. She's still on crutches and will soon graduate to a walking cast, but we get along well and her house is a convenient distance from the school. I decided to wait until summer to look for a place of my own."

"I'm glad you'll still be here in Boise."

"I am too. I've really missed you." Darcy took one last swallow of her milkshake. Setting her glass aside, she said, "Okay, your turn. How do you like being married?"

"It's wonderful." Clare smiled, keeping her thoughts focused on the good parts of her new life. "Living with a man is a lot more demanding than I expected, but Blaine is just thoughtful, and he makes certain I have everything I need. Our apartment is beautiful. Blaine's mother hired a professional decorator so everything matches perfectly. There's a pool we can use in the summertime, a clubhouse, and a weight room. I haven't used any of the exercise equipment yet, but Blaine has a few times. We went to our new ward last week, and our bishop seems really nice."

"Does it seem strange to be in a family ward again? The first time I attended my new ward, it seemed a little weird but kind of nice. I hadn't realized how much I'd missed kids running around and the older people."

"You're not going to the singles ward anymore?" Clare seemed surprised. "How do you expect to meet any single men in a family ward?" she added with a mischievous grin. Seeing the first hint of a blush on Darcy's cheeks, she pounced. "Aha." She laughed. "Who is he?"

"There's a teacher at the high school I've gone out with a few times," Darcy admitted.

"Details, woman! I want details."

"Actually, our waitress is giving us dark looks. I think it's time to pay our bill and move on."

After paying the bill, the two young women strolled slowly toward Darcy's car, laughing and talking as only old friends do. As Darcy unlocked her car, Clare heard her phone ring. Knowing the caller could only be Blaine, she fished it out of her bag as quickly as she could.

"Where are you?" he demanded as soon as she said hello.

"You'll never guess," she said with a laugh. "Darcy picked me up, and we've just had the most delightful time over lunch."

Darcy watched as her friend turned away and lowered her voice. Clare's smile disappeared, and she seemed to withdraw into herself. She wasn't exactly arguing, but she did seem defensive about something. Clare turned farther, and Darcy swallowed a gasp. She'd wondered why her friend had begun wearing such heavy makeup; now she knew. In the bright light of sunshine on snow, it was clear the makeup hid a huge dark spot that seemed to cover most of the right side of Clare's face.

Clare was quiet on the ride back to her condo. Several times Darcy asked if she was all right, and Clare insisted she just had a headache. They pulled up in front of the condo, and Clare scrambled to get out of the car.

"Clare?" Darcy said as Clare stepped to the curb. Clare looked back at her and she spoke softly. "If you ever need me, I'll come."

* * *

David was in the front room chatting with Evan and Karlene when Darcy emerged from her bedroom. She'd dressed in a calf-length skirt of heavy velour that swished against a pair of high-heeled boots as she walked. She'd paired the skirt with a brightly patterned, long-sleeved shirt and added tiny gold hoops to her ears. A shoulder bag matched her boots. David had told her to dress up for their celebration of her contract.

Evan whistled when she walked into the room, and David's eyes spoke their approval. David moved to stand beside her. He took her hand then turned back to speak to Evan, continuing a conversation started before Darcy entered the room. "I think you're underestimating Pauline Prescott. She's cut from a different cloth than her father."

"That may be," Evan conceded. "But it strikes me that there's some-

thing fishy going on for the county attorney to assign her to prosecute a case this big, especially with her brother handling the defense."

"Is that legal?" Darcy gasped.

"I suppose it's legal," Evan grumbled, "but I'm not sure how ethical it is."

"I saw Clare today, and she seemed excited about her husband defending someone named Skidmore in a murder trial. Is that the case Blaine's sister is prosecuting?"

"It's a high-profile case because the victim was wealthy and well known in the state," David said.

"I haven't heard anything about it."

"I hadn't heard about it either until several months after it happened," Karlene told her. "The papers were full of it right while I was in the hospital, but I wasn't reading them or watching the news on television at the time. It's only been the past few weeks that it has been in the news again."

"The murder happened last spring, possibly before you arrived in Boise—I think around the week Karlene had her accident. A woman by the name of Lauren Tisdale was found dead a short distance from a hiking trail north of Boise. She'd been so badly beaten her face was unrecognizable and she'd been shot multiple times. It took almost a week to ID her. The case seemed to be at a standstill until a tip from a convenience store clerk led investigators to Leon Skidmore, a petty crook who usually goes by Skeet and who has been in and out of jail numerous times," Evan explained to Darcy.

"He used the woman's credit card to purchase gas in Elko." David shook his head, indicating his opinion of the suspect's intelligence. Darcy handed him her coat, and he held it for her while she slipped her arms into it.

"Have fun." Karlene smiled as Darcy led the way to the front door.

Darcy paused to turn back to ask Evan, "I know having that woman's credit card looks pretty suspicious, but it isn't enough to convict him of murder, is it?"

"No," Evan agreed. "Skeet's a thief, but he's never been convicted on any type of violence charge. He has a rap sheet a mile long for car and home burglaries, but it doesn't appear he has ever threatened his victims with a gun. It appears the county attorney's office is rushing this case to

trial prematurely, unless they've got some evidence the press hasn't caught wind of."

"Why would the prosecutor's office do that? It seems they'd want to be certain they could get a conviction before setting a trial date." Karlene sounded indignant.

"Jessop Bernard may be behind the rush to court. He's not only the victim's ex-husband but also a county commissioner. He's also up for reelection this year, which would explain why he might be pressing for a quick conviction."

"If Skeet is a petty thief, how can he afford to hire a high-priced attorney like Prescott? Clare told me Blaine's fee is big enough to enable her to quit her job." Darcy might not know a lot about legal fees, but she knew her friend was earning a good salary.

"That puzzles me too," David said. "I met Bernard once at the Prescott home, and he and Garrett seemed to be old friends, so I'm surprised Prescott's firm would consent to defend the man who's charged with the murder of Bernard's wife."

"Isn't the husband the first suspect in cases like this?" Darcy noticed that Karlene looked pale, and she was gripping the arms of her chair so tightly her knuckles had turned white. She hurried back to the woman's side and knelt beside her chair. "Are you all right?" she asked.

Karlene ignored her, focusing her attention on Evan.

"Yes, but Bernard wasn't around the day his ex-wife was killed. His girlfriend and several witnesses placed him in Sun Valley that day," Evan explained. He didn't seem to be aware of Karlene's state.

"The murder was the same day as my accident, wasn't it?" Karlene asked, and he turned toward her.

"Why . . . yes. I believe so." Evan's eyes locked on Karlene's pale face.

"That's where I saw him. He was at the campground when I stopped to visit the restroom and snap a few pictures. He was walking very fast toward the restrooms as I left the women's side. I stopped to avoid bumping into him, but my camera struck his arm. I apologized, but he just kept walking, so I left."

Chapter 12

"YOU SAW SKEET THAT DAY?" Darcy shuddered.

Evan moved closer to Karlene. "It wasn't Skeet you saw that day, was it?"

"No." The woman trembled as though suddenly chilled. "It was the other one. The one we saw on television last week. I never connected the names."

"Jessop Bernard." Evan spoke the name as though it confirmed something he'd suspected all along.

"How could he have been at a campground a few miles from Boise and at Sun Valley too?" David left his place beside the front door and moved closer to the others.

"Somebody lied, or Bernard has a double. I think a trip to the sheriff's office might be a good idea about now." Evan smiled reassuringly at Karlene and rose to his feet. "I'll get our coats. It might be a good idea to take your camera with us," he added.

"That's it! That's why someone tried to break into my house and why he ran me off the road. He wanted my camera! Bernard must think I took his picture that day." Karlene seemed more angry than scared now.

"Did you take his picture?" David asked.

"No." She hesitated. "I don't think so. Not on purpose, anyway. I might have him in a shot I took from the trail earlier, but I was so far away I don't think anyone could identify him in the picture. I didn't mean to include them in the picture, but after I pushed the shutter, I realized there was a couple on a lower loop of the trail. A man was leaning over another figure I assumed was a woman. Thinking they

were indiscreet lovers, I turned my attention in another direction. What if the man was leaning over a dead body?"

"Did you get the picture developed?" Darcy asked. "It's amazing how much photos can be blown up without losing detail."

"No, my camera is one of those new digital cameras, and I usually download the pictures to my computer. I haven't thought about my camera since the accident, but I'm pretty sure I don't have it anymore."

"What makes you think you don't have it anymore?" Evan demanded to know.

"It wasn't with the items the hospital returned to me after the accident."

"We'll see if it was found at the accident scene." Evan sounded doubtful. He turned to David and Darcy. "You two go ahead with your plans for tonight. I'll give the sheriff a call. I know him pretty well from when we were both rookies."

Darcy reluctantly left the house with David. She no longer felt like celebrating. They were almost to the restaurant where David had made reservations when David said, "I wonder if I should call Pauline and tell her what we learned tonight."

Attempting to overcome the pang of jealousy that the mention of Pauline's name produced, Darcy hesitated before speaking. She trusted David and believed him when he said he wasn't romantically interested in the other woman, but she couldn't quite believe Pauline felt the same lack of interest toward him.

"It might be better to wait until we talk to Evan again and learn whether the sheriff accepted Karlene's story."

"You're right. It's just that I would hate for her to look foolish during her first big case for the prosecutor's office. I suspect her brother would like nothing better than to publicly embarrass her."

"You don't like Blaine, do you?" Before David could respond, Darcy chuckled. "I spent months avoiding mentioning him to you, thinking that because he's Pauline's brother, you would defend him."

"That's why you dodged the subject every time I asked about your former roommate. That reminds me. I think your friend might be in serious trouble. I know several women who dated Blaine, and they all ended up with mysterious injuries. His sister used to sport frequent bruises, but she'd never admit their source. Then one day while we

were in high school, Blaine attacked Pauline behind the stadium. He thought they were alone, but I'd only left her long enough to collect some gear. When I got back and saw him punching and kicking her, I reacted violently. I'm ashamed to say I gave him a taste of his own brutality. I was dismissed from the high-school football team because I refused to apologize. Instead, I threatened to hit him twice as hard if he hurt her again."

"That explains the rude comments he made about you the night you rescued me from Mr. Carlson."

David laughed. "I think Blaine's dislike for me is part of the reason Pauline encouraged her family to believe she and I were dating." Darcy joined his laughter, but after a few moments she sobered.

"Clare was wearing a lot of makeup today. I think it was hiding a large bruise on her cheek. Do you think she's really in serious danger?"

"Unfortunately, yes. Blaine has an explosive temper, and he doesn't take responsibility for his own failures. He resents the favoritism he feels his parents—especially his mother—have always shown to their two older children. He could never see that Pauline was as neglected as he was."

"I don't know what to do. I warned Clare over and over that Blaine isn't all he claims to be and that she shouldn't take his abuse. She's so in love with him and in denial that she won't accept anything I say."

Darcy slowly became aware that they were parked in front of the restaurant where she'd once worked. Any other time she would have enjoyed seeing some of the people she'd worked with, especially arriving with David. Now she doubted she'd be able to eat a thing.

"I can cancel the reservation." David held his phone in his hand.

"It's all right. It's just that celebrating my contract doesn't feel as important now when I think of Karlene and Clare both being in danger."

"Let's put both of them out of our minds for an hour or two." There was sympathy in David's voice. "You saw Clare this afternoon, and she was fine. Evan was with Karlene, and I trust him to take care of her. Getting that contract is no little thing in my mind; it means you'll be staying right here where I can see you almost every day."

The hostess greeted Darcy with a hug, and several of the waitresses came to their table to say hello before their dinner was served.

At first, both Darcy and David pointedly talked of other things, but by midway through their entrées, they were again discussing the possibility that Karlene could place Jessop Bernard in the campground near where his ex-wife's, Lauren Tisdale's, body had been found.

"I don't remember much about the stories surrounding their divorce," David said. "But I do remember reading something in the paper about her being an heiress and that she'd never used her husband's name."

"Women keeping the names they're born with, especially if they're famous or come from a family with a prestigious name, is a pretty common occurrence," Darcy pointed out.

"True. And some women can't wait to shed an ex-husband's name along with the marriage."

"That's kind of sad, isn't it?" Darcy aimlessly twirled her fork through the food still on her plate. "Most people grow up with a sense of excitement and anticipation concerning marriage. And I think most people believe their marriages will endure for at least all of this life. Yet look at how many marriages end prematurely with broken dreams, hate, and animosity."

"Selfishness plays a big part in broken marriages as does a failure to plan ahead. My mission president used to say marriage is like everything else in our lives: a failure to plan is the same as planning to fail. He said those who don't have a plan for money management never have enough money to meet their obligations, just like those who don't make plans to deal with moral temptations succumb to those temptations. I really believe that those who rush into marriage without adequate courtship, agreement on major issues, or an understanding of each other's expectations are going to get hurt emotionally and quite likely financially too."

"My parents always stressed the importance of being equally yoked, especially where our faith in God is concerned." She would have said more, but she caught the sound of her cell phone ringing. Pulling it from her coat pocket, she frowned on seeing the name of one of her students appear on the ID screen.

"Miss Olsen?" a tentative voice responded to her greeting. "Mom gave me your number and said to call you. She goes visiting teaching

to your house. And . . . well . . . your house just blew up, and she was afraid you and Sister Roper were in it."

"What!" Darcy couldn't believe what the boy was saying. It had to be some kind of sick joke. But Andy Jacobs, one of her brightest students, wasn't the kind of boy who would make up a wild story. He was in her English class and had always seemed to be levelheaded, if a little shy.

"Mom already called the fire department. Now she's talking to Sister Roper's daughter."

"I'll be right there." She snapped her phone shut and rose to her feet.

"What is it? You're as white as a ghost." David stood, too, and placed an arm around her. Quickly she explained.

David paused only long enough to toss a couple bills on the table before escorting Darcy toward the door.

Evan and Karlene arrived minutes after David pulled onto the street where flames shot thirty feet above Karlene's house. David pulled over half a block away to allow a fire truck to pass, and shut off the engine. "We'll have to walk the rest of the way," he said.

Darcy nodded her head and scrambled from her side of the truck before David could reach her to open her door. For just a moment Darcy experienced déjà vu seeing the flashing lights and firemen unrolling their hoses. The crowd standing in the street and on porches was far larger this time. Last time there was little damage, but this time there was little hope anything belonging to her or Karlene could be saved.

A car with the sheriff's department logo emblazoned on its side passed them, and Darcy recognized Evan and Karlene through a window. David took Darcy's hand, and they hurried forward to join their friends as they stepped from the car parked in front of a hastily erected roadblock. Tears were streaming down Karlene's cheeks. Darcy enfolded the older woman in her arms and held her for long minutes.

The older of the two officers who had sat in the front of the cruiser motioned for the two women to return to the backseat of the car. "We don't know what we're dealing with here yet," he said. "It might be best for the two of you to stay out of sight."

Darcy couldn't help a surge of anger nearly overcoming her as she thought of her clothes, her books, pictures of her family, lesson plans, and so much more gone. She heard a little hiccupping sob escape Karlene's lips and felt ashamed of her self-pity for her own losses. For her friend, it was so much worse: a lifetime of mementos, business records, her computer, furniture, everything.

"I'm so sorry," she murmured as she wrapped her arms around Karlene.

"It's so much to lose. I can hardly take in the enormity of it," Karlene whispered. "Yet I feel such thankfulness that we weren't in the house—that we weren't killed."

Darcy felt her own emotions well to the surface. Choking back tears, refusing to let them fall, she faced how narrow their escape had been. "What if you hadn't remembered about taking that picture? And what if Evan hadn't insisted you go see the sheriff tonight? And if David hadn't offered to take me out to celebrate . . ."

"I think the Lord was watching out for us." Karlene smiled faintly then her smile faded as she turned once more to stare out the window at what had been her home.

Frantic pounding on the car window startled Darcy until she recognized Karlene's daughter, Anne, standing beside the car. She opened the door, and Anne scooted inside to hug her mother. Her cheeks were wet, and she looked as though she'd merely thrown a coat over her pajamas. "Mom, I was so scared when I couldn't find you. One of the officers assured me no one was trapped inside, but I couldn't see you, and I know you don't go out in the evening."

"I was with Evan. He had some business to conduct and insisted I go with him."

"Well, I'm glad he did. He saved your life. Brother Thompson called me, and he was pretty shaken." Anne seemed to suddenly notice Darcy's presence and asked, "Did you go with Mom and Evan?"

Darcy shook her head. Karlene said, "She had a date tonight with David Schoenfeld." Her voice was almost back to normal.

"One of my students called me." She looked through the glass, searching for a glimpse of David. She hoped they hadn't gone to Evan's room over the garage to try to save his belongings. Even though she

could see that the structure was still standing and a stream of water was pouring from a fireman's hose onto the roof, it was likely damaged and might still burst into flame. Almost as though her thoughts had magically drawn him to her, David appeared out of the darkness and confusion. Evan hurried toward her, and the older officer who had arrived in the patrol car with Evan and Karlene walked beside him.

The officer opened the driver's door and asked how they were doing.

"We're fine," Karlene assured him, her usual confidence reasserting itself. "Is the house a complete loss?"

"I'm afraid so." Evan had leaned over the officer's shoulder to speak to Karlene. "You'll need to call your insurance company right away."

"I hadn't replaced my car yet, so I don't need to worry about that, and I was notified yesterday that the replacement check for it is in the bank. What about Darcy's car?"

Karlene's question caused Darcy to jump. She hadn't given her old Escort a thought. Even before the officer said it was a complete loss, she knew it was. It had been parked in the driveway next to the house. The Escort was old and in frequent need of repairs, but it was hers, and she loved it.

Her shoulders sagged. Where would she live now, and how would she get back and forth to school? She didn't even have clothes to wear to work on Monday, even if she could get there.

"Don't worry. It'll all work out. Your car can be replaced." Karlene patted her hand as though she sensed Darcy's gloomy thoughts.

She lost far more than I did, and she's trying to comfort me? Darcy attempted to shake off her self-pity. If Karlene could be optimistic, she could too.

"We need to get you ladies out of the cold," the officer said. "There's nothing you can do here tonight." He didn't add that the bomber might still be in the area and the women might become possible targets if he'd meant for them to die in the explosion and they hadn't, but Darcy sensed that thought was behind the officer's anxious expression.

"Mom will come with me," Anne said. "Darcy can come too if she doesn't mind sleeping in a sleeping bag on the floor."

"No, ma'am," the officer said with a stern look toward Anne. "The county will arrange a place for Mrs. Roper and Miss Olsen to stay. The fire inspector says preliminary assessments indicate this fire was arson, and in light of the other events that have come to our attention, I'm taking both women into protective custody."

Chapter 13

"YOU'RE TAKING THEM TO JAIL?" Anne gasped.

"Oh, no, dear," Karlene said. "The sheriff doesn't mean that at all. He only means he'll find us a safe hotel room. It's best this way. If I stayed with you, I might put you and the children in danger."

"You mean someone really is trying to kill Mom?" Anne's face revealed her shock and verified that she hadn't believed her mother's previous assertions.

"Yes, Anne," Evan interjected. "There's reason to believe this fire was an attempt on your mother's life. It's best that she stay at an undisclosed location until the investigation is complete."

"But how will I know she's all right? Will she be able to call me?"

"I'll arrange for phone calls. Now, if you don't mind, we'd best be on our way." He held the door for Anne to exit the car. She reluctantly climbed out and stood at the curb with hunched shoulders as the car drove away.

As the car sped across town, Darcy opened her cell phone to place a quick call to her parents. In case the fire was on the news or they tried to contact her, she needed to let them know she was safe and would be in touch in a few days. Her mother's quick gasp followed by tears brought her father to the phone.

"I'm fine, really," she told him. "The sheriff's department is merely taking us to a safe house as a precaution." After a tearful farewell, she considered calling Clare. *Chances are I'd get Blaine instead of Clare, and he'd find an excuse to keep her from talking to me anyway.* She closed her phone and put it back in her purse.

* * *

Darcy looked around the cramped room she and Karlene were to share for an unspecified length of time. It boasted two beds a little wider than twin beds with faded maroon bedspreads, separated by a one-drawer nightstand. A long, low dresser with a nineteen-inch television took up half of its surface, and a tiny round table with two uncomfortable-looking chairs completed the room's furniture. A door led to a small, no-frills bathroom, and a single narrow window looked out over a busy street.

The young deputy who escorted them to the room apologized for the spartan quarters. "It's all the county can afford on short notice. Sheriff Langton said he'd work on finding something better. He said, too, that you shouldn't use the phone in this room in case your calls might be traced."

"The room is fine, and we don't plan to make any calls." Karlene sank wearily onto the nearer of the two beds.

"The sheriff said to give you this." The young officer handed a bag to Darcy. She accepted it, and without looking inside, set it on the dresser while she set the security chain on the door as the deputy left.

When the two women were alone, they looked at each other, communicating a multitude of thoughts and feelings without speaking. "I propose we go to bed and try to sleep now," Karlene said with obvious weariness in her voice. "Hopefully we can sort it all out tomorrow."

Darcy picked up the bag the officer left, and after checking its contents, she began divvying up the toothbrushes, flannel pajamas, and hairbrushes the bag contained. As she put the items in the small bathroom, she was pleased to note there was a hair dryer in a wall mount.

A knock on the door startled them awake in the morning.

When Darcy finally opened the door a crack, she discovered a deputy bearing a cardboard breakfast tray. He set the tray down and informed them that though the hotel had no room service, a deputy would bring them meals. He was about to leave when Darcy asked, "Is it all right to use my cell phone? I understand about the room phone, but cell phone calls can't be traced, can they?"

"Actually, miss, with the right equipment, cell phone calls can be traced, but there's no harm in brief calls, like under a minute. However, as a precaution, unless you are placing a call, leave your cell phone off." At least she'd been able to let her parents know she was safe, but she'd have to leave long chats with Clare until after the bomber was caught. She'd probably have to wait anyway since her charger was one of the casualties of the fire and her phone battery was almost dead.

After the deputy left, Darcy and Karlene sat at the small table doing their best to eat a fast food breakfast neither one wanted.

"We can't go to church, so I suppose the next best thing is to see if we can get *Music and the Spoken Word* on TV." Karlene reached for her crutches.

"I'll do it." Darcy jumped up and fiddled with the television until she found a channel that carried the program. As the sound of the great organ on Temple Square filled the room, she felt her spirits rise. A glance at Karlene told her the other woman felt it too.

* * *

Evan arrived Sunday afternoon accompanied by the deputy who had conducted them to the hotel. He entered the room carrying two small suitcases. "Anne collected a few things she thought you might need," he announced as he walked through the door. Darcy was thrilled when she learned one of the cases was for her and that it contained clothes, toiletries, and a few books along with a thin laptop. She'd been trying to reconstruct lesson plans using the tiny tablet and pen from her purse.

"David thought you might have use for the laptop," Evan said.

"The sheriff said it was okay for you to use the computer, but you shouldn't give out this address or use your own user name or Mrs. Roper's in any correspondence," the deputy said. "Mr. Schoenfeld sent you a note with passwords and things like that so you can access the new accounts he set up for you." He handed her an envelope.

"What about my job? I'm a teacher, and I've just started my first contract. I really need to be at school tomorrow."

"We've discussed this," Evan said. "Sheriff Langton doesn't think you're in danger except as someone who might lead the people

responsible for Karlene's accident and the burning of her house to her. He has agreed to allow a deputy to escort you to school tomorrow and return you here after your last class. That's conditional, of course, on your agreement not to discuss anything to do with Mrs. Roper with anyone."

"Not even David?"

"David knows what is going on. Just be sure you can't be overheard."

When Darcy arrived at Boise High School the next morning, she was inundated with expressions of sympathy. It seemed everyone had heard about the fire. She acknowledged the kind remarks directed toward her but resisted everyone's attempts to discuss the cause of the fire or the whereabouts of Karlene.

By the time her first three classes were over, she was exhausted from trying to steer her students away from the fire to parts of speech and the exploits of Lady Macbeth. She was hungry, too, and tired of the fast food deliveries she had survived on all weekend. Setting her cafeteria tray on one of the tables in the faculty room, she picked up her fork and began to eat.

"I was hoping to find you here." She looked up as David joined her at the table. "Are you all right?"

"I'm fine," she told him, "and very much in your debt. I'll pay you back for the computer as soon as I can."

"Don't worry about it. When you're able to replace the items you lost, I'll take it back. I've been planning for some time to get one of those little notebook computers anyway."

"I really do appreciate the use of it."

David looked around and lowered his voice. "Is Karlene all right?"

"Yes. A female deputy is staying with her until I get back."

"Evan is staying with me. His apartment wasn't destroyed, but it sustained quite a bit of smoke and water damage. He said he called Karlene's insurance company for her, and an investigator was due to arrive this morning. He said to tell you not to worry about expenses right now; Karlene's house is well insured, and you'll be reimbursed for your losses."

"I really haven't been worrying about the items I lost. My dad contacted his insurance agent about my car. I'm not ungrateful either

for Anne's thoughtfulness in sending me some of her clothes along with the ones she sent for her mother. I just wish they fit a little better. I'm several inches taller than Anne. I especially wish I could sneak out of here and buy a pair of shoes. High-heel boots are not designed for standing in front of a classroom all day."

"I wouldn't want to try it." David chuckled. "But I think I can solve that problem. There's a computer here in the faculty room. Go online and order whatever you need from a local department store, and after school I'll go pick the items up and have Evan deliver them to the sheriff's office for you."

"Do you think it's safe for me to use my credit card?" Her spirits lifted, though she tried to avoid getting her hopes too high.

"I don't know why not. Even if someone is clever enough to trace your credit card purchases, the information on your account would only lead them to the ruins of Karlene's house."

* * *

Karlene drummed her fingers on the small hotel room table. Darcy suspected that if her legs were completely healed, she'd be pacing the floor. "I'm just so tired of these four boring walls. I'm also tired of being told the sheriff's department is working on it every time I question Evan or one of the deputies about their investigation concerning Jessop Bernard's whereabouts the day his ex-wife was murdered."

"Did they find your camera?"

"No. It isn't among the items collected at the crash site, and there's so much snow in the canyon now that a search there would be a waste of time. I'm afraid if it were found now, it would be useless anyway."

"So it's just your word against Bernard's that he was in the campground that day?"

Before Karlene could answer Darcy, a tap sounded at the hotel room door. It was followed by Evan identifying himself. Karlene released the chain, and Evan stepped into the room followed by Sheriff Langton. Evan went straight to Karlene's side.

The sheriff smiled at her. "Good news. Bernard's alibi for the time of the murder admits she fell asleep right after the two of them returned to their room at about five on the morning of the murder and that she

didn't awake again until midnight. The coroner puts the time of Lauren Tisdale's death around six that evening, so that leaves plenty of time for Jessop Bernard to have driven to the recreation area and returned to Sun Valley before she awoke."

"What about the other people who said they could vouch for Mr. Bernard being in Sun Valley?" Darcy asked.

"We haven't been able to locate Ramon Monterosa, who claims he was with Bernard all evening, but the woman Monterosa was with has a big drug habit and claims she doesn't remember anything about that day. She thinks they played golf until late in the afternoon, but there's no record they were even at the club that day. The bartender at the hotel where Bernard and Monterosa claim they spent the evening remembers seeing Monterosa with another man, but it was a busy night, and he can't swear to the man's identity. He does insist, though, that it was Bernard who ordered drinks sent up to his room around seven. He claims Bernard is a frequent visitor to the hotel and that he often orders drinks over the phone. The county attorney decided there was enough circumstantial evidence that, with an eyewitness as well, it would be feasible to issue a warrant for Bernard's arrest."

"The sheriff picked up Mr. Bernard this morning. He's probably already made bail by now, but there's no reason to think he'll come after you." Evan stood with an arm around Karlene, but he spoke to Darcy. "This case is probably going to drag on for several months, maybe longer, and the sheriff's budget can't support putting you both up indefinitely. Some decisions need to be made."

Darcy couldn't see that anything had really changed. "With Karlene as the only person who can place Jessop Bernard near the crime scene at the time of the murder, isn't she still in danger?"

"My thoughts exactly," Evan said. "I've been doing some work for the department, and the sheriff and I have devised a plan for her protection. Turning his attention back to Karlene, he said, "With your permission, dear, I suggest we spend a few months at my cabin."

"But Evan . . ."

"Now if this were my first proposal, I'd keep it nice and private, but I already asked and you already agreed. We just need to speed up our plans a little."

"Well, yes, but we haven't told our children yet. I don't know how they'll feel about us marrying on such short notice."

"I've already talked with Nora and Mary; they've no objections. They just want me to be happy and for you to be safe. I get along fine with Anne, and I'm sure her first concern will be your safety too. I've arranged for a private plane to meet us at the airport at noon. We can be married tomorrow and just disappear while the investigation continues."

Feeling slightly bemused, Darcy listened to the exchange between the older couple. She'd suspected for a long time that the two would marry, but she'd never considered that she and Karlene would be so abruptly separated. She suddenly faced the overwhelming task of finding a place to live, acquiring a new car, and replacing all she'd lost. A sense of loneliness swept over her. She'd never been all on her own before; first there had been her large, caring family, then Clare, and then Karlene. Now she would be alone.

"Darcy." Her attention was drawn back to the other people in the room. "David has been searching for an apartment for you. He's found a couple for you to look at. He'll meet you at the sheriff's office in about an hour." Maybe she wasn't as completely alone as she had feared.

* * *

Seeing David leaning against a wall watching the door as she entered the sheriff's office a short time later brought a lift to Darcy's step. He hurried toward her, and it seemed the most natural thing in the world for his arms to go around her and tighten in a reassuring embrace.

When she found herself fastening her seat belt in David's truck a few minutes later, the world felt bright and new. Bidding Karlene farewell had been difficult, but she had no qualms about turning the woman's care over to Evan. The two seemed well suited to each other. Taking a deep breath, she looked around like a prisoner set free. Only small heaps of dirty snow remained from the previous week's storm. The sun was shining, the air smelled clean, and a row of small, black-capped birds perched on a nearby fence.

David put the truck in gear, smiling his lopsided grin, and Darcy could swear her pulse leaped into the danger zone. "I've done a little

checking for you on apartments near the high school," he said. "I've found two that look like good possibilities."

"Thank you. I wondered how I was going to get around without a car to check out any available apartments."

"I might have a lead on a car for you, too," David said. "I told you my brother just left for the MTC. He asked Dad to sell his car for him to help out with his expenses. It's a four-year-old PT Cruiser, but it's in good shape and runs well. If you think you'd like to look at it, Dad will drive it here, or we can go there to see it anytime."

"Wonderful! I'd love to see it, but I think I'd better wait until the insurance company reimburses me for my Escort."

David passed the high school and slowed down to make a turn. "Which apartment do you want to look at first? The first is a two-bedroom in a fairly new apartment complex. There are three college students living there now, and they're looking for a fourth roommate. The second is a studio apartment in an older home that has been converted into four single apartments."

The young women looking for a roommate seemed pleasant, and the one she'd share a room with was LDS, but Darcy had a good hunch about the smaller single apartment. Something about the small space felt right. The attic room with its sloping ceiling had two dormer windows on either side. The major portion of the long room held a comfortable seating arrangement with a small kitchen at one side. At the other end of the single room, a folding screen hid a bed and wooden wardrobe. The apartment was within walking distance of the school and a small convenience store.

The only drawback seemed to be two men who shared the apartment beneath hers. Long hair and tattoos didn't instill a great deal of confidence in her. But they seemed friendly without being intrusive and from all appearances seemed to be on good terms with the elderly couple who lived in the apartment next to theirs. And she really liked the small studio apartment. A quick estimate of her living expenses convinced her she could afford it if she put off replacing her car until the insurance check arrived.

* * *

Clare looked up from the bread she was kneading. She'd followed the recipe down to the last detail this time, so there shouldn't be anything Blaine could find fault with. She wished she could call Darcy to make certain she'd done everything right, but Blaine had threatened to take away her phone if she placed any calls without his permission. It was just that she'd never baked bread until this past week, and her first two efforts had been dismal failures. Darcy's mother baked delicious bread, and Darcy had learned from her mother, so her advice would be helpful.

Clare battled with a touch of resentment. She didn't know why Blaine had suddenly decided she should bake their bread; his mother certainly never had. She wished, too, that Blaine and Darcy didn't dislike each other so much. She missed Darcy and often thought longingly of all the things they could do if Blaine didn't fly into a rage every time she mentioned her friend.

Blaine didn't understand her need for another woman to talk to. He rarely spoke to his mother and made no secret of his contempt for his sister and sister-in-law. He didn't even like his secretary. It seemed Clare was the only woman he cared for at all—and sometimes she wondered if he even liked her. She didn't doubt he loved her, but it seemed she never did anything that met his standards.

She was chiding herself for her bout of self-pity when she heard Blaine's telephone ring from the other room. She cringed when she heard Blaine's voice grow hard and cold. It was a warning sign she'd learned to recognize. It was too bad she wasn't as adept at learning which things set off his temper. At least *she* wasn't drawing his ire this time.

A crash came from the living room, followed by the sound of breaking glass. Clare winced. Carefully she finished shaping a loaf of bread dough and dropped it into a pan then began cleaning off the sticky dough that clung to her fingers. Before she finished, Blaine appeared in the doorway wearing a coat. Angrily, he slammed a fist against the side of a cupboard.

Clare turned startled eyes toward her husband. "What's wrong?" she asked with a wave of fear shortening her breath.

"He killed himself! The stupid fool hanged himself!"

"Who?" She placed her arms protectively across her abdomen.

"Skeet! That fool, Leon Skidmore, that's who!" A blow landed against her cheek. A second drove into her chest. The blows kept

coming, and all she could think was that no matter what, she had to protect her baby. Her arms cradled her abdomen. She couldn't raise her arms to ward off Blaine's angry fists, and he was deaf to her pleas to stop. His hands gripped her shoulders, viselike, on her tender skin as he shook her back and forth before flinging her aside. Her head hit the refrigerator, and she slid toward the floor. She was barely conscious of the apartment door slamming shut before a silent blackness settled around her.

Chapter 14

"HERE, CATCH!" DAVID TOSSED A plastic bag toward Darcy.

She caught it and laughed, hugging the bag to her. "Careful," she warned. "Those shoes cost a hundred bucks."

"I wish *I* had new hundred-dollar running shoes!" He pretended to pout.

Darcy shook her head. "I can't believe how well Evan got to know me in such a short time. I think he really understands what running means to me, and he knew I'd spend my money on necessities for my apartment and on clothing I need for work before buying running shoes. With all he has going on right now, I should be the one giving him a gift—a wedding present—instead of the other way around!" She clutched the bag tighter, remembering the envelope Evan had tucked into her pocket minutes before they'd departed from the hotel in the sheriff's car. The note insisted that the hundred-dollar bill in the envelope was meant to replace her lost running shoes.

It took three trips for the two of them to haul Darcy's purchases up the stairs to her new apartment. Though the apartment was furnished, she'd needed to purchase sheets, blankets, towels, groceries, and other household supplies. They'd even visited the store where she'd purchased her cell phone to buy a new battery charger, which she immediately plugged in. When they finished putting everything away, they sprawled side-by-side on the sofa to catch their breath.

"What's that?" She pointed to a box that David had hauled up the stairs on his last trip.

"I don't know," David admitted. "Ted Keely brought it over for you. He said Evan told him you'd be looking for an apartment and that you'd have to start from scratch to furnish it."

Darcy slipped off the sofa to kneel beside the box and laughed when she saw the odd assortment it contained. She reached for a clock radio that looked well used. After examining it a moment, she set it on the floor and pulled an equally battered electric hand mixer from the box. Holding it up for David's inspection, she was startled to hear her phone ring.

She picked up the phone and held it to her ear. At first all she heard was a strange whimpering sound. "Help me, Darcy." She recognized the whispering voice as Clare's.

"Clare, what is it? Are you hurt? Where are you?"

"My apartment . . . baby . . ." Only silence followed.

"What is it? Has Clare been in an accident?" David slid to the floor at Darcy's side.

"I don't know what's wrong, but I think whatever it is, it's bad. She said she's at her apartment and needs help."

He reached for her phone and put it to his ear. He listened a moment then said, "Hang on, Clare. We're on our way." He handed the phone back to Darcy. "Keep the line open while I drive."

They grabbed their coats but didn't stop to put them on as they raced out the door and down the stairs. Darcy scooted across the bench seat, and David had the truck started before she had her seat belt fastened.

"Which way?" David asked when they reached the end of the street. She gave him directions, and he stepped on the gas.

"Clare mentioned a baby. Do you suppose she's having a miscarriage?" Darcy chewed at the inside of her cheek, wishing traffic would thin so that David could drive faster.

"Maybe you should call an ambulance and try to call Blaine," David suggested. "We don't have a key to get in their apartment when we get there." He handed her his phone so she could keep the connection with Clare open on hers.

Darcy briefly wondered if Clare's situation had anything to do with Blaine's temper and whether she'd be bringing more grief to her friend by calling him, but hoping she was wrong, she explained the situation to the 911 operator then keyed in the number to Blaine's office and waited. She was about to give up when a female voice answered. "Blaine Prescott's office. Mr. Prescott cannot take your call right now. He's—"

"This is an emergency. Tell him Darcy Olsen is calling and that his wife is unconscious. He needs to meet the ambulance at his apartment."

"Oh," the woman gasped. "He's seeing a client at the jail, but I'll contact him immediately. I better let his father know too."

The trip across town seemed to take forever. When David parked across the street from the condo, a paramedic unit was already blocking the entry. They rushed toward the door and arrived at Blaine and Clare's apartment just as a man dressed in jeans and a sweatshirt used a pass key to gain entrance. No one challenged them when they followed the paramedics inside. Darcy looked around but didn't see Clare.

"She's in here," one of the paramedics called from the kitchen. The other paramedic and Darcy and David followed his voice.

"Clare!" Darcy screamed when she saw her friend's still form lying on the floor. Her eyes were swollen shut, her body was twisted awkwardly, and blood spattered the refrigerator and pooled on the floor. She started forward, but David held her back.

"Let the paramedics do whatever they need to do," he said, pulling her close to his side.

He was right; she needed to stay back. Biting down on her clenched knuckles to keep from crying, she watched the two paramedics bend over her friend, checking her respiration and pulse. One opened the large black case he'd lugged up the stairs.

When the first paramedic pulled a hypodermic needle and a plastic bag of clear fluid from the case, Darcy spoke up. "I think she might be pregnant."

"This won't injure the fetus if she is," the medic promised as he began setting up the IV.

"Where's my wife? What's going on?" Blaine yelled as he stormed into the kitchen. He was followed by a deputy and his father. Two men followed with a stretcher.

"Stay back," the paramedic kneeling beside Clare snapped as Blaine tried to push him aside.

"She's my wife!" Blaine attempted to insert himself between the paramedic and Clare.

"Blaine!" This time it was Garrett Prescott who spoke in a reprimanding voice to his son. "Let the professionals help her. You can find out what happened and comfort her after they've stabilized her."

"Sir," a paramedic said while facing Blaine. "We're almost ready to transport your wife. We'll meet you at St. Luke's. She's unconscious, but her vital signs are improving. Only a doctor can tell for sure, but I think she and her baby will both make it."

Blaine froze. Darcy could see the shock on his face and guessed he hadn't known Clare might be pregnant. As she stared at him, she noticed several small flecks of coppery red on Blaine's shirt. Were they blood or specks of tomato sauce? She lifted her eyes and met those of the deputy standing on the other side of Blaine. Without saying a word, she knew he'd noticed the spots and was asking himself the same question.

As the stretcher was wheeled past them, Clare's eyes opened to thin slits. "Darcy," she moaned. Instinctively, Darcy reached to clasp her hand. Clare's fingers intertwined with hers, clinging with surprising strength.

Darcy kept pace with the stretcher as Clare was taken down the elevator to the waiting ambulance. She wanted to ride with Clare to the hospital, but Blaine shoved past her, breaking the fragile connection between the friends. He followed Clare into the back of the ambulance.

* * *

Time moved slowly for Darcy. She hadn't been allowed to see Clare since she'd arrived at the hospital. The Prescotts had insisted that only family be admitted to Clare's room or given information concerning her condition. They said it was to protect her privacy, but Darcy suspected it was to protect Brett's campaign from any adverse publicity. Three days had passed, and Darcy's conviction that Blaine had abused Clare only grew.

David met her after her last class on Friday to drive her to the hospital on what they both suspected would be one more futile attempt to see Clare. Darcy carried a pink-and-lavender pot filled with a violet plant. During her lunch hour, she'd walked to a small shop that carried a few plants to purchase it for her friend. They were walking up the front steps of the hospital when a voice hailed David.

"Hi, David." Pauline caught up to them. "Is this the English teacher you told me about at practice last week?" She turned to Darcy as though

expecting an introduction. A flicker of surprise crossed her features. "I know you. You were one of Clare's bridesmaids. Darcy, isn't it?"

"Yes. How are you, Pauline?" Darcy smiled brightly, doing her best to be friendly to Blaine's sister.

Pauline smiled charmingly at Darcy. Her smile didn't seem to be concealing any animosity, so Darcy relaxed a bit. "I assume you're on your way to see Clare?"

"Yes, but I doubt they'll let me in. They seem to be enforcing some kind of family-only rule."

"Why would they do that?" Pauline seemed genuinely puzzled. "This is my first opportunity to visit Clare, but I understand her accident wasn't too serious, and she's healing well. Surely she'll want to see her childhood friend. I understand you were college roommates too."

"Yes." Darcy didn't elaborate.

David pushed the button to summon the elevator. In a casual voice, he turned to Pauline while they waited. "I read in the paper that you were prosecuting Skeet Skidmore for the murder of Lauren Tisdale. Since he's dead now and Jessop Bernard has been charged with the crime, will you continue to handle the case?"

"I'll be assisting with the case, but I won't be the lead attorney." Darcy heard a slight edge of disappointment in the other woman's voice.

"Isn't your father defending Bernard?"

"Yes, their friendship goes way back." A soft chime sounded, and the elevator door opened before them.

As they approached Clare's room, Pauline waved away the nurse who approached them. "We won't stay long."

"I'm sorry, but I'll have to ask you to leave. Mr. Prescott insists that only family be admitted to his daughter-in-law's room." The nurse attempted to stand firm.

Pauline laughed as she produced an ID badge. "I'm Pauline Prescott, and these two are close family friends that I assure you my sister-in-law will be delighted to see."

"I'm sorry. I didn't recognize you, Miss Prescott. Of course, you may go in." The nurse sounded flustered.

Pauline linked an arm through Darcy's and led the way. As she burst through the door, she called out, "Look, sweetie. Guess who I found lurking outside." Her forward stride faltered. Releasing Darcy's arm, she

stepped toward the bed where Clare lay. "What happened to you? Mom said you slipped on something in the kitchen and hit your head against the refrigerator. Those cuts and bruises look a lot more serious than a simple collision with a kitchen appliance."

Tears slipped from Clare's eyes, and she looked away.

Though the blood had been washed away, Clare was a terrible sight. Both eyes were black, and her face was a swollen mass of lumps and bruises. Splotches of black adorned her arms and the patches of skin not completely covered by the hospital gown she wore. A large bandage was wrapped around her head and an IV ran into her arm.

"Clare? I've been so worried about you." Darcy touched Clare gently on her shoulder.

Clare turned slowly and grasped Darcy's hand. "I prayed you would come."

"I would have been here sooner, but the medical staff wouldn't permit anyone other than family in your room. Pauline made an exception for me today." She hid her opinion concerning the ban on visitors by moving several large, expensive floral arrangements aside to make room for the small pot of violets she'd brought for Clare.

"Thank you, Pauline," Clare whispered.

"I was so scared when I found you on the floor in your apartment," Darcy added. "I thought I'd go out of my mind when I wasn't allowed to see you here at the hospital."

"You found me?"

"You don't remember David and I arriving with the paramedics?"

"Blaine said—"

"What happened?" Pauline moved closer to Clare. She looked angry. When Clare didn't answer her question, Pauline went on. "Did my brother beat you?! I've seen a lot of crime scenes, and I've seen accident victims. You need to tell me or the police what happened."

"I-I fell." Clare wouldn't look at Pauline.

"With a little help from my brother, I suspect." Both the statement and the bitterness in Pauline's voice surprised Darcy. Maybe Pauline really was nothing like Blaine.

"Did Blaine do this to you?" Darcy looked into Clare's eyes. Clare made no admission by so much as a nod of her head, but the scared look in her eyes was all the confirmation Darcy needed.

"Clare, listen to me," Darcy pleaded. "You don't have to be Blaine's punching bag. Leave him before he manages to kill you."

"You, of all people, know I can't leave him. He's my husband, and marriage is meant to be forever."

"Not when your life is in danger!" Pauline said.

"You're both being dramatic. My life isn't in danger. Blaine loves me, and he promised . . ." She stopped as though recognizing that by revealing Blaine's promise she'd be admitting he was at fault for her injuries.

"What about your baby? Are you pregnant?" Pauline carefully kept her voice low.

"Yes." Clare's lip trembled. "Blaine wouldn't have . . . If he'd known . . . I should have told him about the baby, but I was waiting for the right moment. The doctor said I didn't lose the baby, and everything appears normal."

"I'm happy for you. You'll be a wonderful mom." Darcy beamed at Clare, and Clare returned the smile.

"I'm so excited. I want half a dozen babies. I always envied your large family, and I want my children to have lots of brothers and sisters."

"Wow! My first nephew or niece. How soon will you know if the baby is a boy or a girl?" Pauline asked. "I can't wait to start buying tiny pink or blue stuff."

David offered his congratulations too, and the four young people talked quietly about babies and families until Clare grew tired. "We'd better go," he suggested.

"Yes, mommies-to-be need lots of rest." Pauline straightened Clare's pillow.

Darcy gave Clare's hand a gentle squeeze. "I'll be back. I won't let the dragons at the gate keep me from checking on you. Now get some rest. Call me anytime. I'll set my phone on vibrate so that if I'm in class, I'll still be able to know you're calling." In a softer voice she added, "Clare, you don't need to stay with that monster. Think about your child, if anything."

Pauline led the way to the elevator. Darcy followed uneasily, her head low. She felt a growing sense of gloom. Clare had married a psychopath, and Darcy had no idea how to help her. Once they were inside the elevator, she was startled by the fierce way Pauline stabbed

the mezzanine button. They rode in silence, but once they reached the first floor, Pauline pointed toward the cafeteria.

"We need to talk." It wasn't an invitation.

David and Darcy exchanged glances as they followed Pauline. When they were settled around a table in an empty corner of the cafeteria, Pauline took a deep breath and looked directly into Darcy's eyes. "How long has this been going on?"

"Almost from the beginning of their relationship," Darcy snapped. Pauline seemed to be blaming her for Clare's condition.

"Why haven't you done something about it?"

Darcy had been angry for a long time, and seeing Clare lying helpless and battered in that hospital bed had ignited her temper. Being questioned by Blaine's sister in such a high-and-mighty manner added fuel to the inferno.

"He's your brother! Why hasn't your family done something about his vicious temper? I'm reasonably certain Clare isn't the first woman that brute has terrorized. If you'd had him committed to a psychiatric facility years ago, Clare wouldn't be lying in that bed covered with the black-and-blue souvenirs of her husband's devotion."

"Take it easy." David pressed a restraining hand on Darcy's arm.

"No. She's right, David." Pauline's shoulders slumped. "My parents dismissed his attacks on me as sibling rivalry. They arranged with the parents of his previous fiancée for her to quietly transfer to another school. There have been rumors from time to time that he 'played rough' with the women he dated. Even if Clare can be persuaded to bring charges against him, Dad will find a way to have them dismissed. You can be sure no photos were taken when Clare was brought into the trauma center."

"You're probably right about your father covering up charges," David agreed. "But photos *were* taken." He held up his cell phone.

Chapter 15

"YOU TOOK PICTURES?" PAULINE AND Darcy reacted simultaneously.

"Yes, both at Clare and Blaine's apartment and a few minutes ago in her hospital room. They won't be as good as pictures taken with a regular camera, but it was all I had."

"It doesn't matter." Darcy slowly shook her head. "You heard Clare. She won't press charges. She's already making excuses for Blaine."

"I'd like a copy of those pictures," Pauline told David. "It's probably true there's nothing we can do now, but I think I'll wander down to the emergency room and see if I can collect any statements or discover whether photos were taken and if so, who took charge of them. No matter what promises a spouse abuser makes, it's only a matter of time until he breaks them."

"How can we just wait for it to happen again? There must be a way to keep Clare safe!" Darcy wanted to scream. There had to be something she could do for Clare.

"Sorry, sweetie." Pauline looked almost as angry as Darcy felt. "Women have made a lot of strides in achieving equality before the law, but no one can force a woman to love wisely." She stood, and Darcy watched her stride from the room with purposeful steps.

"We'd better go." David's words penetrated her thoughts.

"I guess so." She stood, feeling listless and sad.

On the ride back to her apartment, Darcy questioned David about Pauline. "Would she really take Clare's side against her own brother's?"

"Yes, I believe she would. I don't want to betray a friend's confidences, but Pauline has plenty of reasons to want to see Blaine locked

up. She doesn't hold Brett or her parents in high regard either. Garrett and Danielle were never around much while the children were growing up. They took annual trips to Europe, and he was a frequent speaker at colleges and conventions. Though they sometimes took Brett with them, Pauline and Blaine were usually left in the care of various staff members. Pauline is a year older than Blaine but not nearly as big. She suffered a great deal of abuse from him until she went away to law school."

"Why did she come back? Couldn't she practice law somewhere else?"

"Her father laughed at her decision to go to law school, but when she was accepted at Harvard, he made her sign a contract agreeing to work for his firm until her college expenses were paid back. I think pride held her to their bargain."

* * *

Teaching high-school students was proving as rewarding as Darcy had expected. She wasn't so much older than her students that she couldn't enjoy their jokes or appreciate their exaggerated allegiance to the icons of their culture. Their bright minds were a source of delight—particularly in the creative writing course she taught juniors and seniors.

Darcy threw herself wholeheartedly into her work in an attempt to avoid thinking about Clare or Karlene, and when the weather permitted, she ran at the high-school track. Most mornings David ran with her, and there was usually a sprinkling of other serious runners on the track as well.

When she and David had returned to the hospital the day after their visit with Pauline, Clare was no longer there. The only information they could get was that Clare had been released. They had been turned away when they attempted to visit her at the condo she shared with Blaine. Telephone calls went unanswered. Running kept Darcy from dwelling on the frustrating situation.

She was more fortunate in her concern for Karlene. The older woman had called to let her know that they had arrived safely at Evan's cabin and that though there was no cell phone service in the area where they were staying, they'd discovered a delightful place

nearby to eat breakfast a couple of times a week where they could make calls from a landline. She promised to call regularly. They'd talked a few minutes longer, and Darcy expressed her regret that she'd been unable to attend their wedding.

"Evan's daughters took care of everything," Karlene had told her with a laugh. "Mary lives in Las Vegas, and she even selected a beautiful white dress for me to wear. She and the dress were at the temple waiting when we got there. Of course, Evan and I were both sealed to our first spouses so our wedding wasn't for eternity, but it was lovely to be married for time in the temple anyway. If you ever decide to elope, I can guarantee that the Las Vegas Temple is a lovely place to do it." They'd both laughed, and Darcy assured her friend that she had no intention of eloping.

"My parents would kill me if they weren't able to be at my wedding," she'd joked.

Darcy's thoughts returned to Clare's situation as she completed her second mile. "I know it's wrong to hate anyone, but I *hate* Blaine," she admitted to David as they continued to circle the track at a slow jog. The weather had turned warmer, and the first hints of spring were in the air.

"Pauline is aware of the problem, and she drops in to see Clare when she can. She thinks things have been going more smoothly for her the past few weeks. She had a long-overdue talk with her mother, and Danielle has promised to take Clare shopping for maternity clothes, though she doesn't agree the situation with Blaine is as dire as Pauline claims. She actually said there's nothing unusual about marriage partners occasionally striking each other and that if Blaine did hit Clare, it's just one of those things Blaine and Clare will work out as they adjust to marriage."

"That's ridiculous!" Darcy sputtered. "My dad has never hit my mother. I'm sure of it."

"My dad accidentally knocked my mom out once. Dad's really ticklish, and once mom sneaked up behind him to tickle him. He jerked his elbows back and caught her across the bridge of her nose. They still tease each other about it." He chuckled.

"That's not what I mean," Darcy protested.

"I know." David's voice turned serious. "Spousal abuse is a serious problem. At nearly every conference priesthood session as long as I

can remember, the prophet or one of his counselors has stressed the point that men who abuse their wives are not worthy to hold the priesthood or have a temple recommend and that both husbands and wives have a right to feel safe in their homes."

"Clare told me once that she has vague memories of her parents fighting a lot before her father died, but she never mentioned that their fighting was physical. Being a small child when he died, she doesn't remember much."

"It's surprising how much children remember, subconsciously if not consciously," David said. "Remembering her parents' anger with each other might account for why she accepts Blaine's violent outbursts." He paused a moment then added, "On a more pleasant note, I heard from Evan this morning. He sounded happy."

"That's great. It's been several days since I last talked to Karlene. I really miss her. Did he say when they'd be back?"

"No, but he indicated that he's still doing some consulting on the case for the sheriff's department and that a trial date has been set for September. He advised me to keep an eye on you and to check the room over Karlene's garage regularly for any sign of a break-in. He was concerned because Anne has had a couple of suspicious experiences—worrisome enough that her husband has started letting his German shepherd sleep in the house. He's concerned that Bernard might discover where Karlene is and make another attempt to silence her. He said, too, that Sheriff Langton is going to contact the kids who were first on the scene after Karlene's accident and see if any of them will own up to taking Karlene's camera."

"Do you think one of them took it?"

"I don't know. She said she doesn't think she put it back in her bag after she left the picnic site, so it was presumably lying on the front seat. It wasn't on the list of items recovered from the car, so it might have flown out of the car and could be anywhere."

"It'll probably never be found, and Karlene will be the only witness who can testify that Lauren Tisdale's ex-husband was there that day." Darcy couldn't help thinking that if Bernard killed his ex-wife, he had nothing to lose by killing Karlene, too.

"One other thing Evan wanted to tell me is that the autopsy report on Skeet Skidmore indicates he might not have killed himself." David

spoke softly as though concerned that one of the other runners on the track might overhear him.

"What do you mean? He's not still alive, is he?" She didn't think anything about Skeet Skidmore made much sense. She'd puzzled over where a small-time crook got the money to pay Blaine a large retainer. Then there was the matter of Lauren Tisdale's credit card; how did it wind up in his hands? And why did he kill himself just when it appeared someone else might be charged with the murder?

"No, he's dead, but Sheriff Langton found something about the timing of his death suspicious and ordered an investigation. Evan said Blaine refused to cooperate with the investigation, claiming a conflict of interest because his firm is now representing the second defendant in the case."

"It's strange they'd both choose the same lawyer to represent them," Darcy mused.

"Actually, Blaine represented Skeet, and Garrett is representing Bernard. Evan has a theory that Garrett and Jessop expected Blaine to lose Skeet's case and that he was being paid well to do so."

"That's sad, but I wouldn't put anything past Blaine." She headed for the side of the track. "I'd better get dressed. I've only got forty-five minutes until my first class."

"Go ahead. The door is unlocked. I think I'd better start some of my track team toward the locker room too. I don't want them running too long with the temperature this low." He began a faster jog to catch up to two girls who were among the dozen or so students who ran most mornings.

Darcy showered and dressed quickly. Glancing in the mirror, she noted the bright color in her face, one of the benefits of running in the cold. Feeling invigorated, she headed up the stairs to the staff room for an orange and a bagel before heading to class.

She opened the door and barely caught a glimpse of motion before something hit her hard on the head and she crumpled to the floor. Barely conscious of the sound of footsteps quickly receding down the hall, she attempted to drag herself to where she could see who had hit her, but it was no use. By the time she reached the hall, it was empty.

"What happened? Are you all right?" Another teacher, one she

recognized but really hadn't gotten to know well, approached her from the stairwell. She took Darcy's arm and helped her to her feet.

"Thanks. I'm all right. Did you see someone running down the hall?" She attempted to dust off her slacks and straighten her sweater.

"Did someone trip you?" the other teacher asked. "This needs to be reported to the principal."

"I'm not sure what happened. I opened the staff room door and was hit so fast I didn't see anything. I went down, and by the time I collected myself enough to look for the person who hit me, he was gone."

"I still think you should . . ." The woman's voice trailed off, and Darcy turned to see what had alarmed the woman.

There on the floor was Darcy's purse with its contents spilled across the floor. Papers were everywhere, a lipstick tube was almost at her feet, and her phone was barely visible under a sofa. Still in shock, she reached down to gather up a pen and her wallet.

She straightened, holding the items in her hand as though unsure what to do with them.

"Are they yours?" the woman asked.

"Yes. I brought my purse and the papers I graded last night up here before going down to the track to run. They were in my locker."

"I'm calling the principal." The woman stepped to a phone and pushed a few buttons.

Darcy opened her wallet. She didn't carry much cash with her, but the few bills inside seemed to be about what she remembered should be there. Gathering up her empty purse, she placed the pen and her wallet inside before kneeling to begin gathering up her other possessions. The principal and a security guard arrived while she was picking up the scattered papers.

"Are you missing anything?" the principal asked.

"I'm not sure," she admitted. "Nothing seems to be missing, but I don't remember exactly what was in my purse. A letter from my mother might be missing; I don't see it anywhere."

The security guard picked up her cell phone and handed it to her. She looked at it, feeling slightly puzzled. The display on the front showed that it was on. "I'm sure I turned it off before leaving it in my locker. I don't have a good case, and I've dropped it several times

while running, so I turn it off and leave it in my locker when I'm on the track."

"The locker was forced open with some type of metal pry," the security guard called from the other side of the room.

"We've had a few instances of students stealing from teachers in the past," the principal admitted. "But usually the thefts have involved teachers who left purses in plain sight or valuables that have been left on car seats. I don't recall ever having a locker pried open before."

"Your locker is the first one in the row," the security guard pointed out as he wandered back. "I think you walked in just as the kid was getting started. There's no telling how much damage and theft might have occurred if you'd arrived later."

"Were you injured when you were knocked down?" the principal asked. When she indicated that she was fine, he asked her to drop by the office to fill out an incident report before the day was over. He glanced at his watch and stepped briskly from the room with a promise to send someone to repair her locker.

Several other teachers arrived, but not wishing to be the center of attention or to make any more explanations, Darcy gathered up her purse and papers and hurried to her first period class. She almost succeeded in putting the incident out of her mind during the classes she taught, but she found her eyes wandering more than once toward the desk drawer where she'd placed her purse.

Following her fourth period class, she made her way back to the staff room to eat her lunch. She was almost finished when David arrived. He sat beside her and immediately asked about the rumors he'd heard concerning her encounter earlier that morning. When she finished, he said, "I'm glad you weren't hurt and that the thief was interrupted before he actually took anything. It appears to have been a random rather than personal attack. Most of our students are really good kids, but with twelve hundred teenagers, there are always a few that cause problems. I hope this won't cause you to have second thoughts about teaching."

"No, I haven't changed my mind about teaching. I love working with young people, and I'm really not worrying about a repeat of this morning's incident. I plan to get a case for my phone and keep it with me when I run from now on, and I'll just be more careful not to carry

valuables in the future. I guess I just don't understand why he didn't take the cash or my wallet or why he would turn on my phone."

"I don't understand that either. You'd think after all that effort . . . Anyway, I have a few students I need to work with right after school, but I could drop by later and take you to the mall to pick up a case for your phone."

"I can take a bus. I feel guilty tying up so much of your free time running me to the grocery store and on errands like this."

"Don't worry about it. I like being with you, and playing chauffeur lets me spend more time with you than I otherwise might."

"All right. Six okay?"

"Sounds good."

"Oh, and don't eat first. I'll have dinner ready when you get to my apartment."

* * *

Twisting the key in the lock, Darcy opened the door and stepped into her apartment. It was tiny, but she was glad she'd decided to rent it. She looked around at the few furnishings she'd purchased and those her mother and sisters had sent. There was a feeling of home that never failed to lift her spirits when she stepped inside. Today something felt different, but she couldn't put her finger on what it was. Everything looked the same. The apartment was tidy, just the way she'd left it, and there was a faint scent of lavender in the air from her favorite air freshener.

She hung up her coat and changed into jeans before checking her refrigerator and cupboards for the ingredients for a shepherd's pie. While browning the meat with chopped onions, she pulled out instant potatoes and grated cheese for the topping. As she reached back into the refrigerator for eggs, something caught her eye. Just showing beneath the edge of the refrigerator was a piece of paper.

She set down the eggs then used a fingernail to coax the paper out of its hiding place. It turned out to be nothing more than one of those slick little advertising inserts that come with bills. She was about to throw it in the trash when she remembered this one had come with her

credit card bill, and she'd tucked it back in the envelope, wondering if she might be able to take advantage of the Disneyland discount offer next summer. "How did it get over here?" she muttered aloud.

A wave of unease swept over her. Slowly, she walked to the small table she used as a desk. On top was a filing box. The credit card envelope filled the first slot. A chill seemed to fill the room. The credit card bill should have been at the back of the file. She always filed it under V for Visa.

A for AT&T should have been in front. With shaky fingers she thumbed through the few bills in the file. There was no cell phone bill.

Chapter 16

"I DON'T LIKE THIS." DAVID paced the few steps possible in Darcy's small apartment. "First your locker was broken into this morning, and everyone assumed a student was responsible. What if it wasn't a student? Then someone entered your apartment and snooped through items on your desk."

"I can't be sure someone went through the bills on my desk, but I don't know how else to explain my missing cell phone bill and that paper being under the fridge when I'm certain I put it back in the envelope."

"I might be way off base, but Evan said Anne was bothered by a pushy salesman who would have forced his way inside her house but for the dog who suddenly got very aggressive. Then, too, a few days ago while she and the children were out and the dog was locked in the backyard, she returned to find that the lock on her front door had been forced and her husband's desk drawers ransacked. It appears someone is trying to find Karlene through the two people most likely to be in touch with her."

"Oh! That's why my cell phone was turned on! Whoever broke into my locker at work was looking for the area Karlene might have called from. When he found my phone password protected, he threw it aside and came to my apartment looking for a phone bill."

"That's what I'm thinking too."

"He struck out at Anne's house because her husband receives and pays his bills online. Karlene does that too. I remember them mentioning that they liked the convenience of dealing with expenses online because their banks kept tidier records of expenses paid than they could with manual bookkeeping. But how will taking my phone bill help anyone

locate Evan and Karlene? There's nothing on the bill to identify who each caller is, and Karlene always calls from a business phone."

"Anyone who knows anything about you will assume that callers with a Tacoma area code are your family. Local calls can be cross-referenced and easily eliminated. It's the calls coming from other area codes that will catch the thief's attention, and even if they lead an investigator to businesses, they will still reveal the general area where Evan and Karlene are hiding. Finding an exact address may be as simple as checking land deeds for the area or talking to people at the various businesses who might, as people in small towns often do, know exactly where to find Evan's cabin."

"They're in danger, aren't they?" Darcy chewed on the inside of her cheek. "I wish we could call to warn them."

"I'm thinking I should drive up there to let them know they could be in danger. Evan gave me directions before they left in case of an emergency, and I'm a little bit familiar with the area. Dad used to take my brother and me fishing not far from there."

"I'm going with you."

"It could be dangerous."

"I don't care. I can't sit here doing nothing."

"All right. I won't argue, and I'll enjoy the company. Dress in sweats like we were going to the YMCA to workout and pack a change of clothes and what you might need for a night or two in your gym bag. I'll make a few calls while you change." David pulled his phone from the holder at his waist.

Darcy hurried behind the screen that separated her bedroom from the rest of her apartment and pulled out her warmest fleece sweats. The snow was nearly gone from even the north sides of buildings in Boise, but farther north they could still run into late winter storms. Even without fresh snow, Boise's accumulation of snow was usually less than in other parts of the state. She dumped the contents of her gym bag into her clothes hamper and reached for a complete change to shove back inside it. She added the flannel pajamas she'd worn following the destruction of Karlene's house, her toothbrush, her running shoes, and a few toiletries. It only took a moment to don her parka and stuff her phone and wallet into its zippered pockets.

"I'm ready," she announced, stepping from behind the screen just as David tucked his phone back in its case.

"As soon as we get back, I'm installing a better lock on this door," David said as Darcy locked her door behind them.

In minutes they were pulling into the parking lot at the YMCA. Being Friday night, the lot was full, and it took several passes to find a parking spot.

"I didn't think we were really coming here," Darcy said in surprise.

"We're not." He jumped out of the truck and had her door open in seconds. He helped her out then reached for her bag as a large van pulled to a stop behind his truck and two heavily bundled people jumped out, leaving the engine running.

"Quick! Jump in." David tossed their gym bags into the van and slid across the seat, indicating she should follow.

As she settled into the passenger seat she watched the two people they'd passed enter the YMCA building, gym bags in hand. David pressed on the accelerator, and the van leaped ahead. It took a few seconds for Darcy to realize there was something familiar about the van. "Was that Brother Keely and his wife?" She strained to see behind them.

"Uh-huh." David made a sharp turn onto the freeway ramp. He merged with traffic headed east then flashed her a quick grin. "I've always wanted to do that. Besides, I promised Genevieve weeks ago that I'd help her get Ted to the gym."

"I assume that little maneuver was the result of one of your phone calls, but do you think Brother Keely's old van is the best vehicle for such a long trip? I understand we have a steep mountain pass to cross."

"No worries. I set up a couple more vehicle switches just in case someone tries to follow us."

Darcy couldn't help laughing. "I think you've been watching too much TV." She teased David about his super-detective tactics, but she found herself growing nervous anytime a set of headlights stayed visible in the side mirror for more than a few miles.

Two hours later at a service station on Blue Lakes Boulevard in Twin Falls, they switched vehicles with David's parents then headed north in a PT Cruiser. Darcy looked around, spotting a pile of blankets and a cooler in the backseat.

"Nice car," she commented in a dry voice.

"You said you were interested in checking it out," David said, using the same dry tone. "And you know how moms are; no matter

the crisis, they have to make sure their kids are warm and have something to eat. How about peeking inside that ice chest to see what goodies she packed for us. I don't think either of us did justice to the shepherd's pie you made."

Soon they were munching on ham sandwiches, which they washed down with hot chocolate poured from a large insulated jug.

In Shoshone, they made their last vehicle trade. This time when David pulled behind a grocery store on the north end of town, Darcy lost no time shifting their bags to a four-wheel-drive SUV while David and his cousin transferred the blankets and ice chest.

"My, you were a busy boy while I changed my clothes back in Boise." She stifled a giggle as she leaned back in the comfortable bucket seat.

"I only arranged the first two swaps." David chuckled. "Dad called his brother and arranged for my cousin to meet us here with his new SUV he's been bragging about. According to him, it gets great gas mileage, has GPS, a terrific stereo, and is like riding in an armchair."

Warm air blasted from the heater, and light classical music played on the stereo. Darcy felt relaxed and comfortable. Even though she hadn't dated that much, she knew there was something special about the way she felt when she was with David. There was the chemistry thing, which she tried not to think about too much. She even suspected she was falling in love with him, but what impressed her about their relationship the most was that she liked him, really *liked* him. She'd noticed first how comfortable she felt running with him, and she was constantly learning how many other interests they shared, but now she thought having someone she could confide in, someone she trusted completely, someone who shared her convictions, was more important than anything they did together. As she contemplated these things, she felt herself drifting off to sleep.

She awoke when the SUV stopped. She looked around to see they were parked at a service station. "We're not out of gas," David assured her before opening his door. "We'll be going over some mountainous roads from here on, and I'll just feel more comfortable with a full tank. Besides, I thought it might do both of us good to stretch our legs."

Following his lead, she stepped out of the car and was instantly hit by a blast of cold air. Mounds of snow towered over her head and

ringed the service station. She found she had to step carefully to avoid falling on the slippery space between the gas pumps and the building that housed a small store.

While David filled their vehicle, she visited the restrooms and purchased snacks, picking out mostly packaged trail mixes and dried fruit, but she couldn't resist a bag of Oreos, a treat she'd learned David had as great a weakness for as she did. Walking back to the vehicle, she glanced up and down the street and felt a little thrill when she realized she was actually in famed Sun Valley.

David was no longer standing beside the SUV, and she wondered if she should return to the little store. The air was sharp and cold, and she stood gazing at the brightly lit street before noticing a chain of lights on the mountainside. Loud music and laughter came from down the street, and a steady stream of cars flowed both ways on the street before her.

"You'll freeze. Better get inside," David said. He held her door, and she scrambled inside, suddenly anxious for the welcome warmth of the vehicle's heater. She watched David hurry around the front of the SUV and slide back into the driver's seat.

"Here." He tossed something onto her lap before turning the key in the ignition. She glanced down then burst into laughter before scrambling through the bag that held her purchases. "I bought one too." She held up both bags of Oreos.

Munching on the cookies, they continued north. Darcy found a radio station that played livelier music, and they talked about school, David's mission, their families, favorite books, and movies they'd enjoyed. Eventually, their attention turned to Karlene and Evan.

"Do you think they're all right?" Darcy asked.

"I hope so. I just wish there was a way to contact them immediately."

"There aren't many cars on this road, but every time I see another vehicle headed the same direction we are, I worry it might be someone trying to find them or that we might be leading the person who blew up Karlene's house straight to her. I know I teased you about the steps you took to disguise the vehicle we're traveling in, but I'm glad you did it."

"There's a shorter route from Boise to Sun Valley, but the road isn't as good. Still, I worry that whoever broke into your apartment and stole your cell phone bill may have taken that route and is several

hours ahead of us. But worrying won't do any good. Why don't you see if you can sleep for a while? We'll be there in a couple of hours." David took his hand off of the steering wheel to place it on hers for a moment before returning it to the wheel.

"I should relieve you for awhile and let you sleep," Darcy offered.

"I'm okay. It's better that I drive since I've driven this road before."

It was a beautiful night with a nearly full moon turning snow-covered meadows and fir trees alike into glistening silver formations. The night sky sparkled like diamonds on black velvet. As they began the ascent up the mountain, the mounds of snow on either side of the highway seemed to grow taller. Occasionally, a break in the walls of snow revealed a steep drop-off that made her heart pound. Anyone sliding off the road would surely be lost until spring.

Darcy didn't go back to sleep. It was almost midnight when they passed Stanley and closer to one o'clock when they left the highway near the small town of Clayton. The road they entered could barely be classified as a road and had never been plowed. Ruts left by vehicles driving through the snow were the only positive signs that they might actually get through.

"Evan said we turn left after the second bridge." David leaned forward, concentrating on the snow-covered road and searching for landmarks. He drove across a bridge that spanned the Salmon River before continuing. "He also said this road is a private road but that it's used by fishermen in the summer and snowmobilers in the winter and that there are only a handful of cabins along it."

Several times the SUV lurched, and Darcy found herself clutching the armrest, but at last David spotted the second bridge. He almost missed the road that branched to the left. There were no tire tracks, but Darcy could see where snowmobiles had made the turn. She worried about getting stuck in the snow, but David geared down into four-wheel drive, and the SUV continued on until they came to a gate across the road.

David jumped out, pulled a loop of wire up over the heavier of two posts, then lifted the smaller post from the loop that fastened it at the bottom. He signaled for her to move over to the driver's seat and pull the vehicle ahead. After she did so, he closed and fastened the gate, taking his place back behind the wheel.

They crossed a rise, and only a few minutes passed before they both spotted a cabin nestled in a grove of trees. There were no lights on and no vehicle in sight, but David said he was certain it was the cabin Evan had described. The snowmobile tracks went on past the cabin, disappearing over another hill. David turned into the space in front of the cabin and switched off the engine. "This has to be it," he said, but he didn't move to leave the SUV. They sat still, watching the house for several minutes, while the sound of the vehicle's engine died away.

"They're probably asleep."

"It doesn't look like anyone else got here before we did." They spoke at the same time.

"Come on. We'd better wake them." David opened his door.

He'd only taken a few steps when a voice said, "Hold it right there. Step away from your vehicle and keep your hands where I can see them."

Shocked, Darcy looked around, but she couldn't see the owner of the voice.

"Evan, is that you?" David called out but still did as he was told. "It's me. David. Darcy is with me."

"David?" A shadow carrying a rifle separated itself from the trees. "I never expected you to be coming to visit at this hour." The two men approached each other to exchange a hearty back slap before David returned to the truck for Darcy. Evan ushered them inside the cabin, where Darcy and Karlene had a turn to hug each other. Darcy nearly wept with relief seeing that her worst fears hadn't been realized. In fact, Karlene seemed to be in excellent health and extremely happy. She welcomed David and Darcy into the cozy cabin, and Darcy looked around in appreciation at the small but comfortable room decorated with log-style furniture, an abundance of brightly colored rugs, and a stone fireplace.

"What's up?" Evan didn't waste time asking for the reason for their middle-of-the-night visit, and David was equally quick to explain about the stolen cell phone bill.

"You should have called Sheriff Langton. He would have gotten a message to me through the sheriff in Challis."

"I thought of that," David said. "But when I called, I learned the sheriff is in Vegas at a conference, and I wasn't sure if I could trust

anyone else. No one seemed particularly concerned when Anne reported that her house had been broken into two days earlier."

"Anne? Is she all right?" Karlene grasped Evan's arm.

"She's fine," Evan assured her. "I learned of the break-in right after it happened, but I didn't mention it to you because it happened while she and her family were all out, and there was nothing to link it to a search for you. I didn't want to worry you."

"You still should have told me," Karlene grumbled.

"You're right, and this puts a different light on it. The burglar may have been looking for Karlene, or he may have been looking for Darcy's address." Evan frowned.

"Finding me wouldn't have been difficult. The newspaper and television newscasts at the time of the fire mentioned that I teach at Boise High School. Anyone could have simply followed me home from there," Darcy pointed out.

"The question is what do we do now?" Karlene asked, looking from Evan to Darcy and back.

"Assuming you weren't followed," Evan said, "it's going to take a little while for anyone looking for us to narrow the search down to this location. The property isn't registered in my name. When my first wife's father died, leaving this place to us, we put it in our daughters' names. I think we can safely sleep on it until morning then decide what action to take."

"Darcy and I will take the bedroom," Karlene decided. "You two can sleep out here; there are two sofas." She turned to Darcy. "You must be exhausted. Are you hungry, too? Should I fix something before we turn in?"

"David's mother fixed food for us, and we've been snacking on Oreos ever since we left Sun Valley. A place to sleep is all I want," Darcy assured her friend.

"How about you?" Karlene turned to David.

"I'm not hungry, but I am tired. Just point me toward one of those sofas." He grinned.

Chapter 17

IT SEEMED THAT DARCY HAD barely fallen asleep when a persistent buzzing awoke her. Her first instinct was to reach for her alarm clock, then, remembering she wasn't in her apartment, she sat up. Karlene was already up and pulling on sweats over her pajamas. From the other room she heard a rustle of sound, then the click of a closing door.

"What is it?" Darcy whispered.

"Probably just a pesky elk, but something tripped the alarm Evan set down by the gate. It goes off anytime the gate is opened, jumped over, or crawled through, but twice in one night is certainly unusual."

Darcy leaped from bed and reached for her shoes. If the person who cut the gas line and blew up Karlene's house was coming, she wanted to be wearing shoes.

The women rushed into the other room in time to see the shadowy shapes of Evan and David disappearing through the back door of the small cabin. Both were carrying rifles. Karlene didn't turn on a light, and in a whisper she cautioned Darcy to stay away from the windows. They waited for what seemed like hours, but the illuminated dial on Darcy's watch indicated only fifteen minutes had passed.

"Put on your parka," Karlene whispered. "We need to get to the snowmobile shed. If the intruder had been an animal, Evan would have returned by now."

Darcy followed the older woman's instructions, and when she was dressed in her outdoor gear, she followed her out the same back door the men had used. Moving silently in the deep darkness of the cabin's shadow, they crept toward a thick stand of trees. The sharp crunch of their steps in the frozen snow sounded extraordinarily loud, but Karlene

kept moving, and Darcy followed. They seemed to be following a path of sorts. It was darker now than the ride over the mountain had been, and Darcy was glad the moon had drifted behind a cloud, leaving them less visible to anyone who might be watching.

When Karlene paused beside a long, low snowdrift, it took a moment for Darcy to realize they were actually standing at the back of a shed that was burrowed into the hill on which they stood. She couldn't resist looking back the way they had come and was surprised to note they'd been climbing ever since they left the cabin. Either her eyes were accustomed to the darkness now or dawn was approaching. Through the trees she could barely make out the form of a man moving up the road toward the cabin. He carried what appeared to be a heavy object, perhaps a small suitcase, in one hand. She'd known finding Karlene and Evan might be dangerous, but now a terrible awareness of their vulnerability left her shaken.

Evan's voice carried in the clear, cold air as he ordered the man to identify himself. Instead the man disappeared behind a tree. A shot rang out. Silence followed.

After waiting several minutes, Karlene began inching her way forward once more, and Darcy realized she was circling the almost-buried shed to reach the front of it where the door was located. She watched her slide the last few feet then followed. She landed beside the older woman, who was preparing to punch in a code on a small electronic box to open a garage door. The area in front of the door was clear, and the snowmobile tracks she and David had followed earlier led to the door.

"Wait," Darcy whispered, touching Karlene's arm. "The noise will give away our location."

"So will our tracks. There's a clear path from the back door to here," Karlene argued.

More gunfire and shouting on the other side of the cabin brought the argument to a close. Breaking glass and the sound of bullets hitting metal added to the confusion. Karlene pressed the keypad buttons, and the door swept upward almost soundlessly. A large snowmobile was parked facing the open door, and Karlene ran toward it. Darcy noticed in passing that a Jeep was also parked in the shed

but paid it little mind as she leaped astride the snowmobile and clasped her hands around Karlene's waist.

The machine started on the first try, and the two women swept out of the shed with a flurry of snow following behind. They raced along a curve leading back to the road that passed in front of the cabin. Instead of turning toward the cabin, Karlene made a sharp right turn and sped away from it. Darcy wasn't comfortable with running away. If they stayed, perhaps they could help David and Evan in some way. On the other hand, they might only distract them. Evidently Evan had established an escape route for Karlene if she needed it and trained her in the steps she should take. But not knowing if David had escaped the gunfire or if he was lying in the snow wounded—or worse—seemed nearly unbearable.

When they reached a gate, Darcy hopped off the snowmobile. She knew just what to do, though it seemed harder than when she'd watched David release the other gate. After the snowmobile passed through it, she closed it again, hoping that if anyone followed, a fastened gate would slow him down.

Once Darcy was again behind her, Karlene pressed on the gas, and the machine lunged forward. They were climbing higher and at the same time seemed to be circling back toward the road.

"We need to get to a phone," Karlene said.

"I have my cell phone in my pocket." Darcy reached in to grab it.

"It's no use. There isn't any reception here," Karlene said with a hint of fear.

"Wait! Look there!" Darcy pointed to a figure moving through the trees behind the cabin. It became visible as it moved between the bare shapes of deciduous trees then disappeared behind pines. Someone seemed to be following the same path the two women had followed earlier. There was no way to tell whether it was the intruder or one of the men they cared about. A second movement on the trail caught their attention. It appeared to be following the first figure. Darcy clenched her fists in frustration. There was nothing she could do. Karlene was right. They needed to get to a telephone. She started to say so but stopped when a third figure appeared in front of the shed, moving back and forth as though looking for a way to gain entrance. The first of the

two men they'd been watching was almost to the shed now. He seemed to hesitate then pulled back into the trees. The second man left the path abruptly and disappeared into the trees too. Two shots rang out, followed by the stronger crack of rifle fire.

A line of bright light seemed to appear from nowhere in front of the shed that had housed the snowmobile. Darcy barely had time to recognize the streaks as flames before the shed exploded.

Karlene accelerated fast, leaving Darcy barely able to hold on. She heard the word *phone,* but the rest of Karlene's words were lost in the roar of the snowmobile.

Wildly threading their way through trees and around boulders, they eventually reached the road. Karlene increased their speed, and it was all Darcy could do to hold on. They arrived at a ranch house out of breath, and Darcy could tell by Karlene's stricken face that she was as worried about Evan as Darcy was about David. She'd been content to let her relationship with David move slowly, allowing them time to get to know each other. Now she felt a suffocating kind of grief. If she lost David, she wasn't certain she'd be able to go on.

Karlene pushed a doorbell while Darcy hammered on the door. When an older gray-haired man finally came to the door, Karlene brushed at her eyes while asking to use the phone. The man pushed the door open wider, "Come in, Karlene. What happened?"

A gray-haired woman came down the stairs, tying the sash of her robe. She went straight to Karlene and placed an arm around her shoulders. "Are you all right?" she asked.

"Sharon, I've got to call the sheriff." Karlene was shaking now.

"I'll dial for you. He's probably still at home." The woman punched in a number she knew well then handed the telephone to Karlene.

Darcy's eyes wandered around the room while she attempted to listen to Karlene's side of the conversation. It occurred to her that they were standing in an office and that the place they'd come to was the bed-and-breakfast Karlene and Evan had mentioned during their infrequent calls. Obviously they were on good terms with the proprietors and trusted them.

Darcy became aware that the older couple was looking to her for an explanation. "We—my friend and I—came to warn Evan and

Karlene that they were in danger. Then someone came with a gun and there was an explosion." She knew she wasn't making much sense, but all she could think about was getting back to David.

Karlene set the phone back. "The sheriff is on his way. He said he has a deputy who is closer than he is and will be here first." She picked up the gloves she'd set on the desk while speaking on the phone and turned toward the door. "Thanks for your help."

"You better wait for the sheriff," Paul advised.

"I can't. What if Evan and David are hurt? I need to get back there to see if I can help them."

"I can't wait here either," Darcy added.

"All right, just hold on a minute. We'll go in the Suburban. It's faster and will provide a little more protection." Paul reached for a heavy pair of boots. Once they were on his feet, he shrugged into the heavy parka his wife held out for him.

Paul led the way down a hall. Through a couple of open doors Darcy could see attractive bedrooms made up ready for guests. Darcy and Karlene followed Paul through a back door and outside to a parking area where several vehicles waited. They climbed into a large gray Suburban.

Just as they approached the road, a pickup bearing the insignia for the Custer County Sheriff's Office on its door flew past, leaving a swirling cloud of snow in its wake. Paul pulled in behind it, leaving just enough space to be able to see the road. If it weren't for the thick gloves she wore, Darcy knew she'd be chewing her fingernails. She stared out the window and prayed that David and Evan were safe.

The gate was open, and Paul frowned but didn't stop to close it. The pickup truck stopped beside the SUV. When the deputy stepped out of the truck and wasn't met by gunfire, Darcy left the Suburban and hurried to his side. "The explosion was around the corner," she told him. The deputy nodded and headed down a path that disappeared into the trees.

"You'd better drive around." Evan stepped from the side of the cabin and walked toward the deputy. Karlene was out of the Suburban and running toward him. He wrapped an arm around her and bent his head to give her a quick kiss on her cheek. "Take Darcy inside the cabin and wait for me," he told her.

"David? What about David?" Darcy ran after Evan. He stopped, and she stared in horror at his torn and battered parka. Soot and grime covered his face, and there appeared to be blood on his hands.

"David will be okay." At her sharply indrawn breath, he hurried on. "He isn't hurt, but he was closer to the explosion than I was. His ears are still ringing, and he looks worse than I do. He stayed with the body while I came back to wait for the sheriff."

Darcy sagged with relief. David hadn't been killed. "I want to go to him."

Evan shook his head and jumped into the pickup cab.

Darcy straightened as Evan's words penetrated the fog in her mind. Someone was dead. Suddenly she felt sick.

"I'm not staying here and waiting for someone to tell me what's going on," Karlene announced. "I only promised Evan that I would take the snowmobile and get to the closest telephone to call the sheriff if we were under attack or he checked on the alarm and didn't come right back." She started walking up the road in the direction the deputy's truck had taken.

Darcy ran to catch up with her. She wasn't staying behind either. If David was hurt but being macho about it, she would be there to make certain his injuries were properly cared for.

Circling the thick stand of pine that separated the cabin from the snowmobile shed, they reached the bend in the road. Their footsteps faltered as they caught sight of what had been a garage. The roof had collapsed, dumping a ton of snow over the blackened remains of posts, beams, the Jeep, and other unidentifiable black lumps that poked through the tumbled snow. An acrid odor hung in the early-morning air. It took a few seconds before Darcy became aware of Evan, David, and the deputy crouching beside a still form lying on the ground.

On hearing the crunch of snow behind her, Darcy started then cautiously turned her head to see that Paul had followed her and Karlene.

"The sheriff's truck is on its way up the lane," he said. "We best move out of the way."

The three of them moved to the side of the road as a second truck rounded the bend and pulled up beside the deputy's. Two men got

out and joined the three surrounding the body. A few minutes later, David and Evan walked to where the women waited.

The temperature was below freezing, and Darcy's feet and cheeks were almost numb. She looked at David and saw he was shivering and looked a little dazed. His coat was gone! Cuts and red splotches covered his face and hands.

"We need to get you warm!" She took his arm and hurried him back toward the cabin. He didn't protest.

"Darcy! David!" Evan called after them. "Take shelter in Paul's Suburban. Until we get a chance to check the cabin, it might not be safe to go in there."

"Why wouldn't it be safe?" Darcy changed her steps and headed for the large vehicle.

"There might be spilled gas. Anyway, with a broken door and windows, it won't be very warm in there." Evan was keeping pace with them while Karlene and Paul followed closely behind.

Paul was the last one to pile into the Suburban. He lost no time starting the engine, though it took several minutes for even a small amount of heat to begin to creep into the vehicle. Darcy spotted what looked like a blanket in the back and climbed over the seat to get it. Instead of a blanket, she found a couple of large towels which she wrapped around David's shoulders.

"Who spilled gas on my clean floor?" Karlene demanded an answer.

Evan sighed before beginning an explanation. "That fellow left the road and cut through the trees when I challenged him from the trees beside the cabin. We lost sight of him for a little while, so I left David watching the back door and started working my way around to the front. I figured we were too late when I heard glass breaking. I think he tossed something through a window."

David took up the story. "I hurried inside through the back door. It only took a minute to discover that the two of you were gone. I could smell gasoline and figured whatever our intruder had thrown was some kind of gas container. He probably meant to blow up the cabin, but he spotted the two of you on the trail leading to the shed and took off after you before igniting the gas. I didn't know if he was pursuing you or if he might be back to burn the cabin, so I dashed

back outside. I saw the trail leading up the hill and thought I saw something move. I began running. I reached the top of the shed in time to see him splashing gas against the building. I yelled at him, and he dropped the gas can to shoot at me. I don't know if the gas was ignited by his gun or if he deliberately lit it, but there was a line of fire down the side of his pants that led to the shed just before it exploded."

"You could have been killed!" Darcy wrapped her arms around him as though assuring herself he was safe and with her.

"The moment I saw those flames, I leaped as far away from that shed as possible. I think I landed in a bramble bush." He touched several tender spots on his face.

"I'm just guessing, but I think that when he found the cabin empty, he changed his mind about burning it," Evan speculated. "He probably noticed your tracks leading into the woods and followed you to the shed where he saw tracks going in but none coming out, so he splashed gasoline on the front of the building. You can't begin to know how grateful I was to hear the snowmobile engine off in the distance after the sound of the explosion had faded away."

"Why didn't that man hear the engine when Karlene first started the snowmobile?" Darcy wondered.

"I don't know," Evan admitted. "He had thick wool earflaps on his hat and the sound might have been covered by the gunshots we exchanged earlier. The area where the garage was is lower than the cabin, and the hill between the two might have muffled the sound. I didn't hear the snowmobile either until after the explosion."

"Someone was looking out for you," David added.

Paul shifted into reverse. "That young man needs those cuts looked after, and we could all stand a warm breakfast. The sheriff will know where to find you."

When they reached the inn, Sharon took over treating David's scrapes from her abundant first-aid supplies. She had a hot country breakfast prepared and waiting for them, too, replete with sausage and pancakes. Darcy settled next to David in one corner of a sofa and drifted asleep while conversation and speculation about the identity of their attacker continued.

She awoke several hours later when the sheriff and a deputy were

ushered into the room. After introductions, the sheriff took them one by one into another room to receive a formal statement from each person, after which they were allowed to return to the cabin to retrieve their belongings. While Darcy and Karlene packed, the men boarded up the broken window, and a deputy placed padlocks on the door.

David unlocked his cousin's SUV to load his and Darcy's small bags and his mother's cooler inside along with Evan and Karlene's luggage.

"Uh-oh," he groaned. "I'm in big trouble now." A shiny streak ran from near the taillight on the driver's side to the front mirror of his cousin's prized Escalade, and two holes punctured the rear door. The deputy who had accompanied them back to the cabin noted the damage in the notebook he carried.

When the two couples were at last settled in the SUV, David drove carefully down the road that had grown more slippery as the sun began to melt the snow. When he reached the highway, he asked, "Which way?"

"Left," Evan said. "I have a small two-seater plane waiting in Challis."

As they followed the winding highway into the small rural town, a cloud of sadness seemed to hang over the occupants of the vehicle. Darcy knew without asking that there would be no more friendly calls between her and Karlene until after the trial. Wherever the older couple went now, they would take no chances on being traced.

Chapter 18

A ROW OF TULIPS LINED the walkway leading to the house across the street from Darcy's apartment, and the trees in the neighborhood were showing their first pale-green spring color. Winter was finally at an end. Darcy took a few minutes to stretch before setting off down the street at a fast walk. By the time she reached the corner, she shifted to a jog. Instead of turning her feet toward the track, she headed toward the river and the parkway that followed its meandering course.

She missed David. They almost always ran together, and sometimes some of his track athletes ran with them, but today was Saturday, and she was running alone. He and his team were competing in Pocatello, and they'd left for their meet the previous afternoon. As she approached the river, her mind went back to that day almost seven months earlier when she'd run from the apartment she shared with Clare. After all this time, her heart ached as much as it had that day for their lost friendship.

There hadn't been a week since Clare was released from the hospital that Darcy hadn't tried to contact her. She'd reached Blaine a couple of times at first, and he'd insisted Clare was too busy to come to the phone or was sleeping. There was never an answer on Clare's phone. After a while, Clare's and Blaine's phone numbers were listed as out of service. Blaine's secretary refused to put her through to him. She'd gone to Clare's condo and had been turned away by the doorman. She'd even written letters but had received no answer. Pauline, who still played volleyball with David, was the only link she had with Clare, and with Pauline not on good terms with her brother, she had little news to share.

The water was running high in the river, and the grass was green. Several trees sported blossoms. It was a beautiful, peaceful place to run early in the morning. She wished she could relax and enjoy the spring sunshine, but she couldn't keep her thoughts off Clare. Karlene and Evan were another worry. Six weeks had passed since she and David had seen them off in the small plane Evan piloted. Evan had given no indication of where they might go, but she did trust him to protect Karlene until the trial. She just wished it were possible to talk to the older woman about her concern for Clare and to learn whether the man who had died while trying to kill her had been identified.

David had stopped to talk to Sheriff Langton to discover whether the body had been identified, but the sheriff declined to answer his question. He'd even tried to find out a little information through Pauline, but she was equally taciturn on the subject. The only scrap of information either of them had been able to glean was from a newspaper account that said the dead man hadn't been positively identified but was believed to be a former cell mate of Skeet Skidmore.

Darcy turned down a tree-lined path that curved near the river. She was deep in thought, trying to make sense of the connection between Skeet and the attacks against Karlene. As far as she could tell, there was no connection. Jessop Bernard was the man her friend had seen near where Lauren Tisdale was murdered, not Skeet. And Skeet was already dead when someone with a can of gasoline in his hands sneaked toward the cabin where Karlene was staying while she awaited Bernard's trial.

Darcy finished her run and decided to head home a different way.

The trek to her apartment seemed much longer than it had been as she ran the other way. Eventually she reached her street. She hurried forward, but as she drew closer to the apartments, she slowed her steps. Someone was standing on the front porch—someone who looked disturbingly familiar.

It can't be Blaine, she argued with herself. He doesn't even know where I live. Still, she found herself searching for Clare, who was nowhere to be seen. A silver Lexus was parked in the driveway behind the black PT Cruiser she'd purchased from David's dad after their trip to Challis. The PT was parked behind a Harley Davidson motorcycle. The vehicles belonging to the other tenants were either under the

carport roof in the backyard or away. The man who looked like Blaine was talking to one of her downstairs neighbors. Abruptly, the man turned away from her neighbor and climbed into the Lexus. He gunned the engine and backed out of the driveway, his tires squealing.

Darcy was torn. Should she run after the man? If he was Blaine, she might persuade him to let her visit Clare. On the other hand, after what he did to Clare, she didn't want to ever see or speak to the man.

The car tore past her at a speed that far exceeded the posted speed limit for the residential street. The driver didn't glance her way.

A splatter of rain hit the sidewalk in front of her, and she picked up her pace, wondering what had happened to the beautiful spring day she'd been enjoying such a short time ago.

To her surprise, someone held open the front door for her to come inside just as the overhead clouds released a deluge of spring rain. She looked up to see her neighbor grinning at her.

"Thanks!" she gave him a grateful smile.

"I thought that was you." The man she now knew was called Chad grinned, barely restraining an outright laugh at her expense.

She'd met Chad and Devon right after she first moved into her apartment, and though they were always polite when they happened to see each other, the two men who appeared to be in their late thirties or early forties had never made a move toward getting better acquainted, and neither had she. They were both gone a lot on their motorcycles, and though they'd held a couple of noisy parties, their paths hadn't crossed often. She suspected they were as leery of her appearance as she was of theirs. She wasn't exactly scared of the two men, but she'd seen little indication that she had much in common with them.

Now Chad stood with his tattooed arms folded across his broad chest, which was covered only by an open leather vest. The light from the hall fixture behind him glinted off his many body piercings, and several scars gleamed white on his face and chest. He shook his head, and his long, stringy ponytail flipped back and forth.

"What have you done to get that guy in the suit all worked up?" Chad asked. "Don't worry—I didn't tell him a thing."

"He was looking for *me?*" Darcy's heart began to pound. She hadn't been wrong. The man who stood talking to Chad had been Blaine.

"Yeah. Maybe he's a friend of yours, but I didn't take to the way he was pushing his weight around, insisting you were interfering in his business and that he had a right to get what was his from your apartment."

"I don't have anything of his in my apartment!"

"Didn't figure you did. Devon and I caught him sneaking down the stairs once before. We told him then not to come sneaking around when you weren't home. He said he didn't take orders from weirdos. It didn't look like he took anything, so we didn't say anything, but later we heard someone had broken into your place and caused you a lot of trouble. It was right after that you changed your locks."

Darcy wasn't sure which surprised her the most: that Chad knew so much about her business or that it might have been Blaine who'd broken into her apartment. She'd consider his reasons and what he might have done with the information he'd stolen later. Now she was more interested in his reason for coming to see her today.

"I saw you leave this morning in your running clothes," Chad went on, "so I told him you weren't home, but he said there was something in your apartment he needed to get, and he'd just be a minute. We got in a bit of an argument about whether he was coming in or not. He called me a few names I won't repeat to a lady." Blaine was a big man, but Darcy suspected Chad hadn't had a lot of difficulty winning the argument.

"Thank you," she said. "He's married to a friend of mine. He's hurt her pretty badly a few times."

Chad's lip curled. "If I'd known that, I would've punched his lights out. I ain't got no use for yella-bellied cowards that beat on women or kids."

"I appreciate your words." She smiled at him. "He's a prominent attorney, so don't let him goad you into doing anything that might land you in trouble." She picked up her shoes, prepared to climb the stairs to her apartment.

"With your boyfriend being out of town, don't you worry about that lawyer creep. Devon and me'll keep an eye on your place." Chad flexed his considerable muscles, and Darcy didn't know whether to feel reassured or to giggle. She'd never expected a long-haired, tattooed motorcycle rider to volunteer to be her champion.

"Thanks." She fled up the stairs.

In her apartment, she indulged in a long, hot shower. Once she felt warm again and with her hair blown dry, she found herself still puzzling over Blaine's attempted visit to her apartment. What was he looking for? Surely he wouldn't be so unethical as to snoop through her papers in search of a way to trace Karlene, even though his firm was defending Jessop Bernard.

Darcy graded student essays for a while but found it difficult to concentrate. She called her mother, but there was no answer. Being Saturday, her mom was probably doing the weekly shopping or running her younger siblings to various activities.

She found a bag of M&M's in the cupboard. Carrying the open bag, she wandered to the window to look out at the spring flowers just peeping their heads through the ground in the gardens of various neighbors. She scanned the books on her bookshelf and decided she wasn't in the mood for one of her old favorites. For almost half an hour, she thumbed through her scriptures, reading a few verses here and there but failing to internalize the messages as she usually did. At last she picked up a new suspense novel that had caught her eye the last time she and David had visited a bookstore and hoped its plot would prove strong enough to hold her attention.

She curled up on the sofa and had just managed to shut out the questions that swirled through her mind concerning Blaine when the familiar ring of her cell phone startled her into losing her place. Letting the book slide to the floor, she flipped the phone open.

"Hi, Darcy. We took first place!" David's excited voice was a welcome interruption. "We're just getting the kids on the bus, then we'll be on our way home. The kids voted not to stop for a celebration dinner. They're anxious to get home in time for the spring dance scheduled for tonight."

Darcy laughed. "The fact that they'll be greeted as conquering heroes by their classmates couldn't have anything to do with their decision, could it?"

"That and the fact that our first-place sprinter has a date with Jana Meadows, the senior class femme fatale," he conceded. "How about you? Would you like to do a little celebrating tonight? Say dinner about eight?"

"Love to."

After ending the call, she looked down at her book, and her eyes caught sight of the empty M&M bag. She'd emptied the whole bag! Horrified, she gathered up the bag and tossed it into the trash. She didn't usually eat a lot of sweets, which probably showed how much the day's events had upset her. It was probably a good thing she'd skipped lunch and that she and David would be having a late dinner.

* * *

David arrived for their date, and Darcy was glad she'd chosen to wear a dress that always made her feel feminine and attractive. She'd used her curling iron on her hair and applied clear polish to her nails as well. David had dressed up, too, in nice slacks and a sport jacket. He was even wearing a tie.

"You look great." David kissed her lightly and smiled in appreciation.

"Congratulations on the big win," she told him. "I'm anxious to hear all of the details." She thought he looked pretty great too. Whether he was dressed up or in sweaty running shorts and a T-shirt, she was sure he was the handsomest man she'd ever met.

When they reached the bottom of the stairs, Chad opened his door. "Nice win, coach. I just heard on the radio."

"Thanks!"

"You two have fun, and don't worry about a thing," Chad called after them as they exited the front door.

"What's with him?" David laughed as he helped Darcy into his truck. "He usually doesn't say two words when he sees me."

"He actually has a case of hero worship on you," Darcy whispered back. On the drive to the restaurant, she explained about Chad's confrontation with Blaine. Somehow Blaine's visit didn't seem so ominous with David beside her.

"Something's not making a lot of sense here," David said. "But I think I'll mention Blaine's visits to Pauline when we play volleyball next Tuesday."

When they entered an upscale restaurant at the top of a hotel, they both seemed to be parties to a silent pact to put all unanswered

questions aside. A maître d' led them to a table with a view of the city. Creamy linens covered the table, and a chunky candle provided minimal light. Soft music was playing, and Darcy almost pinched herself to see if she was really experiencing the kind of romantic date she'd read only about in novels and witnessed in movies.

Speaking louder than a whisper seemed out of place, so they conversed quietly about the team's chances for a state victory, then they went on to talk about summer plans and long-term dreams. Nighttime stars seemed to meld with city lights. The night was perfect.

A movement from the corner of her eye brought her back to reality. She turned to David, but he was no longer sitting across from her. Instead he knelt before her with a small white box extended toward her on the palm of one hand. She looked at him then at the box, where a diamond sparkled in the candlelight.

"Will you marry me? I promise I'll love you forever." His eyes held hers as the restaurant pianist played "Some Enchanted Evening."

Chapter 19

Darcy floated through the end-of-term activities. Preparing exams and reading essays, signing a contract for the next fall, even worrying about Karlene and Clare seemed to take up less time than staring at the ring on her finger and making plans for her wedding. She and David spent as much time together as possible, running now more than ever.

David was frequently out of town with his track team, but for meets held locally, Darcy was there cheering wildly for his young athletes. Both her students and his seemed to take particular delight in teasing them and showing their enthusiasm for the match between two popular teachers. On evenings or Saturdays when David was away at meets, she spent a lot of time on the phone with her mother, who was thrilled to be helping her daughter plan her wedding.

On the final day of classes, Darcy bid her graduating seniors farewell and told the rest of her students that she expected to see them in the fall. She passed out a summer reading list to the sophomores and juniors who would be returning.

"This isn't a have-to list," she told them. "But anyone who reads any of these books and writes an essay of roughly a thousand words about it will start next semester with ten bonus points for each book read." The list was greeted with mixed cheers and jeers, but she just laughed.

"Miss Olsen?" A pretty girl who usually sat near the back raised her hand. "Will we be invited to your wedding?"

"Our ceremony will be small, with only family and a few especially close friends present," she explained. The girl's face fell. "But you're all

invited to an open house that will be held later here in Boise. My parents will host a big reception in the town where I grew up in Washington, and if any of you are in Tacoma in August, you're invited."

The bell rang, and her students seemed to almost explode from the classroom. A few lingered for private farewells, but soon the classroom was empty. Darcy gave a satisfied sigh. Her first semester of teaching on her own was over, but it had been a satisfying experience.

She reached for a large canvas carryall she'd folded and placed in a desk drawer that morning. She set her grade books in it along with personal books and a few items she'd purchased to illustrate points. She was reaching for a poster at the front of the classroom when she felt a vibration at her waist.

Assuming the caller was David, she opened her phone with a cheerful, "Hi, honey!"

"Darcy," the voice on the other end said in a whisper. "Please come get me."

"Clare?" Darcy gripped the phone tighter. "Of course, I'll come. Where are you?" She strained to hear the address before the line went dead.

She stared at the phone for several seconds before shaking off her stunned state. Without regard to where things landed, she stuffed the items she meant to take with her into the bag and slung it over one shoulder. In seconds she was out the door. She raced to the staff room, where she paused only long enough to get directions from the computer and print out a map of the location Clare had given her.

Ten minutes later while waiting for a light to change, she was staring at the paper where she'd jotted the address Clare had given her. It didn't make sense. Why would Clare be miles from her condo with no transportation?

The light changed, and Darcy pressed on the gas. She wished she'd asked Clare to repeat the address. She wasn't sure she was even in Boise any longer. She'd been so relieved to hear from her friend she hadn't questioned the unfamiliar address.

Following the instructions to the last detail, she turned on to a shabby street then pulled into a parking space beside a rundown café. She left the car running and looked around with a growing sense of

unease. She couldn't imagine Clare asking her to meet her at such a deplorable place. She must have gotten the numbers wrong.

While she wondered what her next step should be, she noticed an invalid woman in a hospital gown wobble toward her on crutches. Darcy felt a wave of pity for the stooped shoulders and humped back. The woman staggered then leaned weakly against the soot-covered café wall.

Darcy was suddenly torn between a desire to help the woman and fear that it might be some kind of trick. What if Blaine had forced Clare to make that call so that he could attempt to make her reveal Karlene's whereabouts? No, she was being melodramatic.

She opened her car door and stepped closer to the woman. "Do you need help? Is there someplace I can take you?"

"Help me." The woman's crutches fell, and she would have fallen, too, if Darcy's instincts hadn't kicked in. She grasped the woman by her arms and found herself staring into Clare's tortured features just before her friend's shadowed blue eyes closed in a faint.

"Clare!" Darcy struggled to keep the other woman from crumpling to the broken concrete beneath their feet. "Clare! Clare! I'm here but you have to stay awake." She looked around in desperation for anyone who might help her get Clare into the car. Traffic whizzed by on the nearby busy street and a black-and-white dog trotted in an unconcerned fashion between two houses at the end of the quiet side street where she had parked.

"I can't carry you, Clare." She knew she sounded desperate, but she really couldn't carry the smaller woman even if she didn't have a heavy cast on one leg and another on an arm. "Put your arm around my neck, and I'll help you walk to my car."

Clare seemed to revive enough to follow Darcy's instructions. After each laborious step, she paused for a moment before attempting the next one. Clare's breathing seemed labored, and Darcy wondered if she should just call an ambulance, but at last they reached the Cruiser and Darcy opened the passenger door. Once she'd carefully backed Clare into the seat and lifted her legs inside, she hurried back for the abandoned crutches.

With the crutches placed across the back seat, Darcy scrambled to her place behind the steering wheel. She took great care to back out

of her parking space without jostling her passenger. Once they were back on the busy street, she glanced over at Clare. She lay against the seat with her eyes closed, looking lost and forlorn. Darcy had to struggle to keep from crying. How had dear, sweet Clare come to this? Clare's eyes flickered, and she seemed to be awake.

"Don't worry about a thing," Darcy attempted to reassure her friend. "We'll be at the hospital in about fifteen minutes."

"No!" Clare struggled to sit up straighter, and Darcy could see a look of terror on her face. "No hospital."

"But Clare . . ."

"I can't let him find me."

"You mean Blaine?"

"You were right." Clare doubled over, clutching her stomach. Darcy had trouble understanding her broken words, delivered between gasping sobs. "He killed my baby."

"He *what?*" Darcy almost lost control of the car. She took the first exit and steered to a quiet spot at the back of a motel. Turning to Clare, she pulled her into an embrace and held her until her heaving shoulders grew calm.

"Now tell me about it." She spoke softly without releasing Clare's shivering form.

"Blaine was so angry because one of his clients killed himself and he didn't get the rest of the big fee he expected. Then he learned his client was actually murdered and that the murder suspect is dead now, too. He accidentally blew himself up while pursuing a witness Blaine's father has been trying to locate." Clare didn't seem to notice Darcy's sharp intake of breath.

"He's been so angry, and every time something has gone wrong, he's taken out his frustration on me. A week ago he learned his father actually set up the big case he was so proud of. Garrett had expected Blaine to lose that case and that his client's conviction would have removed suspicion from his father's client. He said he would have gotten the rest of his fee anyway for doing some work on his dad's case if I'd kept my mouth shut and that it was my fault a witness his father needed was killed. He accused me of spoiling everything for him, and he hit me. I asked him to be careful for the baby's sake, and it just made him angrier. He said I was stupid to get pregnant and that I had no business keeping it a secret so

long." She took a deep breath and went on. "When I came to, I was alone in the condo and having cramps. I was scared, and I didn't know what to do, but I thought that if I didn't get away, my baby would die."

Again Clare's words ended in tears, and Darcy did her best to comfort her.

"I ran away," she whispered. "But I didn't have any money or a place to go. I spent the night at a homeless shelter."

"Why didn't you call me?" Darcy was aghast at what her friend had gone through.

"I didn't have my phone with me, and I was afraid I'd have to give the people there my name if I used their phone. Anyway, I felt so awful. I wasn't thinking clearly. I passed out, and the shelter people took me to the hospital. I had ID with me, and someone called Blaine."

"Oh, Clare, you've been through so much. I'll take care of you now until you're strong enough to be on your own." Darcy stroked her friend's hair in an attempt to soothe her. As she did so, she wondered how safe Clare would be with her since Blaine knew her address, but where else could she take her?

Clare went on as though under some compulsion to get the whole story out. "Blaine took me back to our condo. For almost a week we barely spoke to each other. Then I tried to talk to him. I told him I thought we should see a marriage counselor. He laughed, so I said if he wouldn't see a counselor, then we should talk to our bishop. He threatened to beat me senseless if I said one word to anyone or made any silly accusations. He called me all sorts of vicious things. I know I don't know much about being a good wife, and our troubles were more my fault than his, but a voice in my head seemed to keep saying, 'Get out. Get out now.'

"I didn't go, and I'll regret ignoring that prompting for the rest of my life. Instead I went to our bedroom, put on my shoes, and started hanging up some clothes Blaine had left on the floor. I didn't even hear him come into the bedroom. Later at the hospital he said he thought I was packing to leave him."

"Is that when you lost the baby?"

"Yes. I knew as soon as I woke that the baby was gone. Blaine kept saying, 'Look on the bright side. We can't afford a baby now anyway. We'll have another one later after my career is better established.'"

There were no tears now—just an icy calm. "My doctor came to my room later that morning. He thought I knew there would never be another baby. He told me that I'd hemorrhaged and that he'd had no choice but to operate to save my life. He also said he'd explained everything to my husband, who had promised to break it to me gently. I made up my mind not to go back to the condo."

"You ran away again."

Clare pulled back a few inches and looked directly at Darcy. "I waited a few days. Waiting was hard, but I knew I couldn't survive without money or a place to stay. I tried to call you, but there never seemed to be a dial tone on the phone in my room. Sometimes I wasn't certain I cared about surviving, then one day Blaine left his briefcase in my room while he went to see how soon he could take me home. I knew he kept a small amount of cash in it, so I took some of it. While I was on the floor opening his case, I learned why I wasn't able to call you. Something sticky, probably gum, had been placed over the little wire receptors where the phone plugged into the wall." Clare sagged back against the seat back. "I sneaked out the next morning right after the doctor said my husband was having me transferred to a private nursing home. The money I took only got me as far as that café and one night in the dirty motel behind it. The clerk let me use the phone."

"Don't talk anymore," Darcy whispered in a choked voice. "You need to be in bed. We can talk more when you've rested." She reached to start her car and pulled back onto the highway with extreme care. In moments she regretted not trying to reach David before resuming driving. She was pretty certain Clare was going to need more help than she could give her to get up the stairs to Darcy's apartment.

Clare huddled in her seat with her arms wrapped tightly around her abdomen. Whether some instinct prompted her to protect the child no longer there or if pain was the reason she held herself, Darcy didn't know. Sometimes when she glanced over at her friend, Clare seemed to be sleeping. Other times she stared straight ahead with unfocused eyes.

Chad was in the driveway tinkering with his bike when Darcy pulled in. She was glad to see her neighbor. She shut off the engine, saying, "I'll just be a minute," to Clare.

Darcy approached the large man. "Chad, remember how Blaine Prescott was looking for something when he tried to enter my apartment

a few weeks ago? That something was his wife. She's in my car, and she's been badly beaten."

"You want me to help you get her to a hospital?"

"No, she ran away from the hospital and her husband."

It took only this bare explanation for Chad to step to the side of Darcy's Cruiser, where he opened the passenger door to help Clare out.

"Hey," he said in a soft voice to Clare. Her eyes opened wide, but she didn't speak. "I live in the same building as Darcy. She told me you've been having a rough time and it's doubtful you can climb the stairs to her place. If you'll just put an arm around my neck, I'll have you up there in no time." Her eyes went to Darcy then back to the man leaning toward her. Hesitantly she placed an arm around him, and in one deft motion he scooped her into his arms.

Darcy scrambled to extract the pair of crutches from the backseat and lock the car before beating Chad and Clare to the front door. Chad didn't even seem to be breathing heavy when he paused to let Darcy unlock her apartment door.

"Through there." Darcy indicated the bed behind the screen.

"Right." Chad placed his burden on the bed then looked down at Clare. "Don't you worry about a thing, little lady. You'll be safe here." Clare must have believed him, because in seconds she was asleep.

"Thanks, Chad," Darcy whispered. "I hope you don't get in trouble for helping us. I couldn't think of any other place to take her."

"Like I told the little lady in there," he pointed with his thumb, "you don't have to worry about a thing. I'll be around all weekend, and that smooth-talking bully won't get past me."

"I appreciate your help, Chad."

Chad looked embarrassed. "My father used to knock my mother around every time he had too much to drink. One day when I was about sixteen, she just up and split. She told me good-bye before she lit out and said for me to stay in school. I ain't heard from her since, but I stayed in school 'til I graduated. I got too big for my old man to whip, but I can't ever forgive him for what he did to Ma."

"Thanks for understanding." She supposed she should say something about forgiveness being necessary to begin healing, but she certainly wasn't ready to forgive Blaine yet.

* * *

David knocked softly, but Darcy was listening and went to let him in at once. "Chad stopped me downstairs and warned me what to expect." He spoke in a whisper. "How bad is she?"

Darcy led him to the sofa, where they talked in low voices. "Clare said some things that made me suspect Blaine stole my missing cell phone bill. I know his father's firm is representing Jessop Bernard, and it appears he gave the information he stole to the man who blew up Evan's garage. Blaine told her he's pretty sure the man who died in that explosion also killed Skeet Skidmore."

"I think I better have a talk with Sheriff Langton." David appeared thoughtful. "I'll have to find a way to do it without dragging Clare into it."

Darcy started preparing a light meal. Neither she nor David had eaten dinner, and she was certain Clare had eaten little in the last few days. When the meal was ready, she woke Clare.

"I can sit at the table," Clare protested when Darcy told her she would bring her a tray.

"No, you need all the rest you can get," Darcy insisted. "I'll bring you a tray."

Clare had swallowed several sips of the soup Darcy had heated when she caught sight of David. Her hands began to shake, and soup dribbled from her spoon onto the fresh clothes Darcy had given her. She struggled to leave the bed, and her eyes were wide with fear.

"I'm sure you remember David. He was at your wedding, and he visited you in the hospital when we went there with Pauline. David won't hurt you or tell Blaine you're here," Darcy reassured her.

"He'll tell Pauline, and Blaine will find out. I shouldn't have come here. This is the first place Blaine will look."

Hearing Clare's words, David stepped closer. "Darcy's right. You have nothing to fear from me. I seldom see Pauline, and if I should happen to run into her, I won't mention you without your permission. Besides, she hates Blaine and would never do anything to harm you."

"But . . ." Clare looked confused.

"I wanted to tell you, but I couldn't contact you." Darcy sat beside Clare and clasped her hands. "David and I are engaged. We plan to be married in August."

"I thought Pauline and David were going to get married. Blaine said they've been dating since high school." Clare looked from one to the other, still seeming uncertain whether she could trust David.

"Pauline and I were never serious, but she got a kick out of letting her family think she was considering marrying a high-school coach. I think if you really got to know her, you'd discover she's more your ally than you think. I won't say anything to her without your permission, but I think you should talk to her. I also think she would recommend that you bring abuse charges against Blaine."

"I don't want to see him ever again." The words came out with a whimper. "All I've ever wanted was a family. Now I'll never be a mother."

"I don't think you'll have to see him again. We'll find an attorney who can advise you on that," Darcy said.

"I can't hire an attorney; I don't have any money."

"I know you're not working, but there's your trust fund."

"Blaine had me sign papers so that my trust is deposited in our joint account. Only it isn't really a joint account. He kept forgetting to get the papers for me to sign that would add my name to the account."

"An attorney can fix that," David assured her. "A good divorce lawyer makes freezing assets before the other party can hide them a top priority."

"Divorce! No, I can't get a divorce." The panic was back in Clare's voice.

"Sweetie, I know how you feel about divorce, but you can't stay with Blaine after he's done this to you. You need to put everything about him behind you and start a new life."

"You don't understand. He swore that if I file for divorce, he'll make certain I die for betraying him."

Chapter 20

THE SUN BURNED DOWN ON the small plot of grass behind the duplex where Clare had lived for almost three weeks. There were no trees, but a small square of concrete served as a patio with a worn canvas awning providing a small amount of shade for the plastic table and chairs that were the only furniture there. She brushed a strand of hair out of her eyes with one hand and slowly sipped from the can she held in the other. Neither the cramped duplex nor the tiny yard matched the opulent condo she'd shared with Blaine. Perhaps that's why she found something almost soothing in the stark blandness of her present simple environment. Most of her visible bruises had healed, but she didn't think her mind would ever be the same.

Unexpected sounds such as the neighborhood children lighting firecrackers or a muffler needing repair sent her scurrying indoors much too often. She frequently changed her route to and from work, though she worked just a few blocks from the duplex. David and Darcy, along with her attorney, had found both the duplex and the job for her, and they'd gone to great lengths to conceal her whereabouts.

Her job with a carpet company was going well, though it wasn't as interesting as the one she'd had at the engineering firm in Boise. She liked her boss and the salespeople, but the bookkeeping position wasn't nearly as challenging as her former position. She wasn't certain she was ready for anything challenging, though perhaps some of the shock was beginning to wear off, and she was beginning to face the probability of a lifetime of being alone.

The divorce had gone through without a major incident, and a friend of Darcy's neighbor, Chad, had whisked her out of the court-

room and into a car, escorting her from Idaho within minutes of the final decree.

She'd resisted filing for a divorce for a time, but eventually she'd let David bring Pauline to visit her. She'd been fearful of confiding in Pauline, but gradually she'd come to understand that Pauline had also been one of Blaine's victims. The biggest difference between them was Clare's determination to put Blaine out of her life and Pauline's desire for revenge. In a strange, unexplainable way, the two women seemed to provide a step in the healing process for each other.

Following Pauline's visit, she'd met with the attorney her sister-in-law recommended who didn't appear to be intimidated by the Prescott name or their prestigious law firm. He'd arranged for her to stay with a colleague in Twin Falls during the twenty days between serving Blaine with the divorce papers and their court appearance.

She suspected it was Blaine's parents who had kept him from contesting the divorce or creating a scene when her attorney threatened to make public pictures Clare hadn't even known existed. They'd been willing to agree to almost everything her attorney asked in order to avoid negative publicity during the last months of Brett's campaign. A young deputy had also told the judge about the condition he'd found her in at her condo following one of Blaine's beatings. The deputy and Pauline had both pressed her to file assault charges against Blaine, but she'd only wanted to be free of him. She shuddered, and her hands slipped on the damp can she held as she remembered the look of hate in Blaine's eyes when their eyes met one last time across the courtroom.

"Anyone home?" She looked up to see a man peering over the wooden gate that separated the two backyards. He appeared to be large and had prominent streaks of gray running through his dark hair. Reluctantly, she arose to her feet and approached the gate, feeling the wariness with which she now viewed all large men. "My son lost his Frisbee in your yard. Do you mind if he looks for it?" The man smiled, and she saw nothing hidden behind the smile.

She could see the boy who looked like he might be ten or twelve as she drew closer to the gate. He too was tall, and his dark hair was a little long. It stuck straight up in a rooster tail at the back of his head and almost obscured his eyes in the front. He smiled hopefully at her.

"No, I don't mind." She made up her mind and reached to unlatch her side of the gate. The boy dashed past her, and she followed him with her eyes for a moment.

"I'm Jeffrey Quinn, and that's my son, Jayden." The man brought her attention back to him but without ringing any of her ever-present alarms. "I'm sorry we haven't been by to welcome you to the neighborhood," the man apologized. "My wife's in Boston helping our oldest son and his wife who are expecting a baby at the end of summer. Our daughter-in-law has to stay down until the baby comes, and that's hard to do with an active toddler needing attention, so Kerrie flew back there to help out."

His words caused her pain. She'd never have a toddler or face a difficult pregnancy, and she'd never be a grandmother helping to care for an active grandchild. "I'm C-Carla Wadsworth." Her attorney had advised her to change her name, and the small act did help her feel safer, but sometimes she almost forgot she was Carla now instead of Clare.

"I found it!" Jayden appeared, carrying the Frisbee. She could see why she'd missed noticing it earlier. It was almost the same color as the grass. "Thanks for letting me get it."

"That's all right." She gave the boy one of her rare smiles.

"Your grass is kind of long. I could mow it for you when I mow our side," the boy offered.

She looked at the lawn and felt amazed that she hadn't noticed how long and shaggy it had gotten. She'd looked at it every day without really seeing it. "I guess that would be all right," she told him. "How much do you charge?"

"I won't charge you. Your grass and ours together aren't enough to make one good yard."

Jeffrey Quinn laughed. "We lived out in the country until a few months ago when we decided to build a new home and sold the one we were living in before the new one was ready to move into. Jayden doesn't let us forget how much he misses having more space for activities and friends."

When she heard the roar of a lawnmower a few hours later, she pulled her kitchen curtain aside to watch Jayden make the first couple of rounds then hurried to her refrigerator for a package of frozen ice

cream bars on sticks she'd bought on an impulse a few days earlier. When he finished mowing her small lawn, she waved him closer and invited him to share the ice cream.

"Thanks!" He accepted the offer with an eagerness that amused her. He dropped onto one of the chairs and tore open the wrapper. She hesitated a moment then sat opposite him.

"It's hot this afternoon. You could have waited until morning to the mow the lawns."

"Tomorrow's Sunday." He said it with perfect confidence that she'd know what he meant, and she did. Once she would have assumed the answer was obvious, too, but now she didn't know how she felt about the rules that had once governed her life. To be more accurate, she didn't know how she felt about the Church. She and Blaine had gone to church only once after their marriage, then it seemed there were more reasons to avoid church than for attending. Besides, she'd been reluctant to have the people in their ward see her bruises. She wanted neither their pity nor the embarrassment she knew she'd feel.

"Are you going to church tomorrow?" Jayden asked.

"I don't think so," she said.

"Don't you want to go?"

"I'm not sure."

"I didn't want to go to church when we moved here either. None of my friends were going to be there, and I didn't know anybody. It was pretty bad that first Sunday, but Dad said having a testimony means going to church even when you don't know anybody and there's only a stuck-up girl in your class."

Clare almost smiled.

"You can sit by me. Mom isn't here, and Dad always sits on the stand. All my brothers are gone." A forlorn expression crossed the boy's face.

"I'll go." She found herself wanting to see the boy's smile return. "But I don't even know what time church starts or which building I should go to."

Jayden's face brightened. "The church is two blocks that way." He pointed. "And we have to go really early. Dad has to be there at seven, but sacrament meeting doesn't start until nine. We could walk together."

"Okay, I'll be ready."

Clare found her mood lighter after her conversation with Jayden. She admitted she was lonely and had enjoyed having someone to talk with. She wished she could talk to Darcy, but her lawyer had discouraged her from continuing any relationship that might enable Blaine to find her.

As she prepared her dinner, she thought about going to church and found she did want to go. She wondered what she should say when she was asked about transferring her membership. She couldn't claim to be an investigator, and she couldn't give the membership clerk her real name.

The next morning, Jayden showed up on her front step twenty minutes before church. His white shirt was rumpled and his tie slightly askew. It appeared he'd made an effort to tame his cowlick but hadn't quite succeeded. His eager friendliness reminded her of Darcy's youngest brother, and the wave of homesickness that memory brought almost persuaded her to back out of accompanying Jayden to church, but reluctant to disappoint her young neighbor, she locked her door and matched her steps to his.

A sense of homecoming struck her as she walked through the glass front doors and heard the organ playing a familiar hymn. It didn't take long to confirm her suspicions concerning Jeffrey Quinn. He was the ward bishop. She learned from Jayden that his dad had been a high councilor when they lived at their old house and that he'd been called as bishop of their new ward right after they moved in, even though the family only planned to live there for a year.

Sacrament meeting was like dozens of other such meetings she'd attended since she was a small child, though she was more conscious than she'd ever been of babies crying and toddlers trying to make their escape. As she looked around, she noticed that the ward was unlike any other ward she'd ever attended. There were really young couples with babies and older retirement-age people. Many of the faces represented a variety of nationalities and races. There were almost no school-age children or middle-aged adults.

There was something comforting about hearing concepts she'd heard all her life reiterated by the speakers. She hesitated when the sacrament trays were passed then felt her eyes grow moist when she accepted the sacred emblems. Peace stole into her heart, seeming to promise that comfort would come.

* * *

Clare looked up from her sandwich when the only other woman who worked in her office, Jackie, sat across from her at the single table in the small staff area. Jackie set a large soft drink cup on the table and unwrapped a turkey sandwich.

"I hope you don't mind sharing the table," Jackie said as she drew a yogurt from a paper bag and set it on the table.

Clare shook her head. "I'm happy to have company."

Jackie looked at her oddly, and Clare blushed. She hadn't made any effort to befriend the woman and had restricted her responses to Jackie's overtures to only those subjects that concerned their work.

"I'm sorry," Clare apologized. "I've had a lot on my mind and was recently very ill, but that doesn't excuse my failure to get better acquainted with you."

"Oh, you needn't apologize. I've had my own troubles." Jackie took a spoonful of yogurt. "My husband left me for a younger woman five years ago, and I had nothing but trouble trying to collect child support for our son. Now that he's eighteen, he doesn't appreciate anything I've done for him, and the day after he graduated from high school, he enlisted in the Army. I worry constantly that he'll get killed in a war somewhere."

"Oh! You do have a lot to worry about."

"You know what I've found is the best way to put troubles in perspective?" Jackie took a long swallow of her drink. "Join groups that do things. That's what I've done. Every Tuesday night there's a group of about thirty people who meet to talk about art and look at pictures of beautiful masterpieces. Sometimes we have an artist or college professor give a lecture. But we aren't just interested in art. Every Saturday morning we serve breakfast at the homeless shelter."

"That sounds like an interesting group. I don't have any artistic talent whatsoever, but I've always appreciated classic art. And helping the homeless is certainly a worthwhile act of service." Clare thought Jackie's advice was a lot like she'd heard many times in church; the best way to find yourself is to lose yourself in helping others.

"Would you be interested in joining our group?" Jackie paused with her sandwich halfway to her mouth.

Vague memories of spending a night in a homeless shelter prevented Clare from refusing outright.

Seeing her hesitation, Jackie added, "We're a pretty mixed group. We meet at the Cathedral of the Madeline, but we're not all Catholic. There's a Jewish couple who must be at least sixty. Just come to our meeting tomorrow night and give us a chance."

Clare really did have an interest in art, and Jackie was right about her needing to get out more. Without Darcy's help, she'd be homeless or worse. A group such as Jackie described would also be the last place Blaine would look for her, and she could easily walk or catch a bus to the cathedral. Slowly she nodded her head. "Thank you, I believe I will accept your invitation."

* * *

"It's perfect!" Darcy backed up for a better view of the dress. She'd found the dress in Seattle but had almost passed it up when she discovered it was almost backless. Her mother had noticed how her eyes kept returning to it and had assured her she could fill in the back, making it temple ready. "You're a miracle worker, Mom." She kissed her mom's cheek.

"You better take it off now. David will be here any minute, and you don't want him to see it until tomorrow."

"I'm not superstitious!" Darcy laughed but obediently turned her back so her mother could unbutton the long, white gown. Once the dress was off, and she'd pulled her jeans back on, she watched her mother hang her wedding dress on a hanger and place it beside the bridesmaid dresses Lynette had made for Danene and Tracy.

A wave of sadness dimmed her happiness. There should have been three dresses. Since Clare didn't dare travel to Washington for Darcy's wedding for fear Blaine might be watching, Darcy had decided that her sisters Danene and Tracy would be her only attendants.

The doorbell rang, and Darcy ran to answer the door. In moments she was in David's arms. In all of the excitement of introducing David's parents to hers and David's reunion with her sisters and brothers, it was almost an hour before she found herself alone with him on the back deck.

They stood with their arms intertwined about each other. The scent of pine lingered in the air and mixed with a fresh breeze off the sound. They exchanged a kiss before David said, "I'm sorry about Clare. I know how badly you wanted her to be here."

"I drove down the coast this morning and stopped at a public phone booth to call her at the place where she works. I got the number from her attorney. He said it would be all right to call as long as I called from a phone Blaine couldn't trace. We are both sad that she can't be here, but I really just want her to be safe and have a chance to start over."

"Did she sound okay?" David asked.

"Yes. She seems much better than she did when we last talked, the day her divorce was finalized. She said she's made friends with a little boy who lives next door to her and that the boy's father is the bishop of her ward. She said she has visiting teachers, too, and that she especially likes the older one who is single and works for the Church. Oh, and she's joined an art appreciation group."

"I'm glad she's making friends and beginning to get out. During the almost three weeks she stayed with my cousin after Blaine was served with the divorce papers, she seldom left her room and jumped at every unexpected sound. I've worried a lot about her."

"I worry too. I know she signed a restraining order, and Blaine isn't supposed to have any contact with her, but she doesn't trust him, and I don't either. As much as I wish she was here, I prefer knowing she's safe. Having her here isn't worth the risk involved should Blaine find her."

"I received a surprise telephone call this morning too," David said, changing the subject. She looked up at him with questions in her eyes.

"Evan called. He didn't say where they were, but he did mention they were leaving for another location."

"Is everything all right?" Darcy couldn't help thinking that Karlene was another friend who would miss her wedding.

"He said they're both fine, and they're actually having a good time. Karlene's injuries have healed completely, and she's anxious to return to Idaho to testify. Evan said he keeps in touch with Sheriff Langton and that the autopsy results have identified the man who

tried to kill them at the cabin as Ramon Monterosa. An inmate at the jail has confessed that Monterosa blackmailed him into hanging Skidmore and making it look like suicide."

"Monterosa was Jessop Bernard's friend who insisted Bernard was with him the day Lauren Tisdale was killed. Won't that convince a jury that Bernard was involved in her death?" Darcy wondered.

"It shows there was a connection, but it doesn't place Bernard in the mountains the day his wife died. Skeet and Monterosa were cell mates at the state penitentiary a few years back, and they were suspected of pulling off a string of house burglaries after they were released, but they were never charged with the crimes. Evan thinks Bernard and Monterosa arranged for Skeet to burglarize Tisdale's car and steal her purse so that he would become the chief suspect in the murder."

"Has a trial date been set?" She wondered how much longer Karlene would have to hide.

"Evan said the city attorney's office has requested the earliest possible date, but the defense is requesting more time. He thinks it will probably be January."

"David?" Lynette's voice came from the doorway separating the deck from the family room. "There's a call for you. The caller didn't identify herself, but she said the call was urgent."

Chapter 21

DAVID TOOK A FEW STEPS toward Lynette and accepted the cordless phone she handed him. After identifying himself, he listened for what seemed like a long time. Darcy watched his facial expressions change from interest to excitement then to concern. His tense manner suggested the caller was no casual well-wisher. She didn't pretend that she wasn't listening to David's side of the conversation, but he was doing far more listening than speaking, and she could make little sense of what she heard. Finally he said, "Take it to Sheriff Langton at once. Don't give it to anyone else or tell anyone."

At the mention of the sheriff, Darcy's tension rose.

David was quiet for a long time again, then he said, "Yes, I think she'll be all right. This might be the break we've been hoping for." There was a pause while David's expression changed from concern to a smile. "I'll tell her, and thank you."

He clicked the phone off and stepped closer to Darcy. "Anne made a startling discovery a few minutes ago. She was helping her husband clean out the garage when he found a bag of bloody clothing at the bottom of an old aluminum trash can he uses to collect sawdust when he turns the garage into a woodshop."

"What!?"

"It's okay. Anne recognized the bag as the one the hospital gave her after her mother's accident. The clothes were the ones Karlene was wearing when she reached the emergency room. She thinks she must have been in a hurry, set the bag on a workbench, then accidentally knocked it into the bin and forgot all about it. But the clothes aren't

the important part." His grin was triumphant. "Karlene's camera was in the pocket of her blood-spattered and torn jacket!"

"And you told her to take it to the sheriff. Do you think there's a chance the photos she took that day can still be printed?"

"There's a good possibility. And if Bernard shows up in those pictures . . ."

"The odds are good he'll be convicted, and Karlene and Evan won't need to hide anymore."

"Right, but if word gets out that there's even a possibility those pictures might exist . . . Anne won't be safe until the camera is in the sheriff's hands."

"Poor Anne. She'll be a nervous wreck even with the camera in police custody."

"Anne also wished us happiness and a beautiful day tomorrow for our wedding."

* * *

Darcy liked to lie in bed for several minutes after she first awoke each morning to form a mental to-do list for the day, but she greeted her wedding day with an almost instant leap from bed. She was dressed and ready to leave for the drive from Tacoma to Bellevue in plenty of time. An air of excitement seemed to bounce off the walls as the two families met together for morning prayers, and Terry and Tracy passed around boxes of granola bars in lieu of breakfast.

At the temple, Lynette made a few last-minute adjustments to her daughter's hair and gown. Looking into the mirrors and seeing her mother's reflection beside her own, Darcy felt a lump in her throat. She hoped that when the time came for her to be a mother, she'd be as good a mother as hers had been. She had a sudden glimpse of eternity as she pictured all the mothers and daughters who had brought her to this point in her life, and she made her first vow of the day—she would do all she could to continue the chain.

Nothing had ever touched her as deeply as those moments when she knelt across the altar from David with her hand in his. Peace and joy filled her heart to bursting. The monumental sanctity of becoming

David's eternal partner gave way to smiles and tears as she embraced her family and his.

The day she'd planned for and dreamed of for so long was even better than her dreams. Those dreams hadn't included David, and he was so much more than she could have ever imagined. Before leaving the temple hand in hand with her new husband, she said a silent prayer of gratitude for all the people and teachings that had brought her and David to this glorious day.

After a flurry of picture-taking and a sumptuous dinner in Seattle hosted by David's parents, it was time to return to Tacoma to rest and prepare for the reception.

"Here, take my car." Cody tossed his car keys to David. "I'll ride with the family in the van."

Darcy hugged her brother and whispered a thank-you. Cody usually refused to let anyone drive his precious Mustang.

"Hey, if you make it to Tacoma without adding any new bumps or scratches, I'll even play chauffeur and take you to the airport after the reception. You did remember to go online for your boarding passes, didn't you?"

David patted his pocket.

All the way back to Tacoma, Darcy sat as close to David as the Mustang's bucket seats permitted and marveled that the handsome man beside her was actually her husband.

When they reached the Olsen house, they walked into a whirlwind of activity. Lynette was preparing to drive over to the church to make certain the decorators had followed her instructions. David's mother was accompanying her. His sisters invited Darcy's younger siblings to accompany them and their families to their hotel to relax at the pool for a while. Their husbands announced their intentions of catching up on lost sleep and were soon settled in recliners in front of the television.

David glanced at his watch, then, leaning toward his bride, he spoke softly in her ear. "Remember that beach where we went last Thanksgiving? We've got several hours before we have to dress for the reception. I'd like to spend that time there with you." He dangled Cody's keys before her. "I still have these."

She grinned. "I'll race you getting changed!" She ran for the stairs leading to her room.

Once they got to the beach, they parked the Mustang in the same place they'd left David's truck nine months earlier. There were a couple other cars parked nearby, and a few people could be seen on the beach. Darcy kicked off her sandals and left them in the car. Seeing her action, David did the same. Barefoot, they picked their way across the parking area.

Darcy had learned to treasure the late summer days when the sun shone and fewer clouds and rainstorms dampened the Northwest. This was one of those golden days, and she savored walking beside David with their fingers interlaced as they followed the ribbon of sand toward the rock where they'd watched the sun set that other day.

Darcy strayed toward the water's edge, and David followed. She savored the cool sensation of wet sand between her toes. "It's not as cold as last time," David said as he smiled down at her, "but still cold." He splashed water against her bare ankles. Laughing, she splashed him back. Soon they were running together.

They looked back when they reached the rocky point of land where the forest ended in a jumble of boulders. There were a few people at the far end of the beach, and a couple were swimming in the water. In the distance, a pair of sailboats tilted far to the side as they glided across the water. She could see through the dense growth of trees that separated the strip of beach from the road that a car had parked on the road parallel to the beach. Her attention shifted to the tracks she and David had left in the sand. "Look at the trail we left." She pointed to their footprints.

David leaned back against the large boulder and pulled her into his arms. "I knew that day we first came here that I wanted to see your footprints beside mine for all eternity. That was the day I first knew I wanted us to become more than friends."

"Hello, Miss Olsen. Or should I say Mrs. Schoenfeld?" Darcy saw the man who had addressed her step from behind the rocks. He was of medium height, and his graying hair was professionally styled. She noticed at once that he didn't appear dressed for the beach. His well-tailored slacks, pin-striped shirt, tie, and recently shined shoes immediately put her on edge. There was something familiar about him, but she couldn't place him.

"Do I know you?" she asked.

"Let's just say we have a common interest. Karlene Roper. You tell me where she is, and you can get back to your honeymoon. If you fail to cooperate, instead of being a bride, you'll be a very young widow." Her eyes widened as the man lifted his arm, and she saw a silenced gun pointed toward David.

"But I don't know where she is," Darcy said. "I haven't seen or talked to her for months."

"You were there when she escaped my friend's little trap at that remote cabin, and I think you know where she ran to." The man's voice remained calm and smooth, but Darcy felt her legs begin to tremble, and she was aware that David was slowly pivoting to place himself between her and the gunman. She may not have met him before, but she was certain the man facing her was Jessop Bernard.

"She's telling the truth," David cut in. "The sheriff put Mrs. Roper in a witness protection program, and she's had no contact with Darcy."

"Nonsense. Langton doesn't have that kind of budget. She's with that retired cop friend of hers, and your little bride knows where they are. We'll start with your phones. Set them on the rock between us." He indicated a large rock about halfway between them.

Darcy fumbled for her phone. She'd almost left it behind when she and David had run from the house, then decided that she should take it with her in case her mother had problems with the decorations for the reception and needed to check with her. David took it from her hand and walked forward to gingerly place both cell phones on the designated rock then backed up slowly until he was beside her again. Bernard's gun barrel moved equally slowly as he followed David's movements.

"Our phones will be of no use to you," Darcy told him. "We don't even know how to contact Karlene, and if we did, we wouldn't use our cell phones to contact her after your lawyer stole my phone bill to help you trace her the first time." It was the first sign of surprise or doubt she'd seen on the man's face. Perhaps he hadn't known how Blaine had discovered Karlene's previous location.

"I think you'll suddenly remember where she is when I put a hole in your new husband's knee. Now won't that be too bad for an up-and-coming coach?" He lifted the gun, and Darcy stepped in front of David. David stiffened, and she suspected he wasn't happy with her placing herself in danger to protect him.

"Finding Karlene won't help you. She took pictures of you and your wife that day, so even if you find her, there will still be the pictures." David squeezed her arm, which she figured was disapproval that she had told Bernard about the pictures. There had been plenty of time for Anne to turn the camera over to the sheriff, so she didn't believe she was endangering her, but if the information might convince Bernard that injuring David was a futile gesture, then she wasn't sorry she'd told.

Bernard's calm demeanor exploded. "That camera spent the winter under eight feet of snow. There are no pictures!"

"That's where you're wrong. The emergency room staff saved Karlene's clothing, and it was recently discovered that the camera was safe and dry inside the pocket of the jacket she wore that day."

Bernard narrowed the distance between them. Suddenly he lunged forward, grabbing Darcy's arm and jerking her toward him.

"Where are those pictures?" he snarled. "*If* they even exist."

"I know where they are, but I won't tell you unless you let David go." She knew it was a gamble, but she didn't think Bernard would shoot her as long as he thought she had information he wanted. She hoped, too, that if she drew Bernard's attention to her, David could escape and call the police.

"You'll talk!" Pain exploded across her face as her captor slammed the gun against the side of her face.

She screamed and squirmed, trying to free herself while Bernard yelled threats in her ear. "We'll see how fast you can talk when we get to a more private place." Sparks danced before her eyes as his grip around her neck tightened, and she felt blackness creeping near. More afraid of suffocating than of the gun, she kicked the man's shins, but her bare feet made little impact. Making one last desperate attempt, she bent her knee and drew it swiftly upward.

She hadn't felt herself fall, but her first moment of awareness was of a mouthful of sand. She was lying in an awkward heap with one arm twisted beneath her body, and the grit under her cheek felt damp and sticky. Her lungs screamed for deep, gulping gasps of air, but she forced herself to take shallow breaths. As her senses sharpened, she saw David. He was standing very still. He wasn't looking at her. Instead he was watching something behind her. Some sense of self-preservation warned her not to move or show any sign of awareness, though she

wanted desperately to spit out the sand. She wished David had escaped while Bernard was occupied with her, but she wasn't really surprised to see that he hadn't left her.

"Pick her up. You'll carry her to my car." The order came from behind her, but she knew it was directed at David. She almost uttered a protest. She was slender, but she was five feet ten inches tall—not the kind of girl who could be easily picked up and hauled around even by a man in great physical shape like David.

Beyond David she could no longer see people playing at the far end of the beach, but it wasn't completely deserted. Two carloads of what she took to be teenagers were parked side by side near Cody's Mustang. Faint strains of rock music drifted down the beach to where she lay, filling her with despair. She knew the sound was muted by distance. It was probably blasting loud enough to make the occupants of the cars deaf, also making it impossible for the kids to hear screams or gunshots. Even if she and David managed to escape, there was too much open beach between the man with a gun and Cody's Mustang.

She suddenly noticed a lump beneath her hip. Her fingers inched toward it. A rock was the only possible weapon she could hope for. When her hand closed around the object, she recognized it at once as one of the cell phones. She had no idea how it had gotten beneath her, but she clasped it in grim determination.

David came closer and dropped to one knee. His arms went under her as he picked her up and nestled her against his chest. He straightened in one smooth movement, and she wondered if she'd underestimated his ability to carry her. She let her head loll against his shoulder and her hair fall forward, obscuring most of her face.

David began walking, and she could tell they were moving into the trees instead of back across the beach. They were following a path of sorts, one she remembered from childhood explorations when she and Clare had pretended to be explorers working their way through thick jungle growth and leaping over exposed roots. The path was still rough, and David had to pick his way through thick tangles of Scottish broom and between bramble-infested blackberry bushes.

The car she'd noticed parked along the road was their most likely destination. Even if they found a way to escape, a distance of at least two football fields across open sand separated them from the Mustang.

David stumbled a couple of times, and she was filled with guilt. Maybe she was wrong to pretend to still be unconscious, leaving David in a position to be forced to carry her. Yet if she revealed that she could walk, she feared Bernard would carry out his threat to injure or kill him. He'd probably kill them both anyway since they couldn't give him the information he wanted, and he'd confessed too much to them about his own crimes.

David's steps grew more unsteady. Suddenly he lurched to the side, and she felt herself sliding. As her feet touched the ground, David hissed, "Run!" She needed no second warning. Diving into the thick growth beside the path, she squirmed and wiggled her way through a patch of ferns that towered over her head. A bullet whizzed past her head, and she crawled behind a thick tree trunk.

David! She couldn't see him at first, but then she spotted a clump of ferns swaying where there wasn't the slightest breeze. If he could get through the ferns as she had, the thick tree growth would give them a chance.

Too late! Bernard broke through the thick tangle of bushes. And his gun was pointed straight at the clump of ferns she was certain hid David.

Chapter 22

WITHOUT THINKING BEYOND KNOWING SHE had to stop Jessop Bernard from shooting David, Darcy drew back her arm. She hadn't spent twenty years of her life being a tomboy and playing ball with her dad and brothers for nothing. The cell phone she'd kept clasped in her hand sailed forward in the fastest pitch of her life.

She aimed for his torso, the largest target, and there was a moment of satisfaction as the missile struck and she saw the gunman stumble backward, seeking cover. At the same time he disappeared, she heard a rustle beside her and saw David lunge behind a nearby tree. She pointed to a thick fir tree, and they both began working their way toward it. When they met, they began ducking and twisting to work their way deeper into the forest.

Darcy was aware that the thick growth of trees and shrubs didn't cover a large area. She also had no idea whether the man who pursued them had the ability to track them well. Would their best chance be to work their way back to the road and hope they could flag someone down who might help them? Or should they proceed toward one of the many homes nestled among the trees or along the water? Occasionally she heard sounds behind them that might be Bernard or could have been animals they had startled into flight.

Fearing Bernard might be waiting for them if they attempted to reach the road or return to the area where they'd left the Mustang, Darcy led the way toward the water. The moist ground and thick accumulation of leaves was easier to walk on than the harsher soil in the mountains would be, but her feet still hurt. She avoided looking at them, knowing the sight of the cuts and scratches she'd accumulated would serve only to

increase her awareness of their painful state. David was limping, and she knew he had sustained his share of cuts and jarring scrapes.

Creeping up an incline, they peeked over the crest to see another smaller beach spread before them. At the other end of the short strip of sand, a substantial stream of water dropped in a steep, boulder-strewn plunge toward the larger body of water. There didn't seem to be a road or a house nearby. They lay on their stomachs, hidden by thick vegetation and weighed their options. Though they hadn't heard any sounds of pursuit for some time, they spoke in barely audible whispers.

"I don't think we can cross that river, and if my calculations are right, we're about five miles from the highway," Darcy said. "Maybe we can follow the shoreline back to the other beach."

"Bernard will expect us to return for our car."

"We can't just stay here," Darcy argued. "It'll be dark soon, and if Bernard doesn't find us at the car, he'll come looking here."

"It looks to me like there's some kind of dock or wharf at the north end of that stretch of sand." David pointed. "There might be a boat. Let's go check."

"All right, but let's stay in the trees as long as possible. I don't want to get caught in the open."

David led the way as they skirted the beach, staying in the thick growth that bordered it. Once Darcy thought she heard something behind them. When she turned to look, a deer darted from the trees near where they had lain a short time ago before disappearing again into the thick brush farther away.

They continued on, but Darcy couldn't shake a sense of foreboding. It was almost as though she could sense they were walking toward danger instead of escaping it. It became harder to place one foot in front of the other. Several times David stopped and stood motionless, staring back the way they'd come, though nothing could be seen through the thick growth.

The forest ended in a tumble of blackberry bushes, large rocks, and coarse grass that reached almost to Darcy's thighs.

"Stay here." David's abrupt order startled her. "I'll check it out."

She finally saw what he saw. Two small boats were almost hidden beneath the dock David had spotted earlier.

David hurried down the slope. Taking care to step only on the rocks, she worked her way toward the bushes, picking up several base-ball-sized stones on her way.

From deep inside a thorny thicket, she watched David wade waist deep into the water then tow the two rowboats back to where water lapped against sand. He seemed to be taking an awfully long time examining the boats. She sent a nervous glance back toward the ridge that overlooked the small beach. Seeing nothing but still feeling a creepy unease, she could hardly remain still while she waited for David.

Suddenly David was moving quickly. He set something in one of the boats then pushed it out to deeper water, where a swell caught it and pulled it farther out. He waded back to the other boat, and she expected him to signal for her to join him. Instead he towed it back to the place where it had previously been partially hidden by the worn planks of the dock. He didn't return to shore but stayed in the water. She watched him wade quickly toward a narrow band of rocks and trees that marked the end of the small beach. Then he disappeared behind the wooded point of land.

A breeze ruffled the water, creating crests of white as far as she could see. The little boat David had set free lifted and dipped as the water carried it away. She wondered why David didn't come for her and wondered if he meant for her to make her way to him. She wavered, undecided whether she should remain in her hiding place or begin moving toward the spot were David had disappeared.

The sound of running footsteps pounding along the route David had taken earlier to the dock startled her into acute awareness that their pursuer had caught up to them. Keeping her head low, she saw Bernard pass by without a glance toward where she was hidden. He was making no effort to conceal his presence, and she feared he'd caught sight of David. Her hand coiled around one of the rocks she'd gathered.

Looking decidedly disheveled and with noticeable rips in his once-impeccable slacks and shirt, Bernard rushed straight toward the wooden dock. He stood for several seconds looking out toward the boat that was growing ever smaller. She saw him make a pile of his shoes, the gun, and items from his pocket on a wooden plank. Seconds later he

waded into the water and made his way to the boat David had left behind. As she watched, he secured the items in the boat then drew oars from the bottom of the vessel and used one to push off from the dock. Soon his boat was moving at a rapid pace into the deep water of the sound.

She stifled a nervous giggle. She couldn't believe David had devised such a clever trick or that Bernard had fallen for it. She watched as the small boat moved farther and farther from shore in pursuit of the empty rowboat. Fearing that standing might betray her presence and bring Bernard rushing back to shore, she remained in her cramped position.

The sun's rays were slanting low across the water, obscuring her view, but it seemed that Bernard's boat was riding lower in the water when it reached the shipping lane leading toward Tacoma Harbor. The whitecaps seemed to grow taller, and the small boat disappeared behind a wave. It didn't reappear.

"Both boats were rotten." She hadn't noticed David's approach. He took her hand and helped her to her feet. They held each other for a long time.

"We'd better go," David said at last. He took her hand, and they began the long hike back to the car. When they reached it, they found that two more cars full of teenagers had arrived. They'd built a bonfire and a girl was dancing on the hood of one of the cars with a beer bottle in her hand. When David could make himself heard over the deafening music, he asked if anyone could loan him a cell phone. He made two calls—one to the police and one to Darcy's dad.

They arrived late to their reception. Lynette did her best to salvage some sort of hairstyle for her daughter, but there was no way Darcy could force her cut and swollen feet into the stylish pumps that matched her wedding dress. She couldn't suppress a giggle when she noticed that her groom was also shoeless in the reception line. The huge bruise on Darcy's cheek and a row of scratches across David's elicited stares and wisecracks, but when the bride and groom left the line to sit at a small table with two uniformed policemen for half an hour, their parents and siblings were kept busy spreading just enough of the story to their guests to prevent them from jumping to erroneous conclusions.

* * *

Clare sat on her small patio as the day's light slowly disappeared. The darkness seemed to suit her mood. Today was her best friend's wedding, and she should be there. She imagined Darcy in the kind of dress she had once dreamed of wearing for her own wedding and of floating out of the Seattle Temple on a cloud of happiness beside David with all of her relatives smiling and clicking pictures.

Thoughts of her own wedding brought an ache to her heart. She'd been miserable that day. How could she have been so blind? Why had she let Blaine convince her that temple marriage could wait? Why had she accepted Blaine's excuses and cruelty so readily? At one time she'd thought of herself as a woman who would never tolerate the abuse she had suffered at Blaine's hands.

Somewhere a dog barked, and from someplace closer she caught the scent of charcoal and lighter fluid. The high-pitched shriek of children at play blended with the deep rumble of masculine laughter. A woman called, and a young girl answered. Sometimes she regretted living in a family-oriented neighborhood. It seemed everyone had someone except her. She'd felt happier and had been able to shut out thoughts of Darcy's wedding earlier that morning when she'd stood beside Jackie serving breakfast to the homeless and wishing she could do more for them, but now she could only remember and feel regret.

She'd be the first to admit that Jackie wasn't the sort of friend she would have once picked. The older woman was loud, sometimes used language that Clare found offensive, and the woman admitted that she liked to bar hop most weekends, but she seemed to understand something of Clare's deep hurt. She didn't ask prying questions or judge her. Clare especially appreciated Jackie's introducing her to the art group, where she'd been surprised to find she enjoyed the diverse group and had come to sense that many in the group were struggling to come to terms with hurt or loss. She enjoyed learning about the great masters, and the service project the group supported made her feel needed.

She heard the gate squeak and looked up to see Jayden walking toward her. "Mom and Dad sent me over to ask how you like your steak and to tell you supper is ready."

For a moment she didn't know what to say, then she remembered Jeffrey Quinn's offhand invitation when he and Mark Wright were home teaching two nights ago. She hadn't said she would go, but clearly she was expected at the Quinn home. She rose to her feet and followed her young friend next door.

Over the past few months, she and Jayden had become fast friends. Though his parents had enrolled him in a number of summer activities, he'd often been at loose ends, missing his mother and his friends. The two had embarked on a number of adventures and had each seemed to gain something valuable from their time spent together whether reading a favorite book or devising a super cookie recipe.

Her melancholy receded as she visited with the Quinns, the Wrights, and several other families she'd met at church. Several of Jayden's friends arrived, and she learned the boys were planning a backyard sleepover. She'd only met Kerrie Quinn briefly the previous Sunday, but she felt herself drawn to her. Perhaps it was a noticeable resemblance to Darcy that drew her to the tall, slim woman who made her guests welcome and who seemed to effortlessly manage an array of salads, drinks, and desserts, and took minor mishaps in stride as easily as Lynnette Olsen had always seemed to do.

Long after the other guests had gone, Clare lingered, seated beside Kerrie on a patio glider. Jeffrey stood a few feet away, fussing with the grill, wiping it down, and putting a cover over it. When he finished, he moved closer to the women, where he settled in a high-backed Adirondack chair.

Jayden and two friends from his former neighborhood whose parents had brought them to the Quinn house earlier, complete with sleeping bags, were arguing over the best place to roll out the bags.

"I should go." Clare started to rise.

"No, please don't," Kerrie protested. "I wasn't here when you moved in, and I've been anxious to get to know you. I've heard so much about you and wanted to tell you how much I appreciate the time you've spent with Jayden, talking to him, baking cookies with him, and making him feel important. He came along so much later than our other children who are now all adults that we sometimes forget he's still a child and needs that kind of attention. Anyway, between my being gone most of the summer and living in a new

neighborhood away from his friends, he would have been terribly lonely this summer without you."

"I would have been lonely without him. He's a wonderful boy. You and your husband have done an excellent job raising him."

"Thank you." Kerrie smiled, showing her pleasure at the compliment, though she must have read a note of wistfulness in Clare's voice, because as the boys abandoned their sleeping bags and began a pillow fight, she went on to add, "Before you know it, you'll marry and likely have a boy of your own, and there will be days when you'll have to remind yourself that he's wonderful." She laughed, and her husband joined in before they noticed tears streaming down Clare's face.

The laughter ended abruptly, and Kerrie's arms went around Clare. "What is it? Did I say something I shouldn't have?"

"I'll never have a son like Jayden." She hadn't meant to tell anyone, but something about Kerrie, perhaps her resemblance to Darcy, caused the words to fall from her mouth. "I won't marry again either."

She saw a startled look pass between Kerrie and her husband and realized not even Bishop Quinn had known she'd been married.

"I think you need to talk about it." Bishop Quinn pulled his chair closer to the glider. His eyes were gentle, and her longing to shed the guilt and humiliation that seemed too great a burden for her slender shoulders outweighed her fears. As though a dam had broken, the story burst from her lips. Kerrie hugged her tighter when she spoke of the beatings, the child she'd lost, and the internal damage that ended her hopes of bearing children in the future.

Bishop Quinn reached for a handful of table napkins from the nearby table which he handed to the two women. "Carla," he said in an encouraging voice. She'd grown accustomed to the name and turned her face toward him.

"My name isn't really Carla," she told him.

"I guessed as much when Brother Wright couldn't find a trace of your membership records when the ward requested them, and he mentioned to me that you avoided his questions concerning your former address. I've suspected almost from the day we met that something was troubling you and hoped you would feel comfortable coming to me with your concerns. Would you like to meet with me in my office tomorrow?"

"Yes, I think I would," she committed herself.

"This doesn't have to be the end of your life," Kerrie said. "Life may look hopeless now, but you've already started taking positive steps. You've joined that art group you told me about earlier, and meeting with Jeff tomorrow will begin counseling that can help you heal and gain direction for your life."

* * *

Clare lay awake for a long time after she returned to her side of the duplex. The air was muggy and hot, and the window cooler in the front room did little to ease the stifling heat. She suspected a storm was brewing. She thought about the Quinns and their kindness. Twice she got out of bed to kneel. After praying the second time, she padded across the floor to switch off the cooler and open a few windows, hoping that a slight wind would precede the storm and cool the air.

Laughter and an occasional shout came from the Quinns' backyard, and she smiled, thinking of the fun Jayden and his friends were having. She finally drifted to sleep remembering the sleepovers she and Darcy had shared as children.

Clare awoke knowing something was wrong. She sniffed the air, testing for smoke and assured herself the house wasn't on fire. Her bedroom was dark and still, but she didn't feel reassured. Pushing back the single sheet that covered her, she slipped from bed and crossed to the window. Perhaps the boys sleeping on the lawn next door had disturbed her sleep. Parting the curtains, she peered out, but all seemed peaceful.

She couldn't say what caused her to turn around—a faint whisper of sound, a whiff of cologne, a well-honed sense of self-preservation. A large dark shape nearly filled her bedroom doorway.

"Hello, Clare. Aren't you happy to see me?" Blaine stepped toward her.

Chapter 23

DARCY APPROACHED CLARE'S ROOM WITH trepidation. David clasped her elbow, lending her his support. Clare's attorney had only said that his client was in serious condition when he'd surprised her with a phone call the day before at the hotel where she and David were honeymooning. He'd told Darcy that he had arrived at his office that morning to discover it had been burglarized over the weekend. His files had been scattered, but he and his secretary had finally determined that the only thing missing was his file from the Prescott divorce. Fortunately his secretary had copied contact numbers for Darcy and for his client into her directory. He'd called Clare and been informed by a woman in her office that someone had broken into her home early Sunday morning and nearly killed her. She'd been saved by a neighbor's young son who heard her scream. While David had called the airlines, she'd packed their bags, ending their San Diego honeymoon after only two days.

David pushed open the door and allowed Darcy to precede him into the dimly lit room. She stepped closer to the bed, where she looked down at the ashen face of the woman lying there. Lifting a clenched hand to her mouth, she bit down to stifle the gasp that rose to her lips. The small part of Clare's face that was visible between bandages wasn't recognizable.

"You're a friend of Carla's, the one who helped her escape her husband?" Darcy's attention shifted to a man she hadn't noticed earlier. He stood with his back to a window that looked out over the city. He was of medium height with graying hair. She nodded her head. She'd known months ago that Clare wasn't using her own name.

"We grew up together. Later we were roommates." It seemed a terribly inadequate explanation of her relationship with Clare. Before she could ask the man's identity, he introduced himself as Carla's bishop and next-door neighbor, Jeffrey Quinn. He shook hands with both of them, and they told him their names.

"My son and his friends were sleeping in the backyard," he explained. "They heard her scream, and there were several loud crashes. One of the boys woke me while my son and the other boy ran to help her. They saw a man choking her, so they jumped on his back and probably saved her life."

"Were they hurt? And was her attacker caught?" One question followed another without waiting for an answer to the first.

"Both boys suffered a few painful blows and have king-sized bruises to show off to their friends. And no, her assailant wasn't captured. He nearly knocked me over as he ran from the house as I was entering. I wasn't able to hang onto him."

"It was Blaine. I know it was Blaine."

"Blaine?" Bishop Quinn questioned.

"Blaine was her husband," David explained. "She divorced him because of his physical attacks on her, one of which resulted in the loss of their unborn child. I've been on the phone with the sheriff back home, and he said he went looking for Blaine as soon as he heard about the attack. His father swears Blaine spent the night at his apartment and that they attended church together the next morning. His bishop verified that Blaine was at the eleven o'clock service."

"It's only a six-hour drive from Salt Lake to Boise," Darcy pointed out.

"And the attack occurred before three in the morning," Bishop Quinn added. "Neither I nor any of the boys got a good look at him. We can't identify her attacker."

"That makes it her word against his, and his parents will lie and cover for him just like they did in Boise." David didn't hide his disgust. "Once again, he's going to get away with beating her, and next time he may succeed in killing her."

"Don't be too sure of that." Bishop Quinn's voice was low, but something in the determined look on his face gave Darcy hope.

Clare awoke the next day and confirmed that her attacker had been Blaine, but the officer who interviewed her didn't offer much

hope that he would be arrested. It had been dark. She hadn't seen his face, and he had a strong alibi. With a little persuasion by Bishop Quinn, a guard took up a position at her door, and hospital security took particular interest in who had access to her room. Bishop Quinn also arranged for a counselor from LDS Family Services who specialized in helping abuse victims cope and heal to make regular visits to Clare's room.

Seeing Darcy, Clare attempted to smile.

"Your face?" There was fear in Clare's face when she noticed the bruise on Darcy's cheekbone.

"We ran into a mugger, but David sank his plan. It made us a little late for our wedding reception, but it all worked out. Remind me to fill you in on the details when you're feeling better." She attempted to make light of their ordeal with Jessop Bernard. Present conditions didn't seem right for telling Clare about her own brush with death.

Darcy was surprised by an older woman with brightly dyed red hair and a loud voice who showed up each day to visit with Clare. She spoke in animated terms of a tour she and her friends were planning to cathedrals and museums in Europe and gossiped about homeless people as though they were old friends. Bishop Quinn and his wife were also regular visitors. Several other members of Clare's ward appeared as well. Darcy was glad that when she and David returned to Boise at the end of the week to begin their new teaching year that Clare would not be alone.

The night before their departure for Boise, Darcy asked David, "Do you think that when Blaine stole that file from Clare's attorney and discovered that my parents' address and my phone number were in it, he gave it to Jessop Bernard to get even with me for helping Clare?"

"I don't know," David said. "I've wondered about that, but he could have tracked us to Washington through your school records, or he could have followed me or my family when we drove up. There was even an announcement of our engagement in the school paper."

The phone on the nightstand rang, and David picked it up. "Evan!" he exclaimed. He listened for a minute then said, "We'll meet you downstairs in five minutes."

It didn't take five minutes to reach the lobby, where they received a hearty greeting from Evan and Karlene. Over dinner they learned that the pictures Karlene had taken had been printed and enlarged. Just as

she had suspected, the couple caught by the camera were Jessop Bernard and his wealthy ex-wife, Lauren Tisdale. They also learned that Bernard had been picked up in the sound by a sailing vessel.

"Sheriff Langton reports that Bernard's in bad shape but expected to live," Evan said. "He's being charged with attempted murder and assault by the Tacoma authorities, and Ada County is planning to charge him for his ex-wife's death. With Bernard behind bars and Monterosa dead, Langton figured it would be safe for us to come home. We're thinking of sticking around Salt Lake for a while, but we'll be back in Boise in time for the trial."

Over the next couple of months, Darcy and David made frequent trips to Salt Lake. Each trip found improvement in Clare's condition. It seemed to Darcy that Clare was not only becoming physically stronger, but she detected subtle changes in her self-confidence. Occasionally she even smiled.

When the long Thanksgiving weekend arrived, Darcy and David accepted Evan and Karlene's invitation to spend the holiday with them at their temporary home in the Salt Lake suburbs. They were surprised to find Clare there too. The friends met with hugs and tears.

The Quinn family arrived for dinner. Jayden insisted on sitting beside Clare through dinner, and she seemed pleased with the arrangement. It wasn't until after Clare's former neighbors' departure that Darcy at last found herself alone with Clare in a small sitting room that overlooked the two-story entryway.

Darcy noticed dark shadows under Clare's eyes, and she appeared to be sad. "Are you really well again?" she asked.

"Yes, I believe I am," Clare responded. Her voice was surprisingly strong.

"Are you concerned that Blaine might find you again?"

"Yes. It will be a long time before I stop looking over my shoulder or I'm able to fall asleep in a darkened room again. He'll be even more determined to punish me now that his father has dropped him from his law firm and rumors about him have spread, ruining his chances of gaining the wealth and prestige he craves."

"Evan said he's wanted for questioning here in Utah, and there's the restraining order. He'll be arrested if he goes anywhere near you."

"Restraining orders have failed a lot of women, including me. Blaine's arrogant enough to think he can do as he pleases without getting caught. I don't want to trust my life to a restraining order." Clare stared out the window then lowered her voice to say, "You know I love you very much, and there's no way I can thank you for standing by me even when you knew I was making foolish choices."

"That's what friends do. They believe in each other and trust even when it's hard. I made you a promise that I'd always be there for you, and I will."

"Knowing that will be my greatest comfort in the years ahead. No matter what, I want you to know there'll never be a day I don't think of you and ask God to shower you with blessings. Now tell me all about the new house you and David are buying and about the classes you're teaching."

* * *

A young woman wearing baggy cargo pants and a leather jacket with a backpack flung over one shoulder walked slowly along a row of lockers inside an airport in Ohio. She found the number she sought, bent down, and inserted a key she pulled out from one of her pockets. After brushing her straggling brown hair from her eyes, she removed a package from the locker and dropped it in her backpack with a silent thank-you to a man back in Salt Lake City who owned a small private plane.

She found a phone booth and dropped in a handful of coins.

* * *

On her way home from school, Darcy heard the familiar ring of the cell phone the police in Tacoma had found and returned to her. She pulled into the driveway of the house she and David were purchasing and turned off the engine before reaching for it.

"Hello." She hoped the caller hadn't given up.

"Darcy?" The voice on the other end was unmistakable.

"Clare? Oh, Clare, are you all right? Where are you? I've been going crazy."

"Darcy, I only have a minute before my flight is called. I just wanted to let you know I won't be returning to Boise or Salt Lake. I've changed my name again, and I look different. I'm going to begin a new life as a new person."

"I'll never see you again . . . will I?" There was a catch in Darcy's voice.

"You know as well as I do that Blaine won't stop looking for me, and if he finds me, he'll kill me."

"What about money? How will you get a job?"

"Someone took care of that. Your friend Evan found a way to get my trust fund cashed out. I have that and a whole new identity. I'll be all right."

"Can't you call once in a while to let me know if you're all right?"

"I have to make a complete break. Darcy, you know I have to do this."

"I know. It just seems so unfair." She was crying now.

"I'm no longer bitter," Clare said, "so don't you be. I may still have someone to love someday. Jayden Quinn proved to me last summer that it is possible to love a child who doesn't start out as my own. Who knows, I may find a corn farmer with a dozen motherless children to love."

Darcy chuckled through her tears. "Just make certain your farmer loves you as much as you love him . . . and are you sure about a dozen?"

Now Clare was laughing too. The laughter slowly died.

"Bye, Darcy. I'll love you forever."

"Bye, Clare. I'll pray that you find happiness."

* * *

"Paula Aikens" peered through a grimy window as the train pulled out of Atlanta. The city was green and beautiful, but she was anxious to be on her way. Only one more stop, then she would put down roots, find a home, and look for a job. The town at the end of this journey was large enough that a stranger wouldn't invite notice and small enough not to be considered a major destination by tourists and business conventions. And on a rise just outside of town was a temple, a light on a hill.

CPSIA information can be obtained at www.ICGtesting.com
Printed in the USA
BVOW07s1326061113

335618BV00001B/1/P

PETER D. LITTLE is Professor and Chair of Anthropology and Director of the Program in Development Studies, Emory University. He received his PhD from Indiana University in 1983 and has held visiting appointments at Kyoto University, Oxford University, and the University of Nairobi. During the past twenty-nine years, Dr. Little has conducted research and directed interdisciplinary programs on development and globalization, poverty, political economy of pastoralism, and food insecurity in several African countries, but with primary emphasis on Kenya, Somalia, and Ethiopia. Among his many research awards have been a Guggenheim Fellowship, the *Choice* Academic Book Award, the Talbot Book Prize from the Royal Anthropological Institute, and the Albert and Elizabeth Kirwan Memorial Research Prize. He is the author or editor/coeditor of ten books and more than one hundred journal articles, book chapters, and research papers.